The Works of the Most Reverend John Tillotson, Lord Archbishop of Canterbury. In Twelve Volumes, Containing 254 Sermons and Discourses on Several Occassions; Together With the Rule of Faith; Prayers Composed by him for his own Life; a Discourse to his Ser

SERMONS

ON SEVERAL

SUBJECTS *and* OCCASIONS,

By the moſt Reverend

Dr. *JOHN TILLOTSON,*

LATE

Lord Archbiſhop of *Canterbury.*

VOLUME *the* NINTH.

LONDON:

Printed for *R. Ware, A. Ward, J.* and *P. Knapton, T. Longman,*
R. Hett, C. Hitch, J. Hodges, S. Auſten, J. and *R. Tonſon,*
J. and *H. Pemberton,* and *J. Rivington.*
MDCCXLIII.

SERMON CLVII.

God the first cause, and last end.

ROM. xi. 36.

*For of him, and through him, and to him are all
things, to whom be glory for ever. Amen.*

HAVING confidered the more eminent and
abfolute perfections of the divine nature, as
alfo that which refults from the infinite excellency and
perfection of God compared with the imperfection of
our underftandings, I come in the laft place to treat
of fuch as are merely and purely relative ; as that he
is " the firft caufe, and the laft end" of all things ;
to which purpofe I have chofen thefe words of the
apoftle, for the fubject of my prefent difcourfe ; " For
" of him, and through him, &c."

The dependance of thefe words upon the former
is briefly this. The apoftle had been fpeaking before in this chapter, feveral things that might tend
to raife us to an admiration of the wifdom, and
goodnefs, and mercy of God, in the difpenfation
of his grace, for the falvation of men, both Jews
and Gentiles, and therefore would have us afcribe
this work wholly to God ; the contrivance of it to his
wifdom, and not to our own counfels, v. 34. " For
" who hath known the mind of the Lord ? and
" who hath been his counfellor ?" and the beftow-
ing this grace, to his free goodnefs and mercy, and
not to any defert of ours, v. 35. " Or who hath
" firft given to him, and it fhall be recompenfed to

" him again ?" Yea and not only in the diſpenſation of grace, but of all good things ; not only in this work of redemption, but alſo of creation, GOD is the fountain, and original, and firſt cauſe, from whence every thing proceeds ; and the laſt end, to which every thing is to be referred. " For of him," &c. ἐξ αὐτᾶ, "from him," the efficient cauſe producing all things ; δι᾽ αὐτᾶ, " by or through him," as the efficient conſerving cauſe of all things ; χ) εἰς αὐτὸν, " and to him," as the final cauſe of all things, and the end for which they were made.

The propoſition I ſhall ſpeak to is, that GOD is the firſt cauſe, and laſt end.

Firſt, I ſhall a little explain the terms.

Secondly, confirm the propoſition.

Thirdly, apply it.

Firſt, for the explication of the terms.

I. That GOD is the firſt cauſe, ſignifies,

1. Negatively, that he had no cauſe, did not derive his being from any other, or does depend upon any other being ; but that he was always, and eternally of himſelf.

2. Poſitively, that he is the cauſe of all things beſides himſelf, the fountain and original of all created beings, from whom all things proceed, and upon whom all things depend ; or, that I may uſe the expreſſion of St. John, John i. 3. which I know is appropriated to the ſecond perſon in the Trinity, " By him all things were made, and without him " was nothing made that was made." So that when we attribute to GOD, that he is the firſt, we mean, that there was nothing before him, and that he was before all things, and that all things are by him.

II. The laſt end, that is, that all things refer to him ; that is, the deſign and aim of all things that are made, is the illustration of GOD's glory some way or other, and the manifestation of his perfections.

Secondly, for the confirmation, I shall briefly, according to my usual method, attempt it these two ways.

I. By natural light. The notion of a GOD contains in it all possible perfection. Now the utmost perfection we can imagine, is, for a being to be always of itself, before all other beings, and not only so, but to be the cause of all other beings; that is, that there should be nothing, but what derives it's being from him, and continually depends upon him; from whence follows, that all things must refer to him, as their last end. For every wise agent acts with design, and in order to an end. Now the end is that which is best, which is most worthy the attaining, and that is GOD himself. Now his being and perfections are already, and the best next to the existence of his being and perfections, is the manifestation of them, which is called GOD's glory; and this is the highest end that we can imagine, to which all the effects of the divine power, and goodness, and wisdom, do refer.

And that these titles are to be attributed to GOD, is not only reasonable, when it is revealed and discovered, but was discovered by the natural light of the heathens. Hence it was that Aristotle gave to GOD those titles of the first being, the first cause, and the first mover; and his master Plato calls GOD "the author, and parent of all things, the maker "and architect of the world, and of all creatures; "the fountain and original of all things." Porphyry calls him τὸ πρῶτον, the first, from whence he reasons to this sense, that "he is the ultimate end, "and that all things move towards GOD, that all "motions

SERM.
CLVII.

" motions center in him; becaufe, faith he, it is moft
" proper and natural for things to refer to their ori-
" ginal, and to refer all to him, from whom they
" receive all." Antoninus, the emperor and philofopher, fpeaking of nature (which with the Stoicks
fignifies God) hath thefe words, which are fo very
like thefe of the apoftle, that they may feem to be
taken from him; ἐκ σε͂ πάντα, ἐν σοὶ πάντα, εἰς σὲ
πάντα, " Of thee are all things, in thee are all
" things, to thee are all things."

II. From fcripture. Hither belong all thofe places
where he declares himfelf to be " the firft, and the
" laft," Ifa. xli. 4. " Who hath wrought and done
" it, calling the generations from the beginning ? I
" the Lord, the firft, and with the laft, I am he."
Ifa. xliii. 10. " Before me there was no God formed,"
(or as it is in the margin) " there was nothing form-
" ed of God, neither fhall there be after me." Ifa.
xliv. 6. " I am the firft, and I am the laft, and be-
" fides me there is no God." Ifa. xlviii. 12, 13.
" I am the firft, I am alfo the laft, my hand hath
" laid the foundation of the earth, my right hand
" hath fpread the heavens;" which is as much as
to fay, he hath made the world, and was the firft
caufe of all things. Rev. i. 8. " I am alpha and
" omega, the beginning and the end, faith the
" Lord, which is, and which was, and which is
" to come."

But more exprefly, 1 Cor. viii. 6. " But to us
" there is but one God, the father, of whom are
" all things, and we by him, καὶ ἡμεῖς εἰς αὐτὸν,
" and we to him, and for him." Acts xvii. 24.
" God that made the world, and all things therein."
V. 25. " He giveth to all life, and breath, and all
" things." V. 28. " In him we live, and move,
" and

" and have our being." V. 29. " For as much then
" as we are the off-spring of God."

Hither we may refer those texts which attribute
the same to the second person in the Trinity, as the
eternal wisdom and word of God, whereby all things
were made, John. i. 3. " All things were made by
" him, and without him was nothing made, that
" was made." V. 10. " And the world was made
" by him." 1 Cor. viii. 6. " And one Lord Jesus
" Christ, by whom are all things, and we by
" him." Eph. iii. 9. " God, who created all
" things by Jesus Christ." Col. i. 16. " By him
" were all things created that are in heaven, and
" that are in earth, visible and invisible, whether
" they be thrones, or dominions, or principalities,
" or powers, all things were created by him, and
" for him, and he is before all things, and by him
" all things consist." Heb. i. 2. " By whom also
" he made the worlds." And, v. 3. " Uphold-
" ing all things by the word of his power."

Thirdly and lastly, to apply this doctrine.

Use. First, if God be the first cause of all things,
who did at first produce all creatures, and does since
preserve them and govern them, and disposeth of
all their concernments, and orders all things that befal them, from hence let us learn,

1. With humility and thankfulness to own, and
acknowledge, and admire and bless God as the author and original of our being, as the spring and
fountain of all the blessings and good things that we
enjoy. If we do but consider what these words signify, that God is the first cause of all things, we
shall see great reason to own and acknowledge, to
adore and praise him, and that with the greatest humility ; because we have not given him any thing,
but

but have received all from him ; he is the cauſe of all things, who did freely and of his own good will and pleaſure communicate being to us, without any conſtraint or neceſſity, but what his own goodneſs laid upon him, Rev. iv. 11. " Thou art worthy, O " LORD, to receive glory, and honour, and power ; " for thou haſt created all things, and for thy plea- " ſure they are and were created." We could not, before we were, deſerve any thing from him, or move him by any argument, or importune him by intreaties to make us ; but he freely gave us being ; and ever ſince we depend upon him, and have been preſerved by him, and cannot ſubſiſt one moment without the continued influence of the power and goodneſs which firſt called us out of nothing. He is the author of all the good, and the fountain of all thoſe bleſſings, which for the preſent we enjoy, and for the future hope for.

When he made us at firſt, he deſigned us for happineſs ; and when we by our ſin and wilful miſcar- riage fell ſhort of the happineſs which he deſigned us for, he ſent his ſon into the world for our reco- very, and gave his life for the ranſom of our ſouls. He hath not only admitted us into a new covenant, wherein he hath promiſed pardon, and eternal life to us ; but he hath alſo purchaſed theſe bleſſings for us, by the moſt endearing price, the blood of his own ſon, and hath ſaved us in ſuch a manner as may juſtly aſtoniſh us. Upon theſe conſiderations we ſhould awaken ourſelves to the praiſe of GOD, and with the holy Pſalmiſt, call up our ſpirits, and ſum- mon all the powers and faculties of our ſouls to aſſiſt us in this work, Pſal. ciii. 1, 2, 3, 4, &c. " Bleſs " the LORD, O my ſoul, and all that is within me, " bleſs his holy name ; bleſs the LORD, O my ſoul,
and

" and forget not all his benefits ; who forgiveth all
" thy iniquities, who healeth all thy difeafes, who
" redeemeth thy life from deftruction ; who crown-
" eth thee with loving kindnefs and tender mer-
" cies ;" it is he that " fatisfies our fouls with good
" things," that hath promifed eternal life and happinefs to us, and muft confer and beftow this upon
us ; " Therefore our fouls, and all that is within
" us," fhould " blefs his holy name."

2. If God be the firft caufe, that is, orders all
things that befal us, and by his providence difpofeth
of all our concernments, this fhould teach us with
patience and quietnefs to fubmit to all events, to
all evils and affictions, that come upon us, as being
difpofed by his wife providence, and coming from
him ; we are apt to attribute all things to the next
and immediate agent, and to look no higher than
fecond caufes ; not confidering that all the motions
of natural caufes are directly fubordinate to the firft
caufe, and all the actions of free creatures are under
the government of God's wife providence ; fo that
nothing happens to us befides the defigns and intention of God.

And methinks this is one particular excellency of
the ftile of the fcripture above all other books, that
the conftant phrafe of the facred dialect is to attribute all events (excepting fins only) to God ; fo that
every one that reads it cannot but take notice, that
it is wrote with a more attentive confideration of
God than any other book, as appears by thofe frequent and exprefs acknowledgments of God as the
caufe of all events ; fo that what in other writers
would be faid to be done by this or that perfon, is
afcribed to God. Therefore it is fo often faid, that

the LORD did this and that, stirred up such an enemy, brought such a judgment.   And we shall find
that holy men in scripture make excellent use of this
consideration, to argue themselves into patience and
contentedness in every condition.   So Eli, 1 Sam.
iii. 18. " It is the LORD, let him do what seemeth
" him good."   So Job, he did not so consider the
Sabeans and Chaldeans, who had carried away his
oxen and his camels, and slain his servants ; nor the
wind which had thrown down his house, and killed
his sons and his daughters ; but he looks up to
GOD, the great governor and disposer of all these
events ; " The LORD giveth, and the LORD hath
" taken away, blessed be the name of the LORD."
So David, Psal. xxxvi. 9. " I was dumb, and spake
" not a word, because thou LORD didst it."   So
our blessed SAVIOUR, when he was ready to suffer,
he did not consider the malice of the Jews, which
was the cause of his death, but looks to a higher
hand ; " the cup which my father gives me to
" drink, shall not I drink it ?"

He that looks upon all things as coming from
second causes, and does not eye the first cause, the
good and wise governor, will be apt to take offence
at every cross and unwelcome accident.   Men are
apt to be angry, when one flings water upon them
as they pass in the streets ; but no man is offended
if he is wet by rain from heaven.   When we look
upon evils as coming only from men, we are apt to
be impatient, and know not how to bear them ;
but we should look upon all things as under the government and disposal of the first cause, and the
circumstances of every condition as allotted to us by
the wise providence of GOD ; this consideration,
that

that it is the hand of GOD, and that he hath done it, would ftill all the murmurings of our fpirits. As when a feditious multitude is in an uproar, the prefence of a grave and venerable perfon will hufh the noife, and quell the tumult ; fo if we would but reprefent GOD as prefent to all actions, and governing and difpofing all events, this would ftill and appeafe our fpirits, when they are ready to riot and mutiny againft any of his difpenfations.

Ufe the fecond. If GOD be the laft end of all, let us make him our laft end, and refer all our actions to his glory. This is that which is due to him, as he is the firft caufe, and therefore he does moft reafonably require it of us.

And herein likewife the fcripture doth excel all other books, that is, doth more frequently and exprefly mind us of this end, and calls upon us to propofe it to ourfelves as our ultimate aim and defign. We fhould love him as our chief end, Matth. xxii. 37. " Thou fhalt love the LORD thy GOD " with all thy heart, and with all thy foul, and with " all thy mind." Thus to love GOD is that which, in the language of the fchools, is loving GOD as our chief end. So likewife the apoftle requires, that we fhould refer all the actions of our lives to this end, 1 Cor. x. 31. " Whether ye eat or drink, " do all to the glory of GOD ;" that we fhould " glorify him in our fouls, and in our bodies, which " are his." He is the author of all the powers that we have, and therefore we fhould ufe them for him ; we do all by him, and therefore we fhould do all to him.

And that we may the better underftand ourfelves as to this duty, I fhall endeavour to give fatisfaction to a queftion or two which may arife about it.

Firft,

SERM.
CLVII.

Firft, whether an actual intention of GOD's glory be neceffary to make every action that we do good and acceptable to GOD?

Anfw. 1. It is neceffary that the glory of GOD, either formally or virtually, fhould be the ultimate end and fcope of our lives, and all our actions; otherwife they will be defective in that which in moral actions is moft confiderable, and that is the end. If a man fhould keep all the commandments of the gofpel, this excepted, of making GOD's glory his fupreme end, only with a defign to gain reputation, or fome other advantage in the world, this very thing would vitiate all, and render him unacceptable to GOD.

2. It is very requifite and convenient, as a good fign, that we fhould very frequently, actually think upon, and intend this end; for if it be very much out of our thoughts, we have reafon to be jealous of ourfelves, that we do not intend it at all.

3. It is fo far from being neceffary, that we fhould in every action have this intention of GOD's glory, that it is not morally poffible that we fhould, no more than it is poffible, that a man that goes a journey of a thoufand miles, fhould every ftep he takes have actual thoughts of his journey's end, nor is it more neceffary; for confideration of the end is only fo far neceffary, as it is neceffary to guide and quicken us in the ufe of means; as it is not neceffary for a man to think of his journey's end, farther than to direct and excite him to go thither. And this appears farther by the contrary; it is not neceffary to make a finful action, that a man fhould formally, much lefs actually intend GOD's difhonour; it is enough to conftitute a man a wicked man, if he willingly tranfgrefs GOD's law, the doing whereof

2   does

does by conſequence reflect a diſhonour upon him :
ſo, on the other hand, it is ſufficient to make an action good and acceptable, if it be conformable to
GOD's law, and ſuch as by conſequence redounds to
GOD's glory.

Second queſtion. Whether the glory of GOD
may, or ought to be conſidered, as an end ſeparate
and diſtinct from our own happineſs?

Anſw. I ſhall ſpeak but briefly to this, becauſe I
have elſewhere ſpoken to it ; but in that little which
I have to ſay for ſatisfaction to this queſtion, I will
proceed by theſe ſteps.

I. By the glory of GOD, we mean the demonſtration, or illuſtration, or manifeſtation of ſome or
of all his perfections, more eſpecially his goodneſs,
and mercy, and juſtice, and wiſdom, and power,
and holineſs.

II. It is plain, that the manifeſtation of ſome of
theſe perfections is a thing that may be ſeparated
from the happineſs of a creature ; for his holineſs,
and juſtice, and power, may and ſhall be manifeſted
in the final and eternal ruin of impenitent ſinners.

III. The manifeſtation of any of GOD's perfections, ought many times to be propounded by us as
an end diſtinct and ſeparate from our reſpective happineſs ; ſuch a happineſs, as reſpects only ſome particulars, and ſome particular duration, in oppoſition
to abſolute and eternal happineſs. In this ſenſe our
SAVIOUR ſays, that he " ſought not his own glory,
" but the glory of him that ſent him :" by which
he does not mean, that he quitted everlaſting glory
and happineſs ; but that, in order to the glory of
GOD, he did for a time lay aſide his own glory, and
diveſt himſelf of it while he was in this world ; for
the apoſtle tells us, that he was encouraged to do
                                             this

this out of a respect to a greater glory, Heb. xii. 2.
" Who for the joy that was set before him, endur-
" ed the cross, despising the shame, and is set down
" at the right hand of the throne of GOD." And
in this sense we are to understand the command of
self-denial in the gospel, with reference to our particular or temporal, not our eternal interest ; and that
it is no more, is plain from the argument our SA-
VIOUR uses to encourage this self-denial, the promise of a far greater happiness than that we deny ;
no man that " forsakes father or mother for my
" sake," but shall " have eternal life :" And proportionably we are to understand those commands of
loving CHRIST more than ourselves, that is, more
than any temporal interest.

IV. The manifestation of any of GOD's perfections, neither ought, nor can reasonably be propounded by us, as an end separated from, or opposite to
our eternal blessedness ; that is, we cannot naturally
or reasonably desire the glory of GOD should be advanced, though it were to our final ruin, either by
annihilation, or eternal misery.

1. We cannot either naturally or reasonably desire GOD should be glorified by our annihilation.

(1.) Not naturally. Because such a desire would
be directly contrary to the natural desire of self-pre-
servation, which GOD himself hath planted in us,
and is most intimate and essential to our nature.

(2.) Not reasonably. Because it is utterly unimaginable how GOD can be glorified by the annihilation of a creature. All the attributes that we can
imagine can be manifested herein, are power and so-
vereignty ; his power hath already been as much
manifested in creating and making the creature out
of nothing, as it can be by reducing it into nothing ;

for

for to create is the very fame demonftration of power as to annihilate. And as for his fovereignty,
GOD will never manifeft that in contradiction to his
goodnefs, or wifdom, or any other perfection of the
divine nature. To unmake a creature, and to take
away the being which he had given, would argue
either a failure of his goodnefs toward the creature,
or that he did repent he had made it, which would
reflect upon his wifdom and conftancy. I do not
fay, that in juftice GOD cannot annihilate a creature ;
far be it from me : for what he gave was his own,
and he may without any wrong to the creature take
it again.

2. Much lefs can we naturally defire that GOD
fhould be glorified in our eternal mifery. The
reafons which I gave about annihilation are ftronger
here ; therefore we cannot naturally defire it, nor
reafonably, for the demonftration of his power, or
fovereignty, or juftice, or holinefs, which I think
are all the attributes which we can imagine to be
glorified hereby : not as the manifeftation of his
power ; for that would be as much manifefted in the
happinefs, as mifery of the creature : not of his fovereignty ; for GOD will not manifeft that in contradiction to his goodnefs, upon which nothing can
reflect more, than merely, *pro arbitrio*, for his pleafure, to make an innocent creature for ever miferable : Not his juftice, and holinefs ; for thefe pre-
fuppofe fin and demerit in the creature, out of hatred to which he makes it miferable ; but GOD hath
declared that he efteems himfelf more glorified by
the obedience and happinefs of his creatures, than
by their fin and deftruction ; and if it were reafonable to defire the juftice and holinefs of GOD might
be glorified in my eternal ruin, which I have deferved

ed by fin; this would plainly follow from it, that it
were reafonable " to fin, that juftice might abound,"
which of the two is a greater abfurdity than that
which the apoftle condemns, of " finning, that
" grace may abound."

V. There is a ftrict and inviolable connexion between the greateft glory of GOD, and our obedience
and happinefs : I fay, between his greateft glory ;
becaufe he efteems himfelf more glorified by the
obedience and happinefs of his creatures, than by
their ruin and mifery ; and that we may believe it,
we have his oath for it ; " As I live, faith the LORD,
" I delight not in the death of a finner, but rather
" that he fhould turn, and live." And it is ob-
fervable, that the apoftle, in 1 Cor. x. 31, 32, 33.
" Whether ye eat or drink, or whatfoever ye do,
" do all to the glory of GOD; giving none offence,
" neither to the Jews, nor to the Gentiles, nor to
" the church of GOD ; even as I pleafe all men
" in all things, not feeking mine own profit, but
" the profit of many, that they may be faved,"
explains the glorifying of GOD, by edifying and pro-
moting the falvation of others.

VI. We may confider the glory of GOD as fome
ways diftinct from our happinefs ; that is, we may
confider the manifeftation of his goodnefs, and
mercy, and wifdom, in our happinefs, as that which
refults from it ; but this is not enough to make it a
diftinct end, but the fame diverfly confidered ; as
the publick good is that which refults from the general good of particular perfons, but cannot reafonably be propounded by any man, as an end diftinct
from the general happinefs of particular perfons,
without ruining and deftroying the notion of publick good.

VII. Though

VII. Though confidered as we are particular beings; we can have no greater end than our own happineſs, in which Goᴅ is eminently glorifid ; yet as
we are part of the whole creation-and workmanſhip
of Goᴅ, which is the nobleſt confideration of ourſelves, the glory of Goᴅ, which refults from the manifeſtation of all his perfections in and about his
creatures, is precifely our ultimate end, and yet not
an end really diſtinct from our own happineſs ; and
therefore it is moſt proper, and becoming, and a-
greeable to the wife ſtile of fcripture, to give our
end it's denomination, not from the more particular
and narrow, but the more noble confideration of ourſelves, as we are parts of the whole creation and workmanſhip of Goᴅ ; as it is more generous and becoming for the members of a civil fociety to mention the publick good as their end, than their private
happineſs and advantage, though that be fo really
and effectually promoted by the publick good.

Thus I have finiſhed what I propofed on this argument, and concerning the attributes of Goᴅ in
general ; " Of whom, and through whom, and to
" whom are all things. To him be glory for ever."
Amen.

SERMON CLVIII.

Of doing good.

GALAT. vi. 9, 10.

*Let us not be weary in well-doing, for in due season
we shall reap, if we faint not : as we have therefore opportunity, let us do good unto all men, especially unto them who are of the houshold of faith.*

S E R M.
CLVIII.

A Spital
Sermon,
preached
at Christ-
Church-
on Easter-
Tuesday,
April 14.
1691.

THE apostle in these words recommends unto us a great and comprehensive duty, " the
" doing of good ;" concerning which the text offers
these five particulars to our consideration.

I. The nature of the duty itself, which is called
" well-doing," v. 9. and " doing good," v. 10.

II. The extent of this duty, in respect of it's object, which is all mankind, " Let us do good unto
" all men, especially unto them who are of the
" houshold of faith."

III. The measure of it, "as we have opportunity."

IV. Our unwearied perseverance in it ; " let us
" not be weary in well-doing."

V. The argument and encouragement to it ; because " in due season we shall reap, if we faint not :
" Therefore as we have opportunity, let us do
" good, &c."

I. I will consider the nature of the duty itself ; of
" well-doing," and " doing good." And this I
shall explain to you as briefly as I can, by considering
the extent of the act of doing good, and the excellency of it. And,

1. The extent of the act. It comprehends in it

2   all

all thofe ways wherein we may be beneficial and ufeful to one another. It reaches not only to the bodies of men, but to their fouls, that better and more excellent part of ourfelves; and is converfant in all thofe ways and kinds, whereby we may ferve the temporal, or fpiritual good of our neighbour, and promote either his prefent, or his future and eternal happinefs.

To inftruct the ignorant, or reduce thofe that are in error; " to turn the difobedient to the wifdom of " the juft," and reclaim thofe that are engaged in any evil courfe, by good counfel, and feafonable admonition, and by prudent and kind reproof; to refolve and fatisfy the doubting mind; to confirm the weak; to heal the broken-hearted, and to comfort the melancholy and troubled fpirits : Thefe are the nobleft ways of charity, becaufe they are converfant about the fouls of men, and tend to procure and promote their eternal felicity.

And then " to feed the hungry, to clothe the " naked, releafe the imprifoned ;" to redeem the captives, and to vindicate thofe who are injured and oppreffed in their perfons, or eftates, or reputation ; to repair thofe who are ruined in their fortunes; and, in a word, to relieve and comfort thofe who are in any kind of calamity or diftrefs.

All thefe are but the feveral branches and inftances of this great duty here in the text, of " doing good ;" though it hath, in this place, a more particular refpect to the charitable fupply of thofe, who are in want and neceffity ; and therefore with a more particular regard to that, I fhall difcourfe of it at this time. You fee the extent of the duty. We will, in the

2d place, briefly fay fomething of the excellency

18 P 2   of

of it, which will appear, if we confider, that it is the imitation of the higheft excellency and perfection. To do good, is to be like GOD, who "is good, " and doth good;" and it is to be like him, in that which he efteems his greateft glory. It is to be like the Son of GOD, who, when he was pleafed to take our nature upon him, and live here below, and to dwell amongft us, " went about doing good." And it is to be like the bleffed angels, the higheft rank and order of GOD's creatures ; whofe great employment it is to be miniftring fprits, for the good of men. So that for a man to be kind, and helpful, and beneficial to others, is to be a good angel, and a faviour, and a kind of god too.

It is an argument of a great, and noble, and generous mind, to excite our thoughts and cares to the concernments of others, and to employ our intereft, and power, and endeavours for their benefit and advantage : whereas a low, and mean, and narrow fpirit, is contracted and fhriveled up within itfelf, and cares only for it's own things, without any regard to the good and happinefs of others.

It is the moft noble work in the world, becaufe that inclination of mind, which prompts us to do good, is the very temper and difpofition of happinefs. Solomon, after all his experience of worldly greatnefs and pleafure, at laft pitched upon this, as the great felicity of human life, and the only good ufe that is to be made of a profperous and plentiful fortune. Ecclef. iii. 12. "I know (fays he, fpeaking of riches) " that there is no good in them, but for " a man to rejoice and do good in his life." And certainly the beft way to take joy in an eftate, is to do good with it : and a greater and wifer than Solomon has faid it, even he " who is the power and " wifdom

" wifdom of God" has faid it, that "it is a more
" bleffed thing to give than to receive."

Confider farther, that this is one of the great
and fubftantial parts of religion, and next to the
love and honour, which we pay to Almighty God,
the moft acceptable fervice that we can do to him;
it is one table of the law, and next to the firft and great
commandment, of " loving the Lord our God,"
and very like to it. " And the fecond is like unto
" it," (fays our Saviour) " Thou fhalt love thy
" neighbour as thyfelf;" like to it, in the excellency of it; and equal to it, in the neceffary obligation
of it. " And this commandment (fays St. John, 1 epift:
chap. 4. v. 21.) " have we from him, that he who
" loveth God, love his brother alfo." The firft
commandment indeed excels in the dignity of the
object, becaufe it enjoins the love of God; but the
fecond feems to have the advantage in the reality of it's
effects: for the love of God confifts in our acknowledgment, and honour of him; but our " righte-
" oufnefs and goodnefs extend not to him;" we
can do him no real benefit and advantage: but our
love to men is really ufeful and beneficial to them;
for which reafon, God is contented in many cafes,
that the external honour and worfhip, which he requires
of us by his pofitive commands, fhould give way to
that natural duty of love and mercy which we owe
to one another. " I will have mercy" (fays God in
the prophet Amos) " and not facrifice."

And to fhew how great a value God puts upon
this duty, he hath made it the very teftimony of
our love to himfelf; and for want of it, hath declared that he will reject all our other profeffions and
teftimonies of love to him, as falfe and infincere.
" Whofo hath this worlds good," (faith St. John,

1 epift. iii. 17.) " and feeth his brother have need,
" and fhutteth up his bowels of compaffion from
" him, how dwelleth the love of GOD in him ?"
And again, chap. iv. ver. 20. " If a man fay,
" I love GOD, and hateth his brother, he is a liar ;
" for he that loveth not his brother, whom he hath
" feen, how can he love GOD, whom he hath not
" feen ?"

You fee the duty here recommended, both in the
extent and in the excellency of it ; "let us do good."
I proceed to confider, in the

IId place, the extent of this duty, in refpect of
it's object, which is all mankind, but more efpecially Chriftians, thofe that are of the fame faith and
religion. " Let us do good unto all men, efpecially
" unto thofe that are of the houfhold of faith."
So that the object, about which this duty is converfant, is very large, and takes in all mankind ; " let
" us do good unto all men." The Jews confined
their love and kindnefs to their own kindred and nation ; and becaufe they were prohibited familiarity
with idolatrous nations, and were enjoined to maintain a perpetual enmity with Amalek, and the feven
nations of Canaan, whom GOD had caft out before
them, and devoted to ruin ; they looked upon themfelves as perfectly difcharged from all obligation of
kindnefs to the reft of mankind : and yet it is certain, that they were exprefly enjoined by their law,
to be kind to ftrangers, becaufe they themfelves had
been ftrangers in the land of Egypt. But our SA-
VIOUR hath reftored this law of love and charity to
it's natural and original extent ; and hath declared
every one that is of the fame nature with ourfelves to
be our neighbour, and our brother ; and that he is to
be treated by us accordingly, whenever he ftands

in

in need of our kindnefs and help ; and to fhew that none are out of the compafs of our charity, he hath exprefly commanded us to extend it to thofe who of all others can leaft pretend to it, even our enemies and perfecutors.

So that if the queftion be about the extent of our charity in general, thefe two things are plainly 'enjoined by the chriftian religion.

1. Negatively, That we fhould not hate nor bear ill-will to any man, or do him any harm or mifchief. " Love worketh no evil to his neighbour," (faith the apoftle) Rom. xiii. 10. And this negative charity every man may exercife towards all men, without exception, and that equally, becaufe it does not fignify any pofitive act, but only that we abftain from enmity and hatred, from injury and revenge, which it is in every man's power, by the grace of God, and the due care and government of himfelf, to do.

2. Pofitively, the law of charity requires, that we fhould bear an univerfal good-will to all men, and wifh every man's happinefs, and pray for it, as fincerely as we wifh and pray for our own ; and if we be fincere in our wifhes, and prayers for the good of others, we fhall be fo in our endeavours to procure and promote it.

But the great difficulty is, as to the exercife of our charity, and the real expreffions and effects of it, in doing good to others ; which is the duty here meant in the text, and (as I told you before) does more particularly relate to the relief of thofe who are in want and neceffity. And the reafon of the difficulty is, becaufe no man can do good to all in this kind, if he would ; it not being poffible for any man to come to the knowledge of every man's neceffity and diftrefs ; and if he could, no man's ability can

can poffibly reach to the fupply and the relief of all mens wants. And indeed this limitation the text gives to this duty ; " As we have opportunity (fays the apoftle) " let us do good unto all men ;" which either fignifies, as occafion is offered, or as we have ability of doing, or both; as I fhall fhew afterwards.

So that it being impoffible to exercife this charity to all men that ftand in need of it, it is neceffary to make a difference, and to' ufe prudence and difcretion in the choice of the moft fit and proper objects. We do not know the wants of all men, and therefore the bounds of our knowledge do of neceffity limit our charity within a certain compafs; and of thofe whom we do know, we can relieve but a fmall part for want of ability ; from whence it follows, that though a man were never fo charitably difpofed, yet he muft of neceffity fet fome rules to himfelf, for the management of his charity to the beft advantage. What thofe rules are, cannot minutely and nicely be determined ; when all is done, much muft be left to every man's prudence and difcretion, upon a full view and confideration of the cafe before him, and all the circumftances of it ; but yet fuch general rules may be given, as may ferve for the direction of our practice in moft cafes ; and for the reft, every man's prudence, as well as it can, muft determine the matter. And the rules which I fhall give, fhall be thefe.

Firft, Cafes of extremity ought to take the firft place, and do for that time challenge precedence of all other confiderations. If a perfon be in great and prefent diftrefs, and his neceffity fo urgent, that if he be not immediately relieved, he muft perifh ; this is fo violent a cafe, and calls fo loud for prefent help, that there is no refifting of it, whatever the perfon be ; though a perfect ftranger to us, though
moft

most unworthy, though the greatest enemy we have in the world, yet the greatness of his distress does so strongly plead for him, as to silence all considerations to the contrary ; for after all, he is a man, and is of the same nature with ourselves ; and the consideration of humanity ought, for that time, to prevail over all objections against the man, and to prefer him to our charity, before the nearest relation and friend, who is not in the like extremity. In other cases we not only may, but ought to relieve our friends, and those that have deserved well of us in the first place : but if our enemy be in extremity, then that divine precept takes place, " if thine " enemy hunger, feed him ; if he thirst, give him " drink."

Secondly, In the next place, I think, that the obligation of nature, and the nearness of relation, does challenge a preference ; for there is all the reason in the world, if other things be equal, that we should consider and supply the necessity of those, who are of our blood and kindred, and members of our family, before the necessities of strangers, and those who have no relation to us. There is a special duty incumbent upon us, and another obligation beside that of charity, to have a particular care and regard for them. In this case not only christianity, but nature ties this duty upon us, 1 Tim. v. 8. " If any " man provide not for his own, especially for those " of his own house," for them that are of his family, " he hath denied the faith, and is worse than an " infidel ;" that is, he doth not only offend against the law of christianity, but against the very dictates of nature, which prevail even amongst infidels. And our Saviour hath told us, that when our parents stand in need of relief, it is more acceptable to

CLVIII. GOD, to employ our eftates that way, than to devote them to him, and his immediate fervice ; and that it is a kind of facrilege to confecrate that to GOD, whereby our parents may be profited, and provided for in their neceffity.

Thirdly, the obligation of kindnefs, and benefits, lays the next claim to our charity. If they fall into want, who have obliged us by their former kindnefs and charity, both juftice and charity do challenge from us a particular confideration of their cafe ; and proportionably, if we ourfelves have been obliged to their family, or to any other that are nearly related to them.

Fourthly, thofe " who are of the houfhold of faith," and of the fame religion, and members of the fame myftical body, and do partake of the fame holy myfteries, the body and blood of our bleffed SAVIOUR, the ftricteft bond of love and charity ; thefe fall under a very particular confideration in the exercife of our charity : and of this the apoftle puts us in mind, in the laft words of my text ; " Let " us do good unto all men, efpecially unto thofe " that are of the houfhold of faith." GOD hath a fpecial love and regard for fuch ; and thofe whom GOD loves ought to be very dear to us.

And this, perhaps, was a confideration of the firft rank, in thofe times when Chriftians lived among heathens, and were expofed to continual wants and fufferings ; but it fignifies much lefs now, that Chriftianity is the general profeffion of a nation, and is too often made ufe of to very uncharitable purpofes ; to confine mens bounty and benefits to their own fect and party, as if they, and none but they, were " the houfhold of faith ;" a principle, which I know not whether it hath more of judaifm or of popery in it.   Fifthly,

Fifthly, after thefe, the merit of the perfons who are the objects of our charity, and all the circumftances belonging to them, are to be valued and confidered, and we accordingly to proportion our charity, and the degrees of it. I fhall inftance in fome particulars, by which a prudent man may judge of the reft.

Thofe who labour in an honeft calling, but yet are oppreffed with their charge, or difabled for a time by ficknefs, or fome other cafualty ; thefe many a time need as much, and certainly deferve much better than common beggars ; for thefe are ufeful members of the commonwealth ; and we cannot place our charity better, than upon thefe, who do what they can to fupport themfelves.

Thofe likewife who are fallen from a rich and plentiful condition, without any fault or prodigality of their own, merely by the providence of God, or fome general calamity ; thefe are more efpecially objects of our charity, and liberal relief.

. And thofe alfo, who have been charitable, and have liberally relieved others, when they were in condition to do it ; or the children, or near relations of thofe who were eminently charitable and beneficial to mankind, do deferve a particular regard in our charity. Mankind being (as I may fay) bound in juftice, and for the honour of God's providence, to make good his promife, to preferve fuch from extreme neceffity.

And laftly, thofe, whofe vifible wants, and great age and infirmities, do plead for more than ordinary pity, and do, at firft fight, convince every one that fees them, that they do not beg out of lazinefs, but of neceffity, and becaufe they are not able to do any thing towards their own fupport and fubfiftence.

There are innumerable circumftances more, which it would be endlefs to reckon up ; but thefe which I have mentioned are fome of the chief; and, by proportion to thefe, we may direct ourfelves in other cafes.

Sixthly, thofe whom we certainly know to be true objects of charity, are to be confidered by us, before thofe who are ftrangers to us, and whofe condition we do not know, yea though, in common charity, we do not difbelieve them ; becaufe in reafon and prudence we are obliged to prefer thofe, who are certainly known to us ; fince we find by experience, that there are many cheats and counterfeit beggars, who can tell their ftory, and carry about teftimonials of their own making; and likewife becaufe we run the hazard of mifplacing our charity, when there are objects enough befides, where we are fure we fhall place it right ; and charity mifplaced, as it is in truth and reality no charity in itfelf, fo it is hardly any in us, when we fquander it fo imprudently, as to pafs by a certain and real object, and give it to thofe of whom we are not certain that they are true objects of charity. In this blind way a man " may give all his goods to the poor," as he thinks, and yet do no real charity. And therefore, unlefs we be able to relieve " every one that afks," we muft of neceffity make a difference, and ufe our beft prudence in the choice of the moft proper objects of our charity.

And yet we ought not to obferve this rule fo ftrictly, as to fhut out all whom we do not know, without exception ; becaufe their cafe, if it be true, may fometimes be much more pitiable, and of greater extremity, than the cafe of many whom we do know ; and then it would be uncharitable to reject

such,

such, and to harden our hearts so far against them, as utterly to disbelieve them ; because it is no fault of theirs, that we do not know them ; no, their wants may be real, notwithstanding that ; especially when their extremity seems great, we ought not to stand upon too rigorous a proof and evidence of it, but should accept of a fair probability.

Seventhly, those who suffer for the cause of religion, and are stripped of all for the sake of it, ought to have a great precedence in our charity to most other cases. And this of late hath been, and still is the case of many among us, who have fled hither for refuge, from the tyranny and cruelty of their persecutors, and have been, by a most extraordinary charity of the whole nation, more than once extended to them, most seasonably relieved : but especially by the bounty of this great city, whose liberality, upon these occasions, hath been beyond all example, and even all belief. And I have often thought, that this very thing, next to the mercy and goodness of Almighty God, hath had a particular influence upon our preservation and deliverance from those terrible calamities, which were just ready to break in upon us ; and, were we not so stupidly insensible of this great deliverance which God hath wrought for us, and so horribly unthankful to him, and to the happy instruments of it, might still be a means to continue the favour of God to us. And what cause have we to thank God, who hath allotted to us this more blessed, and more merciful part, to give, and not to receive ; to be free from persecution ourselves, that we might give refuge and relief to those that are persecuted !

III. We must consider the measure of our charity, ὡς καιρὸν ἔχομεν, which our translation renders,

" as

" as we have opportunity;" others, as we have ability : So that this expreſſion may refer, either to the occaſions of our charity, or to the ſeaſon of it, or to the proportion and degree of it.

1. It may refer to the occaſions of our charity, " as we have opportunity, let us do good," that is, according as the occaſions of doing good ſhall preſent themſelves to us, ſo often as an opportunity is offered. And this is an argument of a very good and charitable diſpoſition, gladly to lay hold of the occaſions of doing good ; as it were to meet opportunities when they are coming towards us. This forwardneſs of mind in the work of charity, the apoſtle commends in the Corinthians, 2 Cor. ix. 2. " I know the forwardneſs of your minds, for which " I boaſt of you to them of Macedonia :" And this he requires of all Chriſtians, Tit. iii. 8. that they ſhould " be ready to every good work ;" and 1 Tim. vi. 18. that we be " ready to diſtribute, " willing to communicate." Some are very ready to decline theſe opportunities, and to get out of the way of them ; and when they thruſt themſelves upon them, and they cannot avoid them, they do what they do grudgingly, and not with a willing mind.

2. It may refer to the ſeaſon of this duty, ὡς χαιρὸν ἔχομεν, whilſt we have time, ὡς for ἕως, whilſt this life laſts ; ſo Grotius does underſtand and interpret this phraſe ; and then the apoſtle does hereby intimate to them the uncertainty of their lives, eſpecially in thoſe times of perſecution. And this conſideration holds in all times, in ſome degree, that our lives are ſhort and uncertain ; that it is but a little while that we can ſerve GOD in this kind, namely, while we are in this world, in this vale of miſery and wants. In the next world there will be no occaſion,

no

no opportunity for it; we fhall then have nothing to S E R M.
do, but to reap the reward of the good we have CLVIII.
done in this life, and to receive that bleffed fentence
from the mouth of the great judge of the world,
" Come, ye bleffed of my father, inherit the king-
" dom prepared for you, before the foundation of
" the world : for I was hungry, and ye gave me
" meat, &c." And, *Euge bone ferve !* " Well done,
" good and faithful fervant ! thou haft been faithful
" in a little, and I will make thee ruler over much."
God will then declare his bounty and goodnefs to
us, and open thofe inexhauftible treafures of glory
and happinefs, which all good men fhall partake of,
in proportion to the good which they have done in
this world. Or elfe,

3. (Which I take to be the moft probable meaning of this phrafe,) It may refer to the degree of
this duty, in proportion to our ability and eftate ; as
we have ability, " let us do good unto all men."
And this the phrafe will bear, as learned men have
obferved ; and it is very reafonable to take it in this
fenfe, at leaft as part of the meaning of it, either
expreffed, or implied. For, without this, we cannot
exercife charity, though there were never fo many
occafions for it ; and then this precept will be of
the fame importance with that of the fon of Sirach,
Eccluf. xxxv. 10. " Give unto the moft high ac-
" cording as he hath enriched thee ;" and with that
counfel, Tob. iv. 7. " Give alms, ἐκ τῶν ὑπαρ-
" χόντων, according to thy fubftance," and v. 8.
" If thou haft abundance, give alms accordingly."
And this may be reafonably expected from us ; for
where-ever his providence gives a man an eftate, it
is but in truft for certain ufes and purpofes, among
which charity and alms is the chief : and we muft

be

be accountable to him, whether we have difposed it faithfully to the ends for which it was committed to us. It is an eafy thing, with him, to level mens eftates, and to give every man a competency ; but he does on purpofe fuffer things to be diftributed fo unequally, to try and exercife the virtues of men in feveral ways ; the faith and patience of the poor, the contentednefs of thofe in a middle condition, the charity and bounty of the rich. And, in truth, wealth and riches, that is, an eftate above what fufficeth our real occafions and neceffities, is in no other fenfe a bleffing, than as it is an opportunity put into our hands, by the providence of GOD, of doing more good ; and if we do not faithfully employ it to this end, it is but a temptation and a fnare ; " and " the ruft of our filver and our gold will be a wit- " nefs againft us ;" and we do but " heap up trea- " fures together againft the laft day."

But what proportion our charity ought to bear to our eftates, I fhall not undertake to determine. The circumftances of men have too much variety in them to admit of any certain rule ; fome may do well, and others may do better ; every man as GOD hath put into his heart, and according to his belief of " the recompence which fhall be made at " the refurrection of the juft." I fhall only fay in general, that if there be firft a free and willing mind, that will make a man charitable to his power ; for " the liberal man will devife liberal things." And we cannot propofe a better pattern to ourfelves in this kind, than the king and queen, who are, as they ought to be (but as it very feldom happens) the moft bright and fhining examples of this greateft of all graces and virtues, charity and compaffion to the poor and perfecuted. I proceed to the

IV. Things

IVth thing confiderable in the text, viz. Our unwearied perfeverance in this work of doing good; " let us not be weary in well-doing." After we have done fome few acts of charity, yea, though they fhould be very confiderable, we muft not fit down and fay we have done enough : There will ftill be new objects, new occafions, new opportunities for the exercife of our charity, fpringing up and pre- fenting themfelves to us. Let us never think that we can do enough in the way of doing good. The beft and the happieft beings are moft conftant and unwearied in this work of doing good. The holy angels of God are continually employed in miniftring for the good of " thofe, who fhall be heirs of falva- " tion :" and the Son of God, when he appeared in our nature, and " dwelt among us," that he might be a perfect and familiar example to us of all holi- nefs and virtue, " he went about doing good" to the bodies, and to the fouls of men. How diligent and unwearied was he in this work ! It was his employ- ment and his pleafure, his meat and drink, the joy and the life of his life. And God himfelf, though he is infinitely and perfectly good in himfelf, yet he ftill continues " to do good," and is never weary of this bleffed work. It is the nature, and the per- fection, and the felicity of God himfelf; and how can we be weary of that work, which is an imita- tion of the higheft excellency and perfection, and the very effence of happinefs !

. V. And laftly, here is the argument and encou- ragement to the chearful difcharge of this duty, " becaufe in due feafon we fhall reap, if we faint " not ; therefore, as we have opportunity, let us do " good unto all men. In due feafon we fhall reap ;" that is, fooner or later, in this world, or in the

I

other, we shall receive the full reward of our well-doing.

And now I have explained this duty to you, as plainly and briefly as I could, the hardest part of my task is yet behind, to persuade men to the practice of it; and to this purpose I shall only insist upon the promise in the text, " be not weary in well-doing ; " for in due season ye shall reap, if ye faint not :" We shall reap the pleasure and satisfaction of it in our own minds, and all the other mighty advantages of it in this world, and the vast and unspeakable reward of it in the other.

First, We shall reap the pleasure and satisfaction of it in our own minds; and there is no sensual pleasure that is comparable to the delight of doing good. This Cato makes his boast of, as the great comfort and joy of his old age, *conscientia benè actæ vitæ, multorumque benefactorum recordatio jucundissima.* The remembrance of a well-spent life, and of many benefits and kindnesses done by us to others, is one of the most pleasant things in the world. Sensual pleasures soon die and vanish, but that is not the worst of them, they leave a sting behind them ; and when the pleasure is gone, nothing remains but guilt, and trouble, and repentance : whereas the reflection upon any good we have done, is a perpetual spring of peace and pleasure, to us, and no trouble and bitterness ensues upon it ; the thoughts of it lie even and easy in our minds ; and so often as it comes to our remembrance, it ministers fresh comfort to us.

Secondly, We shall likewise reap other mighty advantages by it in this world. It is the way to derive a lasting blessing upon our estates. What we give in alms and charity is consecrated to God, and is one of the chiefest and most acceptable sacrifices in
the

the chriftian religion: fo the apoftle tells us, Heb. xiii. 16. " To do good, and to communicate, for- " get not ; for with fuch facrifices God is well " pleafed." It is like the firft-fruits under the law, which being dedicated and offered up to God, did derive a bleffing upon their whole harveft.

And it procures for us alfo the bleffing and pray- ers of thofe to whom we extend our charity ; their bleffing, I fay, upon us and ours, and all that we have : and " is it a fmall thing in our eye, to have" (as Job fpeaks) " the bleffing of them, who are "ready to perifh, to come upon us?" " The fervent " prayer" of the poor for us " availeth much ;" for God hath a fpecial " regard to the prayers of the de- " ftitute, and his ear is open to their cry."

Few men have faith to believe it, but certainly charity is a great fecurity to us in the times of evil, and that not only from the fpecial promife and pro- vidence of God, which is engaged to preferve thofe from want, who are ready to relieve the neceffity of others, Prov. xi. 25. " The liberal foul fhall be " made fat ; and he that watereth, fhall be watered " alfo himfelf," and Prov. xxviii. 27. " He that " giveth unto the poor fhall not lack. He fhall not " be afraid in the evil time, and in the days of dearth " he fhall be fatisfied," fays the Pfalmift. But be- befides the promife and providence of God, our cha- rity and alms are likewife a great fecurity to us, from the nature and reafon of the thing itfelf. Whofo- ever is charitable to others, does wifely befpeak the charity and kindnefs of others for himfelf, againft the day of neceffity ; for there is nothing that makes a man more and furer friends, than our bounty ; this will plead for us, and ftand our friend in our great- eft troubles and dangers ; " for a good man," faith

1 C R,   the

the apoſtle, that is, for one that is ready to oblige others by great kindneſſes and benefits, " one would " even dare to die." It has ſometimes happened, that the obligation which a man hath laid upon others by a chearful and ſeaſonable charity, hath, in time of danger and extremity, done him more kindneſs than all his eſtate could do for him. " Alms," ſaith the wiſe man, " hath delivered from death."

And in times of publick diſtreſs, and when we are beſet with cruel and powerful enemies, who, "if " GOD were not on our ſide, would ſwallow us up " quick," the publick charity of a nation does many times prove it's beſt ſafeguard and ſhield. There is a moſt remarkable paſſage to this purpoſe, Eccluſ. xxix. 11, 12, 13. " Lay up thy treaſure accord- " ing to the commandments of the moſt High, and " it ſhall bring thee more profit, than gold. Shut " up alms in thy ſtore-houſes, and it ſhall deliver " thee from all affliction. It ſhall fight for thee a- " gainſt thine enemies, better than a mighty ſhield " and a ſtrong ſpear."

And of this I doubt not but we of this nation, by the great mercy and goodneſs of Almighty GOD, have had happy experience in our late wonderful de- liverance, under the conduct and valour of one of the beſt and braveſt of princes, and to whom, by too many among us, the moſt unworthy and unthank- ful returns have been made, for the unwearied pains he hath undergone, and for the deſperate hazards he hath expoſed himſelf to for our ſakes, that ever were made to ſo great and generous a benefactor ; ſo great a benefactor, I ſay, not only to theſe nations, but to all Europe, in aſſerting and vindicating their liberties againſt the inſolent tyranny and pride of one of the greateſt oppreſſors of mankind ; of whom I

        may

may fay, as Job does of the Leviathan, Job xli. 33. 34. " Upon earth there is not his like. He behold- " eth all high things; he is king over all the children of pride."

And beyond all this, the bleffing of God does defcend upon the pofterity of thofe who are eminently charitable, and great benefactors to mankind. This David obferves in his time ; " I have been " young" (fays he) "and now am old ; yet have " I not feen the righteous forfaken, nor his feed " begging bread ;" and what he means by the righteous man, he explains in the next words, " he is " ever merciful, and lendeth."

I fhall only add upon this head, that the practice of this virtue will be one of our beft comforts at the hour of death, and that we fhall then look back upon all the good we have done in our life with the greateft contentment and joy imaginable. Xenophon, in his Cyrus, which he defigned for the perfect idea of a good prince, reprefents him in the laft minutes of his life, addreffing himfelf to God to this purpofe, " Thou knoweft that I have been a lover of " mankind ; and now that I am leaving this world, " I hope to find that mercy from thee, which I have " fhewed to others." Thefe words that excellent heathen hiftorian thought fit to come from the mouth of fo excellent a prince, as he had defcribed him, juft as he was leaving the world ; by which we may fee, what the light of nature thought to be the beft comfort of a dying man. This brings me to the

Third and laft particular which I mentioned, the vaft and unfpeakable reward, which this grace and virtue of charity will meet with in the other world. It will plead for us at the day of judgment, and procure for us a moft glorious " recompence at the " refurrection

refurrection of the juft," and that proportionable to the degrees of our charity ; 2 Cor. ix. 6. " He " which foweth fparingly, fhall reap alfo fparingly :" " and he which foweth bountifully, fhall reap boun- " tifully ;" and from this confideration, the apoftle encourageth our perfeverance in well-doing ; " let us " not be weary in well-doing, for in due feafon we fhall " reap, if we faint not ;" that is, we fhall certainly meet with the reward of it, if not in this world, yet in the other.

And now that I have declared this duty to you, together with the mighty pleafure, and advantages, and rewards of it, I crave leave to prefent you with fome of the beft occafions, and opportunities of the exercife and practice of it. And for your encourage- ment hereto, I fhall read to you the prefent ftate of the chief hofpitals belonging to this great city, and of the difpofal of their charity for the laft year.

And now I have laid before you thefe great objects of your charity, and the beft arguments I could think of to incline and ftir up your minds to the exercife of this excellent grace and virtue ; as there is no time left for it, I having, I am afraid, already tired your patience, fo, I hope, there is no need to prefs this duty any farther upon you, fince you are willing and forward of yourfelves, and fo very ready to every good work. This great city hath a double honour due to it, of being both the greateft benefactors in this kind, and the moft faithful managers, and dif- pofers of it ; and I am now in a place moft proper for the mention of CHRIST's Hofpital, a proteftant foundation of that moft pious and excellent prince Edward VI. which, I believe, is one of the beft in- ftances of fo large and fo well-managed a charity, this day in the world.

And

And now to conclude all : if 'any of you know any better employment than " to do good ;" any work that will give truer pleafure to our minds ; that hath greater and better promifes made to it, " the promifes of the life that now is, and that " which is to come ;" that we fhall reflect upon with more comfort, when we come to die ; and that through the mercies and merits of our bleffed SAVIOUR, will ftand us in more ftead at the day of judgment ; let us mind that work : but if we do not, let us apply ourfelves to this bufinefs of charity with all our might, and " let us not be weary in well- " doing, becaufe in due feafon we fhall reap, if we " faint not."

" Now the GOD of peace, who brought again " from the dead our LORD JESUS CHRIST, the " great fhepherd of the fheep, through the blood " of the everlafting covenant, make you perfect in " every good work, to do his will, through JESUS " CHRIST, to whom with thee, O father, and the " Holy Ghoft, be all honour and glory, thankfgiv- " ing and praife, both now and for ever," Amen.

SERMON CLIX.
The neceffity of repentance and faith.

ACTS xx. 21.
Teftifying both to the Jews, and alfo to the Greeks, re-
pentance toward GOD, and faith toward our LORD
JESUS CHRIST.

TO have feen St. Paul in the pulpit, was one of thofe three things which St. Auguftine thought worth the wifhing for.   And fure it were very defirable

SERM. rable to have ſeen this glorious inſtrument of GOD,
CLIX. who did ſuch wonders in the world, to have heard
that plain and powerful eloquence of his, which was
ſo " mighty through GOD, for the caſting down of
" ſtrong holds, and the ſubduing of men to the
" obedience of the goſpel;" to have beheld the
zeal of this holy man, who was all on fire for GOD,
with what ardency of affection, and earneſtneſs of
expreſſion, he perſuaded men to come in to CHRIST,
and entertain the goſpel. This were very deſirable ;
but ſeeing it is a thing we cannot hope for, it ſhould
be ſome ſatisfaction to our curioſity, to know what
St. Paul preached, what was the main ſubject of his
ſermons, whither he referred all his diſcourſes, and
what they tended to. This he tells us in the words
that I have read to you, that the main ſubſtance of
all his ſermons was " repentance toward GOD, and
" faith toward our LORD JESUS CHRIST."

The occaſion of the words was briefly this ; St.
Paul being in his journey to Jeruſalem, and intending to be there by the day of Pentecoſt, that he
might not be hindred in his journey, he reſolves to
paſs by Epheſus, and only to call to him the elders of
the church to charge them with their duty, and the
care of the church ; and to engage them hereto, he
tells them how he had carried and demeaned himſelf
among them, v. 18. with what diligence and vigi-
lance he had watched over them, with what affection and earneſtneſs he had preached to them, v. 19,
20. And here in the text he tells them, what had
been the ſum of his doctrine, and the ſubſtance of
thoſe many ſermons he had preached among them,
and what was the end and deſign of all his diſcourſes,
viz. To perſuade men to " repentance toward GOD,
" and faith toward our LORD JESUS CHRIST ; teſ-
" tifying both to the Jews and Greeks, &c. I ſhall

I shall explain the words a little, and then fix up-on the observations which I intend to speak to, because I design this only as a preface to some larger discourses of faith and repentance.

For explication. Testifying, the word is διαμαρτυρόμεν⊙, which signifies to testify, to prove a thing by testimony ; so it is used, Heb. ii. 6. " But one " in a certain place testifieth, saying." In heathen writers the word is often used in a law sense, for contesting by law, and pleading in a cause ; and from hence it signifies, earnestly to contend or persuade by arguments and threatenings. In the use of the LXX. it signifies to protest, to convince, to press earnestly, to persuade. It is used most frequently by St. Luke in a very intense signification, and is sometimes joined with exhorting, which is an earnest persuading to a thing, Acts ii. 40. " And with " many other words did he testify and exhort, say- " ing, save yourselves from this untoward genera- " tion ;" and with preaching, Acts viij. 25. " And " when they had testified and preached the word of " the Lord ;" and so Acts xviii. 5. " Being pressed " in spirit, he testified to the Jews, that Jesus was " the Christ." Being pressed in spirit, signifies intention and vehemency in testifying to them, that he did vehemently endeavour to convince them ; it seems to be equivalent to the expression, v. 28. where it is said, " Apollos did mightily convince the Jews that " Jesus was the Christ ;" that is, did use such persuasions and arguments as were sufficient to convince ; and to mention no more, Acts xxviii. 23. " He " expounded and testified the kingdom of God, " persuading them concerning Jesus."

S. Paul in his epistle to Timothy useth these words in a most vehement sense, for giving a solemn charge,

SERM. 1 Tim. v. 21. "I charge thee before God and the
CLIX. " Lord Jesus Christ," the word is διαμαρτύρο-
μαι; and fo 2 Tim. ii. 14. " charging them before
" the Lord, that they ftrive not about words ;"
and fo 2 Tim. iv. 1. " I charge thee before God
" and the Lord Jesus Christ ;" and here in the
text the word feems to be of a very high and intenfe
fignification, becaufe of the circumftances mentioned
before and after ; he tells us before, that he taught
them " at all feafons," v. 18. " publickly and from
" houfe to houfe," v. 20. And afterwards at the
" 31ft. v. that " he warned them day and night
" with tears." So that "teftifying to the Jews re-
" pentance and faith," muft fignify his preffing and
perfuading of them with the greateft vehemency, to
turn from their fins, and believe on the Lord Jesus
Christ ; his charging on them thefe things as their
duty, his pleading with them the neceffity of faith
and repentance, and earneftly endeavouring to convince them thereof.

" Repentance toward God, and faith toward our
" Lord Jesus Christ :" what is the reafon of
this appropriation of repentance and faith, the one
as properly refpecting God, and the other our Lord
Jesus Christ ? I anfwer. Repentance doth properly refpect God, becaufe he is the party offended,
and to whom we are to be reconciled ; the faith of
the Gofpel doth properly refer to the Lord Jesus
Christ, as the chief and principal object of it; fo
that by " teftifying to them repentance toward
" God, &c. we are to underftand that the apoftle
did earneftly prefs and perfuade them to repent of
their fins, whereby they had offended God, and to
believe on the Lord Jesus Christ, as the Meffias,
the perfon that was ordained of God, and fent to be
the Saviour of the world,   From

.From the words thus explained, this is the obfervation that doth naturally arife,

That repentance and faith are the fum and fubftance of the gofpel; and that minifters ought with
all earneftnefs and vehemency to prefs people to repent and believe, to charge them with thefe as their
duty, and by all means to endeavour to convince
them of the neceffity of them.

In the handling of this I fhall do thefe two things.

Firft, fhew you what is included in repentance and
faith, that you may fee that they are the fum of the
gófpel. And,

Secondly, fhew you the neceffity of them.

Firft, What is included in thefe.

I. Repentance ; this properly fignifies a change of
mind, a conviction that we have done amifs, fo as
to be truly forry for what we have done, and heartily to wifh that we had not done it. To repent, is to alter our mind, to have other apprehenfions of things
than we had, to look upon that now as evil, which
we did not before; from whence follows forrow for
what we have done, and a refolution of mind for the
future not to do again that which appears now to us
to be fo evil, that we are afhamed of it, and troubled for it, and wifh we had never done it. So that
repentance implies a conviction that we have done
fomething that is evil and finful, contrary to the law
we are under, and thofe obligations of duty and gratitude that lie upon us, whereby GOD is highly provoked and incenfed againft us, and we in danger of
his wrath, and the fad effects of his difpleafure; upon which we are troubled, and grieved, and afhamed for what we have done, and wifh we had been
wifer, and had done otherwife ; hereupon we refolve never to do any thing that is finful, that is con-

trary

trary to our duty and obligations to God, and by which we may provoke him againft us. Thefe two things are contained in a true repentance, a deep fenfe of, and forrow for the evils that are paft, and the fins that we have committed ; and a firm purpofe and refolution of obedience for the future, of abftaining from all fin, and doing whatever is our duty ; the true effect of which refolution, is the breaking off the practice of fin, and the courfe of a wicked life, and a conftant courfe of obedience.

II. Faith in CHRIST is an effectual believing the revelation of the gofpel, the hiftory and the doctrine of it ; the hiftory of it, that there was fuch a perfon as JESUS CHRIST, that he was the true Meffias, prophefied of and promifed in the Old Teftament, that he was born and lived and preached, and wrought the miracles that are recorded, that he was crucified and rofe again, and afcended into heaven, that he was " the Son of God," and fent by him into the world, by his doctrine to inftruct, and by the example of his life to go before us in the way to happinefs, and by the merit and fatisfaction of his death and fufferings, to appeafe and reconcile God to us, and to purchafe for us the pardon of our fins and eternal life, upon the conditions of faith and repentance and fincere obedience ; and that to enable us to the performance of thefe conditions, he promifed, and afterward fent his holy Spirit, to accompany the preaching of his gofpel, and to affift all Chriftians to the doing of that which God requires of them ; this is the hiftory of the gofpel.

Now the doctrine of it contains the precepts and promifes and threatenings of it, and faith in CHRIST includes a firm belief of all thefe ; of the precepts of the gofpel as the matter of our duty, and the

rule

rule of our life ; and of the promiſes and threatenings of the goſpel, as arguments to our duty, to
encourage our obedience, and deter us from ſin. So
that he that believes the LORD JESUS, believes him
to be the great guide and teacher ſent from GOD, to
bring and conduct men to eternal happineſs, and that
therefore we ought to hearken to him and follow
him ; this is to believe his prophetical office. He believes that he is " the author of ſalvation," and hath
purchaſed for us forgiveneſs of ſins, ranſom from
hell, and eternal life and bleſſedneſs upon the conditions before mentioned, and therefore that we ought
to rely upon him only for ſalvation, to own him for
our SAVIOUR, and to beg of him his holy Spirit,
which he hath promiſed to us, to enable us to perform the conditions required on our part ; this is to
believe his prieſtly office. And laſtly, he believes
that the precepts of the goſpel, being delivered to
us by the Son of GOD, ought to have the authority
of laws upon us, and that we are bound to be obedient to them ; and for our encouragement if we
be ſo, that there is a glorious and eternal reward promiſed to us ; and for our terror if we be not, there
are terrible and eternal puniſhments threatened to us ;
to which rewards, the LORD JESUS CHRIST at the
day of judgment will ſentence men, as the great
judge of the world ; and this is to believe the kingly
office of CHRIST. And this is the ſum of that
which is meant by " faith toward the LORD JESUS
" CHRIST," which the apoſtle ſaith was one ſubject
of his preaching.

And the proper and genuine effect of this faith is
to live as we believe, to conform our lives to the
doctrine, to the truth whereof we aſſent. Hence it is
that true Chriſtians, that is, thoſe who faſhioned their

-I
lives

lives according to the goſpel, are called believers ;
and the whole of chriſtianity is many times contained in this word believing, which is the great principle
of a chriſtian life. As in the old teſtament all religion is expreſſed by " the fear of GOD ;" ſo in the
new, by " faith in CHRIST."

And now you ſee what is included in repentance
and faith, you may eaſily judge whether theſe be not
the ſum of the goſpel, that men ſhould forſake their
ſins and turn to GOD, and believe in the revelation of
the goſpel concerning JESUS CHRIST, that is, heartily entertain and ſubmit to it. What did CHRIST
preach to the Jews, but that they ſhould repent of
their ſins, and believe on him as the Meſſias ? And
what did the apoſtles preach, but to the ſame purpoſe? When St. Peter preached to the Jews, Acts ii.
the effect of his ſermon and the ſcope of it was to
perſuade them " to repent and be baptized in the
" name of JESUS," that is, to profeſs their belief in
him, v. 38. And ſo Acts iii. 19. This is the concluſion of his diſcourſe, " repent therefore and be
" converted," and then he propounded CHRIST to
them as the object of their faith, being the great
prophet that was propheſied of by Moſes, who ſhould
" be raiſed up among them," v. 22. So likewiſe
St. Paul when he preached to the Jews and Gentiles,
theſe were his great ſubjects, Acts xvii. 30. This
is the concluſion of his ſermon to the Athenians, to
perſuade them to repent by the conſideration of a
future judgment ; and to perſuade them to believe
on the LORD JESUS CHRIST, who was to be the
judge of the world, from the miracle of his reſurrection ; " But now he commands all men every
" where to repent, becauſe he hath appointed a day,
" &c. whereof he hath given aſſurance unto all men,
" in

" in that he hath raifed him from the dead." So
that you fee that thefe are the great doctrines of the
gofpel, and were the fum of the apoftles preaching;
all their fermons were perfuafives to thefe two duties
of repentance and faith.

Secondly, for the neceffity of thefe doctrines. They
are neceffary for the efcaping of eternal mifery, and
attaining of everlafting happinefs. And this will appear, by confidering the nature of them, and the
relation they have to both thefe.

For the avoiding of eternal punifhment, it is ne-
eeffary the guilt fhould be removed, which is an obligation to punifhment, and that cannot be but by
pardon ; and fure we cannot imagine that GOD will
ever pardon us without repentance ; he will never
remit to us the punifhment of fin, fo long as we tell
him we are not at all troubled for what we have done,
and we are of the fame mind ftill, and will do the
fame again ; and till we repent, we tell GOD this,
and we may be fure GOD will not caft away his par-
dons upon thofe that defpife them ; fo that repentance
is neceffary to the efcaping of hell.

And faith in CHRIST is neceffary to it ; for if this
be the method of GOD's grace, not to pardon fin
without fatisfaction, and JESUS CHRIST hath made
fatisfaction for fin by the merit of his fufferings, and
if it be neceffary that we fhould believe this, that the
benefit hereof may redound to us ; then faith in
CHRIST is neceffary to the obtaining of the pardon
of fin, by which the guilt of fin is removed, that
is, our obligation to eternal punifhment.

And then for attaining falvation. CHRIST having
in the gofpel revealed to us the way and means to
eternal happinefs, it is neceffary that we fhould believe this revelation of the gofpel by JESUS CHRIST,

in

in order to this end.   So that you see the necessity
of faith and repentance, because without these we
can neither escape misery, nor attain to happiness.

I should now come to draw some inferences from
this discourse, but I will first give satisfaction to a
query or two, to which this discourse seems to have
given occasion.

1. Query. You will say, why do I call repentance
a doctrine of the gospel ? It is a doctrine of nature.
Natural religion tells us, that when we have offended God, we ought to be sorry for it, and resolve to
amend and reform.

Ans. I do not make the doctrine of repentance
proper to the gospel, as if it had not been revealed
to the world before ; but because it is a doctrine
which the gospel very much presseth and persuadeth
men to, and because the great motives and enforcements of it are peculiar to the gospel,   So that the
doctrine of repentance, considered with those powerful reasons and arguments to it which the gospel furnisheth us withal, is in this sense proper to the gospel, and not known to the world before.

There are two motives and enforcements to repentance which the gospel furnisheth us with.

1. Assurance of pardon and remission of sins in
case of repentance, which is a great encouragement
to repentance, and which, before the gospel, the
world had never any firm and clear assurance of.

2. Assurance of eternal rewards and punishments
after this life, which is a strong argument to persuade men to change their lives, that they may a-
void the misery that is threatened to impenitent sinners, and be qualified for the happiness which it pro-
miseth to repentance and obedience.   And this the
apostle tells us in the formentioned place, Acts xvii.
30, 31.

30, 31. is that which doth, as it were, make repentance to be a new doctrine that did come with the goſpel into the world, becauſe it was never before enforced with this powerful argument ; " the times " of that ignorance God winked at ; but now he " calls upon all men every where to repent ; be- " cauſe, &c." When the world was in ignorance, and had not ſuch aſſurance of a future ſtate, of eternal rewards and puniſhments after this life, the arguments to repentance were weak and feeble in compariſon of what they now are, the neceſſity of this duty was not ſo evident. But now God hath aſſured us of a future judgment, now exhortations to repentance have a commanding power and influence upon men ; ſo that repentance, both as it is that which is very much preſſed and inculcated in the goſpel, and as it hath it's chief motives and enforcements from the goſpel, may be ſaid to be one of the great doctrines of the goſpel.

Query 2. Whether the preaching of faith in CHRIST, among thoſe who are already Chriſtians, be at all neceſſary ? Becauſe it ſeems very improper, to preſs thoſe to believe in CHRIST, who are already perſuaded that he is the Meſſias, and do entertain the hiſtory and doctrine of the goſpel.

Anſ. The faith which the apoſtle here means, and which he would perſuade men to, is an effectual belief of the goſpel ; ſuch a faith as hath real effects upon men, and makes them to live as they believe ; ſuch a faith as perſuades them of the need of theſe bleſſings that the goſpel offers, and makes them to deſire to be partakers of them, and in order thereto to be willing to ſubmit to thoſe terms and conditions of holineſs and obedience, which the goſpel requires. This is the faith we would perſuade men to, and there is nothing more neceſſary to be preſſed upon the greateſt part of Chriſtians than this ; for how few are there, among thoſe who profeſs to believe the goſpel, who believe it in this effectual manner, ſo as to conform themſelves to it ? The faith which moſt Chriſtians pretend to is merely negative ; they do not diſbelieve the goſpel, they do not conſider it, nor trouble themſelves about it, they do not care, nor are concerned whether it be true or not ; but they have not a poſitive belief of it, they are not poſſeſſed with a firm perſuaſion of the truth of thoſe matters which are contained in it ; if they were, ſuch a perſuaſion would produce real and poſitive effects. Every man naturally deſires happineſs, and it is impoſſible that any man that is poſſeſſed with this belief, that in order to happineſs it is neceſſary for him to do ſuch and ſuch things ; and that if he omit or neglect them he is unavoidably miſerable, that he ſhould not do them. Men ſay they believe this or that, but you may ſee in their lives, what it is they believe. So that the preaching of this faith in CHRIST, which is the only true faith, is ſtill neceſſary.

I. Infer. " If repentance towards GOD, and faith in " the LORD JESUS CHRIST," be the ſum and ſubſtance of the goſpel, then from hence we may infer the excellency of the chriſtian religion, which inſiſts only upon thoſe things that do tend to our perfection and our happineſs. Repentance tends to our recovery, and the bringing of us back as near as may be to innocence. *Primus innocentiæ gradus eſt non peccaſſe*; *ſecundus, pœnitentia :* and then " faith in the LORD " JESUS CHRIST," though it be very comprehenſive, and contains many things in it, yet nothing but what is eminently for our advantage, and doth very much conduce to our happineſs. The hiſtorical part

of

of the gospel acquaints us with the person and actions of our SAVIOUR, which conduceth very much to our understanding of the author and means of our salvation. The doctrinal part of the gospel contains what GOD requires on our part, and the encouragements and arguments to our duty, from the consideration of the recompence and rewards of the next life. The precepts of CHRIST's doctrine are such as tend exceedingly to the perfection of our nature, being all founded in reason, in the nature of GOD, and of a reasonable creature ; I except only those positive institutions of the christian religion, the two sacraments, which are not burthensom, and are of excellent use. This is the first.

II. We may learn from hence what is to be the sum and end of our preaching, to bring men to repentance and a firm belief of the gospel ; but then it is to be considered, that we preach repentance, so often as we preach either against sin in general, or any particular sin or vice ; and so often as we persuade to holiness in general, or to the performance of any particular duty of religion, or to the exercise of any particular grace ; for repentance includes the forsaking of sin, and a sincere resolution and endeavour of reformation and obedience. And we preach repentance so often as we insist upon such considerations and arguments, as may be powerful to deter men from sin, and to engage them to holiness. And we preach "faith towards our LORD JESUS CHRIST," so often as we declare the grounds of the christian religion, and insist upon such arguments as tend to make it credible, and are proper to convince men of the truth and reasonableness of it, so often as we explain the mystery of CHRIST's incarnation, the history of his life, death, resurrection, ascension, and

18 T 2 intercession,

interceffion, and the proper ends and ufe of thefe ; fo often as we open the method of GOD's grace for the falvation of finners, the nature of the covenant between GOD and us, and the conditions of it, and the way how a finner is juftified and hath his fins pardoned, the nature and neceffity of regeneration and fanctification ; fo often as we explain the precepts of the gofpel, and the promifes and threatenings of it, and endeavour to convince men of the equity of CHRIT's commands, and to affure them of the certainty of the eternal happinefs which the gofpel promifes to them that obey it, and of the eternal mifery which the gofpel threatens to thofe that are difobedient; all this is preaching "faith in our LORD " JESUS CHRIST."

III. This may correct the irregular humours and itch in many people, who are not contented with this plain and wholefom food, but muft be gratified with fublime notions and unintelligible myfteries, with pleafant paffages of wit, and artificial ftrains of rhetorick, with nice and unprofitable difputes, with bold interpretations of dark prophecies, and peremptory determinations of what will happen next year, and a punctual ftating of the time when Anti-chrift fhall be thrown down, and Babylon fhall fall, and who fhall be employed in this work. Or if their humour lies another way, you muft apply yourfelf to it, by making fharp reflections upon matters in prefent controverfy and debate, you muft dip your ftile in gall and vinegar, and be all fatyr and invective againft thofe that differ from you, and teach people to hate one another, and to fall together by the ears ; and this men call gofpel preaching, and fpeaking of feafonable truths.

Surely St. Paul was a gofpel preacher, and fuch

an

an one as may be a pattern to all others ; and yet he
did none of these ; he preached what men might
underftand, and what they ought to believe and
practife, in a plain and unaffected and convincing
manner ; he taught "fuch things as made for peace,"
" and whereby he might edify and build up men in
" their holy faith." The doctrines that he preached will never be unfeafonable, that men fhould leave
their fins, and believe the gofpel, and live accordingly.

And if men muft needs be gratified with difputes
and controverfies, there are thefe great controverfies
between God and the finner to be ftated and determined ; whether this be religion, to follow our own
lufts and inclinations, or to endeavour to be like God,
and to be conformed to him, in goodnefs, and mercy, and righteoufnefs, and truth, and faithfulnefs ?
Whether Jesus Christ be not the Meffias and Saviour of the world ? Whether faith and repentance and
fincere obedience be not the terms of falvation, and the
neceffary conditions of happinefs ? Whether there
fhall be a future judgment, when all men fhall be
fentenced according to their works ? Whether there
be heaven and hell ? Whether good men fhall be
eternally and unfpeakably happy, and wicked men
extremely and everlaftingly miferable ? Thefe are the
great controverfies of religion, upon which we are
to difpute on God's behalf againft finners. God
afferts, and finners deny thefe things, not in words,
but which is more emphatical and fignificant, in their
lives and actions. Thefe are practical controverfies
of faith, and it concerns every man to be refolved
and determined about them, that he may frame his
life accordingly.

And fo for repentance ; God fays, repentance is a
forfaking of fin, and a thorough change and amendment

SERM.
CLIX.
ment of life ; the finner fays, that it is only a formal confeffion, and a flight afking of God forgivenefs : God calls upon us fpeedily and forthwith to
repent; the finner faith it is time enough, and it
may fafely be deferred to ficknefs or death ; thefe are
important controverfies, and matters of moment.
But men do not affect common truths ; whereas thefe
are moft neceffary : And indeed whatever is generally ufeful and beneficial, ought to be common, and
not to be the lefs valued, but the more efteemed for
being fo.

And as thefe doctrines of faith and repentance are
never unfeafonable, fo are they more peculiarly proper when we celebrate the holy facrament, which
was inftituted for a folemn and ftanding memorial
of the chriftian religion, and is one of the moft
powerful arguments and perfuafives to repentance
and a good life.

The faith of the gofpel doth more particularly
refpect the death of Christ ; and therefore it is called " faith in his blood," becaufe that is more efpecially the object of our faith ; the blood of Christ,
as it was a feal of the truth of his doctrine, fo it is
alfo a confirmation of all the bleffings and benefits
of the new covenant.

And it is one of the greateft arguments in the world
to repentance. In the blood of Christ we may
fee our own guilt, and in the dreadful fufferings of
the Son of God, the juft defert of our fins; " he
" hath born our griefs, and carried our forrows, he
" was wounded for our tranfgreffions, and bruifed
" for our iniquities ; therefore the commemoration
of his fufferings fhould call our fins to remembrance,
the reprefentation of his body broken, fhould melt
our hearts ; and fo often as we remember that " his
" blood

" blood was fhed for us, our eyes" fhould " run " down with rivers of tears ;" fo often as we " look " upon him whom we have pierced," we fhould " mourn over him." When the fon of GOD fuffered, " the rocks were rent in funder ;" and fhall not the confideration of thofe fufferings be effectual to break the moft ftony and obdurate heart?

. What can be more proper when we come to this facrament, than the renewing of our repentance ? When we partake of this paffover, we fhould " eat " it with bitter herbs." The moft folemn expreffions of our repentance fall fhort of thofe fufferings, which our bleffed SAVIOUR underwent for our fins. If " our head were waters, and our eyes fountains " of tears," we could never fufficiently lament the curfed effects and confequences of thofe provocations which were fo fatal to the Son of GOD. ·

And that our repentance may be real, it muft be accompanied with the refolution of a better life ; for if we return to our fins again, " we trample under " foot the Son of GOD, and profane the blood of " the covenant," and out of " the cup of falvation " we drink our own damnation," and turn that which fhould fave us into an inftrument and feal of our own ruin.

SERMON CLX.

Of confeffing and forfaking fin, in order to pardon.

PROV. xxviii. 13.

*He that covereth his fins fhall not profper: but who-
fo confeffeth and forfaketh them, fhall have mercy.*

SERM.
CLX.

Preached
on Afh-
wednef-
day.

SINCE we are all finners, and liable to the juftice of GOD, it is a matter of great moment
to our comfort and happinefs, to be rightly inform-
ed by what means, and upon what terms, we may
be reconciled to GOD, and find mercy with him.
And to this purpofe the text gives us this advice and
direction, " whofo confeffeth and forfaketh his fins
" fhall have mercy."

In which words there is a great bleffing and benefit declared and promifed to finners, upon certain
conditions. The bleffing and benefit promifed, is
" the mercy and favour of GOD," which comprehends all the happy effects of GOD's mercy and goodnefs to finners. And the conditions upon which this
bleffing is promifed are two, "confeffion of our fins,
" and forfaking of them;" and thefe two contain in
them the whole nature of that great and neceffary
duty of repentance, without which a finner can have
no reafonable hopes of the mercy of GOD.

I. Here is a bleffing or benefit promifed, which is
" the mercy and favour of GOD." And this in the
full extent of it, comprehends all the effects of the
mercy and goodnefs of GOD to finners, and doth primarily import the pardon and forgivenefs of our fins.

And

And this probably Solomon did chiefly intend in this expreffion; for fo the mercy of GoD doth moft fre-quently fignify in the old teftament, viz. the forgive-nefs of our fins. And thus the prophet explains it, Ifa. lv. 7. " Let the wicked forfake his ways, and " the unrighteous man his thoughts, and let him " return unto the LORD, and he will have mercy, " and to our GOD, for he will abundantly pardon."

But now fince the clear revelation of the gofpel, the mercy of GoD doth not only extend to the par-don of fin, but to power againft it ; becaufe this al-fo is an effect of GoD's free grace and mercy to finners, to enable them, by the grace of his holy Spirit, to mafter and mortify their lufts, and to per-fevere in goodnefs to the end.

And it comprehends alfo our final pardon and ab-folution at the great day, together with the glorious reward of eternal life, which the apoftle expreffeth, by " finding mercy with the LORD in that day." And this likewife is promifed to repentance, Acts iii. 19. " Repent ye therefore, and be converted, " that your fins may be blotted out, when the times " of refrefhing fhall come from the prefence of the " LORD, and he fhall fend JESUS CHRIST, who " before was preached unto you ;" that is, that when JESUS CHRIST who is now preached unto you fhall come, you may receive the final fentence of abfolu-tion and forgivenefs.

And thus much fhall fuffice to have fpoken of the bleffing and benefit here promifed, the mercy of GoD ; which comprehends all the bleffed effects of the divine grace and goodnefs to finners, the prefent pardon of fin, and power to mortify fin, and to per-fevere in a good courfe, and our final abfolution by

SERM.
CLX.
the sentence of the great day, together with the merciful and glorious reward of eternal life.

II. We will consider in the next place, the conditions upon which this blessing is promised, and they are two, the confessing and forsaking of our sins, " Whoso confesseth and forsaketh his sin, shall have " mercy;" and these two do contain and constitute the whole nature of repentance, without which a sinner can have no reasonable hopes to find mercy with God. I begin with the

First, the confession of our sins; by which is meant a penitent acknowledgment of our faults to God; to God I say, because the confession of our sins to men is not, generally speaking, a condition of the forgiveness of them, but only in some particular cases, when our sins against God are accompanied and complicated with scandal and injury to men. In other cases the confession of our sins to men is not necessary to the pardon of them; as I shall more fully shew in the progress of this discourse.

All the difficulty in this matter is, that the confession of our sins is opposed to the covering and concealing of them: " he that covereth his sin shall " not prosper: but whoso confesseth them shall have " mercy." But no man can hope to hide his sin from God, and therefore confession of them to God cannot be here meant. But this objection, if it be of any force, quite excludeth confession to God, as no part of Solomon's meaning; when yet confession of our sins to God is granted, on all hands, to be a necessary condition of the forgiveness of them. And to take away the whole ground of this objection; men are said in scripture, when they do not confess their sins and repent of them, to hide and conceal them from God: not to acknowledge them is as if

a man

a man went about to cover them. And thus David oppofeth confeffion of fins to God, to the hiding of them, Pfal. xxxii. 5. " I acknowledged my fin unto " thee, and mine iniquity have I not hid : I faid I " will confefs my tranfgreffions unto the Lord." So that this is no reafon, why the text fhould not be underftood of the confeffing of our fins to God.

But becaufe the neceffity of confeffing our fins to men (that is, to the prieft) in order to the forgive- nefs of them, is a great point of difference between us and the church of Rome, it being by them efteem- ed a neceffary article of faith, but by us, fo far from being neceffary to be believed, that we do not be- lieve it to be true ; therefore for the clear ftating of this matter, I fhall briefly enquire into thefe two things.

I. Whether confeffion of our fins to the prieft, as taught and practifed in the church of Rome, be ne- ceffary to the forgivenefs of them.

II. How far the difclofing and revealing of our fins to the minifters of God is convenient upon o- ther accounts, and for other purpofes of religion.

I. Whether confeffion of our fins to the prieft, and the manner in which it is taught and practifed in the church of Rome, be neceffary to the forgivenefs of them. What manner of confeffion this is, the council of Trent hath moft precifely determined, viz. " Secret confeffion to the prieft alone, of all " and every mortal fin, which upon the moft dili- " gent fearch and examination of our confciences " we can remember ourfelves to be guilty of, fince " our baptifm; together with all the circumftances " of thofe fins, which may change the nature of " them; becaufe without the perfect knowledge of " thefe, the prieft cannot make a judgment of the

" nature

SERM. " nature and quality of men's fins, nor impofe fit-
CLX. " ting penance for them." This is the confeffion
of fins required in the church of Rome, which the
fame council of Trent, without any real ground from
fcripture or ecclefiaftical antiquity, doth moft confi-
dently affirm, " to have been inftituted by our LORD,
" and by the law of GOD to be neceffary to falvati-
" on, and to have been always practifed in the ca-
" tholick church."

I fhall as briefly as I can examine both thefe pretences, of the divine inftitution, and conftant practice of this kind of confeffion.

Firft, for the divine inftitution of it, they mainly
rely upon three texts; in the firft of which there is
no mention at all of confeffion, much lefs of a particular confeffion of all our fins with the circumftances
of them; in the other two there is no mention of
confeffion to the priefts: and yet all this ought clearly to appear in thefe texts, before they can ground a
divine inftitution upon them; for a divine inftitution
is not to be founded upon obfcure confequences, but
upon plain words.

The firft text, and the only one upon which the
council of Trent grounds the neceffity of confeffion,
is, John xx. 23. " Whofefoever fins ye remit, they
" are remitted; and whofefoever fins ye retain, they
" are retained:" It is a fign they were at a great
lofs for a text to prove it, when they are glad to
bring one that hath not one word in it concerning
confeffion, nor the leaft intimation of the neceffity of it.

But let us fee how they manage it to their purpofe. The apoftles and their fucceffors (faith Bellar-
mine) by this power of remitting and retaining fins,
are conftituted judges of the cafe of penitents; but
they cannot judge without hearing the caufe, and
this

this infers particular confeſſion of ſins to the prieſt, from whence he concludes it neceſſary to the forgiveneſs of ſins.

But do not the miniſters of the goſpel exerciſe this power of remitting ſins in baptiſm? And yet particular confeſſion of all ſins to the prieſt is not required, no not in the church of Rome, in the baptiſm of adult perſons. And therefore according to them, particular confeſſion of ſin to the prieſt is not necefſary to his exerciſing the power of remitting ſins, and conſequently the neceſſity of confeſſion cannot be concluded from this text.

And to ſhew how they are puzzled in this matter, Vaſquez by a ſtrange device concludes the neceſſity of confeſſion from the power of retaining ſins; for (ſays he) if the prieſt have a power of retaining ſins, that is of denying pardon and abſolution to the penitent, then he may impoſe confeſſion as a condition of forgiveneſs, and not abſolve the penitent upon other terms. But ſuppoſing the prieſt to have this unreaſonable power, this makes confeſſion no otherwiſe neceſſary by divine inſtitution, than going to Jeruſalem or China is, in order to the forgiveneſs of our ſins, or ſubmitting to any other fooliſh condition, that the prieſt thinks fit to require; for according to this way of reaſoning, this power of retaining ſins makes every fooliſh thing, that the prieſt ſhall impoſe upon the penitent, to be neceſſary by divine command and inſtitution.

But the truth is, this power of remitting and retaining ſins is exerciſed by the miniſters of the goſpel, in the adminiſtration of the ſacraments, and the preaching of the goſpel, which is called " the word " of reconciliation, the miniſtry whereof is commit " ted to them.", And thus the ancient fathers underſtood

derſtood it; and as a great divine told them in the council of Trent, it was perhaps never expounded by any one father concerning the buſineſs of confeſſion.

The ſecond text they alledge to this purpoſe is 1 John i. 9. " If we confeſs our ſins, he is faithful " and juſt to forgive us our ſins." Here indeed is confeſſion; but general, not particular, as appears by the oppoſition, " If we ſay that we have no ſin, " we deceive ourſelves, and the truth is not in us : " but if we confeſs our ſins," that is, if we acknowledge our ſelves to have been ſinners. And then there is not a word of confeſſing to the prieſt; the confeſſion here meant is plainly to GOD, becauſe it follows, " he is faithful and juſt to forgive us our " ſins," that is GOD, who is neceſſarily underſtood in the former part of the ſentence ; as if it had run thus, " if we confeſs our ſins to GOD, he is faithful " and juſt to forgive us our ſins."

The third text is, Jam v. 16. " Confeſs your " faults one to another, and pray one for another." And here again there is only mention of confeſſion, but not a word of the prieſt : and for another reaſon, if I had been to adviſe them, they ſhould not have preſt this text for their ſervice in this cauſe, becauſe it does them as much hurt as good ; for it is certain, the duty of confeſſion here enjoined is reciprocal and mutual, " confeſs your ſins one to another :" ſo that if by virtue of this text the people are bound to confeſs their ſins to the prieſt, the prieſt is hereby as much obliged to confeſs his ſins to the people ; which I dare ſay is more than they have a mind to prove from this text. The plain meaning whereof is this, that as Chriſtians ſhould be ready to perform all mutual offices of charity, ſo to aſſiſt and comfort one

another,

another by their counfel and prayers. And therefore the apoftle advifeth Chriftians when they are fick, if at the fame time they be under any fpiritual trouble, by reafon of the guilt of any fin lying upon their confciences, to lay open their cafe to one another, that fo they may have the help of one anothers advice and prayers; " confefs your faults one " to another, and pray one for another, that ye " may be healed," both of your bodily and fpiritual diftemper. Not that the prieft or minifter is here excluded; St. James had fpoken of that particular before, that when " any was fick," he fhould " fend " for the elders of the church," that he might in the firft place have the benefit of their counfel and prayers; and then becaufe private Chriftians may alfo be ufeful to one another in this kind, he adds, that they fhould alfo lay open their condition and troubles " to one another," that fo they might have the help of one anothers advice and prayers; and very probably all the confeffion here meant of private Chriftians to one another, is of the offences and injuries they may have been guilty of, one towards another; that they fhould be reconciled upon this occafion, and as a teftimony of their charity, fhould " pray one for another;" whereas they are bound " to fend for the elders of the church," and they are " to pray over them," as an act not only of charity, but of fuperiority, and by virtue of their office in the church, a more efpecial bleffing being to be expected from their prayers.

Thefe three texts are the main arguments from fcripture, which they of the church of Rome bring to prove their auricular or fecret confeffion to be of divine inftitution; and woful proofs they are: which fhews what miferable fhifts they are reduced to, who refolve to maintain a bad caufe. I pro-

I proceed in the second place, to discover the falshood of their other pretences, that this kind of confession hath always been practised in the catholick church; and not only so, but believed absolutely necessary to the remission of mens sins, and their eternal salvation.

The truth of the whole matter is this: publick confession and penance for open and scandalous crimes was in use, and with great strictness observed in the first ages of Christianity; and there was then no general law or custom, that exacted secret confession of sins to the priest, as a necessary part of repentance, and condition of forgiveness: afterward publick penance was by degrees disused, which plainly shews, that, in the opinion of the church, this discipline, how useful soever, was not of absolute necessity to restore men to the favour of God.

In place of this came in private confession to the priest, particularly appointed to this office, and called the penitentiary; but upon occasion of a scandal that happened, this also was abrogated by Nectarius bishop of Constantinople; which shews that neither was this necessary. And this act of Nectarius was justified by his successor St. Chrysostom, who does over and over most expresly teach, that confession of our sins to men is not necessary to the forgiveness of them, but that it is sufficient to confess them to God alone; so that St. Chrysostom does plainly stand condemned by the decrees of the council of Trent.

And thus for several ages the matter rested, till the degeneracy of the church of Rome growing towards it's height, about the IX. and X. centuries, some began to contend for the necessity of secret confession; and this in the year 1215. in the IV. council of Lateran under Pope Innocent III. was decreed and established.   And

· And this is the firſt publick law that was made in the chriſtian church concerning this matter, not-withſtanding all the boaſts of the council of Trent, about the antiquity of this inſtitution and practice; for Gratian, who lived about fifty years before this council, tells us, that in his time ſeveral wiſe and religious men were of the contrary opinion, and did not hold confeſſion neceſſary by virtue of any divine law. Afterwards in the council of Florence, and eſpecially in that of Trent, this decree of the council of Lateran was confirmed and enlarged in many particulars, of which I have already given ſome account.

And whereas they pretend for themſelves the univerſal practice not only of the paſt, but preſent church, we are able to ſhew from clear teſtimony of their own writeis, that confeſſion, as taught and practiſed in the church of Rome, is no where elſe in uſe at this day, neither among the Abyſſines, nor Indians of St. Thomas, nor the Neſtorians, nor the Armenians, nor the Jacobites, churches of great antiquity and vaſt extent. And as for the Greek church, if we may believe Gratian, and the author of the gloſs upon the canon law, the Greeks had anciently no tradition concerning the neceſſity of confeſſion, nor do they at this day agree with the Roman church in all points concerning it.

So that, in ſhort, there is no nation nor church throughout the whole world, that bears the name of chriſtian, the Roman church only excepted, that doth fully embrace and maintain the whole doctrine of the council of Trent, concerning confeſſion ; and yet, according to their principles, the whole is of equal neceſſity to be believed, as any part of it. With what face then do they declare, that this manner of con-

feffion always was, and ftill is obferved in the catholick, that is, in the whole chriftian church ?

I have not time to fhew the great and manifold inconveniencies and mifchiefs of this practice : how
infinite a torture it is to the confciences of men, by
entangling them in endlefs doubts and fcruples ; and
how great a fcandal it is to the chriftian profeffion, in
the lewd management of it by the priefts, is evident
from the two bulls of pope Pius IV. and Gregory XV.
which mention things too fhameful to be declared ;
not to infift upon other horrible abufes of it to the
vileft and wickedeft purpofes ; not fo much to direct
the confciences of men, as to dive into their fecrets,
of which there are fo many plain and notorious inftances, that they are paft denial.

The other thing pretended for it is, that it is a
great reftraint upon men from fin. And very probably it is fo, to modeft and well difpofed perfons :
but experience fhews how quite contrary an effect it
hath upon others, who are the far greateft part of
mankind. Does not all the world fee in the popifh
countries, in the time of their carnival, juft before
Lent, the anniverfary feafon of confeffion, how fcandalous a liberty men take of doing lewd and wicked
things ; and that for this very reafon, becaufe their
confciences are prefently to be eafed and fcoured (as
they call it) by confeffion and abfolution ? And they
therefore take the opportunity to gratify their lufts,
and fill up the meafure of their iniquity at that time ;
becaufe with one labour they can fet their confciences
right, and clear them of all guilt. And they look
upon this as a fpecial piece of fpiritual good hufban-
dry, to quit their fcores with God at once, that fo
they may have no occafion to trouble him, nor the
prieft, nor themfelves again for a good while after.

So

So that confeſſion, inſtead of being a reſtraint from
ſin, gives great encouragement to it, by deluding
men into a vain hope of obtaining the pardon of
their ſins from time to time, though they ſtill continue in the practice of them ; by which device,
mens ſins are at once remitted and retained ; the
prieſt remits them by abſolution, and the penitent retains them, by going on ſtill in the commiſſion of
them, in hope of obtaining a new abſolution as often as occaſion ſhall require.   I proceed to the

IId Enquiry, namely, how far the diſcloſing and
revealing our ſins to the miniſters of God, may be
convenient upon other accounts, and to other purpoſes of religion ? To which the anſwer is very plain
and ſhort ; ſo far as is neceſſary either to the direction, or the eaſe of mens conſciences.

There are many caſes wherein men, under the
guilt and trouble of their ſins, can neither appeaſe
their own minds, nor ſufficiently direct themſelves,
without recourſe to ſome pious and prudent guide ;
in theſe caſes, men certainly do very well, and many
times prevent a great deal of trouble and perplexity
to themſelves, by a timely diſcovery of their condition to ſome faithful miniſter, in order to their direction and ſatisfaction, without which they ſhall
never perhaps be able to clear themſelves of the ob-
ſcurity and entanglement of their own minds, but
by ſmothering their trouble in their own breaſts,
ſhall proceed from one degree of melancholy to another, till at laſt they be plunged either into diſtrac-
tion or deſpair ; whereas the diſcovery of their condition in time, would prove a preſent and effectual
remedy.   And to this purpoſe, a general confeſſion
is for the moſt part ſufficient ; and where there is occaſion for a more particular diſcovery, there is no

need

need of raking into the particular and foul circumſtances of mens ſins, to give that advice which is neceſſary for the cure and eaſe of the penitent ; a thing
ſo far from being deſirable, that it muſt needs be very
grievous to every modeſt and good man.

And thus far confeſſion is not only allowed, but
encouraged among proteſtants.   In the Lutheran
churches, Chemnitius tells us, that private general
confeſſion is in uſe and practice.   And Calvin freely
declares, that he is ſo far from being againſt peoples
repairing to their paſtors to this purpoſe, that he
earneſtly wiſheth it were every where obſerved before the receiving of the ſacrament.   And the ſame
is the ſenſe of our own church, laying no neceſſity
upon men in this matter, but adviſing, eſpecially
before the ſacrament, thoſe who have any trouble
upon their conſciences, to repair to ſome diſcreet
and faithful miniſter of GOD's word, for advice and
ſatisfaction.   And thus all the good uſe, which can
be made of confeſſion, may be had in our church,
without the ill effects and conſequences of the Romiſh
confeſſion, and without laying a yoke upon the conſciences of men, which our SAVIOUR never laid.

And now I have, as briefly and as plainly as I
could, ſtated this controverſy between us and the
church of Rome, concerning the neceſſity and uſe of
ſecret confeſſion to the miniſters of GOD, as the proper guides and directors of our conſciences.   But it
is granted on all hands, that confeſſion of our ſins to
GOD is neceſſary ; and there is no doubt but it is
here intended in the text, viz. a penitent acknowledgment of our ſins ; the nature whereof I ſhall
briefly explain to you.

And it muſt not only be a general confeſſion that
we are ſinners ; but there muſt be a particular acknowledgment

ledgment of our fins to God, fo far as upon a particular difcuffion and examination of our confciences,
we can call them to remembrance ; efpecially our
moft heinous fins, which our confciences will not fuffer
us to forget, muft be particularly acknowledged, with
the feveral aggravations of them.

And this confeffion muft be accompanied with
fuch a fhame and forrow for our fins, as produceth in
us a fincere refolution to leave them, and to betake
ourfelves to a better courfe.   Thefe are the principal
ingredients of a penitent confeffion.

1. There muft be a fhame, without which there is
no hope of amendment. Confeffion always fuppofeth
conviction of a fault ; and he that is truly convinced
that he hath done amifs, cannot but be afhamed of
what he hath done. And thus the penitents in fcripture were wont to make confeffion of their fins to
God ; Ezra ix. 6. " O my God, fays he, I am
" afhamed, and blufh to lift up my face to thee my
" God." So Jeremiah, ch. iii. 25. " We lie down
" in our fhame, and our confufion covereth us ;
" for we have finned againft the Lord."   And fo
likewife Daniel, chap. ix. 5.   " We have finned,
" and have committed iniquity, and done wicked-
" ly ; unto us belongeth confufion of face."   And
thus our Saviour defcribes the penitent behaviour
of the publican, as afhamed to look up to that God
whom he had offended, Luke xviii. 13.   " He
" would not lift up fo much as his eyes to heaven ;
" but fmote upon his breaft, faying, God be mer-
" ciful to me a finner."

2. Confeffion muft be always accompanied with
great forrow for our fins, confidering the great difhonour we have brought to God, and the danger
into which we have brought ourfelves ; " I will
" declare

SERM. " declare mine iniquity, says David, and I will be
CLX. " forry for my fin."

And this forrow muft be proportionable to the
degree of our fin. If we have been very wicked,
and have finned greatly againft the LORD, and
" have multiplied our tranfgreffions" and continued
long in an evil courfe, have neglected GOD, and
" forgotten him days without number," the meafure of our forrow muft bear fome proportion to the
degree of our fins: if they have been " as fcarlet
" and crimfon," (as the prophet expreffeth it) that
is, of a deeper dye than ordinary, our forrow muft
be as deep as our guilt ; for it is not a flight trouble
and a few tears that will wafh out fuch ftains.

Not that tears are abfolutely neceffary, though
they do very well become, and moft commonly accompany a fincere repentance. All tempers are not
in this alike ; fome cannot exprefs their forrow by
tears, even then when they are moft inwardly and
fenfibly grieved. But if we can eafily fhed tears upon
other occafions ; certainly " rivers of tears" ought
to " run down our eyes," becaufe we have broken
GOD's laws, the reafonable, and righteous, and good
laws of fo good a GOD, of fo gracious a fovereign,
of fo mighty a benefactor, of the founder of our
being, and the perpetual patron and protector of our
lives : but if we cannot command our tears, there
muft however be great trouble and contrition of fpirit, efpecially for great fins ; to be fure to that degree as to produce the

3. Property I mentioned of a penitent confeffion,
namely, a fincere refolution to leave our fins, and
betake ourfelves to a better courfe. He does not
confefs his fault, but ftand in it, who is not refolved
to amend. True fhame and forrow for our fins is
                                                    utterly

utterly inconfiftent with any thought of returning to
them. It argues great obftinacy and impudence to
confefs a fault and continue in it. Whenever we
make confeffion of our fins to God, "furely it is
" meet to fay unto him, I will not offend any more ;
" that which I know not, teach thou me ; and if I
" have done iniquity, I will do no more."

This is the firft part of repentance mentioned in
the text, the firft condition of our finding mercy
with God, the penitent acknowledgment of our fins
to him. I proceed to the

Second condition required to make us capable of
the mercy of God, which is the actual forfaking of
our fins ; " whofo confeffeth and forfaketh them
" fhall have mercy." I fhall not go about to explain what is meant by " forfaking fin," it is that
which every body can underftand, but few will do ;
there lies all the difficulty. I fhall only put you in
mind, that forfaking of fin comprehends our return
to our duty, that neceffarily follows from it. In fins
of commiffion, he that hath left any vice, does thereby become mafter of the contrary virtue. *Virtus eft*
vitium fugere; not to be drunk, is to be fober ; not
to opprefs, or defraud, or deal falfly, is to be juft
and honeft : and for fins of omiffion, the forfaking
of them is nothing elfe, but the doing of thofe duties which we omitted and neglected before. And
therefore what Solomon here calls " forfaking of
" fin," is elfewhere in fcripture more fully expreffed, by " ceafing to do evil, and learning to do
" well," Ifa. i. 16. By forfaking our fins, and turning to God ; Ifa. lv. 7. " Let the whicked man
" forfake his ways, and the unrighteous man his
" thoughts, and let him return unto the Lord."
By turning from all our fins, and keeping all God's

3

laws

SERM. laws and ftatutes; Ezek. xviii. 21. " If the wicked
CLX.   " will turn from all his fins which he hath commit-
    " ted, and keep all my ftatutes, and do that which
    " is lawful and right."

And this is a moft effential part of repentance,
and a neceffary condition of our finding mercy with
GOD. That part of repentance which I have mentioned and infifted upon before, the penitent acknowledgment of our fins to GOD, with fhame and forrow for them, and a firm purpofe and refolution to
leave them ; all this is but preparatory to the actual
forfaking of them : that which perfects and com-
pletes repentance, is " to turn from our evil ways,"
and " to break off our fins by righteoufnefs."

And thefe terms of confeffing and forfaking
our fins, are reafonable in themfelves, and honourable to GOD, and profitable to us; and upon lower terms we have no reafon to expect the mercy
of GOD, nor in truth are we capable of it, either by
the prefent forgivenefs of our fins, or the final ab-
folution of the great day, and the bleffed reward of
eternal life. GOD peremptorily requires this change
as a condition of our forgivenefs and happinefs ; " re-
" pent and be converted, that your fins may be
" blotted out," Acts iii. 19. " If thou wilt enter
" into life, keep the commandments," Matth. xix.
17. " Without holinefs no man fhall fee the LORD,"
Heb. xii. 14. And why fhould any man hope for
the mercy of GOD upon other terms than thofe
which he hath fo plainly and peremptorily declared ?

It is a mean and unworthy thought of GOD, to
imagine that he will accept men to his favour and
eternal life upon other terms than of better obedience. Will any wife father or prince accept lefs from
his children and fubjects ? Will they be fatisfied with
                                    fighs

fighs and tears, as well as with obedience ? And well
pleafed if they be but melancholy for their faults,
though they never mend them ? We muft not impute that to GOD, which would be a defect of wifdom and good government in any father or prince
upon earth. GOD values no part of repentance upon any other account, but as it tends to reclaim us
to our duty, and ends in our reformation and a-
mendment.

This is that which qualifies us for the happinefs of
another life, and " makes us meet to be made par-
" takers of the inheritance of the faints in light."
And without this, though GOD fhould be pleafed to
forgive us, yet we could not forgive ourfelves; and
notwithftanding the legal difcharge from guilt, the
fting of it would remain, and we fhould, like our
firft parents after they had finned, run away and
hide ourfelves from GOD, though he fpake never fo
kindly to us. GOD hath placed in every man's mind
an inexorable judge, that will grant no pardon and
forgivenefs but to a reformed penitent, to him that
hath fuch a fenfe of the evil of his paft life, as to become a better man for the future.

And whoever entertains any other notion of the
grace and mercy of GOD to finners, confounds the
nature of things, and does plainly overthrow the
reafon of all laws, which is to reftrain men from
fin : but when it is committed, to pardon it without
amendment, is to encourage the practice of it, and
to take away the reverence and veneration of thofe
laws, which feem fo feverely to forbid it. So that
next to impunity, the forgivenefs of mens fins upon
fuch eafy and unfit terms gives boldnefs and encouragement to fin, and muft neceffarily in the opinion
of men leffen the honour and efteem of GOD's laws.

And thus I have considered and explained both the blessing and benefit which is here promised and declared, viz. " the mercy and favour of GOD," which comprehends both the present forgiveness of our sins, and power against them, and grace to persevere in goodness to the end, and our final absolution at the great day, and the glorious and merciful reward of eternal life : and likewise the conditions upon which this blessing is promised, viz. the penitent acknowledgment of our sins to GOD, with such shame and sorrow for them, as produceth a sincere resolution of leaving them, and returning to a better course, and the actual forsaking of them, which involves in it our actual return to our duty, and a constant and sincere obedience to the laws of GOD in the future course of our lives.

I shall now make some application of this discourse to ourselves. I am sure we are all nearly concerned in it. The best of us have many sins to confess and forsake ; some of us very probably have need to change the whole course of our lives, to put us into a capacity of the mercy of GOD. This work can never be unseasonable ; but there cannot be a more proper time for it, than when we are solemnly preparing ourselves to receive the holy sacrament ; in which as we do commemorate the great mercy of GOD to mankind, so we do likewise renew and confirm our covenant with him, that holy covenant wherein we engage ourselves to forsake our sins, as ever we expect the forgiveness of them at GOD's hand.

To persuade us hereto, be pleased to consider the reasonableness of the thing, the infinite benefit and advantage of it ; and which is beyond all other arguments, the absolute necessity of it, to make us
capable

capable of the mercy and forgiveness of God, in this world and the other, and "to deliver us from " the wrath which is to come," and from those terrible storms of vengeance, which will infallibly fall upon impenitent sinners : so that we have all the reason and all the encouragement in the world, to resolve upon a better course. Upon this condition, the mercy of God is ready to meet and embrace us, God will pardon our greatest provocations, and be perfectly reconciled to us. So he hath declared by the prophet, Isaiah i. 16. " Wash ye, make you clean, " put away the evil of your doings from before " mine eyes, cease to do evil, learn to do well. " Come now and let us reason together, saith the " Lord ; though your sins be as scarlet, they shall be " as white as snow ; though they be red as crimson, " they shall be as wool." And what greater encouragement can we desire, than that upon so easy and advantageous terms, God should be so ready to have an end put to all controversies and quarrels between him and us ?

" I beseech you therefore, brethren, by the mer- " cies of God," to take up a serious resolution " to " break off your sins by repentance," and to reform whatever, upon due search and trial of your ways, you shall find to be amiss in your lives.

" I beseech you by the mercies of God," that mercy which naturally " leads to repentance," and which is " long-suffering to us-ward," on purpose " that " we may not perish, but come to repentance ;" which hath spared us so often, and is not yet exhausted and tired out by our intolerable obstinacy, and innumerable provocations ; that mercy which moved the Son of God to become man, to live among us, and to die for us ; who now as it were speaks to us

18 Y 2   from

from the cross, extending his pierced hands, and
painful arms to embrace us, and through the gasping
wounds of his side let us see the tender and bleeding
compassion of his heart; that mercy which if we
now despise it, we shall in vain one day implore, and
catch hold of, and hang upon, to save us from sink-
ing into eternal perdition ; that mercy, which how
much soever we now presume upon, will then be so
far from interposing between us and the wrath of
God, that it will highly inflame and exasperate it :
for whatever impenitent sinners may now think, they
will then certainly find that the divine justice, when
it is throughly provoked, and whetted by his abused
mercy and goodness, will be most terribly severe,
and like a razor set with oil, will cut the keener for
it's smoothness.

" Consider this all ye that forget God, left he
" tear you in pieces, and there be none to deliver :
" consider and shew yourselves men, O ye trans-
" gressors !"

We do consider all this (may some perhaps say)
but we have been great sinners, so great, that we
doubt whether our case be not already desperate.

This, if it be sensibly said, with deep sorrow and
contrition, with that shame and confusion of face,
which becomes great offenders, is a good confession,
and the best reason in the world, why ye should now
" break off your sins :" for if what you have already done, do really make your case so doubtful
and difficult ; do not by sinning yet more and more
against the Lord, make it quite desperate and past
remedy; do but you repent, and God will yet " re-
" turn and have mercy upon you." And do not
say you cannot do it, when it must be done, or you
are undone. Power and necessity go together : when

3

men

men are hard preffed they find a power which they thought they had not ; and when it comes to the pufh, men can do that which they plainly fee they either muft do,, or be ruined for ever.

But after all this, I am very fenfible how great a need there is of God's powerful affiftance in this cafe, and that it is not an ordinary refolution, and common meafure of God's grace, that will reclaim thofe who have been long habituated to an evil courfe.

Let us therefore earneftly beg of him, that he would make thefe counfels effectual, that he would " grant us repentance unto life," that he would make us all fenfible of our faults, forry for them, and refolved to amend them ; and let us every one put up David's prayer to God for ourfelves, " deal " with thy fervant according to thy mercy, and " teach me thy ftatutes ; order my fteps in thy " word, and let not any iniquity have dominion over " me; teach me, O Lord, the way of thy ftatutes, " that I may keep them unto the end."

. I have now done ; I am only to mind you of another duty, which is to accompany our repentance, and fafting, and prayer, as a teftimony of the fincerity of our repentance, and one of the beft means to make our fafting and prayer acceptable to God, and to turn away his judgments from us, and that is charity and alms to the poor, whofe number is very great among us, and their neceffities very preffing and clamorous, and therefore do call for a bountiful fupply.

And to convince men of the neceffity of this duty, and the efficacy of it in conjunction with our repentance and fafting, and prayers, I fhall only offer to your confideration a few plain texts of fcripture,

which

SERM. which need no comment upon them. Dan. iv.
CLX. 27. It is the prophet's advice to Nebuchadnezzar;
" Break off thy ſins by righteouſneſs, and thine ini-
" quity by ſhewing mercy to the poor ; if ſo be it
" may be a lengthening of thy tranquillity. Acts x.
4. the angel there tells Cornelius, " Thy prayers and
" thine alms are come up for a memorial before GOD."
Iſa. lviii. 5. " Is not this the faſt which I have
" choſen, to looſe the bands of wickedneſs, to un-
" do the heavy burthens, and to let the oppreſſed
" go free, and that ye break every yoke? Is it not
" to deal thy bread to the hungry, and that thou
" bring the poor that are caſt out, to thy houſe ;
" when thou ſeeſt the naked, that thou cover him,
" and that thou hide not thyſelf from thy own fleſh ?
" Then ſhall thy light break forth as the morning,
" and thine health ſhall ſpring forth ſpeedily, and
" thy righteouſneſs ſhall go before thee, and the
" glory of the LORD ſhall be thy reward : then ſhalt
" thou call, and the LORD ſhall anſwer thee; thou
" ſhalt cry, and he ſhall ſay, here I am:"   To
which I will only add that gracious promiſe of our
SAVIOUR ; " bleſſed are the merciful, for they ſhall
" find mercy ;" and that terrible ſentence in St.
James, " He ſhall have judgment without mercy,
" that hath ſhewed no mercy."

SERMON CLXI.

Of confeſſion, and ſorrow for ſin.

PSAL. xxxviii. 18.

I will declare mine iniquity, and be ſorry for my ſin.

IN this pſalm David does earneſtly beg mercy and S E R M. CLXI. forgiveneſs of God, and in order to the obtaining of it, he declares both his ſins, and his repentance for them in theſe words, which contain in them two of the neceſſary ingredients, or at leaſt concomitants of a true repentance, viz. confeſſion of ſin, and ſorrow for it.

I ſhall ſpeak ſomething of the firſt of theſe, viz. confeſſion of ſin : but the ſecond, viz. ſorrow for ſin, ſhall be the main ſubjeÛt of my diſcourſe.

I. Confeſſion of ſin; " I will declare mine iniqui- " ty," or as it is in the old tranſlation, " I will con- " feſs my wickedneſs." Of which I ſhall ſpeak un- der theſe three heads.

I. What confeſſion of ſin is.

II. How far it is neceſſary.

III. What are the reaſons and grounds of this neceſſity.

I. What confeſſion of ſin is. It is a declaration or acknowledgment of ſome moral evil or fault to another, which we are conſcious to ourſelves we have been guilty of. And this acknowledgment may be made by us, either to God or man. The ſcripture mentions both. Confeſſion of our ſins to God is very frequently mentioned in ſcripture, as the firſt and neceſſary part of repentance ; and ſometimes,

SERM.
CLXI.
times, and in some cases, confession to men is not only recommended, but enjoined.

II. How far confession of our sins is necessary. That it is necessary to confess our sins to GOD, the scripture plainly declares, and is I think a matter out of all dispute. For it is a necessary part of repentance, that we should confess our sins to GOD, with a due sense of the evil of them; and therefore the scripture maketh this a necessary qualification, and condition of pardon and forgiveness. Prov. xxviii. 13. " Whoso confesseth and forsaketh his sins, shall " have mercy." 1 John i. 9. " If we confess our " sins, he is faithful and just to forgive us our sins, " and to cleanse us from all unrighteousness;" implying that if we do not confess our sins to GOD, the guilt of them will still remain; to GOD I say, for of confession to him St. John plainly speaks, when he says, " He is faithful and just;" Who? GOD surely; who though he be not named before, yet is necessarily understood in the words before; " If we " confess our sins," i. e. to GOD, " he is faithful " and just."

A general confession of our sins is absolutely necessary; and in some cases a particular acknowledgment of them, and repentance for them, especially if the sins have been great and deliberate and presumptuous; in this case a particular confession of them, and repentance for them, is necessary so far as we can particularly recollect them, and call them to remembrance: whereas for sins of ignorance and infirmity, of surprize and daily incursion, for lesser omissions, and the defects and imperfections of our best actions and services, we have all the reason that can be to believe, that GOD will accept of a general confession of them, and repentance for them. And

if

if any man afk me, where I find this diftinction in
fcripture, between a general and particular repentance ; I anfwer, that it is not neceffary it fhould be
any where expreffed in fcripture, being fo clearly
founded in the nature and reafon of the thing ; becaufe in many cafes it is not poffible that we fhould
have a particular knowledge and remembrance of all
our particular fins ; as is plain in fins of ignorance,
fince our very calling them by that name does neceffarily fuppofe that we do not know them. It is
impoffible we fhould remember thofe fins afterwards,
which we did not know when they were committed : and therefore either a general repentance for
thefe, and the other fins I mentioned of the like nature, muft be fufficient, in order to the pardon of
them ; or we muft fay, that they are unpardonable,
which would be very unreafonable, becaufe this would
be to make leffer fins more unpardonable than thofe
which are far greater.

And yet though this difference between a general and
particular repentance be no where exprefly mentioned in fcripture, there does not want foundation for it
there. Pfal. xix. 12. " Who can underftand his
" errors ? Cleanfe thou me from fecret fins," (i. e.)
fuch as we do not difcern and take notice of, when
they are committed : and yet David fuppofeth, that
upon a general acknowledgment of them, and repentance for them, we may be cleanfed from them ;
though we cannot make a particular acknowledgment
of them, and exercife a particular repentance for
them, becaufe they are fecret, and we do not particularly underftand what they are.

As for our confeffing our fins to men, both fcripture and reafon do in fome cafes recommend and enjoin it. As,

Of confeſſion, and ſorrow for ſin.

1. In order to the obtaining of the prayers of good men for us. James v. 16. " Confeſs your ſins " one to another ;" he ſaid before, " the prayer of " faith ſhall ſave the ſick, and the Lord ſhall raiſe " him up." This in all probability is meant of the miraculous power of prayer, which St. Chryſoſtom reckons among the miraculous gifts of the Spirit, be- ſtowed upon Chriſtians in the firſt ages of the church : and this is very much countenanced and confirmed by what preſently follows after this command of " confeſſing our ſins one to another, and praying " one for another," and given as the reaſon of it ; " for the effectual fervent prayer of a righteous " man availeth much," the original is δέησις ἐνερ- γεμένη, the inſpired prayer, which, in the verſe be- fore, is called " the prayer of faith," meaning that miraculous faith, in the power whereof Chriſtians did obtain of God whatever they were inſpired to aſk of him ; according to our Saviour's promiſe in the goſpel, concerning the efficacy of the prayers of Chriſtians, which we find mentioned among the other miraculous powers, which were to be conferred upon them by the coming of the Holy Ghoſt.

2. Confeſſion of our ſins to men is likewiſe reaſon- able, in order to the eaſe and ſatisfaction of our minds, and our being directed in our duty for the future. In this caſe common reaſon and prudence, without any precept of ſcripture, will direct men to have recourſe to this remedy, viz. to diſcover and lay open our diſ- eaſe to ſome ſkilful ſpiritual phyſician, to ſome faith- ful friend or prudent guide, in order to ſpiritual ad- vice and direction, for the peace and ſatisfaction of our minds. And then,

3. In caſe our ſins have been publick and ſcanda- lous, both reaſon and the practice of the chriſtian

2   church

church do require, that when men have publickly offended, they fhould give publick fatisfaction, and open teftimony of their repentance.

But as for private and auricular confeffion of our fins to a prieft in all cafes, and as of abfolute neceffity to our obtaining pardon and forgivenefs from God, as the church of Rome teacheth, this is neither neceffary by divine precept, nor by any conftitution and practice of the ancient chriftian church, as I have fhewn in my former difcourfe.

Not to mention the bad confequence of this practice, and the impious and dangerous ufe which hath been made of this feal of confeffion, for the concealing and carrying on of the moft wicked and barbarous defigns ; and the debauching of the penitents, by drawing them into the commiffion of the fame and greater fins, than thofe which they confeffed, which the more devout perfons of that church have frequently complained of. I proceed now to fhew briefly in the

IIId Place, the grounds and reafons of the neceffity of confeffing our fins to God ; and I fhall but juft mention them.

1. From the precept and command of God ; for which I have already produced clear proof of fcripture.

2. From the nature of the thing, becaufe without this there can be no repentance towards God. He that will not fo much as own the faults which he hath been guilty of, can never repent of them. If we will not confefs our fins to God, we are never like to be forry for them. Thus much for the firft thing in the text, the confeffion of our fins. I proceed now to the

Second ingredient of repentance mentioned in the text, which is forrow for fin ; " I will declare mine
" iniquity,

" iniquity, and be forry for my fin." In the handling of this argument, I fhall

I. Confider the nature of this paffion of forrow.

II. The reafon and grounds of our forrow for fin.

III. The meafure and degrees of it.

IV. How far the outward expreffion of our inward grief by tears is neceffary to a true repentance.

I. For the nature of this paffion. Sorrow is a
trouble or difturbance of mind, occafioned by fomething that is evil, done or fuffered by us, or which
we are in danger of fuffering, that tends greatly to
our damage or mifchief: fo that to be forry for a
thing, is nothing elfe but to be fenfibly affected with
the confideration of the evil of it, and of the mifchief and inconvenience which is like to redound to
us from it : which if it be a moral evil, fuch as fin
is, to be forry for it, is to be troubled that we have
done it, and to wifh with all our hearts that we had
been wifer, and had done otherwife ; and if this forrow be true and real, if it abide and ftay upon us,
it will produce a firm purpofe and refolution in us,
not to do the like for the future.

It is true indeed, that we are faid to be forry for
the death and lofs of friends ; but this is rather the
effect of natural affection than of our reafon, which
always endeavours to check and moderate our grief
for that which we cannot help, and labours by all
means to turn our forrow into patience : and we are
faid likewife to grieve for the miferies and fufferings
of others ; but this is not fo properly forrow as pity
and compaffion. Sorrow rather refpects ourfelves,
and our own doings and fufferings. I proceed in the

IId Place to enquire into the reafons and grounds
of our forrow for fin ; and they, as I have already
hinted, are thefe two ; the intrinfical, or the confequent

quent evil of fin ; either the evil of fin in itfelf, or
the mifchiefs and inconveniencies which it will bring
upon us. For every one that is forry for any fault
he is guilty of, is 'fo upon one of thefe two accounts ; either upon the fcore of ingenuity, or of
intereft ; either becaufe he hath done a thing which
is unworthy in itfelf, or becaufe he hath done fomething which may prove prejudicial to himfelf ; either
out of a principle of love and gratitude to God, or
from a principle of felf-love. And though the former of thefe be the better, the more generous principle
of forrow ; yet the latter is ufually the firft ; becaufe it is the more fenfible, and toucheth us more
nearly : for fin is a bafe and ill-natured thing, and
renders a man not fo apt to be affected with the injuries he hath offered to God, as with the mifchief
which is likely to fall upon himfelf. And therefore
I will begin with the latter, becaufe it is ufually the
more fenfible caufe of our trouble and forrow for fin.

1. The great mifchief and inconvenience that fin
is like to bring upon us. When a man is thoroughly convinced of the danger into which his fins have
brought him, that they have " made him a child of
" wrath," and " a fon of perdition," that he is
thereby fallen under the heavy difpleafure of Almighty God, and liable to all thofe dreadful curfes which
are written in his book, that ruin and deftruction
hang over him, and that nothing keeps him from eternal and intolerable torments, but the patience and
long-fuffering of God, which he does not know how
foon it may ceafe to interpofe between him and the
wrath of God, and let him fall into that endlefs and
infupportable mifery, which is the juft portion and
defert of his fins ; he that lays to heart the fad eftate
and condition into which he hath brought himfelf by
fin,

us to happinefs, by the moft ftupendous and amazing condefcenfion of love and goodnefs that ever
was, even by giving his only Son to die for us.

And can we reflect upon all this, and not be forry
and grieved at our very hearts, that we fhould be fo
evil to him, who hath been fo good to us ; that we
fhould be fo undutiful to fo loving a father, fo un-
kind to fo faithful and conftant a friend, fo ungrateful
and unworthy to fo mighty a benefactor ? If any
thing will melt us into tears, furely this will do it,
to confider that we have finned againft him, who
made us, and continually preferves us, and after all
our unkindnefs to him, did ftill retain fo great a love
for us, as to redeem us from hell and deftruction,
by the death and fuffering of his Son, and notwithftanding all our offences does ftill offer us pardon
and peace, life and happinefs. Such confiderations
as thefe, ferioufly laid to heart, fhould, one would
think, break the hardeft heart, and make tears to
gufh even out of a rock. I proceed in the

IIId Place to confider the meafure and degree of
our forrow for fin. That it admits of degrees,
which ought to bear fome proportion to the heinouf-
nefs of our fins, and the feveral aggravations of them,
and the time of our continuance in them, is out of
all difpute : for though the leaft fin be a juft caufe of
the deepeft forrow ; yet becaufe our greateft grief
can never bear a due proportion to the vaft and infinite evil of fin, God is pleafed to require and accept fuch meafures of forrow, as do not bear an
exact correfpondence to the malignity of fin, provided they be according to the capacity of our nature,
and in fome fort proportioned to the degree and aggravations of our fins ; i. e. Though the higheft degree of our forrow doth neceffarily fall below the evil

of

ſin, and the miſchiefs which attend him every moment of his continuance in that ſtate, and how near
they are to him, and that there is but a ſtep between
him and death, and hardly another between that and
hell, he cannot ſurely but be very ſorry for what he
hath done, and be highly diſpleaſed and offended
with himſelf, that he ſhould be the author of his
own ruin, and have co tributed as much as in him
lies to his everlaſting undoing.

2. Another and better principle of ſorrow for ſin,
is ingenuity; becauſe we are ſenſible, that we have
carried ourſelves very unworthily towards GOD, and
have been injurious to him, who hath laid all poſſible obligations upon us: for he hath made us, and
hath given us our beings, and hath charged his
watchful providence with the continual care of us;
his bounty hath miniſtred to the neceſſities and comforts of our life; all the bleſſings that we enjoy, are
the effects of his mere love and goodneſs, without
any hope of requital, or expectation of any other
return from us, than of love, of gratitude, and o-
bedience; which yet are of no advantage to him,
but very beneficial and comfortable to ourſelves:
for he does not expect duty and obedience from us,
with any regard of benefit to himſelf, but for our
ſakes, and in order to our own happineſs.

Nay, his kindneſs did not ſtop here, but after we
had abuſed him by our repeated provocations, yet he
ſtill continued his care of us; and when we had
farther provoked him to withdraw his love, and to
call in his abuſed goodneſs, and had done what lay
in us to make ourſelves miſerable, he would not ſuffer us to be undone, but found out a ranſom for us,
and hath contrived a way for the pardon of all our
offences, and to reconcile us to himſelf, and to reſtore

us

of the leaft fin ; yet God requires that we fhould be more deeply affected with fome fins than others.

But what is the loweft degree which God requires in a true penitent, and will accept, as it is impoffible for me to tell, fo it is unprofitable for any body to know : for no man can reafonably make this enquiry with any other defign, than that he may learn how he may come off with God upon the cheapeft and eafieft terms. Now there cannot be a worfe fign, that a man is not truly fenfible of the great evil of fin, than this, that he defires to be troubled for it as little as may be, and no longer than needs muft : and none furely are more unlikely to find acceptance with God, than thofe who deal fo nearly, and endeavour to drive fo hard a bargain with him.

And therefore I fhall only fay this in general, concerning the degrees of our forrow for fin ; that fin being fo great an evil in itfelf, and of fo pernicious a confequence to us, it cannot be too much lamented and grieved for by us : and the more and greater our fins have been, and the longer we have continued and lived in them, they call for fo much the greater forrow, and deeper humiliation from us : for the reafoning of our Saviour concerning Mary Magdalene, " She loved much, becaufe much was " forgiven her," is proportionably true in this cafe, thofe who have finned much, fhould forrow the more.

And then we muft take this caution along with us, that if we would judge aright of the truth of our forrow for fin, we muft not meafure it fo much by the degrees of fenfible trouble and affliction, as by the rational effects of it, which are hatred of fin, and a fixed purpofe and refolution againft it for the future : for he is moft truly forry for his mifcarriage, who looks upon what he hath done amifs with abhorrence

rence and detestation of the thing, and wisheth he had not done it, and censures himself severely for it, and thereupon resolves not to do the like again. And this is the character which St. Paul gives of a godly sorrow, 2 Cor. vii. 10. that " it worketh repent-
" ance," μεʃάνοιαν, it produceth " a real change
" in our minds," and makes us to alter our purpose and resolution: and though such a person may not be so passionately and sensibly afflicted for sin, yet it appears by the effect, that he hath a deeper and more rational resentment of the evil of it, than that man who is sad and melancholy and drooping for never so long a time, and after all returns to his former sinful course ; the degree of his sorrow may appear greater, but the effect of it is really less.

IV. As for the outward expressions of our grief and sorrow. The usual sign and outward expression of sorrow is tears ; but these being not the substance of our duty, but an external testimony of it, which some tempers are more unapt to than others ; we are much less to judge of the truth of our sorrow for sin by these, than by our inward sensible trouble and affliction of spirit. Some persons are of a more tender and melting disposition, and can command their tears upon a little occasion, and upon very short warning ; and such persons that can weep for every thing else that troubles them, have much more reason to suspect the truth of their sorrow for sin, if this outward expression of it be wanting. And we find in scripture, that the sorrow of true penitents does very frequently discover itself by this outward sign of it. Thus when Ezra and the people made confession of their sins to God, it is said, that " they wept very
" sore," Ezra x. Peter when he reflected upon that great sin of denying his master, it is said, " He

SERM. " went forth and wept bitterly." David alſo was
CLXI. abundant in this expreſſion of his grief. In the book
of Pſalms he ſpeaks frequently of his ſighs and groans,
and of " watering his couch with his tears :" yea ſo
ſenſibly was he affected with the evil of ſin, that he
could ſhed tears plentifully for the ſins of others,
Pſal. cxix. 136. " Rivers of waters run down mine
" eyes, becauſe men keep not thy law." In like
manner Jeremiah tells us, that " his ſoul did weep
" in ſecret places, for the pride and obſtinacy of the
" Jews;" that " his eye did weep ſore, and run
" down with tears ;" Jer. xiii. 17. And ſo likewiſe St. Paul, Philip iii. 18, 19. " There are many
" that walk, of whom I have told you often, and
" now tell you even weeping, that they are enemies
" to the croſs of CHRIST." And there ſeems to be
this natural reaſon for it, that all great and perma-
nent impreſſions upon the mind, all deep inward re-
ſentments have uſually a proportionable effect upon
the body, and the inferior faculties.

But though this happen very frequently, yet it is
not ſo conſtant and certain : for all men have not the
ſame tenderneſs of ſpirit, nor are equally prone to
tears ; nay though a man can weep upon natural accounts, as upon the loſs of a child, or near relation,
or an intimate friend, or when he lies under a ſharp
bodily pain, yet a man may truly repent, though he
cannot expreſs his ſorrow for ſin the ſame way, provided he give teſtimony of it by more real effects :
and therefore the rule, which is commonly given by
caſuiſts in this caſe, ſeems to be more enſnaring than
true and uſeful : namely, " That that man that can
" ſhed tears upon account of any evil leſs than that
" of ſin, (as certainly all natural evils are) ought
" to queſtion the truth of his repentance for any ſin
" that

" that he hath committed, if he cannot ſhed tears
" for it." This I think is not true, becauſe there is
ſcarce any man of ſo hard and unrelenting a ſpirit,
but the loſs of a kind father, or a dear child, or
other near relation, will force tears from him: and yet
ſuch a man, if it were to ſave his ſoul, may not be
able at ſome times to ſhed a tear for his ſins. And
the reaſon is obvious; becauſe tears do proceed from
a ſenſitive trouble, and are commonly the product of
a natural affection; and therefore it is no wonder,
if they flow more readily and eaſily upon a natural
account; becauſe they are the effect of a cauſe ſuitable to their nature. But ſorrow for ſin, which hath
more of the judgment and underſtanding in it, hath
not it's foundation in natural affection, but in reaſon; and therefore may not many times expreſs itſelf in tears, though it may produce greater and
more proper effects.

So that upon the whole matter, I ſee no reaſon to
call in queſtion the truth and ſincerity of that man's
ſorrow and repentance, who hates ſin and forſakes it,
and returns to GOD and his duty, though he cannot
ſhed tears, and expreſs the bitterneſs of his ſoul for
his ſin, by the ſame ſignifications that a mother doth
in the loſs of her only ſon. He that cannot weep
like a child may reſolve like a man, and that undoubtedly will find acceptance with GOD. A learned divine hath well illuſtrated this matter by this ſi-
militude. Two perſons walking together eſpy a
ſerpent, the one ſhrieks and cries out at the ſight of
it, the other kills it: ſo is it in ſorrow for ſin; ſome
expreſs it by great lamentation and tears, and vehement tranſports of paſſion; others by greater and
more real effects of hatred and deteſtation, by forſaking their ſins, and by mortifying and ſubduing

their lusts : but he that kills it does certainly best express his inward displeasure and enmity against it.

The application I shall make of what hath been said upon this argument, shall be in two particulars.

I. By way of caution, and that against a double mistake about sorrow for sin.

1. Some look upon trouble and sorrow for sin, as the whole of repentance.

2. Others exact from themselves such a degree of sorrow, as ends in melancholy, and renders them unfit both for the duties of religion, and of their particular calling. The first concerns almost the generality of men ; the latter but a very few in comparison.

1. There are a great many, who look upon trouble and sorrow for their sins, as the whole of repentance, whereas it is but an introduction to it. It is that which works repentance ; but is not repentance itself. Repentance is always accompanied with sorrow for sin ; but sorrow for sin does not always end in true repentance : sorrow only respects sins past ; but repentance is chiefly preventive of sin for the future. And God doth therefore require our sorrow for sin, in order to our forsaking of it. Heb. vi. 1. Repentance is there called " repentance from " dead works." It is not only a sorrow for them, but a turning from them.

There is no reason why men should be so willing to deceive themselves, for they are like to be the losers by it : but so we see it is, that many men are contented to be deceived to their own ruin ; and among many other ways, which men have to cheat themselves, this is none of the least frequent, to think that if they can but shed a few tears for sin upon a death-bed, which no doubt they may easily do, when they see their friends weeping about them,

and

and apprehend themfelves to be in imminent danger, not only of death, but of that which is more terrible, the heavy difpleafure, and the fiery indignation of Almighty God, " into whofe hands it is a fear- " ful thing to fall ;" I fay, they think that if they can but do thus much, God will accept this for a true repentance, and hereupon grant them pardon and eternal life. And upon thefe fond hopes, they adjourn their repentance, and the reformation of their lives to a dying hour.

Indeed if I were to fpeak to a man upon his death- bed, I would encourage him to a great contrition and forrow for his fins, as his laft and only remedy, and the beft thing he can do at that time ; but on the other hand, when I am fpeaking to thofe that are well and in health, I dare not give them the leaft en- couragement to venture their fouls upon this, becaufe it is an hazardous, and almoft defperate remedy ; efpecially when men have cunningly and defignedly contrived to rob God of the fervice of their lives, and to put him off with a few unprofitable fighs and tears at their departure out of the world. Our Saviour tells us, that it is " not every one, that fhall fay un- " to him Lord! Lord! that fhall enter into the " kingdom of heaven ;" and that there is a time, when " many fhall feek to enter in, but fhall not " be able."

The fum of this caution is, that men fhould take heed of miftaking forrow for fin, for true repentance, unlefs it be followed with the forfaking of fin and the real reformation of our lives. Ahab humbled himfelf, but we do not find that he was a true peni- tent. Judas was forry for his fin, and yet for all that was " the fon of perdition." Efau is a fad type of an ineffectual forrow for fin, Heb. xii. where the

apoftle

SERM. apostle tells us, that " he found no place for repen-
CLXI. " tance," that is, no way to change the mind of
his father Isaac, " though he sought it carefully with
" tears." If sorrow for sin were repentance, there
would be store of penitents in hell ; for there is the
deepest and most intense sorrow, " weeping and
" wailing and gnashing of teeth."

2. Another mistake which men ought to be cau-
tioned against in this matter, is of those who exact
from themselves such a degree of sorrow for sin, as
ends in deep melancholy, as renders them unfit both
for the duties of religion, and of their particular callings. But because there are but very few who fall
into this mistake, I shall need to say the less to it.
This only I shall say, that those who indulge their
sorrow to such a degree, as to drown their spirits,
and to sink them into melancholy and mopishness,
and thereby render themselves unserviceable to GOD,
and unfit for the necessities of this life, they commit one sin more to mourn for, and overthrow the
end of repentance by the indiscreet use of the means
of it. For the end of sorrow for sin, is the forsaking of it, and returning to our duty : but he that
sorrows for sin, so as to unfit him for his duty, defeats his own design, and destroys the end he aims at.

II. The other part of the application of this discourse should be, to stir up this affection of sorrow
in us. And here, if I had time, I might represent
to you the great evil of sin, and the infinite danger
and inconvenience of it. If the holy men in scripture, David, and Jeremiah, and St. Paul, were so
deeply affected with the sins of others, as to shed
rivers of tears at the remembrance of them ; how
ought we to be touched with the sense of our own
sins, who are equally concerned in the dishonour
brought

brought to God by them, and infinitely more in the S E R M.
danger they expofe us to ! can we weep for our dead _{CLXI.}
friends ? And have we no fenfe of that heavy load
of guilt, of that body of death, which we carry a-
bout with us ? Can we be fad and melancholy for
temporal loffes and fufferings, and refufe to be comforted ? And is it no trouble to us to have loft heaven
and happinefs, and to be in continual danger of the
intolerable fufferings and endlefs torments of another world ?

   I fhall only offer to your confideration, the great
benefit and advantage which will redound to us from
this " godly forrow ; it worketh repentance to fal-
" vation, not to be repented of," faith St. Paul. If
we would thus " fow in tears," we fhould " reap
" in joy." This forrow would but " continue for
" a time," and " in the morning" of the refurrection there would be joy to all eternity, " joy un-
" fpeakable and full of glory." It is but a very
little while, and thefe " days of mourning will be
" accomplifhed ;" and then " all tears fhall be wip-
" ed from our eyes ; and the ranfomed of the Lord
" fhall come to Sion with fongs, and everlafting
" joy fhall be upon their heads. They fhall obtain
" joy and gladnefs, and forrow and fighing fhall
" flee away. Bleffed are they that mourn, for they
" fhall be comforted : but wo unto you that laugh,
" for ye fhall mourn and weep." If men will rejoice in the pleafures of fin, and " walk in the ways
" of their hearts, and in the fight of their eyes ;"
if they will " remove forrow from their heart," and
put away all fad and melancholy thoughts from
them, and are refolved to harden their fpirits againft
the fenfe of fin, againft the checks and convictions
of their own confciences, and the fuggeftions of
God's

God's holy Spirit, againft all the arguments that God
can offer, and all the methods that God can ufe to
bring them to repentance; let them "know, that for
" all thefe things God will bring them into judg-
" ment;" and becaufe they would not give way to
a timely and feafonable forrow for fin, they fhall lie
down in eternal forrow, "weeping and wailing and
" gnafhing of teeth fhall be their portion for ever."
From which fad and miferable eftate, beyond all
imagination, and paft all remedy, God of his infinite goodnefs deliver us all, for Jesus Christ's
fake.

"To whom, &c.

SERMON CLXII.

The unprofitablenefs of fin in this life,
an argument for repentance.

JOB xxxiii. 27, 28.

*He looketh upon men, and if any fay, I have finned,
and perverted that which was right, and it profited me not ; he will deliver his foul from going into the pit, and his life fhall fee the light.*

SERM.
CLXII.

Preached
on Afh-
wednef-
day. 1689.

THE great folly and perverfenefs of human nature is in nothing more apparent than in this,
that when in all other things men are generally led
and governed by their interefts, and can hardly be
impofed upon by any art, or perfuaded by any folici-
tation, to act plainly contrary to it ; yet in matter
of their fin and duty, that is, in that which of all
other is of greateft concernment to them, they have
little

little or no regard to it ; but are fo blinded and be-
witched with " the deceitfulnefs of fin," as not to
confider the infinite danger and difadvantage of it;
and at the fame time to caft the commandments of
God, and the confideration of their own happinefs
behind their backs.

And of this every finner, when he comes to himfelf, and confiders what he hath done, is abundantly
convinced; as appears by the confeffion and acknowledgment, which is here in the text put into the
mouth of a true penitent ; " I have finned, and
" perverted that which was right, and it profited me
" not, &c."

In which words here is a great blefling and benefit
promifed on God's part, and condition required on
our part.

Firft, The blefling or benefit promifed on God's
part, which is deliverance from the ill confequences
and punifhment of fin ; " he will deliver his foul
" from going into the pit, and his life fhall fee the
" light," that is, he will deliver him from death
and damnation.   And though perhaps temporal
death be here immediately intended, yet that is a
type of our deliverance from eternal death; which is
exprefly promifed in the gofpel.

Secondly, Here is a condition required on our
part ; " If any fay, I have finned, and perverted
" that which was right, and it profited me not."
In which words there are contained,

I. A penitent confeffion of our fins to God ; for
" he looketh upon men, and if any fay, I have fin-
" ned," that is, make a penitent confeffion of his
fin to God.

II. A true contrition for our fin, not only for
fear of the pernicious confequences of fin, and the

punifhment that will follow it, implied in thefe words,
" and it profited me not," this is but a very imperfect contrition : but from a juft fenfe of the evil nature of fin, and the fault and offence of it againft
God, that we have done contrary to right and our
duty. " If any fay, I have finned, and perverted
" that which was right." Here you fee that true
and perfect contrition for our fins, is made a neceffary
condition of the bleffing and benefit here promifed,
viz. deliverance from the punifhment due to them.

III. Here is a defcription of the evil nature of fin,
it is " a perverting of that which is right." Sin is a perverting of the conftitution and appointment of God,
and of the nature and order of things. God hath
given man a law and rule to walk by, but " the
" foolifhnefs of man perverteth his way." The great
lines of our duty are plain and vifible to all men ;
and if we would attend to the direction of our own
minds, concerning good and evil, every man would
be " a law to himfelf." " He hath fhewed thee, O
" man, what is good." That which is right and
juft and good is plain and obvious, and offers itfelf firft to us ; and whenever we fin, we go out of
the right way that lies plain before us, and " turn
" afide into crooked paths." But when we do that
which is right, we act agreeably to the defign and
frame of our beings, and comply with the true nature and order of things ; we do what becomes us,
and are what we ought to be : but fin perverts the
nature of things, and puts them out of courfe ;
" I have finned and perverted that which was right."

IV. You have here an acknowledgment of the
mifchievous and pernicious confequences of fin ; " I
" have finned and perverted that which was right,
" and it profited me not." Which laft words are a

3

μειωσις,

μειωσις, in which much lefs is faid than is meant and intended ; " It profited me not," that is, it was fo far from being of advantage, that the effects and confequences of it were very pernicious and deftructive.

And this is not only true as to the final iffue, and event of an evil courfe in the other world ; but I fhall endeavour to fhew, that even in refpect of this world, and the prefent life, the practice of fome fins is plainly mifchievous to the temporal interefts of men ; that others are wholly unprofitable ; and that thofe which pretend to bring fome benefit and advantage, will, when all accounts are caft up, and all circumftances duly weighed and confidered, be found to do far otherwife.

Firft, I fhall fhew, that the practice of fome vices is evidently mifchievous and prejudicial to us, as to this world ; as all thofe vices which fall under the cognizance of human laws, and are punifhed by them: murder, theft, perjury, fedition, rebellion, and the like ; thefe cannot be denied to be of pernicious confequence to men, and therefore the great patrons of vice feldom plead for thefe, the inconvenience of them is fo palpable, that fome feel it, and all may fee it every day.

But befides thefe, there are many other forts of fin, which human laws either take no notice of, or do not fo feverely punifh, which yet in their natural confequences are very pernicious to our prefent intereft ; either they are a difturbance to our minds, or dangerous to our health, or ruinous to our eftate, or hurtful to our reputation, or it may be at once prejudicial to us, in all, or moft of thefe refpects ; and thefe are the greateft temporal inconveniencies that men are liable to.

All irregular paffions, as wrath, malice, envy,

19 B 2 impa-

impatience and revenge, are not only a disturbance to ourselves, but they naturally draw upon us hatred and contempt from others. Any one of these paſsions is enough to render a man uneaſy to himſelf, and to make his converſation difguſtful and troubleſom to all that are about him ; for all men naturally hate all thoſe, who are of an envious, or malicious, or revengeful temper, and are apt to riſe up and ſtand upon their guard againſt them. Anger and impatience are great deformities of the mind, and make a man look as ugly, as if he had a wry and diſtorted countenance ; and theſe paſsions are apt to breed in others a ſecret contempt of us, and to bring our prudence into queſtion, becauſe they are ſigns of a weak and impotent mind, that either hath loſt, or never had the government of itſelf.

There are other vices, which are plainly pernicious to our health, and do naturally bring pains and diſeaſes upon men ; ſuch are intemperance and luſt: and though ſome may pretend to govern themſelves, in the practice of theſe, with ſo much moderation and difcretion, as to prevent the notorious bad conſequences of them, yet there are very few or none that do ſo ; this is ſeldom more than a ſpeculation, and men that allow themſelves in any lewd or intemperate courſe, will find it very hard to govern themſelves in it ; for after men have forfeited their innocence, and broke in upon their natural modeſty, they are apt by degrees to grow profligate and deſperate. If a man gives way but little to his own vicious inclinations, they will ſoon get head of him, and no man knows how far they will hurry him at laſt.

Beſides, that the vices I am ſpeaking of, intemperance and luſt, have other great inconveniencies attending them, they expoſe men more frequently,

than

than moft other vices, to occafions of quarrel, in which men often lofe their own lives, or take away other mens, by which they fall under the danger of the law, and the ftroke of publick juftice ; or if they efcape that, (as too often they do) they cannot fly from their own confciences, which do commonly fill them with the horror and torment of fuch an action all their days ; fo pernicious are the ufual confequences of thefe vices, of which we fee fad inftances every day.

Nor are thefe vices lefs hurtful to mens eftates ; for they are extremely expenfive and wafteful, and ufually make men carelefs of all their bufinefs and concernments, liable to be cheated by thofe, whom they are forced to truft with their affairs, becaufe they will not mind them themfelves, and to be abufed by crafty men, who watch the opportunities of their folly and weaknefs, to draw them into foolifh bargains. It is an old obfervation, that more men perifh by intemperance, than by the fword ; and I believe it is as true, that more eftates are diffipated and wafted by thefe two riotous vices, than by all other accidents whatfoever.

And there is fcarce any notorious vice, by which men do not greatly fuffer in their reputation and good name, even when the times are worft and moft degenerate ; any wicked courfe, whether of debauchery or injuftice, is a blemifh to a man's credit, not only in the efteem of the fober and virtuous, but even of thofe who are loofe and extravagant ; for men are fooner brought to practife what is bad, than to approve of it, and do generally think all fin and wickednefs to be a ftain upon them, whatever in a fwaggering humour they may fay to the contrary. A clear evidence of this is, that men do fo ftudioufly endeavour

deavour to conceal their vices, and are so careful that as few as may be should be conscious to them, and are so confounded if they be discovered, and so out of all patience when they are upbraided with them; a plain acknowledgment, that these things are shameful in themselves, and whatever face men may put upon things, that they do inwardly and at the bottom of their hearts believe, that these practices are deservedly of bad reputation, and do, in the general opinion of mankind, leave a blot upon them.

Secondly, There are other sins, which though they are not usually attended with consequences so palpably mischievous, yet are plainly unprofitable, and bring no manner of advantage to men.

Of this sort is all kind of profaneness, and customary swearing in common conversation, there is neither profit nor pleasure in them. What doth the profane man get by his contempt of religion ?' He is neither more respected nor better trusted for this quality ; but on the contrary, it is many times really to his prejudice, and brings a great odium upon him, not only from those who sincerely love religion, but from others also; though they are conscious to themselves, that they do not love religion as they ought, yet they have a veneration for it, and cannot endure that any one should speak slightly of it.

And it is as hard to imagine, where the pleasure of profaneness lies. Men cannot but at first have a great reluctancy in their minds against it, and must offer considerable violence to themselves, to bring themselves to it ; and when it is grown more familiar, and their consciences are become more seared and insensible, yet whenever they are alone and serious, or when any affliction or calamity is upon them, they are full of fears and anguish, their guilt

stares

ftares them in the face, and their confciences are raging and furious.

And as all kind of profaneneſs is unprofitable, ſo
more eſpecially cuſtomary ſwearing in ordinary converſation, upon every occaſion of paſſion, or any
other trivial cauſe, nay it may be without cauſe, out
of mere habit and cuſtom. Now what can poſſibly
be imagined to be the profit or pleaſure of this vice?
ſenſual pleaſure in it there can be none, becauſe it is
not founded in the temper of the body : a man may
be naturally prone to anger or luſt ; but no man I
think is born with a ſwearing conſtitution.

And there is as little profit as pleaſure in it ; for
the common and trivial uſe of oaths makes them perfectly inſignificant to their end, and is ſo far from
giving credit to a man's word, that it rather weak-
ens the reputation of it.

Thirdly, Thoſe vices which pretend to be of advantage to us, when all accounts are caſt up, and all
circumſtances duly conſidered, will be found to be
quite otherwiſe. Some vices pretend to bring in
profit, others to yield pleaſure ; but upon a thorough
examination of the matter, theſe pretences will vaniſh and come to nothing.

The vices which pretend to be moſt profitable are
covetouſneſs and oppreſſion, fraud and falſhood, and
perfidiouſneſs : but if we look well into them, we
ſhall find that either they do not bring the advantages they pretend to bring ; or that the inconveniencies which attend them are as great or greater, than
the advantages they bring ; or elſe that the practice
of the oppoſite virtues would be of much greater
advantage to us.

1. Some of theſe vices do not bring the advantages
they pretend to do. Covetouſneſs may increaſe a

man's

man's eſtate, but it adds nothing to his happineſs and contentment ; for though his eſtate grow never ſo much, his want is ſtill as great as it was before, and his care and trouble continually greater ; ſo that ſo long as he continues covetous, the more rich, the leſs happy.

And then for fraud and falſhood ; they are not of that real and laſting advantage, that cunning but ſhort-ſighted men are apt to imagine. Nothing is truer than that of Solomon, " the lying tongue is " but for a moment." A man can practiſe the arts of falſhood and deceit but for a little while, before they will be diſcovered ; and when they are diſcovered, they are ſo far from being any advantage to him, that they turn to his prejudice, and the cunning man begins to be in a bad caſe, and he that was wont to over-reach others, is at laſt caught himſelf.

2. Several of theſe vices are attended with inconveniencies, as great or greater than the advantages they bring. If a man increaſe his eſtate by injuſtice and oppreſſion, yet he loſeth his reputation. Beſides that all fraudulent and unjuſt courſes are apt to entangle a man in a great many inconveniencies, and to expoſe him to troubleſom ſuits, for the keeping of what he hath unjuſtly gotten ; it is very often ſeen, that what is gotten by injuſtice is ſpent in law ; and though it may be thoſe whom he hath wronged never recover their right, yet firſt or laſt the unjuſt man is put to more trouble and vexation about it, than the thing is worth. This Solomon obſerves, Prov. xv. 16. " In the revenue of the wicked there is " trouble."

The perfidious man by betraying a friend or a truſt, may perhaps make ſome preſent advantage : but then by ſuch a villainy he makes himſelf odious

to

to all mankind, and by this means, at one time or other, prevents himfelf of greater advantages which he might have had another way ; and perhaps at laft is miferably crufhed by thofe whom he betrayed, who, in the change and revolution of human affairs, may fome time or other have the opportunity of being revenged.   Or elfe,

3. The practice of the oppofite virtues would be of far greater advantage to us.

Truth and fidelity are in common experience found to be a better and furer way of thriving, and more like to laft and hold out, than fraud and falfhood; and as honefty is a furer way of raifing an eftate, fo it brings along with it greater fecurity of the quiet enjoyment of it.   There is never any real occafion, and feldom any colour and pretence of bringing fuch a man into trouble ; for which reafon Solomon fays, " Better is the little which the righteous man hath, " than great poffeffions without right :" becaufe, though it be but little, yet it will wear like fteel, and he is like to enjoy it quietly, and may increafe it ; whereas the unjuft man is continually in danger of lofing what he hath gotten.

And if this be the cafe, it is very plain, that thofe vices which pretend to bring the greateft advantage, are really unprofitable ; and to thefe kind of vices the text feems to point more particularly ; " if any " fay, I have finned, and perverted that which was " right, and it profited me not, &c."

But perhaps though there be no profit in any finful courfe, yet there may be fome pleafure.   That comes next to be examined , and I doubt not to make it evident, that there is no fuch pleafure in fin, as can make it a reafonable temptation to any man to venture upon it.   The vices which pretend to bring

the greateft pleafure, are lewdnefs, and intemperance, and revenge.

The two firft of thefe are the higheft pretenders
to pleafure : but GOD knows, and the finner himfelf
knows, how thin and tranfitory this pleafure is, how
much trouble attends it, and how many fighs and
groans follow it, and whatever pleafure they may
minifter to the fenfe, they bring a great deal of anguifh and perplexity to the mind ; fo that the trouble which they caufe, does more than countervail
the pleafure which they bring : and they do not only difturb the mind, but they difeafe the body. How
many are there, who for the gratifying of an inor-
dinate luft, and for the incomprehenfible pleafure of
a drunken fit, have endured the violent burnings of
a fever, or elfe have confumed the remainder of
their days in languifhing ficknefs and pain ?

And the reafon of all this is plain, becaufe all the
pleafures of fin are violent, and forced, and unnatural, and therefore not like to continue ; they are
founded in fome difeafe and diftemper of our minds,
and therefore always end in pain and fmart.

And as for revenge ; it is indeed a very eager and
impatient defire : but fo far furely from being a
pleafure, that the very thoughts of it are extremely
troublefom, and raife as great ftorms in the mind of
a man, as any paffion whatfoever : and I never heard
of the pleafure of being in a ftorm ; it is pleafant
indeed to be out of it, when others are in it. And
when revenge hath fatisfied itfelf, and laid it's enemy bleeding at it's foot, the man that executed it
commonly repents himfelf the next moment, and
would give all the world to undo what he hath
done ; fo that if there be any pleafure in revenge,
it is fo flitting and of fo fhort a continuance, that

3.   we

we know not where to fix it ; for there is nothing but tumult and rage before the execution of it, and after it nothing but remorfe and horror ; fo that if it be a pleafure, it is but of one moment's continuance, and lafts no longer than the act is a doing ; and what man in his wits would purchafe fo fhort a pleafure at fo dear a price ? This is moft certainly true, and if it were well confidered, fufficient to convince any reafonable man of the unreafonablenefs of this paffion.

Cain is a fearful inftance of this kind, who after he had drawn his brother into the field, and flain him there, how was he tormented with the guilt of what he had done, and forced to cry out, " my pu- " nifhment is greater than I can bear," (or as fome tranflations render the words) " mine iniquity is " greater than that it can be forgiven !" Gen. iv. 13. " From thy face, (fays he to GOD, in the anguifh of his foul) " from thy face fhall I be hid, and I " fhall be a fugitive and a vagabond in the earth ; " and it fhall come to pafs that every one that find- " eth me fhall flay me, v. 14. Every one that find- " eth me," how fearful did his guilt make him ! when probably there was then but one man in the world be- fides himfelf. And I may fay of this fort of men, as St. Jude does of thofe in his time, Jude v. 11. " Wo " unto them, for they have gone in the way of Cain," they are guilty of his crime, and his doom fhall be theirs.

And here I cannot but take notice of a great evil that grows daily upon us, and therefore deferves with the greateft feverity to be difcountenanced and pu- nifhed, I mean that of duels, than which what can be more unchriftian ? And what can be more unrea- fonable, than for men upon deliberation, and after the heat of paffion is over, to refolve to fheath their fwords in one another's bowels, only for a hafty word ?

And which is yet more unreaſonable, that becauſe
two men are angry, and have quarrelled with one
another, and will fight it out, that therefore two
more, who have no quarrel, no kind of diſpleaſure
againſt one another, muſt fight too, and kill one
another if they can for no reaſon, and upon no provocation.   Theſe falſe rules of honour will not paſs
in another world in the higheſt and greateſt court of
honour, from whence there is no appeal.

I ſhall conclude this whole argument with that excellent ſaying of Cato, reported in A. Gellius, " co-
" gitate cum animis veſtris, &c." " conſider (ſays
" he) with yourſelves, if ye be at any trouble and
" pain to do a good action, the trouble will be ſoon
" over ; but the pleaſure and comfort of what ye
" have done well, abides with you all your days :
" but if to gratify yourſelves, you do any thing
" that is wicked, the pleaſure will quickly vaniſh ;
" but the guilt of it will ſtick by you for ever."

And is it not then much better to prevent all this
trouble, by denying ourſelves theſe ſinful pleaſures,
which will follow us with guilt whilſt we live, and
fill us with horror and deſpair when we come to die ?

I ſhall now make ſome reflections upon what has
been delivered, and ſo conclude.

Firſt, What hath been ſaid upon this argument,
ought particularly to move thoſe who have ſo great a
conſideration of this preſent life, and the temporal
happineſs of it, that the practice of all virtues is a
friend to their temporal, as well as eternal welfare,
and all vice is an enemy to both.

Secondly, This likewiſe takes off all manner of
excuſe from ſin and vice.   It pretends not to ſerve
the ſoul, and to profit our future happineſs in another
world ; and if it be an enemy alſo to our preſent
wel-

welfare in this world, what is there to be said for it?

Thirdly, (which I desire to insist a little longer upon) all the arguments which I have used, to convince men of the folly of a wicked course, are so many strong and unanswerable reasons for repentance; for when a man is convinced, that " he hath done foolishly, and to his own prejudice, that he hath sinned, . " and that it profited him not," what can he do less, than to be heartily sorry for it, and ashamed of it, and resolved to do better for the future? Nothing surely is more reasonable than repentance; and yet how hard is it to bring men to it? Either men will mistake the nature of it, and not do it effectually; or they will delay it, and not do it in time.

I. Men mistake the nature of repentance; and there are two great mistakes about it.

1. Of those who make the great force and virtue of it to consist, not so much in the resolution of the penitent, as in the absolution of the priest. And this the church of Rome, in their doctrine concerning repentance, does. For their sacrament of penance (as they call it) they make to consist of two parts; the matter of it, which consists in these three acts of the penitent, confession, contrition, and satisfaction; and the form of it, which is the absolution of the priest, in which they make the main virtue and force of repentance to consist; *in quâ præcipuè ipsius vis sita est*, are the very words of the council of Trent. And here is a wide difference betwixt us; for though the comfort of the penitent may in some case consist in the absolution of the priest, yet the virtue and efficacy of repentance does not at all consist in it, but wholly in the contrition and sincere resolution of the penitent, as the scripture every where declares: and to think otherwise, is of
dangerous

dangerous confequence; becaufe it encourageth men to hope for the benefit of repentance, that is, the pardon and forgivenefs of their fins, without having truly repented. And indeed the council of Trent have fo framed their doctrines in this point, that any one may fee, that they did not matter how much they abated on the part of the penitent, provided the power of the prieft be but advanced, and kept up in it's full height.

2. The other miftake is of thofe, who make repentance to confift in the bare refolution of amendment, though it never has it's effect; that is, though the finner either do not what he refolved, or do it only for a fit, and during his prefent trouble and conviction.

There is one cafe indeed, and but one, wherein a refolution not brought to effect is available, and that is, when nothing hinders the performance and execution of it, but only want of time and opportunity for it; when the repentance is fincere, and the refolution real, but the man is cut off between the actual reformation which he intended, and which God, who fees things certainly in their caufes, knows would have followed, if the man had lived to give demonftration of it. But this is nothing to thofe who have the opportunity to make good their refolution, and do not: for, becaufe the refolution which would have been performed, had there been time and opportunity, is reckoned for a true repentance, and accepted of God as if it had been done; therefore the refolution which was not brought to effect when there was time and opportunity for it, hath not the nature of true repentance, nor will it be accepted of God.

I will add but one thing more upon this head, becaufe

caufe I doubt it is not always fufficiently confidered; and that is this, that a fincere refolution of a better courfe does imply a refolution of the means, as well as of the end; he that is truly refolved againft any fin, is likewife refolved againft the occafions and temptations that would lead and draw him to it; otherwife he hath taken up a rafh and foolifh refolution, which he is not like to keep, becaufe he did not refolve upon that which was neceffary to the keeping of it. So he that refolves upon any part of his duty, muft likewife refolve upon the means which are neceffary to the difcharge and performance of it; he that is refolved to be juft in his dealing, and to pay his debts, muft be diligent in his calling, and mind his bufinefs, becaufe without this he cannot do the other; for nothing can be more vain and fond, than for a man to pretend that he is refolved upon doing his duty, when he neglects any thing that is neceffary to put him into a capacity, and to further him in the difcharge of it. This is, as if a man fhould refolve to be well, and yet never take phyfick, or be carelefs in obferving the rules which are prefcribed in order to his health. So for a man to refolve againft drunkennefs, and yet to run himfelf upon the temptations which naturally lead to it, by frequenting the company of lewd and intemperate perfons, this is, as if a man fhould refolve againft the plague, and run into the peft-houfe. Whatever can reafonably move a man to be refolved upon any end, will, if this refolution be wife and honeft, determine him as ftrongly to ufe the means which are proper and neceffary to that end.

These are the common miftakes about this matter, which men are the more willing to run into, becaufe they are loth to be brought to a true repentance;

ance ; the nature whereof is not difficult to be underſtood, (for nothing in the world is plainer ;) only men are always ſlow to underſtand what they have
no mind to put in practice.   But,

II. Beſides theſe miſtakes about repentance, there
is another great miſcarriage in this matter, and that
is the delay of repentance ; men are loth to ſet about
it, and therefore they put it upon their laſt hazard,
and reſolve then to huddle it up as well as they can :
but this certainly is great folly, to be ſtill making
more work for repentance, becauſe it is to create ſo
much needleſs trouble and vexation to ourſelves ; it
is to go on ſtill in playing a fooliſh part, in hopes to
retrieve all by an after-game ; this is extremely dangerous, becauſe we may certainly ſin, but it is not
certain we ſhall repent, our repentance may be prevented, and we may be cut off in our ſins ; but if
we ſhould have ſpace for it, repentance may in pro-
ceſs of time grow an hundred times more difficult
than it is at preſent.

But if it were much more certain, and more eaſy
than it is, if it were nothing but a hearty ſorrow and
ſhame for our ſins, and an aſking God forgiveneſs
for them, without being put to the trouble of reforming our wicked lives, yet this were great folly,
to do thoſe things which will certainly grieve us after we have done them, and put us to ſhame, and
to aſk forgiveneſs for them.   It was well ſaid of old
Cato, *næ tu ſtultus es homuncio, qui malis veniam
precori, quam non peccare* ; " thou art a fooliſh man
" indeed, who chuſeſt rather to aſk forgiveneſs,
" than not to offend."

At the beſt, repentance implies a fault ; it is an
after-wiſdom, which ſuppoſeth a man at firſt to have
plaid the fool ; it is but the beſt end of a bad buſineſs ;

bufinefs ; a hard fhift, and a defperate hazard, which a man that had acted prudently would never have been put to ; it is a plaifter after we have dangeroufly wounded ourfelves : but certainly it had been much wifer, to have prevented the danger of the wound, and the pain of curing it. A wife man would not make himfelf fick if he could, or if he were already fo, would not make himfelf ficker, though he had the moft effectual and infallible remedy in the world in his power : but this is not the cafe of a finner, for repentance as well as faith is the gift of GOD.

Above all, let me caution you, not to put off this great and neceffary work, to the moft unfeafonable time of all other, the time of ficknefs and death, upon a fond prefumption, that you can be reconciled to GOD when you pleafe, and exercife fuch a repentance as will make your peace with him at any time.

I am heartily afraid, that a very great part of mankind do mifcarry upon this confidence, and are fwallowed up in the gulf of eternal perdition, with this plank in their arms. The common cuftom is (and I fear it is too common) when the phyfician hath given over his patient, then, and not till then, to fend for the minifter ; not fo much to enquire into the man's condition, and to give him fuitable advice, as to minifter comfort, and to fpeak peace to him at a venture.

But let me tell you, that herein you put an extreme difficult tafk upon us, in expecting that we fhould pour wine and oil into the wound before it be fearched, and fpeak fmooth and comfortable things to a man, that is but juft brought to a fenfe of the long courfe of a lewd and wicked life, impenitently continued in. Alas ! what comfort can we give to men in fuch a cafe ? We are loth to drive them to deſpair; and yet we muſt not deſtroy them by preſumption; pity and good nature do ſtrongly tempt us to make the beſt of their caſe, and to give them all the little hopes, which with any kind of reaſon we can, and God knows it is but very little that we can give to ſuch perſons upon good ground; for it all depends upon the degree and ſincerity of their repentance, which God only knows, and we can but gueſs at. We can eaſily tell them what they ought to have done, and what they ſhould do if they were to live longer, and what is the beſt that they can do in thoſe ſtraights into which they have brought themſelves, viz. to exerciſe as deep a ſorrow and repentance for their ſins as is poſſible, and to cry mightily to God for mercy, in and through the merit of our bleſſed Saviour. But how far this will be available in theſe circumſtances we cannot tell; becauſe we do not know, whether if the man had lived longer, this repentance and theſe reſolutions which he now declares of a better courſe, would have been good.

And after all is done that can be done in ſo ſhort a time, and in ſuch circumſtances of confuſion and diſorder, as commonly attend dying perſons, I doubt the reſult of all will be this; that there is much more ground of fear than hope concerning them; nay perhaps, while we are preſſing the dying ſinner to repentance, and he is bungling about it, he expires in great doubt and perplexity of mind what will become of him; or if his eyes be cloſed with more comfortable hopes of his condition, the next time he opens them again, he may find his fearful miſtake, like the rich man in the parable, who when he was " in hell, lift up his eyes being in " torment."

This is a very diſmal and melancholy conſideration,

and

and commands all men prefently to repent, and not
to put off the main work of their lives to the end of
them, and the time of ficknefs and old age. Let
us not offer up a carcafs to GOD inftead of a living
and acceptable facrifice: but let us turn to GOD, in
the days of our health and ftrength, "before the
" evil days come, and the years draw nigh, of which
" we fhall fay we have no pleafure in them ; before
" the fun and the moon and the ftars be darkned ;"
as Solomon elegantly expreffeth it, Ecclef. xii. 1, 2.
before all the comforts of life be gone, before our
faculties be all ceafed and fpent, before our underftandings be too weak, and our wills too ftrong ;
our underftandings be too weak for confideration, and
the deliberate exercife of repentance, and our wills
too ftrong and ftiff to be bent and bowed to it.

Let us not deceive ourfelves, heaven is not an
hofpital made to receive all fick and aged perfons,
that can but put up a faint requeft to be admitted
there ; no, no, they are never like to fee the kingdom of GOD, who inftead of feeking it in the firft
place, make it their laft refuge and retreat ; and
when they find the fentence of death upon them,
only to avoid prefent execution, do bethink themfelves of getting to heaven, and fince there is no
other remedy, are contented to petition the great
king and judge of the world, that they may be
tranfported thither.

Upon all thefe confiderations, let us ufe no delay
in a matter of fuch mighty confequence to our eternal happinefs, but let the counfel which was given to
Nebuchadnezzar be acceptable to us ; let us "break
" off our fins by righteoufnefs, and our iniquities
" by fhewing mercy to the poor ; if fo be it may
" be a lengthening of our tranquillity." Repentance

and alms do well together; "let us break off our "sins by righteousness, and our iniquities by shew- "ing mercy to the poor;" especially upon this great occasion, which his majesty's great goodness to those distressed strangers, that have taken sanctuary among us, hath lately presented us withal, "re- "membring that we also are in the body," and liable to the like sufferings; and considering on the one hand, that gracious promise of our LORD, "Blessed are the merciful, for they shall receive "mercy;" and on the other hand, that terrible threatening in St. James, "He shall have judg- "ment without mercy, that hath shewed no mercy."

To conclude, from all that hath been said, let us take up a present resolution of a better course, and enter immediately upon it, "to day whilst it is call- "ed to day, lest any of you be hardened through "the deceitfulness of sin. O that men were wise, "that they understood this, that they would consi- "der their latter end! And grant we beseech thee "Almighty GOD, that we may all know and do, "in this our day, the things which belong to our "peace, for thy mercy's sake in JESUS CHRIST, "to whom with thee, O Father, and the Holy "Ghost, be all honour and glory now and for ever." Amen.

SERMON CLXIII.

The shamefulness of sin, an argument for repentance.

ROM. vi. 21, 22.

What fruit had ye then in those things, whereof ye are now ashamed? For the end of those things is death. But now being made free from sin, and become servants to GOD, ye have your fruit unto holiness, and the end everlasting life.

THERE are two passions which do always in some degree or other accompany a true repentance, viz. Sorrow and shame for our sins; because these are necessary to engage men to a resolution of making that change wherein repentance does consist : for till we are heartily sorry for what we have done, and ashamed of the evil of it, it is not likely that we should ever come to a firm and steady purpose of forsaking our evil ways, and betaking ourselves to a better course.

And these two passions of sorrow and shame for our sins, were wont anciently to be signified by those outward expressions of humiliation and repentance, which we find so frequently mentioned in scripture, of " being clothed in sackcloth" as a testimony of our sorrow and mourning for our sins, and of " be-" ing sprinkled upon the head, and covered over " with filth and dirt, with dust and ashes," in token of our shame and confusion of face for all our iniquities and transgressions. Hence are those expressions in scripture of " repenting in sackcloth and ashes, of " lying down in our shame, and being covered with " confusion,"

SERM. CLXIII.

The first sermon on this text.

" confusion," in token of their great sorrow and shame for the manifold and heinous sins, which they had been guilty of.

Of the former of these, viz. trouble and sorrow
for our sins, I have very lately * treated ; and of the latter, I intend now by God's assistance to speak, viz. shame for our sins, and that from these words which I have recited to you ; " what fruit had ye then in " those things?" &c. In which words the apostle makes a comparison between an holy and virtuous, and a sinful and vicious course of life, and sets before us a perfect enumeration of the manifest inconveniencies of the one, and the manifold advantages of the other.

First, The manifest inconveniencies of a vicious and sinful course ; and the apostle mentions these three.

I. It is unprofitable, it brings no manner of present benefit and advantage to us, if all things be rightly calculated and considered. " What fruit had ye " then in those things?" Then (i. e.) at the time when you committed those sins, had you any present advantage by them? No, certainly ; but quite contrary.

II. The reflection upon our sins afterwards is cause of shame and confusion to us; " What fruit " had ye then in those things, whereof ye are now " ashamed?"

III. The final issue and consequence of these things is very dismal and miserable ; " the end of those " things is death." Let us put these things together, and see what they amount to : No fruit then when ye did these things, and shame now when ye come afterwards to reflect upon them, and death and misery at the last.

Secondly,

Secondly, Here is likewife on the other hand reprefented to us the manifold benefits of an holy and virtuous life. And that upon thefe two accounts.

I. Of the prefent benefit of it, which the apoftle calls here, fruit; " ye have your fruit unto holinefs."

II. In refpect of the future reward of it; " and " the end everlafting life." Here is a confiderable earneft in hand, and a mighty recompence afterwards, infinitely beyond the proportion of our beft actions and fervices, both in refpect of the greatnefs and the duration of it, " everlafting life;" for a few tranfient and very imperfect actions of obedience, a perfect and immutable and endlefs ftate of happinefs. I fhall begin with the

Firft of the two general heads, viz. the manifeft inconveniencies of a finful and vicious courfe ; and the apoftle I told you in the text takes notice of three.

I. It is unprofitable, and if all things be rightly calculated and confidered, it brings no manner of prefent advantage and benefit to us. " What fruit had " ye then in thofe things?" Then (i. e.) when ye committed thofe fins, had you any prefent advantage by them ? No, certainly, quite contrary ; as if the apoftle had faid, if you ferioufly reflect upon your former courfe of impiety and fin, wherein you have continued fo long, you cannot but acknowledge that it brought no manner of advantage to you ; and when all accounts are truly caft up, you muft, if you will confefs the truth, own that you were in no fort gainers by it : For the words are a μείωσις, and the apoftle plainly intends more than he expreffeth, " What fruit had ye then in thofe things?" (i. e.) the wicked courfe which ye formerly lived in, was fo far from being any ways beneficial to you, that it was on the contrary upon all accounts extremely to your prejudice and difadvantage. And

And this is not only true in respect of the final issue and consequence of a sinful and vicious course of life, that no man is a gainer by it at the long run; and if we take into our consideration another world, and the dreadful and endless misery which a wicked and impenitent life will then plunge men into (which in the farther handling of this text will at large be spoken to, being the last of the three particulars under this first general head :) But it is true likewise, even in respect of this world, and with regard only to this present and temporal life, without looking so far as the future recompence and punishment of sin in another world.

And this would plainly appear, by an induction of these three particulars.

1. It is evident that some sins are plainly mischievous to the temporal interest of men, as tending either to the disturbance of their minds, or the endangering of their healths and lives, or to the prejudice of their estates, or the blasting of them in their reputation and good name.

2. That there are other sins, which though they are not so visibly burdened and attended with mischievous consequences, yet they are plainly unprofitable, and bring no manner of real advantage to men, either in respect of gain or pleasure; such are the sins of profaneness, and customary swearing in common conversation.

3. That even those sins and vices, which make the fairest pretence to be of advantage to us, when all accounts are cast up, and all circumstances duly weighed and considered, will be found to be but pretenders, and in no degree able to perform and make good what they so largely promise before hand, when they tempt us to the commission of them.   There
are

are fome vices, which pretend to bring in great pro-fit, and tempt worldly-minded men, whofe minds are difpofed to catch at that bait; fuch are the fins of covetoufnefs and oppreffion, of fraud and falfhood and perfidioufnefs. And there are others which pretend to bring pleafure along with them, which is almoft an irrefiftible temptation to voluptuous and fenfual men; fuch are the fins of revenge, and intemperance, and luft. But upon a particular examination of each of thefe, it will evidently appear, that there is no fuch profit or pleafure in any of thefe vices, as can be a reafonable temptation to any man to fall in love with them, and to engage in the commiffion and practice of them. But I fhall not now inlarge upon any of thefe, having lately difcourfed upon them from another text. I fhall therefore proceed to the

II. Inconvenience which I mentioned of a finful and vicious courfe, viz. that the reflection upon our fins afterwards, is caufe of great fhame and confufion to us. "What fruit had you then in thofe things, "whereof you are now afhamed?" And this is a very proper argument for this feafon; becaufe the paffion of fhame, as it is a natural and ufual con-fequent of fin, fo it is a difpofition neceffarily required to a true repentance.

Preached in Lent.

Moft men when they commit a known fault are apt to be afhamed, and ready to blufh whenever they are put in mind of it, and charged with it. Some perfons indeed have gone fo far in fin, and have waded fo deep in a vicious courfe, as to be confirmed and hardened in their wickednefs to that degree as to be paft all fhame, and almoft all fenfe of their faults; efpecially in regard of the more common and ordinary vices, which are in vogue and fafhion, and in the commiffion whereof they are countenanced and encouraged by company and example, fuch were thofe of whom the prophet fpeaks, Jer. vi. 15. " Were they afhamed, " when they had committed abomination? nay, " they were not afhamed, neither could they blufh."

But yet even thefe perfons, when they come to be fenfible of their guilt, fo as to be brought to repentance, they cannot then but be afhamed of what they have done. For what face foever men may fet upon their vices, fin is fhameful in itfelf, and fo apt to fill men with " confufion of face," when they ferioufly reflect upon it, that they cannot harden their foreheads againft all fenfe of fhame. And whatever men may declare to the contrary, this is tacitly acknowledged by the generality of men, in that they are fo folicitous and careful to conceal their faults from the eyes of others, and to keep them as fecret as they can; and whenever they are difcovered and laid open, 'tis matter of great trouble and confufion to them; and if any one happen to upbraid and twit them with their mifcarriages of any kind, they cannot bear with patience to hear of them.

There are indeed fome few fuch prodigies and monfters of men, as are able after great ftruglings with their confciences, to force themfelves to boaft impudently of their wickednefs, and " to glory in " their fhame;" not becaufe they do really and inwardly believe their vices to be an honour and glory to them, but becaufe confcious to themfelves that they have done fhameful things, and believing that others know it, they put on " a whore's forehead," and think to prevent the upbraiding of others, by owning what they have done, and feeming to glory in it: but yet for all that, thefe perfons, if they would confefs the truth, do feel fome confufion in
them-

themfelves, and they are inwardly fenfible of the infamy and reproach of fuch actions, for all they would feem to the world to bear it out fo well : For when all is done, there is a wide difference between the impudence of a criminal, and the confidence and affurance of a clear confcience, that is fully fatisfied of it's own innocence and integrity. The confcientious man is not afhamed of any thing that he hath done: but the impudent finner only feems not to be fo, but all the while feels a great deal of confufion in his own mind. The one is fenfible and fatisfied that there is no caufe for fhame : the other is confcious to himfelf that there is caufe, but he offers violence to himfelf, and fuppreffes all he can the fenfe and fhew of it, and will needs face down the world, that he hath no guilt and regret in his own mind for any thing that he hath done.

Now that fin is truly matter of fhame, will be very evident, if we confider thefe two things.

Firft, If we confider the nature of this paffion of fhame.

Secondly, If we confider what there is in fin, which gives real ground and occafion for it.

Firft, For the nature of this paffion. Shame is the trouble or confufion of mind, occafioned by fomething that tends to our difgrace and difhonour, to our infamy and reproach. Now there is nothing truly and really matter of fhame and reproach to us, but what we ourfelves have done, or have been fome way or other acceffary to the doing of, by our own fault or neglect, and by confequence what it was in our power and choice not to have done: For no man is afhamed of what he is fure he could not help. Neceffity, unlefs it be wilful and contracted, and happens through fome precedent occafion and

19 E 2   fault

fault of our own, does take away all juft caufe of fhame.

And nothing likewife is matter of fhame, but fomething which we ought not to do, which mifbecomes us, and is below the dignity and perfection of our nature, and is againft fome duty and obligation that is upon us to the contrary; and confequently is a reproach to our reafon and underftanding, a reflection upon our prudence and difcretion, and at firft fight hath an appearance of ruggednefs and deformity.

And all actions of this nature do receive feveral aggravations, with refpect to the perfons againft whom, and in whofe prefence, and under whofe eye and knowledge thefe fhameful things are done. Now I fhall fhew in the

Second place, That fin contains in it whatfoever is juftly accounted infamous, together with all the aggravations of fhame and reproach that can be imagined. And this will appear by confidering fin and vice in thefe two refpects;

I. In relation to ourfelves.

II. In refpect to God, againft whom, and in whofe fight it is committed.

I. In relation to ourfelves, there are thefe four things which make fin and vice to be very fhameful.

1. The natural ruggednefs and deformity of it.

2. That it is fo great a difhonour to our nature, and to the dignity and excellency of our being.

3. That it is fo great a reproach to our reafon and underftanding, and fo foul a reflection upon our prudence and difcretion.

4. That it is our own voluntary act and choice.

Every one of thefe confiderations render it very fhameful, and all of them together ought to fill the finner with " confufion of face." I fhall fpeak to them feverally.

1. The natural ruggednefs and deformity of fin and vice render it very fhameful. Men are apt to be afhamed of any thing in them, or belonging to them, that looks ugly and monftrous, and therefore they endeavour with great care and art to conceal and diffemble their deformity in any kind. How ftrangely do we fee men concerned, with all their diligence and fkill, to cover and palliate any defect or deformity in their bodies; an ill face, if they could, however a foul and bad complexion, or blind or fquinting eye, a crooked body or limb, or whatever is ill-favoured or monftrous. Now in regard of our fouls and better part, fin hath all the monftroufnefs and deformity in it, which we can imagine in the body, and much more; and it is as hard to be covered from the eye of difcerning men, as the deformity of the body is; but impoffible to be concealed from the eye of GOD, to whom " darknefs " and light," fecret and open are all one. But then the moral defects and deformities of the mind have this advantage above the natural defects and deformities of the body, that the former are poffible to be cured by the grace of GOD, in conjunction with our own care and endeavour : Whereas no diligence or fkill can ever help or remove many of the natural defects and deformities of the body.

Sin is the blindnefs of our minds, the perverfenefs and crookednefs of our wills, and the monftrous irregularity and diforder of our affections and appetites; it is the mif-placing of our powers and faculties, the fetting of our wills and paffions above our reafon; all which is ugly and unnatural, and, if we were truly fenfible of it, matter of great fhame and reproach to us. There

There is hardly any vice, but at first sight hath an odious and ugly appearance to a well disciplined and innocent mind, that hath never had any acquaintance with it. And however familiarity and custom may abate the sense of it's deformity, yet it is as it was before, and the change that is made in us does not alter the nature of the thing. Drunkenness and furious passion, pride and falshood, covetousness and cruelty, are odious, and matter of shame, in the sincere and uncorrupted opinion of all mankind. And though a man, by the frequent practice of any of these vices, and a long familiarity with them, may not be so sensible of the deformity of them in himself, yet he quickly discerns the uglinest of them in others, whenever they come in his way, and could with salt and sharpness enough upbraid those whom he sees guilty of them, but that he is inwardly conscious, that the reproach may be so easily returned, and thrown back upon himself. However this is a natural acknowledgment of the deformity and shamefulness of sin and vice.

2. They are likewise shameful, because they are so great a dishonour to our nature, and to the dignity and excellency of our being. We go below ourselves, and act beneath the dignity of our nature, when we do any thing contrary to the rules and laws of it, or to the revealed will of God; because these are the bounds and limits which God and nature hath set to human actions; and are the measures of our duty, i. e. what is fit and becoming for us to do, and what not. So that all sin and vice is base and unworthy, and beneath the dignity of our nature; it argues a corrupt and diseased constitution and habit of mind, a crooked and perverse disposition of will, and a sordid and mean temper of spirit.

I   And

And therefore the fcripture doth frequently reprefent a ftate of fin and wickednefs, by that which is
accoupted the bafeft and meaneft condition among
men, by a ftate of fervitude and flavery, efpecially
if it had been our choice, or the evident and neceffary confequence of our wilful fault : for we do as
bad as chufe it, when we wilfully bring it upon ourfelves. So that to be a finner, is to be a flave to
fome vile luft, appetite, or paffion, to fome unnatural or irregular defire ; it is to fell ourfelves into
bondage, and to part with one of the moft valuable
things in the world, our liberty, upon low and unworthy terms. Such a ftate and condition does unavoidably debafe and debauch our minds, and break
the force and firmnefs of our fpirits, and robs us, as
Dalilah did Sampfon, of our ftrength and courage,
of our refolution and conftancy; fo that men have
not the heart left to defign and endeavour in good
earneft their own refcue out of this mean and miferable eftate, into which by their own folly and fault
they have brought themfelves.

When men are engaged into a cuftom of finning,
and have habituated themfelves to any vicious courfe,
how do they betray their weaknefs and want of refolution, by being at the beck of every foolifh luft,
and by fuffering themfelves to be commanded and
hurried away by every unruly appetite and paffion,
to do things which they know to be greatly to their
harm and prejudice, and which they are convinced
are mean and fordid things, and fuch as they are a-
fhamed that any wife man fhould fee them doing !
and there is no greater argument of a pitiful and degenerate fpirit, than to commit fuch things as a man
would blufh to be furprized in, and would be mightily troubled to hear of afterwards. And which is
more,

more, after he hath been convinced by manifold experience, that they are a shame and disgrace to him, and make him to hang down his head, and let fall his countenance, whenever he is in better company than himself; yet after this to go and do the same things again, which he is sensible are so shameful, and to be so impotent, and to have so little command of himself, as not to be able to free himself from this bondage, nor the heart to pray to GOD that by his grace he would enable him thereto.

And that sin is of this shameful nature, is evident, in that the greatest part of sinners take so much care and pains to hide their vices from the sight and notice of men, and to this purpose chuse darkness and secret places of retirement to commit their sins in. The apostle takes notice, that thus much modesty was left even in a very wicked and degenerate age, 1 Thes. v. 7. "They that be drunk (says he) "are drunk in the night." Now all this is a plain acknowledgment, that sin is a spurious and degenerate thing, that it misbecomes human nature, and is below the dignity of a reasonable creature : otherwise why should men be so solicitous and concerned to cover their faults from the sight of others? If they are not ashamed of them, why do they not bring them into the broad light, and shew them openly, if they think they will endure it ?

So true is that observation which Plato makes, that though a man were sure that GOD would forgive his sins, and that men should never know them, yet there is that baseness in sin, that a wise man, that considers what it is, would blush to himself alone to be guilty of it ; and though he were not afraid of the punishment, would be ashamed of the turpitude and deformity of it.

Did

Did but a man confider ferioufly with himfelf, how mean and unmanly it is for a man to be drunk ; and what an apifh and ridiculous thing he renders himfelf to all fober men that behold him, and with what contempt and fcorn they entertain fuch a fight; and how brutifh it is to wallow in any unlawful luft, and how much a man defcends and ftoops beneath himfelf ; what fhameful fear and cowardice he betrays when he is frighted to tell a lie out of fear, or tempted thereto for fome little advantage ; and yet is fo inconfiftent with himfelf, as to have, or to pretend to have the courage to fight any man, that fhall tell him fo fawcy a truth, as that he told a lie.

Would but a man think before-hand, how unworthy, and how unequal a thing it is to defraud or cheat his brother, or to do any thing to another man, which he would be loth in the like cafe that he fhould do to him ; how bafe a thing it is, for a man to be perfidious and falfe to his promife or truft ; how monftrous to be unthankful to one that hath highly obliged him, and every way and upon all occafions deferved well at his hands ; and fo I might inftance in all other forts of fins ; I fay, he that confiders this well and wifely, though there were no law againft fin, and (if it were a poffible cafe, and fit to be fuppofed) though there were no fuch being as God in the world, to call him to account and punifh him for it, yet out of mere generofity and greatnefs of mind, out of pure refpect to himfelf, and the dignity and rank of his being, and of his order in the world, out of very reverence to human nature, and the inward perfuafion of his own mind, (however he came by that perfuafion) concerning the indecency and deformity and fhamefulnefs of the thing ; I fay, for thefe reafons, if there were no other, a man would ftrive with himself, with all his might, to refrain from sin and vice, and not only blush, but abhor to think of doing a wicked action.

3. Sin will yet farther appear shameful, in that it is so great a reproach to our underftandings and reafons, and so foul a blot upon our prudence and difcretion. *Omnis peccans aut ignorans eft, aut incogitans,* is a faying, I think, of one of the fchool-men; (as one would guefs by the Latin of it) " Every finner " is either an ignorant, or an inconfiderate perfon." Either men do not underftand what they do, when they commit fin ; or if they do know, they do not actually attend to, and confider what they know. Either they are habitually or actually ignorant of what they do ; for fin and confideration cannot dwell together; it is so very unreafonable and abfurd a thing, that it requires either grofs ignorance, or ftupid inadvertency, to make a man capable of committing it. Whenever a man fins, he muft either be deftitute of reafon, or muft lay it afide or afleep for the time, and so fuffer himfelf to be hurried away, and to act brutifhly, as if he had no underftanding.

Did but men attentively confider what it is to offend God, and to break the laws of that great lawgiver, who " is able to fave or to deftroy," they would difcern so many invincible objections againft the thing, and would be filled with fuch ftrong fears and jealoufies of the fatal iffue and event of it, that they would not dare to venture upon it. And therefore we find the fcripture so frequently refolving the wickednefs of men into their ignorance and inconfideratenefs, Pfal. xiv. 4. " Have all the workers of " iniquity no knowledge ?" intimating that by their actions one would judge so. And the fame account

God

GOD himfelf alfo gives elfewhere of the frequent difobedience and rebellion of the people of Ifrael, Deut.
xxxii. 28, 29. " They are a nation void of coun-
" fel, neither is there any underftanding in them.
" Oh ! that they were wife, that they underftood
" this, that they would confider their latter end !"
Knowledge and confideration would cure a great part
of the wickednefs that is in the world ; men would
not commit fin with fo much greedinefs, would they
but take time to confider and bethink themfelves
what they do.

Have we not reafon then to be afhamed of fin,
which cafts fuch a reproach of ignorance and rafh-
nefs upon us ? And of imprudence likewife and in-
difcretion ? Since nothing can be more directly and
plainly againft our greateft and beft intereft both of
body and foul, both here and hereafter, both now
and to all eternity. And there is nothing that men
are more afhamed of, than to be guilty of fo great
an imprudence, as to act clearly againft their own
intereft, to which fin is the moft plainly crofs and
contrary, that it is poffible for any thing to be. No
man can engage and continue in a finful courfe, without being fo far abufed and infatuated, as to be contented to part with everlafting happinefs, and to be
undone and miferable for ever ; none but he that
can perfuade himfelf againft all the reafon and fenfe
of mankind, that there is pleafure enough in the
tranfient acts of fin, to make amends for eternal
forrow, and fhame, and fuffering. And can fuch a
thought as this enter into the heart of a confiderate
man ? Epicurus was fo wife, as to conclude againft
all pleafures that would give a man more trouble and
difturbance afterwards ; againft all pleafures that had
pain and grief confequent upon them : and he for-

bids his wife man to tafte of them, or to meddle
with them ; and had he believed any thing of a future ftate, he muft, according to his principle, have
pronounced it the greateft folly that could be, for
any man to purchafe the pleafures and happinefs of a
few years, at the dear rate of eternal mifery and torment. So that if it be a difgrace to a man to act
imprudently, and to do things plainly againft his intereft, then vice is the greateft reproach that is poffible.

The fourth and laft confideration, which renders
fin fo fhameful to us, is, that it is our own voluntary act and choice. We chufe this difgrace, and
willingly bring this reproach upon ourfelves. We
pity an ideot, and one that is naturally deftitute of
underftanding, or one that lofeth the ufe of his reafon
by a difeafe or other inevitable accident: but every
one defpifeth him who befots himfelf, and plays the
fool out of carelefnefs and a grofs neglect of himfelf.
And this is the cafe of the finner ; there is no man
that finneth, but becaufe he is wanting to himfelf ;
he might be wifer and do better, and will not ; but
he chufes his own devices, and voluntarily runs himfelf upon thofe inconveniencies, which it was in his
power to have avoided.

Not but that I do heartily own and lament the
great corruption and degeneracy of our nature, and
the ftrong propenfions which appear fo early in us to
that which is evil: but God hath provided a remedy
and cure for all this : For fince " the grace of God
" which brings falvation unto all men hath appear-
" ed," under the influence and through the affiftance of that grace, which is offered to them by the
gofpel, men may " deny ungodlinefs and worldly
" lufts, and live foberly, righteoufly, and godly
" in this prefent world." For I make no doubt,
                                                    but

but fince. God has entered into a new covenant of grace with mankind, and offered new terms of life and falvation to us; I fay, I doubt not, but his grace is ready at hand, to enable us to perform all thofe conditions which he requires of us, if we be not wanting to ourfelves.

There was a way of falvation eftablifhed, before the gofpel was clearly revealed to the world; and they who under that difpenfation, whether Jews or Gentiles, fincerely endeavoured to do the will of God, fo far as they knew it, were not utterly defti-tute of divine grace and affiftance : but now there is a more plentiful effufion of God's grace and holy fpirit; fo that whoever under the gofpel fins delibe-rately, fins wilfully, and is wicked, not for want of power but of will to do otherwife. And this is that which makes fin fo fhameful a thing, and fo very reproachful to us, that we deftroy ourfelves by our own folly and neglect of ourfelves, and become mi-ferable by our own choice, and when the grace of God hath put it into our power to be wife and to be happy.

I fhould now have proceeded to the fecond thing I propofed, which was to confider fin in relation to God, and to fhew that it is no lefs fhameful in that refpect, than I have fhewn it to be with regard to ourfelves : but this I fhall refer to another oppor-tunity.

SERMON CLXIV.

The shamefulness of sin, an argument for repentance.

ROM. vi. 21, 22.

What fruit had ye then in those things, whereof ye are now ashamed? For the end of those things is death. But now being made free from sin, and become servants to GOD, ye have your fruit unto holiness, and the end everlasting life.

ERM.
CLXIV.
he second
rmon on
is text.

IN these words the apostle makes a comparison, between an holy and virtuous, and a sinful and vicious course of life, and sets before us a perfect enumeration of the manifold inconveniencies of the one, and the manifold advantages of the other.

I began with the first of these, viz. to shew the manifest inconveniencies of a sinful and vicious course. I am upon the second inconvenience of a sinful course, viz. that the reflection upon it afterwards is cause of great shame and " confusion of face" to us; and that

First, In relation to ourselves. Which I have dispatched, and proceed now in the

Second place, To consider sin in respect of GOD, against whom, and in whose sight and presence it is committed; and upon examination it will appear to be no less shameful in this respect than the other.

There are some persons before whom we are more apt to be ashamed and blush, than before others; as those whom we reverence, those to whom we are greatly obliged, and those who are clear of those

faults

faults which we are guilty of ; and thofe who hate or greatly diflike what we do ; efpecially if they be prefent with us, and in our company ; if they ftand by us, and obferve, and take notice of what we do, and are likely to publifh our folly and make it known, and have authority and power to punifh us for our faults ; we are afhamed to have done any thing that is vile and unworthy before fuch perfons. Now to render fin the more fhameful, God may be confidered by us under all thefe notions, and in all thefe refpects.

1. Whenever we commit any fin, we do it before him, in his prefence, and under his eye and knowledge, to whom of all perfons in the world we ought to pay the moft profound reverence. I remember Seneca fomewhere fays ; that " there are fome per- " fons, *quorum interventu perditi quoque homines vi-* " *tia fupprimerent,* that they are fo awful and fo " generally reverenced for the eminency of their " virtues, that even the moft profligate and impu- " dent finners will endeavour to fupprefs their vices, " and refrain from any thing that is notorioufly " bad, and uncomely, whilft fuch perfons ftand by " them, and are in prefence." Such an one was Cato among the Romans. The people of Rome had fuch a regard and reverence for him, that if he appeared, they would not begin or continue their ufual fports, till he was withdrawn from the theatre, thinking them too light to be acted before a perfon of his gravity and virtue: and if they were fo much awed by the prefence of a wife and virtuous man, that they were afhamed to do any thing that was unfeemly before him; how much more fhould the prefence of the holy God, who is " of purer eyes " than to behold iniquity," make us blufh to do

any

R M.
XIV.
any thing that is lewd and vile in his fight, and fill us with fhame and " confufion of face" at the thoughts of it? Now whenever we commit any fin, God looks upon us; and he alone is an ample theatre indeed. That he obferves what we do, ought to be more to us, than if the eyes of all the world befides were gazing upon us.

2. He likewife is incomparably our greateft benefactor, and there is no perfon in the world, to whom in any degree we ftand fo much obliged, as to him; and from whom we can expect and hope for fo much good, as from him; the confideration whereof muft make us afhamed, fo often as we confider, and are confcious to ourfelves, that we have done any thing that is grievous and difpleafing to him.

We are wont to have a peculiar reverence for thofe to whom we are exceedingly beholden, and to be much afhamed to do any thing before them, which may fignify difrefpect, and much more enmity againft them; becaufe this would be horrible ingratitude, one of the moft odious and fhameful of all vices. And is there any one to whom we can ftand more obliged, than to him that made us, than to the author and founder of our beings, and the great patron and preferver of our lives; and can there then be any before whom, and againft whom we fhould be more afhamed to offend? When the prodigal in the parable would fet forth the fhamefulnefs of his mifcarriage, he aggravates it from hence, that he had offended againft and before one to whom he had been fo infinitely obliged: " Father, fays he, " I have finned againft heaven, and in thy fight."

3. We are afhamed likewife to be guilty of any fault or crime before thofe perfons who are clear of it, or of any thing of the like nature themfelves.

Men

Men are not apt to be afhamed before thofe who are their fellow-criminals, and involved with them in the fame guilt, becaufe they do not ftand in awe of them, nor can have any reverence for them. Thofe, who are equally guilty, muft bear with one another. We are not apt to fear the cenfures and reproofs of thofe, who are as bad as ourfelves; but we are afhamed to do a foul and unworthy action, before thofe who are innocent and free from the fame, or the like fins and vices which we are guilty of.

Now whenever we commit any fin, it is in the prefence of the holy GOD, who hath no part with us in our crimes, whofe nature is removed at the fartheft diftance from fin, and is as contrary to it as can be. " There is no iniquity with the LORD our " GOD." And therefore of all perfons in the world we fhould blufh to be guilty of it before him.

4. We are apt alfo to be afhamed to do any thing before thofe who diflike and deteft what we do. To do a wicked action before thofe who are not offended at it, or perhaps take pleafure in it, is no fuch matter of fhame to us. Now of all others, GOD is the greateft hater of fin, and the moft perfect enemy to it in the whole world. Hab. i. 13. " Thou art of " purer eyes, than to behold evil, and canft not look " on iniquity," i. e. with patience, and without an infinite hatred and abhorrence of it. Such is the unfpotted purity and perfection of the divine nature, that it is not poffible that GOD fhould give the leaft countenance to any thing that is evil. Pfal. v. 4, 5. " Thou art not a God," fays David there to him, " that haft pleafure in iniquity, neither " fhall evil dwell with thee: The wicked fhall not " ftand in thy fight; thou hateft all workers of " iniquity."

5. We are afhamed likewife to do any thing that is evil and unfeemly before thofe, who we are afraid will publifh our faults to others, and will make known and expofe the folly of them. Now whenever we fin, it is before him who will moft certainly one day bring all our works of darknefs into the open light, and expofe all our fecret deeds of difhonefty upon the publick ftage of the world, and make all the vileft of our actions known, and lay them open, with all the fhameful circumftances of them, before men and angels, to our everlafting fhame and confufion. This is the meaning of that proverbial fpeech, fo often ufed by our SAVIOUR, " There is " nothing covered that fhall not be revealed, nei- " ther hid that fhall not be made manifeft." All the fins which we now commit with fo much caution, in fecret and dark retirements, fhall in that great day of revelation, when the fecrets of all hearts fhall be difclofed, be fet in open view, and in fo full and ftrong a light, that all the world fhall fee them ; and that which was plotted and contrived in fo much fecrecy, and hardly whifpered in this world, fhall then " be proclaimed aloud," and as it were " upon the " houfe tops."

6. And laftly, We are afhamed and afraid to commit a fault before thofe, who we believe will call us to an account for it, and punifh us feverely. A man may fuffer innocently and for a good caufe ; but all fuffering in that cafe is by wife and good men efteemed honourable and glorious, and though we are condemned by men, we are acquitted in our own confciences : But that which is properly called punifhment is always attended with infamy and reproach ; becaufe it always fuppofeth fome fault and crime, as the ground and reafon of it. Hence it is

3   that

that in this world men are not only afraid, but a-
fhamed to commit any fault before thofe, who they
think have authority and power to punifh it. He is
an impudent villain indeed, that will venture to cut
a purfe in the prefence of the judge.

Now whenever we commit any wickednefs, we
do it under the eye of the great Judge of the world,
who ftedfaftly beholds us, and whofe omnipotent
juftice ftands by us ready armed and charged for our
deftruction, and can in a moment cut us off. Every
fin that we are guilty of, in thought, word or deed, is
all in the prefence of the holy, and juft, and powerful
GOD; whofe power enables him, and whofe holinefs
and juftice will effectually engage him, one time or
other, if a timely repentance doth not prevent it, to
inflict a terrible punifhment upon all the workers of
iniquity.

You fee then by all that hath been faid upon this
argument, how fhameful a thing fin is, and what
" confufion of face" the reflection upon our wicked
lives ought to caufe in all of us. " What fruit had
" ye then in thofe things, whereof ye are now afham-
" ed?" If ever we be brought to true repentance
for our fins, it cannot but be matter of great fhame
to us.

We find in fcripture that fhame doth continually
accompany repentance, and is infeparable from it.
This is one mark and character of a true penitent,
that he is afhamed of what he hath done. Thus
Ezra, when he makes confeffion of the fins of the
people, he teftifies and declares his fhame for what
they had done; " I faid, O my GOD! I am afham-
" ed, and blufh to lift up mine eyes to thee my
" GOD; for our iniquities are increafed over our
" heads, and our trefpaffes are grown up to the

19 G 2   " heavens,"

" heavens," Ezra ix. 6. And may not we of this
nation at this day take thefe words unto ourfelves,
confidering to what a ftrange height our fins are
grown, and how iniquity abounds among us? So
likewife the prophet Jeremiah, when he would exprefs the repentance of the people of Ifrael, Jer. iii.
25. " We lye down (fays he) in our fhame, and
" our confufion covereth us, becaufe we have finned
" againft the LORD our GOD." In like manner
the prophet Daniel, after he had in the name of the
people made humble acknowledgment of their
manifold and great fins, he takes fhame to himfelf
and them, for them. Dan. ix. 5. " We have fin-
" ned, fays he, and have committed iniquity, and
" have done wickedly, and have rebelled in depart-
" ing from thy precepts, and from thy judgments.
" O LORD, righteoufnefs belongeth to thee ; but
" unto us confufion of face, as at this day ; to the
" men of Judah, and to the inhabitants of Jerufa-
" lem, and unto all Ifrael, that are near, and that are
" far off, through all the countries whither thou haft
" driven them, becaufe of their trefpafs, which they
" have trefpaffed againft thee : O LORD ! to us be-
" longeth confufion of face, to our kings, to our
" princes, and to our fathers, becaufe we have fin-
" ned againft thee." By which we may judge, how
confiderable and effential a part of repentance, this
holy man efteemed fhame, for the fins they had
been guilty of, to be. And indeed upon all occafions of folemn repentance and humiliation for fin,
this taking fhame for their fins is hardly ever omitted, as if there could be no fincere confeffion of fin
and repentance for it, without teftifying their fhame,
and " confufion of face" upon the remembrance of
their fins.

Now.

Now to ftir up this affection of fhame in us, let
me offer to you thefe three confiderations.

I. Confider what great reafon we have to be heartily afhamed of all the fins and offences which we
have been guilty of againft GOD.   It was a good old
precept of philofophy, That we fhould reverence
ourfelves, i. e. that we fhould never do any thing
that fhould be matter of fhame and reproach to us
afterwards, nothing that mifbecomes us, and is unworthy of us.

I have fhewn at large, that all fin and vice is a
difhonour to our nature, and beneath the dignity of
it; that it is a great reproach to our reafon, and directly contrary to our true and beft intereft ; that it
hath all the aggravating circumftances of infamy and
fhame ; that every fin that was at any time committed by us, was done in the prefence of one, whom of
all perfons in the world we have moft reafon to reverence, and againft him, to whom of all others we
ftand moft obliged for the greateft favours, for innumerable benefits, for infinite mercy and patience and
forbearance towards us, in the prefence of the holy and
juft GOD, who is at the fartheft diftance from fin,
and the greateft and moft implacable enemy to it in
the whole world ; and who will one day punifh all
our faults, and expofe us to open fhame for them ;
who will " bring every work into judgment, and
" every fecret fin" that ever we committed, and take
vengeance upon us for all our iniquities.   So that
whenever we fin, we fhamefully intreat ourfelves,
and give the deepeft wounds to our reputation in the
efteem of him, who is the moft competent judge of
what is truly honourable and praife-worthy, and
clothe ourfelves with fhame and difhonour.

We are afhamed of poverty, becaufe the poor man
is

is defpifed, and almoft ridiculous in the eye of the proud and covetous rich man, " whofe riches are his " high tower,"and make him apt to look down upon the poor man that is below him, with contempt and fcorn; we are afhamed of a dangerous and contagious difeafe, becaufe all men fly infectious company: but a man may be poor or fick by misfortune; but no man is wicked, but by his own fault and wilful choice. Ill-natured and inconfiderate men will be apt to contemn us for our poverty and affliction in any kind: but by our vices we render ourfelves odious to God, and to all good and confiderate men.

II. Confider that fhame for fin now, is the way to prevent eternal fhame and confufion hereafter. For this is one great part of the mifery of another world, that the finner fhall then " be filled with everlafting " fhame and confufion" at the remembrance of his faults and folly. The eternal mifery of wicked men is fometimes in fcripture reprefented, as if it confifted only or chiefly in the infamy and reproach which will then overwhelm them, when all their crimes and faults fhall be expofed and laid open to the view of the whole world, Dan. xii. 2. where the general refurrection of the juft and unjuft is thus defcribed; " Many of them that fleep in the duft of the earth " fhall awake, fome to everlafting life, and fome to " everlafting fhame and contempt:" where everlafting life and everlafting fhame are oppofed, as if eternal fhame were a kind of perpetual death.

In this world finners make a hard fhift, by concealing or extenuating their faults, as well as they can, to fupprefs or leffen their fhame; they have not now fo clear and full a conviction of the evil and folly of their fin; God is pleafed to bear with them, and to fpare them at prefent, and they do not yet feel the
difmal

difmal effects and confequences of a wicked life: but in the next world, when " the righteous judgment " of God is revealed," and the full vials of his wrath fhall be poured forth upon finners, they fhall then " be clothed with fhame as with a garment, and " be covered with confufion:" then they will feel the folly of their fins, and have a fenfible demon-ftration within themfelves of the infinite evil of them; their own confciences will then furioufly fly in their faces, and with the greateft bitternefs and rage up-braid and reproach them with the folly of their own doings; and fo long as we are fenfible, that we fuffer for our own folly, fo long we muft unavoidably be afhamed of what we have done. So that if finners fhall be everlaftingly tormented in another world, it neceffarily follows, that they fhall be eternally con-founded.

Is it not then better to remember our ways now, and to be afhamed and repent of them, than to bring everlafting fhame and confufion upon ourfelves, be-fore God, and angels, and men? This is the argu-ment which St. John ufeth, to take men off from fin, and to engage them to holinefs and righteoufnefs of life; 1 Joh. ii. 28. " That when he fhall appear," that is, when he fhall come to judge the world, " we " may have confidence, and not be afhamed before " him at his coming."

III. And laftly, Confider that nothing fets men at a farther diftance from repentance, and all hopes of their becoming better, and brings them nearer to ruin, than impudence in a finful courfe. There are too many in the world, who are fo far from being afhamed of their wickednefs, and blufhing at the mention of their faults, that they boaft of them, and glory in them. God often complains of this in the

people

SERM.
CLXIV.

people of Ifrael, as a fad prefage of their ruin, and an ill fign of their defperate and irrecoverable condition : Jer. iii. 3. " Thou hadft a whore's forehead, " and refufedft to be afhamed ;" and Jerem. vi. 15. " Were they afhamed, when they committed abo- " minations ? Nay, they were not afhamed, neither " could they blufh: therefore they fhall fall among " them that fall, and in the time that I vifit them " they fhall be caft down." Hear likewife how the apoftle doth lament the cafe of fuch perfons, as are incurable and paft all remedy : Philip iii. 18, 19. " There are many of whom I have told you often, " and now tell you, even weeping, that they are " enemies to the crofs of CHRIST ; whofe end is " deftruction, whofe God is their belly, whofe glory " is in their fhame." Such perfons who glory in that which ought to be their fhame, what can their end be but deftruction ?

There is certainly no greater argument of a degenerate perfon, and of one that is utterly loft to all fenfe of goodnefs, than to be void of fhame : and as on the one hand, they muft be very towardly, and well difpofed to virtue, who are drawn by ingenuity, and meer fenfe of obligation and kindnefs ; fo on the other hand, they muft be very ftupid and infenfible, who are not wrought upon by arguments of fear, and fenfe of fhame. There is hardly any hopes of that man, who is not to be reclaimed from an evil courfe, neither by the apprehenfion of danger, nor of difgrace, and who can at once fecurely neglect both his fafety and reputation.

Hear how the prophet reprefents the deplorable cafe of fuch perfons, Ifa. iii. 9. " The fhew of their " countenance bears witnefs againft them ;" in the Hebrew it is, " The hardnefs of their countenance
" doth

" doth teftify againft them, and they declare their
" fin as Sodom, they hide it not. Wo unto their
" fouls, for they have rewarded evil to themfelves."
When men are once arrived to that pitch of impiety,
as to harden their foreheads againft all fenfe and fhew
of fhame, and fo as to be able to fet a good face upon the fouleft matter in the world; " wo unto
" them," becaufe their cafe feems then to be defperate, and paft all hopes of recovery. For who can
hope, that a man will forfake his fins, when he is
not fo much as afhamed of them? But yet one would
think, that thofe that are not afhamed of their impiety, fhould be afhamed of their impudence, and
fhould at leaft blufh at this, that they can do the
vileft and the moft fhameful things in the world without blufhing.

To conclude this whole difcourfe, let the confideration of the evil and fhamefulnefs of fin have this
double effect upon us, to make us heartily afhamed
of the paft errors and mifcarriages of our lives, and
firmly refolved to do better for the future.

I. To be heartily afhamed of the paft errors of
our lives. So often as we reflect upon the manifold
and heinous provocations of the divine majefty, which
many of us have been guilty of in the long courfe of
a wicked life, together with the heavy aggravations
of our fins, by all the circumftances that can render
them abominable and fhameful, not only in the eye
of GOD and men, but of our own confciences likewife; we have great reafon to humble ourfelves before GOD, in a penitent acknowledgment of them, and
every one of us to fay with Job, " Behold I am vile,
" what fhall I anfwer thee? I will lay mine hand
" upon my mouth, I abhor myfelf, and repent in
" duft and afhes;" and with Ezra, " O my GOD!

R M. " I am ashamed, and blush to lift up my face to
LXIV " thee, my God ; for our iniquities are increased over
      " our heads, and our trespass is grown up unto the
      " heavens : And now, O my God, what shall we
      " say after this ? for we have forsaken thy command-
      " ments ;" and with holy Daniel, " we have sinned,
      " and have committed iniquity, and have done
      " wickedly ; O Lord ! righteousness belongeth un-
      " to thee, but unto us confusion of face."   Thus
we should reproach and upbraid ourselves in the presence of that holy God, whom we have so often and
so highly offended, and against whom we have done
as evil things as we could, and say with the prodigal
son in the parable ; " Father, I have sinned against
      " heaven and before thee, and am no more worthy
      " to be called thy son."

If we would thus take shame to ourselves, and
humble ourselves before God, he would " be merci-
      " ful to us miserable sinners ;" he would " take away
      " all iniquity, and receive us graciously ;" and so
soon as ever he saw us coming towards him, would
meet us with joy, and embrace us in the arms of his
mercy.   And then,

II. As we should be heartily ashamed of the past
errors and miscarriages of our lives, so we should
firmly resolve, by God's grace, to do better for the
future ; never to consent to iniquity, or to do any
thing which we are convinced is contrary to our duty, and which will be matter of shame to us, when
we come to look back upon it, and make our blood
to rise in our faces at the mention or intimation of it ;
which will make us to sneak, and " hang down our
      " heads," when we are twitted and upbraided with
it, and which, if it be not prevented by a timely
humiliation and repentance, will fill us with horror

                          3   and

and amazement, with shame and confusion of face, both at the hour of death, and in the day of judgment.

So that when we look into our lives, and examine the actions of them, when we consider what we have done, and what our doings have deserved, we should, in a due sense of the great and manifold miscarriages of our lives, and from a deep sorrow and shame and detestation of ourselves for them ; I say, we should, with that true penitent described in Job, take words to ourselves, and say, " surely it is meet " to be said unto God, I will not offend any more ; " that which I know not, teach thou me ; and if I " have done iniquity, I will do no more." And thus I have done with the second inconvenience of a sinful and vicious course of life, viz. that the reflection upon it afterwards causeth shame ; " What fruit " had you then in those things, whereof ye are now " ashamed ?"

SERMON CLXV.

The final issue of sin, an argument for repentance.

ROM. vi. 21, 22.

What fruit had ye then in those things, whereof ye are now ashamed ? For the end of those things is death. But now being made free from sin, and become servants to God, ye have your fruit unto holiness, and the end everlasting life.

THESE words are a comparison between an holy and virtuous and a sinful and vicious course of life, and set before us the manifest inconveniencies

veniencies of the one, and the manifold advantages
of the other. I have entered into a difcourfe upon
the firft of thefe heads, viz. The manifeft inconveniencies of a finful and vicious courfe : and the
text mentions thefe three.

I. That it is unprofitable.

II. That the reflection upon it afterwards is matter of fhame. Thefe two I have fpoken largely to.
I fhall now proceed to the

III. And laft inconvenience, which the text mentions, of a finful and vicious courfe of life, viz. that
the final iffue and confequence of thefe things is very
difmal and miferable ; " the end of thofe things is
" death." No fruit then when ye did thefe things ;
fhame now that you come to reflect upon them ; and
mifery and death at the laft.

There are indeed almoft innumerable confiderations and arguments to difcourage and deter men from
fin ; the unreafonablenefs of it in itfelf ; the injuftice
and difloyalty, and ingratitude of it in refpect to
God ; the ill example of it to others ; the cruelty
of it to ourfelves ; the fhame and difhonour that attends it ; the grief and forrow which it will coft us,
if ever we be brought to a due fenfe of it ; the trouble and horror of a guilty confcience, that will perpetually haunt us ; but above all the miferable event
and fad iffue of a wicked courfe of life continued in,
and finally unrepented of. The temptations to fin
may be alluring enough, and look upon us with a
fmiling countenance, and the commiffion may afford us a fhort and imperfect pleafure : but the remembrance of it will certainly be bitter, and the end
of it miferable.

And this confideration is of all others the moft
apt to work upon the generality of men, efpecially

upon the more obstinate and obdurate sort of sinners, and those whom no other arguments will penetrate; that whatever the present pleasure and advantage of sin may be, it will be bitterness and misery in the end.

The two former inconveniencies of a sinful course, which I have lately discoursed of, viz. That sin is unprofitable, and that it is shameful, are very considerable, and ought to be great arguments against it to every sinner, and considerate man : and yet how light are they, and but as the very small dust upon the balance, in comparison of that insupportable weight of misery which will oppress the sinner at last ! " Indignation and wrath, tribulation and an-" guish upon every soul of man that doth evil." This, this is the sting of all, that " the end of these " things is death."

It is very usual in scripture to express the greatest happiness, and the greatest misery, by life and death; life being the first and most desirable of all other blessings, because it is the foundation of them, and that which makes us capable of all the rest. Hence we find in scripture, that all the blessings of the gospel are summed up in this one word, " John xx. 31. " These things are written, that you might believe " that Jesus is the Christ, the Son of God, and " that believing ye might have life through his " name." 1 John iv. 9. " In this was manifest the " love of God towards us, because that God sent his " only begotten Son into the world, that we might " live through him." So that under this term or notion of life, the scripture is wont to express all happiness to us, and more especially that eternal life which is the great promise of the gospel. And this is life by way of eminency ; as if this frail and mortal and miserable life, which we live here in this world, did not deserve that name. And

And on the other hand, all the evils which are consequent upon sin, especially the dreadful and lasting misery of another world, are called by the name of death, " the end of these things is death." So the apostle, here in the text, and v. 23. " The " wages of sin is death," not only a temporal death, but such a death as is opposed to eternal life ; " The " wages of sin is death : but the gift of GOD is eter- " nal life through JESUS CHRIST our LORD." So that death here in the text is plainly intended to comprehend in it all those fearful and astonishing miseries, wherewith the wrath of GOD will pursue and afflict sinners in another world.

But what and how great this misery is, I am not able to declare to you ; " it hath" no more " en- " tered into the heart of man," than those great and glorious things which " GOD hath laid up for them " that love him :" and as I would fain hope, that none of us here shall ever have the sad experience of it ; so none but those who have felt it, are able to give a tolerable description of the intolerableness of it.

But by what the scripture hath said of it in general, and in such metaphors as are most level to our present capacity, it appears so full of terror, that I am loth to attempt the representation of it. There are so many other arguments, that are more human and natural, and more proper to work upon the reason and ingenuity of men ; as the great love and kindness of GOD to us ; the grievous sufferings of his Son for us ; the unreasonableness and shamefulness of sin ; the present benefit and advantage, the peace and pleasure of an holy and virtuous life ; and the mighty rewards promised to it in another world, that one would think these should be abundantly sufficient to prevail with men to gain them to goodness

nefs, and that they need not to be frighted into it, and to have the law laid to them, as it was once given to the people of " Ifrael, in thunder and light-
" ning, in blacknefs, in darknefs and tempeft," fo as to make them "exceedingly to fear and tremble."
And it feems a very hard cafe, that when we have to deal with men, fenfible enough of their intereft in other cafes, and diligent enough to mind it, we can-not perfuade them to accept of happinefs, without fetting before them the terrors of eternal darknefs, and thofe amazing and endlefs miferies, which will certainly be the portion of thofe who refufe fo great an happinefs; this I fay feems very hard, that men muft be carried to the gate of hell, before they can be brought to fet their faces towards heaven, and to think in good earneft of getting thither.

And yet it cannot be diffembled, that the nature of men is fo degenerate, as to ftand in need of this argument ; and that men are fo far engaged in an evil courfe, that they are not to be reclaimed from it by any other confideration, but of the endlefs and unfpeakable mifery of impenitent finners in another world. And therefore God, knowing how necef-fary this is, doth frequently make ufe of it ; and our bleffed Saviour, than whom none was ever more mild and gentle, doth often fet this confideration be-fore men to take them off from fin, and to bring them to do better. And this St. Paul tells us, Rom. i. 18. is one principal thing which renders the go-fpel fo powerful an inftrument for the reforming and faving of mankind, becaufe " therein the wrath of
" God is revealed from heaven, againft all ungod-
" linefs and unrighteoufnefs of men."

So that how harfh and unpleafant foever this argu-ment may be, the great ftupidity and folly of fome men,

men, and their inveterate obstinacy in an evil course
makes it necessary for us to press it home, that those
who will not be moved, and made sensible of the
danger and inconvenience of sin by gentler arguments,
may be roused and awakened by the terrors of eternal misery.

That the last issue and consequence of a wicked
life will be very miserable, the general apprehension
of mankind concerning the fate of bad men in another world, and the secret misgivings of mens consciences, gives men too much ground to fear. Besides that the justice of divine providence, which is
not many times in this world so clear and manifest,
does seem to require that there should be a time of
recompence, when the virtue and patience of good
men should be rewarded, and the insolence and obstinacy of bad men should be punished. This cannot but appear very reasonable to any man, that
considers the nature of God, and is persuaded that
he governs the world, and hath given laws to mankind, by the observance whereof they may be happy,
and by the neglect and contempt whereof they must
be miserable.

But that there might remain no doubts upon the
minds of men, concerning these matters, God hath
been pleased to reveal this from heaven, by a person
sent by him on purpose to declare it to the world;
and to the truth of these doctrines concerning a future state and a day of judgment, and recompences,
God hath given testimony by unquestionable miracles wrought for the confirmation of them, and particularly by " the resurrection of Jesus Christ
" from the dead, whereby he hath given an assu-
" rance unto all men, that he is" the person " or-
" dained by God to judge the world in righteousness,
" and

" and to render to every man according to his deeds ;
" to them who by patient continuance in well-do-
" ing feek for glory, and honour and immortality,
" eternal life; but to them who obey not the truth,
" but obey unrighteoufnefs, indignation and wrath,
" tribulation and anguifh upon every foul of man
" that doeth evil."

So that how quietly foever wicked men may pafs
through this world, or out of it, (which they feldom
do) mifery will certainly overtake their fins at laft ;
unfpeakable and intolerable mifery, arifing from the
anguifh of a guilty confcience, from a lively apprehenfion of their fad lofs, and from a quick fenfe of
the fharp pain which they labour under ; and all this
aggravated and fet off with the confideration of paft
pleafure, and the defpair of future eafe. Each of
thefe is mifery enough, and all of them together do
conftitute and make up that difmal and forlorn ftate,
which the fcripture calls hell and damnation.

I fhall therefore briefly reprefent (for it is by no
means defirable to dwell long upon fo melancholy
and frightful an argument)

Firft, The principal ingredients which conftitute
this miferable ftate. And,

Secondly, The aggravations of it.

Firft, The principal ingredients which conftitute
this miferable ftate ; and they are thefe three which
I have mentioned.

I. The anguifh of a guilty mind.

II. The lively apprehenfions of the invaluable happinefs which they have loft.

III. A quick fenfe of the intolerable pains which
they lie under.

I. The anguifh of a guilty confcience. And this
is natural; for there is a worm that abides in a guilty

R M. confcience, and is continually gnawing it. This is
LXV. that our SAVIOUR calls " the worm that dies not."
And though GOD fhould inflict no pofitive punifhment upon finners, yet this is a revenge which every
man's mind would take upon him ; for things are
fo ordered by GOD, in the original frame and confti-
tution of our minds, that on the one hand peace and
pleafure, contentment and fatisfaction do naturally
arife in our minds from the confcience of well-doing,
and fpring up in the foul of every good man : and
on the other hand, no man knowingly does an evil
action, but his guilty confcience galls him for it, and
the remembrance of it is full of bitternefs to him.

And this the finner feels in this world ; he difguif-
eth and diffembleth his trouble as much as he can,
and fhifts off thefe uneafy thoughts by all the diver-
fions he can devife, and by this means palliates his
difeafe, and renders his condition in fome fort tolerable unto himfelf : but when he is alone, or caft upon the bed of ficknefs, and his thoughts are let loofe
upon him, and he hath nothing to give them a diverfion, how does his guilt ferment and work ! and
the fever, which lurked before, does now fhew itfelf, and is ready to burn him up ; fo that nothing
can appear more difmal and ghaftly, than fuch a man
does to himfelf.

And much more, when finners come into the other
world, and are entered into the regions of darknefs,
and the melancholy fhades, where evil fpirits are
continually wandring up and down ; where they
can meet with nothing either of employment or pleafure, to give the leaft diverfion to their penfive minds ;
where they fhall find nothing to do, but to reflect
upon, and bemoan themfelves ; where all the wicked actions that ever they committed fhall come frefh

2   into

into their minds, and ſtare their conſciences in the face. It is not to be imagined, what ſad ſcenes will then be preſent to their imaginations, and what ſharp reflections their own guilty minds will make upon them, and what ſwarms of furies will poſſeſs them.

So ſoon as ever they are entered upon that ſtate, they will then find themſelves forſaken of all thoſe comforts which they once placed ſo much happineſs in ; and they will have nothing to converſe with, but their own uneaſy ſelves, and thoſe that are as miſerable as themſelves, and therefore uncapable of adminiſtring any comfort to one another. They will then have nothing to think on, but what will trouble them ; and every new thought will be a new increaſe of their trouble. Their guilt will make them reſtleſs, and the more reſtleſs they are, the more will their minds be enraged ; and there will be no end of their vexation, becauſe the cauſe and ground of it is perpetual. For there is no poſſible way to get rid of guilt, but by repentance ; and there is no encouragement, no argument to repentance, where there is no hope of pardon. So that if God ſhould hold his hand, and leave ſinners to themſelves, and to the laſhes of their own conſcience, a more ſevere and terrible torment can hardly be imagined, than that which a guilty mind would execute upon itſelf.

II. Another ingredient into the miſeries of ſinners in another world, is the lively apprehenſion of the invaluable happineſs which they have loſt by their own obſtinacy and fooliſh choice. In the next world wicked men ſhall be for ever ſeparated from God, who is the fountain of happineſs, and from all the comforts of his preſence and favour. This, our Saviour tells us, is the firſt part of that dreadful ſentence that ſhall be paſſed upon the wicked at the great

day; "depart from me;" which words, though
they do not signify any positive infliction and torment, yet they import the greatest loss that can be
imagined. And it is not so easy to determine which
is the greatest of evils, loss or pain. Indeed to a
creature that is only endowed with sense, there can
be no misery but that of pain and suffering : but to
those who have reason and understanding, and are
capable of knowing the value of things, and of re-
flecting upon themselves in the want of them, the
greatest loss may be as grievous and hard to be born
as the greatest pain.

It is true, that sinners are now so immers'd in the gross
and sensual delights of this world, that they have no
apprehension of the joys of heaven, and the pleasures
of God's presence, and of the happiness that is to be
enjoyed in communion with him, and therefore they
are not now capable of estimating the greatness of this
loss. But this insensibleness of wicked men continues no
longer than this present state, which affords them variety of objects of pleasure and of business to divert
them and entertain them : but when they come into
the other world, they shall then have nothing else to
think upon, but the sad condition into which they
have brought themselves, nothing to do but to pore
and meditate upon their own misfortune, when they
shall lift up their eyes, and with the rich man in the
parable, in the midst of their torments, look up to
those who are "in Abraham's bosom;" and their
misery will be mightily increased by the contemplation of that happiness which others enjoy, and themselves have so foolishly forfeited and fallen short of;
insomuch that it would be happy for them, if that
God, from whose presence they are banished, that
heaven from which they have excluded themselves,
and

and that everlasting glory, which they have despised and neglected, might be for ever hid from their eyes, and never come into their minds.

III. This is not all, but besides the sad apprehension of their loss, they shall endure the sharpest pains. These God hath threatened sinners withal, and they are in scripture represented to us, by the most grievous and intolerable pains that in this world we are acquainted withal, as by the pain of burning. Hence the wicked are said " to be cast into the lake, " which burns with fire and brimstone, and into " the fire which is not quenched:" which, whether it be literally to be understood or not, is certainly intended to signify the most severe kind of torment; but what that is, and in what manner it shall be inflicted, none know but they that feel it, and lie under it. The scripture tells so much in general of it, as is enough to warn men to avoid it; that it is the effect of a mighty displeasure, and of anger armed with omnipotence, and consequently must needs be very terrible, more dreadful than we can now conceive, and probably greater than can be described by any of those pains and sufferings which now we are acquainted withal ; for " who knows the power of God's " anger," and the utmost of what almighty justice can do to sinners? Who can comprehend the vast significancy of those expressions, " fear him, who af- " ter he hath killed can destroy both body and soul " in hell ?" and again, " it is a fearful thing to fall " into the hands of the living God ?" One would think this were misery enough, and needed no farther aggravation ; and yet it hath two terrible ones, from the consideration of past pleasures which sinners have enjoyed in this world, and from an utter despair of future ease and remedy.

1. From

1. From the confideration of the paft pleafures which finners have enjoyed in this life. This will make their fufferings much more fharp and fenfible ; for as nothing commends pleafure more, and gives happinefs a quicker tafte and relifh, than precedent fufferings and pain, there is not perhaps a greater pleafure in the world, than the ftrange and fudden eafe which a man finds after a fharp fit of the ftone or colick, or after a man is taken off the rack, and nature which was in an agony before is all at once fet at perfect eafe : fo on the other hand, nothing exafperates fuffering more, and fets a keener edge upon mifery, than to ftep into afflictions and pain immediately out of a ftate of great eafe and pleafure. This we find in the parable was the great aggravation of the rich man's torment, that he had firft " re-" ceived his good things," and was afterwards tormented. We may do well to confider this, that thofe pleafures of fin which have now fo much of temptation in them, will in the next world be one of the chief aggravations of our torment.

2. The greateft aggravation of this mifery will be, that it is attended with the defpair of any future eafe ; and when mifery and defpair meet together, they make a man completely miferable. The duration of this mifery is expreffed to us in fcripture, by fuch words as are ufed to fignify the longeft and moft interminable duration. " Depart ye curfed into ever-" lafting fire, Matt. xxv. 41. Where the worm dieth " not, and the fire is not quenched," Mark ix. 43. And 2 Theff. 1. 7. it is there faid, that thofe " who " know not God, and obey not the gofpel of his " Son, fhall be punifh'd with everlafting deftruc-" tion, from the prefence of the Lord, and from " the glory of his power." And in Rev. xx. 10.

That

That " the wicked fhall be tormented day and night
" for ever and ever." And what can be imagined
beyond this? This is the perfection of mifery, to lye
under the greateft torment, and yet be in defpair of
ever finding the leaft eafe.

And thus I have done with the firft thing I propounded to fpeak to from this text, viz. the manifeft inconveniencies of a finful and vicious courfe of
life; that it brings no prefent benefit or advantage
to us; that the reflection upon it caufeth fhame; and
that it is fearful and miferable in the laft iffue and confequence of it. " What fruit had you," &c.

I fhould now have proceeded to the fecond part
of the text, which reprefents to us the manifold advantages of an holy and virtuous courfe of life;
ver. 22. " But now being made free from fin, and
" become the fervants of righteoufnefs, ye have your
" fruit unto holinefs," there's the prefent advantage
of it; " and the end everlafting life," there's the future reward of it. But this is a large argument,
which will require a difcourfe by itfelf, and therefore
I fhall not now enter upon it; but fhall only make
fome reflections upon what hath been faid, concerning
the miferable iffue and confequence of a wicked life
impenitently perfifted in.

And furely if we firmly believe and ferioufly confider thefe things, we have no reafon to be fond of
any vice; we can take no greater comfort or contentment in a finful courfe. If we could for the
feeming advantage and fhort pleafure of fome fins,
difpenfe with the temporal mifchiefs and inconveniencies of them, which yet I cannot fee how any prudent and confiderate man could do: if we could
conquer fhame, and bear the infamy and reproach
which attends moft fins, and could digeft the up-
braidings

braidings of our own consciences, so often as we call them to remembrance, and reflect seriously upon them ; though for the gratifying an importunate inclination, and an impetuous appetite, all the inconveniencies of them might be born withal ; yet methinks the very thought of the end and issue of a wicked life, that " the end of these things is death," that " indignation and wrath, tribulation and an" guish," far greater than we can now describe, or imagine, " shall be to every soul of man that doth " evil," should over-rule us. Though the violence of an irregular lust and desire are able to bear down all other arguments, yet methinks the eternal interest of our precious and immortal souls should still lye near our hearts, and affect us very sensibly. Methinks the consideration of another world, and of all eternity, and of that dismal fate which attends impenitent sinners after this life, and the dreadful hazard of being miserable for ever, should be more than enough to dishearten any man from a wicked life, and to bring him to a better mind and course.

And if the plain representations of these things do not prevail with men to this purpose, it is a sign that either they do not believe these things, or else that they do not consider them ; one of these two must be the reason why any man, notwithstanding these terrible threatnings of God's word, does venture to continue in an evil course.

It is vehemently to be suspected, that men do not really believe these things, that they are not fully persuaded that there is another state after this life, in which the righteous God " will render to every " man according to his deeds :" and therefore so much wickedness as we see in the lives of men, so much infidelity may reasonably be suspected to lye
lurking

lurking in their hearts. They may indeed feeming-
ly profefs to believe thefe things ; but he that would
know what a man inwardly and firmly believes,
fhould attend rather to his actions, than to his verbal
profeffions : For if any man lives fo, as no man that
believes the principles of the chriftian religion in reafon can live, there is too much reafon to queftion
whether that man doth believe his religion ; he may
fay he does, but there is a far greater evidence in the
cafe than words ; the actions of the man are by far
the moft credible declarations of the inward fenfe and
perfuafion of his mind.

Did men firmly and heartily believe that there is
a God that governs the world, and regards the actions of men, and that " he hath appointed a day
" in which he will judge the world in righteoufnefs,"
and that all mankind fhall appear before him in
that day, and every action that they have done in
their whole lives fhall be brought upon the ftage, and
pafs a ftrict examination and cenfure, and that thofe
who have made confcience of their duty to God and
men, and have " lived foberly, righteoufly, and
" godly in this prefent world," fhall be unfpeakably
and eternally happy in the next ; but thofe who have
lived leud and licentious lives, and perfifted in an
impenitent courfe, fhall be extremely and everlaftingly miferable, without pity, and without comfort,
and without remedy, and without hope of ever being otherwife ; I fay, if men were fully and firmly
perfuaded of thefe things, it is not credible, it is
hardly poffible that they fhould live fuch profane
and impious, fuch carelefs and diffolute lives, as we
daily fee a great part of mankind do.

That man that can be awed from his duty, or
tempted to fin by any of the pleafures or terrors of

this world, that for the present enjoyment of his lusts can be contented to venture his soul, what greater evidence than this can there be, that this man does not believe the threatnings of the gospel, and how " fearful a thing it is to fall into the hands of the " living God?" That man that can be willing to undergo an hard service for several years, that he may be in a way to get an estate, and be rich in this world; and yet will not be persuaded to restrain himself of his liberty, or to deny his pleasure, or to check his appetite or lust, for the greatest reward that God can promise, or the severest punishment that he can threaten; can any man reasonably think, that this man is persuaded of any such happiness or misery after this life, as is plainly revealed in the gospel, that " verily there is a reward for the righteous, and " verily there is a God that judgeth the earth?" For what can he that believes not one syllable of the bible, do worse than this comes to?

A strong and vigorous faith even in temporal cases, is a powerful principle of action, especially if it be backed and enforced with arguments of fear. He that believes the reality of a thing, and that it is good for him, and that it may be attained, and that if he do attain it, it will make him very happy, and that without it he shall be extremely miserable; such a belief and persuasion will put a man upon difficult things, and make him to put forth a vigorous endeavour, and to use a mighty industry for the obtaining of that, concerning which he is thus persuaded.

And the faith of the gospel ought to be so much the more powerful, by how much the objects of hope and fear, which it presents to us, are greater and more considerable. Did men fully believe the hap-

piness

pinefs of heaven, and the torments of hell, and were they as verily perfuaded of the truth of them, as if they were before their eyes, how infignificant would all the terrors and temptations of fenfe be to draw them into fin, and feduce them from their duty?

But although it feems very ftrange, and almoft incredible, that men fhould believe thefe things, and yet live wicked and impious lives; yet becaufe I have no mind, and God knows there's no need to increafe the number of infidels in this age, I fhall chufe rather to impute a great deal of the wickednefs that is in the world, to the inconfideratenefs of men, than to their unbelief. I will grant that they do in fome fort believe thefe things, or at leaft that they do not difbelieve them; and then the great caufe of mens ruin muft be, that they do not attend to the confequence of this belief, and how men ought to live that are thus perfuaded. Men ftifle their reafon, and fuffer themfelves to be hurried away by fenfe, into the embraces of fenfual objects and things prefent, but do not confider what the end of thefe things will be, and what is like to become of them hereafter; for it is not to be imagined, but that man who fhall calmly confider with himfelf what fin is, the fhortnefs of its pleafure, and the eternity of its punifhment, fhould ferioufly refolve upon a better courfe of life.

And why do we not confider thefe things, which are of fo infinite concernment to us? What have we our reafon for, but to reflect upon ourfelves, and to mind what we do, and wifely to compare things together, and upon the whole matter to judge what makes moft for our true and lafting intereft? to confider our whole felves, our fouls as well as our bodies; and our whole duration not only in this world, but in the other, not only with regard to time, but to eternity? to look before us to the laft iffue and event of our actions, and to the fartheft confequence of them, and to reckon upon what will be hereafter, as well as what is prefent ; and if we fufpect or hope or fear, efpecially if we have good reafon to believe a future ftate after death, in which we fhall be happy or miferable to all eternity, according as we manage and behave ourfelves in this world, to refolve to make it our greateft defign and concernment while we are in this world, fo to live and demean ourfelves, that we may be of the number of thofe that fhall be accounted worthy to efcape that mifery, and to obtain that happinefs, which will laft and continue for ever.

And if men would but apply their minds ferioufly to the confideration of thefe things; they could not act fo imprudently as they do; they would not live fo by chance and without defign, taking the pleafure that comes next, and avoiding the prefent evils which prefs upon them, without any regard to thofe that are future, and at a diftance, though they be infinitely greater and more confiderable : If men could have the patience to debate and argue thefe matters with themfelves, they could not live fo prepofteroufly as they do, preferring their bodies before their fouls, and the world before God, and the things which are temporal before the things that are eternal.

Did men verily and in good earneft believe but half of that to be true, which hath now been declared to you, concerning the miferable ftate of impenitent finners in another world, (and I am very fure, that the one half of that which is true concerning that ftate hath not been told you) I fay, did we in any meafure believe what hath been fo imperfectly reprefented, " what manner of perfons fhould we all be,
" in

" in all holy converfation and godlinefs, waiting for
" and haftening unto" (that is, making hafte to make
the beft preparation we could for) " the coming of
" the day of God!"

I will conclude all with our Saviour's exhorta-
tion to his difciples, and to all others ; " watch ye
" therefore and pray always, that ye may be ac-
" counted worthy to efcape all thefe things, and to
" ftand before the Son of man : To whom, with
" the Father and the Holy Ghoft, be all honour and
" glory, world without end. Amen."

SERMON CLXVI.

The prefent and future advantage of an holy and virtuous life.

ROM. vi. 21, 22.

*What fruit had ye then in thofe things, whereof ye
are now afhamed ? For the end of thofe things is
death. But now being made free from fin, and
become fervants to God, ye have your fruit unto
holinefs, and the end everlafting life.*

I HAVE feveral times told you, that the apoftle
in thefe words makes a comparifon between an
holy and virtuous, and a finful and vicious courfe of
life, and fets before us the manifeft inconveniencies
of the one, and the manifold advantages of the other.

SERM
CLXVI.
The fourth
fermon on
this text.

I have finifhed my difcourfe upon the firft part of
the comparifon ; the manifeft inconveniencies of a
finful and vicious courfe. I proceed now to the other
part of the comparifon, which was the   Second

Second thing I propounded to fpeak to from thefe words, viz. the manifold benefits and advantages of an holy and virtuous courfe; and that upon thefe two accounts.

Firft, Of the prefent benefit and advantage of it, which the apoftle here calls fruit, " ye have your fruit " unto holinefs."

Secondly, In refpect of the future reward of it, " and the end everlafting life." So that here is a confiderable earneft in hand, befides a mighty recompence afterwards, infinitely beyond the proportion of our beft actions and fervices, both in regard of the greatnefs and duration of it, " everlafting life;" that is, for a few tranfient acts of obedience, a perfect and immutable and endlefs ftate of happinefs. And thefe two the apoftle mentions in oppofition to the inconveniencies and evil confequences of a wicked and vicious courfe; " what fruit had you then in thofe " things? &c."

But before I come to fpeak to thefe two particulars, I fhall take notice of the defcription which the apoftle here makes, of the change from a ftate of fin and vice to a ftate of holinefs and virtue. " But now being made free from fin, and be- " come the fervants of GOD;" intimating that the ftate of fin is a ftate of fervitude and flavery, from which repentance and the change which is thereby made does fet us free; " but now being made " free from fin." And fo our SAVIOUR tells us, that " whofoever committeth fin is the fervant of " fin;" and this is the vileft and hardeft flavery in the world, becaufe it is the fervitude of the foul, the beft and nobleft part of ourfelves; it is the fubjection of our reafon, which ought to rule and bear fway over the inferior faculties, to our fenfual

fual appetites and brutiſh paſſions ; which is as uncomely a ſight, as to ſee beggars ride on horſe-back,
and princes walk on foot.   And as inferior perſons,
when they are advanced to power, are ſtrangely inſolent and tyrannical towards thoſe that are ſubject
to them ; ſo the luſts and paſſions of men, when they
once get the command of them, are the moſt domi-
neering tyrants in the world; and there is no ſuch
ſlave as a man that is ſubject to his appetite and luſt,
that is under the power of irregular paſſions and vicious inclinations, which tranſport and hurry him to
the vileſt and moſt unreaſonable things.   For a wicked man is a ſlave to as many maſters as he hath paſſions and vices ; and they are very imperious and exacting, and the more he yields to them, the more they
grow upon him, and exerciſe the greater tyranny
over him : and being ſubject to ſo many maſters, the
poor ſlave is continually divided and diſtracted between their contrary commands and impoſitions ; one
paſſion hurries him one way, and another as violently drives him another ; one luſt commands him upon ſuch a ſervice, and another it may be at the ſame
time calls him to another work.   His pride and ambition bids him ſpend and lay it out, whilſt his covetouſneſs holds his hand faſt cloſed ; ſo that he knows
not many times how to diſpoſe of himſelf or what to
do, he muſt diſpleaſe ſome of his maſters, and what
inclination ſoever he contradicts, he certainly diſ-
pleaſeth himſelf.

And that which aggravates the miſery of his condition is, that he voluntarily ſubmits to this ſervitude.   In other caſes men are made ſlaves againſt their
wills, and are brought under the force and power of
others, whom they are not able to reſiſt : but the
ſinner chuſeth this ſervitude, and willingly puts his
                                                              neck

neck under this yoke. There are few men in the world so sick of their liberty, and so weary of their own happiness, as to chuse this condition : but the sinner sells himself, and voluntarily parts with that liberty, which he might keep, and which none could take from him.

And which makes this condition yet more intolerable, he makes himself a slave to his own servants, to those who are born to be subject to him, to his own appetites and passions ; and this certainly is the worst kind of slavery, so much worse than that of mines and gallies, as the soul is more noble and excellent than the body.

Men are not usually so sensible of the misery of this kind of servitude, because they are govern'd by sense more than reason : But according to a true judgment and estimation of things, a vicious course of life is the saddest slavery of all others. And therefore the gospel represents it as a design every way worthy of the Son of God, to come down from heaven, and to debase himself so far, as to assume our nature, and to submit to the death of the cross, on purpose to rescue us from this slavery, and to assert us into " the liberty of the sons of God." And this is the great design of the doctrine of the gospel, to free men from the bondage of their lusts, and to bring them to the service of God, " whose service is " perfect freedom." And therefore our Saviour tells us, John viii. 31, 32. That " if we continue in " his word," i. e. if we obey his doctrine, and frame our lives according to it, it will make us free ; " ye " shall know (says he) the truth, and the truth shall " make you free." And if we observe it, the scripture delights very much to set forth to us the benefits and advantages of the christian religion by the meta-

phor

phor of liberty and redemption from captivity and
flavery. Hence our SAVIOUR is often called the re-
deemer and deliverer, and is faid to have " obtained
" eternal redemption for us." And the publifhing
of the gofpel is compared to the proclaiming of the
year of jubilee among the Jews, when all perfons that
would were fet at liberty. Ifa. lxi. 1, 2. " The Spi-
" rit of the LORD is upon me," faith the prophet
fpeaking in the perfon of the Meffiah, " becaufe he
" hath anointed me to proclaim liberty to the cap-
" tives, and the opening of the prifon to them that
" are bound, to proclaim the acceptable year of the
" LORD." And it is probable that upon this account likewife the chriftian doctrine or law is by St.
James called " the royal law of liberty."

This is the great defign of chriftianity, to fet men
free from the flavery of their lufts ; and to this end
the apoftle tells us, Tit. ii. 13. that " CHRIST gave
" himfelf for us, that he might redeem us from all
" iniquity, and purify to himfelf a peculiar people,
" zealous of good works." And herein the great
mercy and compaffion of GOD towards mankind appeared, in that he fent his Son to refcue us from that
fervitude, which we had fo long groaned under, that
" being made free from fin, we might become the
" fervants of GOD, and the fervants of righteoufnefs."

And this he hath done not only by the price of
his blood, but by the power and purity of his doctrine, and the holy example of his life, and by all
thofe confiderations which reprefent to us the mifery
of our finful ftate, and the infinite danger of continuing in it : and on the other hand, by fetting before
us the advantages of a religious and holy life, and
what a bleffed change we make, when we quit the
fervice of fin, and become the fervants of GOD. It

SERM.
CXLVI.

will not only be a mighty prefent benefit to us, but will make us happy to all eternity ; and thefe are the two confiderations which at firft I propounded to fpeak to at this time.

First, The prefent benefit of an holy and virtuous life, which the apoftle here calls fruit ; ". But now " being made free from fin, and become the fer- " vants of God, ye have your fruit unto holinefs."

Secondly, The future reward and recompence of 'it ; " and the end everlafting life."

Firft, Let us confider the prefent benefit and advantage of an holy and virtuous life, which the apoftle here calls fruit. If all things be truly confidered, there is no advantage comes to any man by a wicked and vicious courfe of life. A wicked life is no prefent advantage ; the reflection upon it afterwards is fhameful and troublefom ; and the end of it miferable. But on the contrary, the advantages of an holy and good life are many and great even in this world, and upon temporal accounts, abftracting from the confideration of a future reward in the world to come.

I fhall inftance in five or fix eminent advantages, which it ufually brings to men in this world.

I. It brings great peace and contentment of mind.

II. It is a very fit and proper means to promote our outward temporal intereft.

III. It tends to the lengthening our days, and hath frequently the bleffing of long life attending upon it.

IV. It gives a man great peace and comfort when he comes to die.

V. After death it tranfmits a good name and reputation to pofterity.

VI. It derives a bleffing upon our pofterity after us. And thefe are certainly the greateft bleffings that

that a wife man can aim at, and defign to himfelf in this world. Every one of thefe taken feverally is very confiderable ; but all of them together complete a man's temporal felicity, and raife it to as high a pitch as is to be expected in this world.

I. A religious and virtuous courfe of life is the beft way to peace and contentment of mind, and does commonly bring it. And to a wife man, that knows how to value the eafe and fatisfaction of his own mind, there cannot be a greater temptation to religion and virtue, than to confider that it is the beft and only way to give reft to his mind. And this is prefent fruit and ready payment ; becaufe it immediately follows, or rather accompanies the difcharge of our duty. " The fruit of righteoufnefs is peace," faith the prophet ; and the apoftle to the Hebrews fpeaks of " the peaceable fruits of righteoufnefs," meaning that inward peace which a righteous man hath in his own mind.

A man needs not to take pains, or to ufe many arguments, to fatisfy and content his own mind, after he hath done a good action, and to convince himfelf, that he hath no caufe to be troubled for it , for peace and pleafure do naturally fpring from it : nay, not only fo, but there is an unexpreffible kind of pleafure and delight, that flows from the teftimony of a good confcience. Let but a man take care to fatisfy himfelf in the doing of his duty, and whatever troubles and ftorms may be raifed from without, all will be clear and calm within : for nothing but guilt can trouble a man's mind, and fright his confcience, and make him uneafy to himfelf ; that indeed will wound his fpirit, and fting his very foul, and make him full of fearful and tormenting thoughts. This Cain found after he had committed that crying

fin

SERM.   fin of murdering his brother. Gen. iv. 6. "The
CLXVI.   " Lord faid unto Cain, why art thou wrath ? And
" why is thy countenance fallen ? His guilt made
him full of wrath, and difcontent filled his mind with
vexation, and his countenance with fhame and confufion.   When a man's confcience is awakened to a
fenfe of his guilt, it is angry and froward, and harder to be ftilled than a peevifh child : but the practice
of holinefs and virtue does produce juft the contrary
effects ; it fills a man's mind with pleafure, and
makes his countenance chearful.

And this certainly, if it be well confidered, is no
fmall and contemptible advantage. The peace and
tranquillity of our minds is the great thing, which all
the philofophy and wifdom of the world did always
defign to bring men to, as the very utmoft happinefs
that a wife man is capable of in this life ; and it is
that which no confiderate man would part with, for
all that this world can give him. The greateft fortune in this world ought to be no temptation to any
man in his wits, to fubmit to perpetual ficknefs and
pain for the gaining of it ; and yet there is no difeafe
in the world, that for the fharpnefs of it is comparable to the fting of a guilty mind, and no pleafure
equal to that of innocence and a good confcience.
And this naturally fprings up in the mind of a good
man, where it is not hindred either by a melancholy
temper, or by falfe principles in religion, which fill
a man with groundlefs fears and jealoufies of the love
and favour of God towards him ; and excepting thefe
two cafes, this is the ordinary fruit of an holy and
good courfe, which is not interrupted by frequent
falling into fin, and great omiffions and violations of
our duty : for in this cafe the interruptions of our
peace and comfort will naturally be anfwerable to the
inequality of our obedience.   II. Be-

II. Befides the prefent and ineftimable fruit of holinefs, the quiet and fatisfaction of our own minds; it is likewife a proper means to promote our intereft and happinefs in this world. For as every vice is naturally attended with fome temporal inconvenience of pain or lofs; fo there is no grace or virtue, but does apparently conduce to a man's temporal felicity. There are fome virtues which tend to the health of his body, and the prolonging of his life, as temperance and chaftity; others tend to riches and plenty, as diligence and induftry in our callings; others to the fecure and peaceable enjoyment of what we have, as truth and fidelity, juftice and honefty in all our dealings and intercourfe with men. There are other virtues that are apt to oblige mankind to us, and to gain their friendfhip and good will, their aid and affiftance, as kindnefs, and meeknefs, and charity, and a generous difpofition to do good to all, as far as we have power and opportunity. In a word, there is no real intereft of this world, but may ordinarily be as effectually promoted and purfued to as great advantage, by a man that exercifes himfelf in the practice of all virtue and goodnefs, and ufually to far greater advantage, than by one that is intemperate and debauched, deceitful and difhoneft, apt to difoblige and provoke, four and ill-natured to all mankind: for there is none of thefe vices, but is to a man's real hinderance and difadvantage, in regard of one kind of happinefs or another, which men aim at and propofe to themfelves in this world.

III. A religious and virtuous courfe of life doth naturally tend to the prolonging of our days, and hath very frequently the blefling of health and long life attending upon it. The practice of a great many virtues is a great prefervative of life and health, as the due go-

vernment

vernment of our appetites and paffions, by temperance and chaftity and meeknefs, which prevent the
chief caufes from within of bodily difeafes and diftempers ; the due government of our tongues and converfation in refpect of others, by juftice and kindnefs, and abftaining from wrath and provocation,
which are a great fecurity againft the dangers of outward violence, according to that of St. Peter, 1 Epift.
iii. 10. " He that will love life and fee good days,
" let him refrain his tongue from evil, and his lips
" that they fpeak no guile ; let him efchew evil,
" and do good, let him feek peace and enfue it."

And befide the natural tendency of things, there
is a fpecial bleffing of GOD, which attends good
men, and makes " their days long in the land which
" the LORD their GOD hath given them."

IV. There is nothing gives a man fo much comfort when he comes to die, as the reflection upon an
holy and good life : and then furely above all other
times comfort is moft valuable, becaufe our frail and
infirm nature doth then ftand moft in need of it.
Then ufually mens hearts are faint and their fpirits
low, and every thing is apt to deject and trouble
them ; fo that we had need to provide ourfelves of
fome excellent cordial againft that time ; and there
is no comfort like to that of a clear confcience, and
of an innocent and ufeful life. This will revive and
raife a man's fpirits under all the infirmities of his
body, becaufe it gives a man good hopes concerning
his eternal ftate, and the hopes of that are apt to
fill a man with " joy unfpeakable and full of glory."

The difference between good and bad men is never
fo remarkable in this world, as when they are upon
their death-bed. This the fcripture obferves to us,
Pfal. xxxvii. 37. " Mark the perfect man, and be-
" hold

" hold the upright, for the end of that man is peace."

With what triumph and exultation doth the blef-fed apoftle St. Paul, upon the review of his life, dif-courfe concerning his death and diffolution? 2 Tim. iv. 6, 7, 8. " I am now ready, fays he, to be offered " up, and the time of my departure is at hand : " I have fought a good fight, I have finifhed my " courfe, I have kept the faith ; henceforth there is " laid up for me a crown of righteoufnefs, which the " LORD, the righteous judge, will give me at that " day." What would not any of us do to be thus affected when we come to leave the world, and to be able to bear the thoughts of death and eternity with fo quiet and well fatisfied a mind ! Why, let us but endeavour to live holy lives, and to be ufeful and ferviceable to GOD in our generation, as this holy apoftle was, and we fhall have the fame ground of joy and triumph which he had. For this is the proper and genuine effect of virtue and goodnefs ; " the " work of righteoufnefs is peace, and the effect of " righteoufnefs quietnefs and affurance for ever." All the good actions that we do in this life are fo many feeds of comfort fown in our own confciences, which will fpring up one time or other, but efpecial-ly in the approaches of death, when we come to take a ferious review of our lives ; for then mens con-fciences ufe to deal plainly and impartially with them, and to tell them the truth ; and if at that time more efpecially " our hearts condemn us not, then may we " have comfort and confidence towards GOD."

V. An holy and virtuous life doth tranfmit a good name and reputation to pofterity. And this Solomon hath determined to be a much greater happinefs, than for a man to leave a great eftate behind him : a good name, fays he, " is rather to be chofen than

" great

" great riches." Pious and virtuous men do commonly gain to themfelves a good efteem and reputation in this world, while they are in it ; but the virtues of good men are not always fo bright and fhining, as to meet with that refpect and acknowledgment which is due to them in this world. Many times they are much clouded by the infirmities and paffions which attend them, and are fhadowed by fome affected fingularities and morofities, which thofe which have lived more retired from the world are more liable to. Befides that the envy of others, who are not fo good as they, lies heavy upon them, and does deprefs them. For bad men are very apt to mifinterpret the beft actions of the good, and put falfe colours upon them, and when they have nothing elfe to object againft them, to charge them with hypocrify and infincerity ; an objection as hard to be anfwered, as it is to be made good, unlefs we could fee into the hearts of men.

But when good men are dead and gone, and the bright and fhining example of their virtues is at a convenient diftance, and does not gall and upbraid others, then envy ceafeth, and every man is then content to give a good man his due praife, and his friends and pofterity may then quietly enjoy the comfort of his reputation, which is fome fort of blefling to him that is gone. This difference Solomon obferves to us between good and bad men ; " the memory of the juft is blefled, or well fpoken " of : but the name of the wicked fhall rot."

VI. And laftly, religion and virtue do derive a blefling upon our pofterity after us. " Oh, that " there were fuch an heart in them," faith Mofes concerning the people of Ifrael, " that they would " fear me, and keep all my commandments always,
" that

" that it might be well with them and with their
" children for ever !" And to this purpofe there are
many promifes in fcripture of God's " blefling the
" pofterity of the righteous," and " his fhewing
" mercy to thoufands of the children of them that
" love him, and keep his commandments."

And this is a great motive to obedience, and
touches upon that natural affection which men bear
to their children ; fo that if we have any regard to
them, or concernment for their happinefs, we ought
to be very careful of our duty, and afraid to offend
God ; becaufe according as we demean ourfelves towards him, we entail a lafting blefling or a great
curfe upon our children ; by fo many and fo ftrong
bonds hath God tied our duty upon us, that if we
either defire our own happinefs, or the happinefs of
thofe that are deareft to us, and part of ourfelves, we
muft " fear God and keep his commandments."

And thus I have briefly reprefented to you fome
of the chief benefits and advantages which an holy
and virtuous life does commonly bring to men in this
world, which is the firft encouragement mentioned
in the text ; " Ye have your fruit unto holinefs."

Before I proceed to the fecond, I fhall only juft
take notice, by way of application, of what has
been faid on this argument.

1. That it is a great encouragement to well-doing,
to confider that ordinarily piety and goodnefs are no
hindrance to a man's temporal felicity, but very
frequently great promoters of it ; fo that excepting
only the cafe of perfecution for religion, I think I
may fafely challenge any man, to fhew me how the
practice of any part or duty of religion, how the
exercife of any grace or virtue is to the prejudice of a
man's temporal intereft, or does debar him of any

E R M.
CLXVI

true pleafure, or hinder him of any real advantage, which a prudent and confiderate man would think fit to chufe. And as for perfecution and fufferings for religion, God can reward us for them, if he pleafe, in this world ; and we have all the affurance that we can defire, that he will do it abundantly in the next.

2. The hope of long life, and efpecially of a quiet and comfortable death, fhould be a great encouragement to an holy and virtuous life. He that lives well, takes the beft courfe to live long, and lays in for an happy old age, free from the difeafes and infirmities which are naturally procured by a vicious youth, and likewife free from the guilt and galling remembrance of a wicked life. And there is no condition, which we can fall into in this world, that does fo clearly difcover the difference between a good and bad man, as a death-bed : for then the good man begins moft fenfibly to enjoy the comforts of well-doing, and the finner to tafte the bitter fruits of fin. What a wide difference is then to be feen, between the hopes and fears of thefe two forts of perfons ! and furely next to the actual poffeffion of bleffednefs, the good hopes and comfortable profpect of it are the greateft happinefs ; and next to the actual fenfe of pain, the fear of fuffering is the greateft torment.

Though there were nothing beyond this life to be expected, yet if men were fure to be poffeffed with thefe delightful or troublefom paffions when they come to die, no man that wifely confiders things would, for all the pleafures of fin, forfeit the comfort of a righteous foul, leaving this world full of the hope of immortality ; and endure the vexation and anguifh of a guilty confcience, and that infinite terror and amazement which fo frequently poffeffeth the foul of a dying finner.

2

3. If

3. If there be any fpark of a generous mind in us, it fhould animate us to do well, that we may be well fpoken of when we are gone off the ftage, and may tranfmit a grateful memory of our lives to thofe that fhall be after us. I proceed now to the

Second thing I propofed, as the great advantage indeed, viz. the glorious reward of a holy and virtuous life in another world, which is here called everlafting life; " and the end everlafting life:" by which the apoftle intends to exprefs to us, both the happinefs of our future ftate, and the way and means whereby we are prepared and made meet to be made partakers of it; and that is by the conftant and fincere endeavours of an holy and good life. For it is they only that " have their fruit unto holinefs," whofe end fhall be " everlafting life." I fhall fpeak briefly to thefe two, and fo conclude my difcourfe upon this text.

I. The happinefs of our future ftate, which is here exprefs'd by the name of " everlafting life;" in very few words, but fuch as are of wonderful weight and fignificancy: For they import the excellency of this ftate, and the eternity of it. And who is fufficient to fpeak to either of thefe arguments? Both of them are too big to enter now into the heart of man, too vaft and boundlefs to be comprehended by human underftanding, and too unwieldy to be managed by the tongue of men and angels, anfwerable to the unfpeakable greatnefs and glory of them. And if I were able to declare them unto you, as they deferved, you would not be able to hear me. And therefore I fhall chufe to fay but little upon an argument, of which I can never fay enough, and fhall very briefly confider thofe two things which are comprehended in that fhort defcription, which the text gives

us

us of future happinefs, by the name of " everlafting life," viz. the excellency of this ftate, and the
eternity of it.

1. The excellency of it, which is here reprefented
to us under the notion of life, the moft defirable of
all other things, becaufe it is the foundation of all
other enjoyments whatfoever. Barely to be in being,
and to be fenfible that we are fo, is but a dry notion
of life. The true notion of life is to be well and to
be happy, *vivere eft benè valere*. They who are in
the moft miferable condition that can be imagined,
are in being, and fenfible alfo that they are miferable. But this kind of life is fo far from coming under the true notion of life, that the fcripture calls it
" the fecond death." Rev. xxi. 8. It is there faid,
that " the wicked fhall have their part in the lake
" that burneth with fire and brimftone, which is the
" fecond death." And chap. xx. ver. 6. " Bleffed
" and holy is he, that hath part in the firft refur-
" rection, on fuch the fecond death fhall have no
" power." So that a ftate of mere mifery and torment is not life but death ; nay, the fcripture will
not allow the life of a wicked man in this world to
be true life, but fpeaks of him as dead. Eph. ii. 1.
fpeaking of the finners among the Gentiles, " You,
" faith the apoftle, hath he quickened, who were
" dead in trefpaffes and fins." And which is more
yet, the fcripture calls a life of finful pleafures (which
men efteem the only happinefs of this world) the
fcripture, I fay, calls this a death, 1 Tim. v. 6. " She
" that liveth in pleafures, is dead whilft fhe liveth."
A lewd and unprofitable life, which ferves to no good
end and purpofe, is a death rather than a life. Nay,
that decaying and dying life which we now live in
this world, and which is allayed by the mixture of
fo

so many infirmities and pains, of so much trouble and sorrow; I say, that even this sort of life, for all that we are so fondly in love with it, does hardly deserve the name of life. But the life of the world to come, of which we now speak, this is life indeed; to do those things which we were made for, to serve the true ends of our being, and to enjoy the comfort and reward of so doing, this is the true notion of life; and whatever is less than this, is death, or a degree of it, and approach towards it. And therefore very well may heaven and happiness be described by the notion of life, because " truly to live" and " to be happy" are words that signify the same thing.

But what kind of life this is, I can no more describe to you in the particularities of it, than Columbus could have described the particular manners and customs of the people of America, before he or any other person in these parts of the world had seen it or been there. But this I can say of it in general, and that from the infallible testimony of the great Creator and glorious inhabitants of that blessed place, that it is a state of pure pleasure and unmingled joys, of pleasures more manly, more spiritual, and more refined, than any of the delights of sense, consisting in the enlargement of our minds and knowledge to a greater degree, and in the perfect exercise of love and friendship, in the conversation of the best and wisest company, free from self-interest, and all those unsociable passions of envy and jealousy, of malice and ill-will, which spoil the comfort of all conversation in this world; and, in a word, free from all other passion or design, but 'an ardent and almost equal desire to contribute all, that by all means possible they can, to the mutual happiness of one another: For charity reigns in heaven, and is the brightest

grace

grace and virtue in the firmament of glory, far out-
shining all other; as St. Paul, who had himself been
taken up into the third heaven, does exprefly declare
to us.

Farther yet, this bleffed ftate confifts more particularly in thefe two things: In having our bodies
raifed and refined to a far greater purity and perfection, than ever they had in this world; and in the
confequent happinefs of the whole man, foul and body, fo ftrictly and firmly united as never to be parted
again, and fo equally match'd as to be no trouble or
impediment to one another.

(1.) In having our bodies raifed and refined to a
far greater purity and perfection, than ever they had
in this world. Our bodies, as they are now, are unequally tempered, and in a perpetual flux and change,
continually tending to corruption, becaufe made up of
fuch contrary principles and qualities, as by their perpetual conflict are always at work, confpiring the ruin
and diffolution of them; but when they are raifed
again, they fhall be fo tempered and fo refined, as
to be free from all thofe deftructive qualities, which
do now threaten their change and diffolution: and
though they fhall ftill confift of matter, yet they fhall
be purified to that degree, as to partake of the immortality of our fouls, to which they fhall be united,
and to be of equal duration with them. So the fcripture tells us, 1 Cor. xv. 52, 53. " That our dead
" bodies fhall be raifed incorruptible: for this cor-
" ruptible muft put on incorruption, and this mor-
" tal muft put on immortality."

Our bodies when they are laid down in the grave
are vile carcafes, but they fhall be raifed again beau-
tiful and glorious, and as different from what they
were before, as the heavenly manfions in which they
are

are to refide for ever are from that dark cell of the grave out of which they are raifed ; and fhall then be endowed with fuch a life, and ftrength, and vigour, as to be able without any change or decay to abide and continue for ever in the fame ftate.

Our bodies in this world are grofs flefh and blood, liable to be affected with natural and fenfual pleafures, and to be afflicted with natural pains and difeafes, to be prefs'd with the natural neceffities of hunger and thirft, and obnoxious to all thofe changes and accidents to which all natural things are fubject: But " they fhall be raifed fpiritual bodies," pure and refined from all the dregs of matter ; they fhall not hunger, nor thirft, nor be difeafed, or in pain any more.

" Thefe houfes of clay, whofe foundation is in " the duft," are continually decaying, and therefore ftand in need of continual reparation by food and phyfick: but " our houfe which is from heaven" (as the apoftle calls it) fhall be of fuch lafting and durable materials, as not only time, but even eternity itfelf, fhall make no impreffion upon it, or caufe the leaft decay in it. " They (fays our bleffed SA-" VIOUR) who fhall be accounted worthy to obtain " that world, and the refurrection from the dead, " cannot die any more : but fhall be like the angels, " and are the children of GOD," i. e. fhall in fome degree partake of the felicity and immortality of GOD himfelf, " who is always the fame, and whofe " years fail not." Nay, the apoftle exprefly tells us, that our bodies after the refurrection fhall be fpiritual bodies, fo that we fhall then be as it were all fpirit, and our bodies fhall be fo raifed and refined, that they fhall be no clog or impediment to the operation of our fouls. And it muft needs be a great comfort to us whilft we are in this world, to live in
the

the hopes of so happy and glorious a change ; when we consider how our bodies do now oppress our spirits, and what a melancholy and dead weight they are upon them, how grievous an incumbrance and trouble and temptation they are for the most part to us in this mortal state.

(2.) The blessedness of this state consists likewise in the consequent happiness of the whole man, soul and body, so strictly and firmly united as never to be parted again, and so equally matched as to be no trouble and impediment to one another.

In this world the soul and body are for the most part very unequally yoked, so that the soul is not only darkened by the gross fumes and clouds which rise from the body, but loaded and oppress'd by the dull weight of it, which it very heavily lugs on and draws after it ; and the soul likewise, and the vicious inclinations and the irregular passions of it, have many times an ill influence upon the body and the humours of it. But in the next world they shall both be purified, the one from sin, and the other from frailty and corruption, and both be admitted to the blessed fight and enjoyment of the ever-blessed God.

But the consideration of this (as I said before) is too big for our narrow apprehensions in this mortal state, and an argument not fit to be treated of by such children, as the wisest of men are in this world ; and whenever we attempt to speak of it, we do but lisp like children, and understand like children, and reason like children about it. " That which is im-
" perfect must be done away," and our souls must be raised to a greater perfection, and our understandings filled with a stronger and steadier light, before we can be fit to engage in so profound a contemplation. We must first have been 'in heaven,
and

and poffefs'd of that felicity and glory which is there
to be enjoyed, before we can either fpeak or think
of it in any meafure as it deferves. In the mean
time, whenever we fet about it, we fhall find our faculties opprefs'd and dazzled with the weight and
fplendor of fo great and glorious an argument; like
St. Paul, who, when " he was caught up into pa-
" radife," faw and heard thofe things, which, when
he came down again into this world, he was not able
to exprefs, and which it was not poffible for the
tongue of man to utter.

So that in difcourfing of the ftate of the bleffed,
we muft content ourfelves with what the fcripture
hath revealed in general concerning it ; that it is a
ftate of perfect freedom from all thofe infirmities and
imperfections, thofe evils and miferies, thofe fins and
temptations which we are liable to in this world. So
St. John defcribes the glory and felicity of that ftate,
as they were in vifions reprefented to him, Rev. xxi.
2, 3, 4. " And I, John, faw the holy city, the new
" Jerufalem, prepared as a bride adorned for her
" hufband. And I heard a great voice out of hea-
" ven, faying, Behold! the tabernacle of God is
" with men, and he will dwell with them, and they
" fhall be his people, and God himfelf fhall be with
" them, and be their God. And God fhall wipe
" away all tears from their eyes ; and there fhall be
" no more death, neither forrow, nor crying, nei-
" ther fhall there be any more pain : for the former
" things are paffed away ;" that is, all thofe evils
which we faw or fuffered in this world, fhall for ever
vanifh and difappear, and, which is the great privilege and felicity of all, that there fhall no fin be
there, ver. 27. " There fhall in no wife enter into it
" any thing that defileth," and confequently there

shall be no misery and curse there. So we read,
chap. xxii. 3, 4. " And there shall be no more curse;
" but the throne of God and of the Lamb shall be
" in it, and his servant shall serve him, and they
" shall see his face." In which last words our employment and our happiness are express'd ; but what
in particular our employment shall be, and wherein
it shall consist, is impossible now to describe ; it is
sufficient to know in the general, that our employment shall be our unspeakable pleasure, and every
way suitable to the glory and happiness of that state,
and as much above the noblest and most delightful
employments of this world, as the perfection of our
bodies, and the power of our souls, shall then be
above what they are now in this world.

For there is no doubt, but that he who made us,
and endued our souls with a desire of immortality, and so large a capacity of happiness, does understand very well by what way and means to make us
happy, and hath in readiness proper exercises and employments for that state, and every way more fitted
to make us happy, than any condition or employment in this world is suitable to a temporal happiness : employments that are suitable to " the spirits
" of just men made perfect," united to bodies purified and refined almost to the condition of spirits ;
employments which we shall be so far from being
weary of, that they shall minister to us a new and
fresh delight to all eternity ; and this perhaps, not so
much from the variety, as from the perpetual and
growing pleasure of them.

It is sufficient for us to know this in the general,
and to trust the infinite power and wisdom and goodness of God, for the particular manner and circumstances of our happiness ; not doubting but that he,
who

who is the eternal and inexhauftible fpring and fountain of all happinefs, can and will derive and convey
fuch a fhare of it to every one of us as he thinks fit,
and in fuch ways as he, who beft underftands it, is
beft able to find out.

In a word, the happinefs of the next life fhall be
fuch as is worthy of the great King of the world to
beftow upon his faithful fervants, and fuch as is infinitely beyond the juft reward of their beft fervices;
it is " to fee GOD," i. e. to contemplate and love
the beft and moft perfect of beings, and " to be for
" ever with the LORD, in whofe prefence is fulnefs
" of joy, and at whofe right hand there are plea-
" fures for evermore."

I will fay no more upon this argument, left I
fhould fay lefs, and becaufe whoever ventures to
wade far into it, will foon find himfelf out of his
depth, and in danger to be fwallowed up and loft
in that great abyfs, which is not to be fathomed by
the fhallow faculties of mortal men.

I fhall therefore only mention the

2. Thing I propofed to fpeak to, viz. the eternity of this happinefs; " and the end everlafting
" life:" by which the apoftle intends to exprefs the
utmoft perfection, but not the final period of the
happinefs of good men in another world. For to a
perfect ftate of happinefs thefe two conditions are requifite, that it be immutable, and that it be interminable, that it can neither admit of a change nor of an
end. And this is all that I fhall fay of it, it being
impoffible to fay any thing that is more intelligible
and plain, concerning that which is infinite, than that
it is fo. I fhould now have proceeded to the

II. Thing I propofed, viz. by what way and
means we may be prepared, and made meet to be

19 N 2. made

S E R M. made partakers of this happinefs; and that is (as I
LXVI. have told you all along) by the conftant and fincere
endeavour of an holy and good life; for the text
fuppofeth that they only who are " made free from
" fin," and " become the fervants of GOD," and
who " have their fruit unto holinefs," are they whofe
end fhall be everlafting life. But this is an argument which I have had fo frequent occafion to fpeak
to, that I fhall not now meddle with it.   All that I
fhall do more at prefent fhall be to make an inference or two from what hath been faid upon this argument.

I. The confideration of the happy ftate of good
men in another world, cannot but be a great comfort
and fupport to good men under all the evils and fufferings of this prefent life.   Hope is a great cordial
to the minds of men, efpecially when the thing hoped
for does fo vaftly outweigh the prefent grievance and
trouble.   The holy fcriptures, which reveal to us
the happinefs of our future ftate, do likewife affure
us that there is no comparifon between the afflictions
and fufferings of good men in this world, and the reward of them in the other.   " I reckon (faith St.
" Paul) Rom. viii. 8. that the fufferings of this pre-
" fent time, are not worthy to be compared with the
" glory that fhall be revealed in us."

Particularly the confideration of that glorious
change which fhall be made in our bodies at the refurrection, ought to be a great comfort to us under
all the pains and difeafes which they are now liable
to, and even againft death itfelf.   One of the greateft burdens of human nature, is the frailty and infirmity of our bodies, the neceffities which they are
frequently prefs'd withal, the difeafes and pains to
which they are liable, and " the fear of death," by

reafon.

reafon whereof a great part of mankind are " fubject
" to bondage ;" againft all which this is an everlafting fpring of confolation to us, that the time is coming when we fhall have other fort of bodies, freed
from that burden of corruption which we now groan
under, and from all thofe miferies and inconveniencies which flefh and blood are now fubject to. For
the time will come, when " thefe vile bodies," which
we now wear, " fhall be changed, and fafhioned like
" to the glorious body of the Son of GOD ;" and
when they fhall be raifed at the laft day, they fhall
not be raifed fuch as we laid them down, vile and
corruptible, but immortal and incorruptible : for the
fame power which hath raifed them up to life, fhall
likewife change them, and put a glory upon them
like to that of the glorified body of our LORD ; and
when this glorious change is made, ", when this cor-
" ruptible hath put on incorruption, and this mortal
" hath put on immortality, then fhall come to pafs
" the faying that is written, death is fwallowed up
" in victory ;" and when this laft enemy is perfectly
fubdued, we fhall be fet above all the frailties and
dangers, all the temptations and fufferings of this
mortal ftate ; there will then be no " flefhly lufts"
and brutifh paffions " to war againft the foul ;" no
" law in our members" to rife up in rebellion againft
" the law of our minds ;" no difeafes to torment us,
no danger of death to terrify us ; all the motions
and paffions of our outward man fhall then be perfectly fubject to the reafon of our minds, and our
bodies fhall partake of the immortality of our fouls.
How fhould this confideration bear us up under all
the evils of life and the fears of death, that the refurrection will be a perfect cure of all our infirmities
and difeafes, and an effectual remedy of all the evils

that

that we now labour under; and that it is but a very little while that we shall be troubled with these frail, and mortal, and vile bodies, which shall shortly be laid in the dust, and when they are raised again, shall become spiritual, incorruptible, and glorious.

And if our bodies shall undergo so happy a change, what happiness may we imagine shall then be conferred upon our souls, that so much better and nobler part of ourselves! as the apostle reasons in another case, " Doth GOD take care of oxen ?" Hath he this consideration of our bodies, which are but the brutish part of the man ? What regard will he then have to his own image, that spark of divinity which is for ever to reside in these bodies ? If upon the account of our souls, and for their sakes, our bodies shall become incorruptible, spiritual and glorious ; then certainly our souls shall be endued with far more excellent and divine qualities : if our bodies shall in some degree partake of the perfection of our souls in their spiritual and immortal nature ; to what a pitch of perfection shall our souls be raised and advanced ! even to an equality with angels, and to some kind of participation of the divine nature and perfection, so far as a creature is capable of them.

II. The comparison which is here in the text, and which I have largely explained, between the manifest inconveniencies of a sinful and vicious course, and the manifold advantages of an holy and virtuous life, is a plain direction to us which of these two to chuse. So that I may make the same appeal that Moses does, after that he had at large declared the blessings promised to the obedience of GOD's laws, and the curse denounced against the violation and transgression of them, Deut. xxx. 19. " I call hea-
" ven and earth to record against you this day, that
" I have

" I have set before you life and death, blessing and
" cursing; therefore chuse life," that you may be
happy in life and death, and after death to all eternity. I know every one is ready to chuse happiness,
and to say with Balaam, " Let me die the death of
" the righteous, and let my latter end be like his :"
but if we do in good earnest desire the end, we must
take the way that leads to it; we must " become
" the servants of God, and have our fruit unto ho-
" liness," if ever we expect, that " the end shall
" be everlasting life."

SERMON CLXVII.

The nature and necessity of holy resolution.

JOB xxxiv. 31, 32.

*Surely it is meet to be said unto God, I have born
chastisement, I will not offend any more : That which
I see not, teach thou me; if I have done iniquity,
I will do no more.*

THESE words are the words of Elihu, one
of Job's friends, and the only one who is
not reproved for his discourse with Job, and who
was probably the author of this ancient and most
eloquent history of the sufferings and patience of
Job, and of the end which the Lord made with
him ; and they contain in them a description of the
temper and behaviour of a true penitent. " Surely
" it is meet, &c."

In which words we have the two essential parts of
a true repentance. First,

SERM. CLXVII. The first sermon on this text.

First, An humble acknowledgment and confession of our sins to GOD, " Surely it is meet to be said " unto GOD, I have born chastisement."

Secondly, A firm purpose and resolution of a-mendment and forsaking of sin for the future, " I " will not offend any more ; if I have done iniqui-" ty, I will do no more."

First, An humble acknowledgment and confession of our sins to GOD ; " Surely it is meet to be said " unto GOD, I have born chastisement," that is, have sinned and been justly punished for it, and am now convinced of the evil of sin, and resolved to leave it ; " I have born chastisement, I will offend " no more."

Of this first part of repentance, viz. an humble confession of our sins to GOD, with great shame and sorrow for them, and a thorough conviction of the evil and danger of a sinful course, I have already treated at large.   In these repentance must begin, but it must not end in them : for a penitent con-fession of our sins to GOD, and a conviction of the evil of them, signifies nothing, unless it brings us to a resolution of amendment, that is, of leaving our sins, and betaking ourselves to a better course. And this I intend, by GOD's assistance, to speak to now, as being the

Second part of a true repentance here described in the text, viz.   A firm purpose and resolution of a-mendment and forsaking of sin for the future ; and to express it the more strongly and emphatically, and to shew the firmness of the resolution, it is repeat-ed again, " I will not offend any more ;" and then in the next verse, " I have done iniquity, I will " do no more."   And this is so necessary a part of repentance, that herein the very essence and formal nature

nature of repentance does conſiſt, viz. in the firm and ſincere purpoſe and reſolution of a better courſe.

In the handling of this argument, I ſhall do theſe ſix things.

I. I ſhall ſhew what reſolution is in general.

II. What is the ſpecial object of this kind of reſolution.

III. What is implied in a ſincere reſolution of leaving our ſins and returning to God.

IV. I ſhall ſhew that in this reſolution of amendment, the very eſſence and formal nature of repentance does conſiſt.

V. I ſhall offer ſome conſiderations to convince men, both of the neceſſity and fitneſs of this reſolution, and of keeping ſtedfaſtly to it. " Surely it is " meet to be ſaid unto God, I will not offend " any more."

VI. I ſhall add ſome brief directions concerning the managing and maintaining of this holy and neceſſary reſolution.

I. What reſolution in general is. It is a fix'd determination of the will about any thing, either to do it, or not to do it, as upon due deliberation we have judged and concluded it to be neceſſary or convenient to be done, or not to be done by us: and this ſuppoſeth three things.

1. Reſolution ſuppoſeth a precedent deliberation of the mind about the thing to be reſolved up. For no prudent man does determine or reſolve upon any thing, till he have conſidered the thing, and weighed it well with himſelf, and have fully debated the neceſſity and expedience of it ; what advantage he ſhall have by the doing of it, and what danger and inconvenience will certainly or very probably redound to him by the neglect and omiſſion of it. For pe-

remptorily to determine and resolve upon any thing, before a man have done this, is not properly resolution, but precipitancy and rashness.

2. Resolution supposeth some judgment pass'd upon the thing, after a man hath thus deliberated about it ; that he is satisfied in his mind one way or other concerning it, that his understanding is convinced. either that it is necessary and convenient for him to do it, or that it is not ; and this is sometimes called resolution, but is not that resolution which immediately determines a man to action. This judgment of the necessity and fitness of the thing is not the resolution of the will, but of the understanding ; for it does not signify that a man hath fully determined to do the thing, but that he hath determined with himself that it is reasonable to be done, and that he is no longer in doubt and suspence whether it be best for him to do it or not, but is in his mind resolved and satisfied one way or other. And these are two very different things ; to be resolved in one's judgment, that is, to be convinced that a thing is fit and necessary to be done, and to be resolved to set upon the doing of it ; for many men are thus convinced of the fitness and necessity of the thing, who yet have not the heart, cannot bring themselves to a firm and fixed resolution to set upon the doing of it. So that an act of the judgment, must go before the resolution of the will : for as he is rash that resolves to do a thing before he hath deliberated about it ; so he is blind and wilful that resolves to do a thing before his judgment be satisfied, whether it be best for him to do it or not.

3. If the matter be of considerable moment and consequence, resolution supposeth some motion of the affections ; which is a kind of bias upon the
will,

will, a certain propension and inclination that a man SF M. feels in himself, either urging him to do a thing, or withdrawing him from it. Deliberation and judgment, they direct a man what to do, or leave undone; the affections excite and quicken a man to take some resolution in the matter, that is, to do suitably to the judgment his mind hath pass'd upon the thing. For instance; a great sinner reflects upon his life, and considers what he hath done, what the course is that he lives in, and what the issue and consequence of it will probably or certainly be, whether it will make him happy or miserable in the conclusion; and debating the matter calmly and soberly with himself, he is satisfied and convinced of the evil and danger of a wicked life, and consequently that it is best for him to resolve upon a better course, that is, to repent. Now these thoughts must needs awaken in him fearful apprehensions of the wrath of Almighty God, which is due to him for his sins and hangs over him, and which he is every moment in danger of, if he goes on in his evil course. These thoughts are apt likewise to fill him with shame and confusion, at the remembrance of his horrible ingratitude to God his maker, his best friend and greatest benefactor, and of his desperate folly in provoking omnipotent justice against himself; whereupon he is heartily grieved and troubled for what he hath done; and these affections of fear and shame and sorrow being once up, they come with great violence upon the will, and urge the man to a speedy resolution of changing his course, and leaving the way he is in, which he is fully convinced is so evil and dangerous; and of betaking himself to another course, which he is fully satisfied will be much more for his safety and advantage.

So that resolution in general, is a fix'd determination of the will; that is, such a determination as is not only for the present free from all wavering and doubting, but such as cannot prudently be altered, so long as reason remains. For the man who upon full deliberation and conviction of his mind resolves upon any thing, cannot without the imputation of fickleness and inconstancy quit that resolution, so long as he hath the same reason which he had when he took it up, and is still satisfied that the reason is good. For instance; The man who hath taken up a resolution to be sober, because of the ugliness and unreasonableness of drunkenness, and the temporal inconveniencies and eternal damnation which that sin exposeth a man to; if these reasons be true and good, can never prudently alter the resolution which he hath taken, and return to that sin again.

· II. Let us consider what is the special object or matter of this resolution, wherein the formal nature of repentance does consist, what it is that a man when he repents resolves upon ; and that I told you is to leave his sin, and to return to God and his duty ; and this is the resolution which the penitent here described in the text takes up, " I will not of-
" fend any more. That which I see not, teach thou
" me; and if I have done iniquity, I will do no
" more." He resolves against all known sin, " I
" will not offend any more;" and if through ignorance he had sinned and done contrary to his duty, he desires to be better instructed, that he may not offend again in the like kind, " That which I see
" see not, teach thou me ; and if I have done ini-
" quity, I will do no more."

- So that the true penitent resolves upon these two things.

    1. To forsake his sin.   And
· -2. To return to God and his duty.   1. To

1. To forsake his sin : and this implies the quitting of his sinful course whatever it had been ; and that not only by abstaining from the outward act and practice of every sin, but by endeavouring to crucify and subdue the inward affection and inclination to it.

. And it implies farther, the utter forsaking of sin ; for repentance is not only a resolution to abstain from sin for the present, but never to return to it again. Thus Ephraim, when he repented of his idolatry, he utterly renounced it, saying, " What have I to do " any more with idols?" Hof. xiv. 8. He that truly repents, is resolved to break off his sinful course, and to abandon those lusts and vices which he was formerly addicted to, and lived in.

2. The true penitent resolves likewise to return to God and his duty : he does not stay in the negative part of religion, he does not only resolve not to commit any sin, but not to neglect or omit any thing that he knows to be his duty ; and if he has been ignorant of any part of his duty, he is willing to know it, that he may do it ; he is not only determined to forsake his sin, which will make him miserable, but to return to God, who alone can make him happy : he is now resolved to love God, and to serve him as much as he hated and dishonoured him before ; and will now be as diligent to perform and practise all the duties and parts of religion, as. he was negligent of them before, and as ready to do all the good he can to all men in any kind, as he was careless of these things before : these in general are the things which a true penitent resolves upon. I proceed to the

III. Thing I proposed to consider, namely what is implied in a sincere resolution of leaving our sins,

and

and returning to God and our duty. And this holy
reſolution, if it be thorough and ſincere, does imply
in it theſe three things.

1. That it be univerſal.

2. That it be a reſolution of the means as well as
of the end.

3. That it preſently comes to effect, and be ſpeedily and without delay put in execution.

1. A ſincere reſolution of amendment muſt be univerſal: a reſolution to forſake all ſin, and to return to
our whole duty, and every part of it ; ſuch a reſolution as that of holy David, "to hate every falſe way,
" and to have reſpect to all God's commandments."

This reſolution muſt be univerſal in reſpect of the
whole man, and with regard to all our actions. In
reſpect of the whole man ; for we muſt reſolve not only
to abſtain from the outward action of ſin, but this reſolution muſt have it's effect upon our inward man, and
reach our very hearts and thoughts ; it muſt reſtrain
our inclinations, and " mortify our luſts and cor-
" rupt affections, and renew us in the very ſpirit of
" our minds," as the apoſtle expreſſes it.

And it muſt be univerſal, in reſpect of all our
actions. For this is not the reſolution of a ſincere
penitent, to abſtain only from groſs and notorious,
from ſcandalous and open ſins ; but likewiſe to refrain from the commiſſion of thoſe ſins which are
ſmall in the eſteem of men, and not branded with a
mark of publick infamy and reproach ; to forbear
ſin in ſecret, and when no eye of man ſees us and
takes notice of us. This is not a ſincere reſolution,
to reſolve to practiſe the duties and virtues of religion
in publick, and to neglect them in private ; to reſolve to perform the duties of the firſt table, and to
paſs by thoſe of the ſecond ; to reſolve to ſerve God,
and

and to take a liberty to defraud and cozen men ; to honour our father which is heaven, and to injure and hate our brethren upon earth ; " to love our neigh-
" bour, and to hate our enemy," as the Jews did of old time ; to resolve against swearing, and to allow ourselves the liberty to speak falsely, and to break our word ; to flee from superstition, and to run into faction ; to abhor idols, and to commit sacrilege ; to resolve to be devout at church, and deceitful in our shops ; to be very scrupulous about lesser matters, and to be very zealous about indifferent things ; " to tithe mint and anise and cummin,
" and to omit the weightier matters of the law,
" mercy and fidelity and justice ;" to be very rigid in matters of faith and opinion, but loose in life and practice.

No ; the resolution of a sincere penitent must be universal and uniform : it must extend alike to the forbearing of all sin, and the exercise of every grace and virtue, and to the due practice and performance of every part of our duty. The true penitent must resolve for the future to abstain from all sin, " to be
" holy in all manner of conversation, and to abound
" in all the fruits of righteousness, which by JESUS
" CHRIST are to the praise and glory of GOD."
For if a man do truly repent of his wicked life, there is the very same reason why he should resolve against all sin, as why he should resolve against any ; why he should observe all the commandments of GOD, as why he should keep any one of them. For as St. James reasons concerning him that wilfully breaks any one commandment of GOD, that " he is guilty
" of all, and breaks the whole law ;" because the authority of GOD is equally stampt upon all his laws, and is violated and contemned by the wilful transgres-

J   sion

sion of any one of them; " For he that hath said,
" thou shalt not kill, hath likewise said, thou shalt
" not commit adultery, and thou shalt not steal :"
so he that resolves against any one sin, or upon performance of any one part of his duty, ought for the
very same reason to make his resolution universal;
because one sin is evil and provoking to God, as
well as another; and the performance of one part of
our duty good and pleasing to him, as well as another, and there is no difference. So that he that
resolves against any sin, upon wise and reasonable
grounds, because of the evil of it, and the danger
of the wrath of God to which it exposeth us, ought
for the same reason to resolve against all sin; because
it is damnable to commit adultery, and to steal, as
well as to kill ; and that resolution against sin, which
is not universal, it is a plain case that it is not true
and sincere, and that it was not taken up out of the
sense of the intrinsical evil of sin, and the danger of
it in respect of God and the judgment of another
world ; (for this reason holds against every sin, and
remains always the same) but that it was taken up
upon some inferior consideration, either because of
the shame and infamy of it among men, or because
of some other temporal inconvenience, which if the
man could be secured against, he would presently
break his resolution, and return to the commission of
that sin, with as much freedom as any other.

2. A sincere resolution implies a resolution of the
means as well as of the end. He that is truly and
honestly resolved against any sin, is likewise resolved
to avoid as much as is possible the occasions and
temptations which may lead or draw him to that sin;
or if they happen to present themselves to him, he is
resolved to stand upon his guard, and to resist them.

In

In like manner he that sincerely resolves upon doing his duty in any kind, must resolve upon the means that are requisite and necessary to the due discharge and performance of that duty. As he that resolves against that needless and useless sin of swearing in common conversation, must resolve also " to set a " guard before the door of his lips," seeing it is certain that it requires great care and attention, at least for some competent time, to get rid of a habit.

When David resolved " not to offend with his " tongue," he resolved at the same time to be very watchful over himself, Psal. xxxix. 1. " I said I will " take heed to my ways, that I offend not with my " tongue : I will keep my mouth as with a bridle, " while the wicked is before me." For a man to resolve against any sin or vice, and yet to involve himself continually in the occasions, and to run himself into the company and temptations, which do naturally, and will almost necessarily lead and betray him into those sins, is a plain evidence of insincerity. This I take for a certain rule, that whatever can reasonably move a man to resolve upon any end, will, if his resolution be sincere and honest, determine him every whit as strongly to use all those means which are necessary in order to that end. But of this I have spoken elsewhere.

3. A sincere resolution of leaving our sins, and returning to God and our duty, does imply the present time, and that we are to resolve speedily and without delay to put this resolution in practice; that we are peremptorily determined not to go one step farther in the ways of sin, not to neglect any duty that God requires of us, not for one moment; but immediately and forthwith to set upon the practice of it, so soon as occasion and opportunity is offer'd

to us. And the reason of this is evident; because the very same considerations that prevail upon any man to take up this resolution of amendment, and changing the course of his life, are every whit as prevalent to engage him to put this resolution presently in practice and execution.

I deny not, but a man may resolve upon a thing for the future, and when the time comes may execute his resolution, and this resolution may for all that be very sincere and real, though it was delayed to a certain time; because he did not see reason to resolve to do the thing sooner: but it cannot be so in this case of repentance; because there can no good reason be imagined, why a man should resolve seven years hence to change his course, and break off his sinful life, but the very same reason will hold as strongly, why he should do it presently and without delay; and over and besides this, there are a great many and powerful reasons and considerations, why he should rather put this good resolution in present execution, than put it off and defer it to any farther time whatsoever.

What is it that puts thee upon this resolution of leaving thy sins, and urgeth thee to do it at all? Art thou resolved to leave sin, because it is so great an evil? Why it is so for the present; the evil of it is intrinsical to it, and cleaves to the very nature of it, and is never to be separated from it: so that this is a present reason, and as strong against it now, as ever it will be hereafter: nay it is stronger at present; because if it be so great an evil, the sooner we leave it, the better.

Or dost thou resolve to forsake sin, because thou art apprehensive of the danger and mischief of it, that it will expose thee to the wrath of God, and to
the

the endleſs and intolerable miſery of another world? Why this reaſon likewiſe makes much more for the preſent leaving of it: becauſe the longer thou continueſt in a ſinful and impenitent ſtate, the greater is thy danger, and the greater penalty thou wilt moſt certainly incur; by delaying to put this good reſolution in practice, thou doſt increaſe and multiply the cauſes of thy fear. For hereby thou provokeſt God more, and every day doſt incenſe his wrath more and more againſt thee; thou prepareſt more and more fuel for " everlaſting burnings," and " treaſureſt up for thy ſelf more wrath, againſt the " day of wrath, and the revelation of the righteous " judgment of God." Nay thou doſt not only increaſe and aggravate, but thou doſt hereby haſten thine own miſery and ruin, and takeſt the moſt effectual courſe that is poſſible, to bring thine own fears, and the vengeance of Almighty God, ſo much the ſooner upon thee. For nothing provokes God to take a ſpeedier courſe with ſinners, and does more quicken the pace of his judgments, than wilful continuance in ſin.

And yet farther; if thy reſolution be valuable and conſiderable to thee, thou takeſt the moſt effectual courſe in the world to fruſtrate and defeat it. Thou art fully reſolved to leave thy ſins hereafter, and thou thinkeſt thou haſt reaſon for it: but by continuing in them for the preſent, thou provokeſt the juſtice of Almighty God to cut thee off, before thy reſolution hath taken effect.

Again; doſt thou reſolve to leave thy ſins one time or other, becauſe thereby thou hopeſt to put thy ſelf into a capacity of pardon and mercy, and of eternal life and happineſs? Why this reaſon ſhould move thee to do the thing as ſoon as is poſſible; be-

cauſe

SERM.
CLXVII

cause the sooner thou forsakest thy sins, thou hast the greater hope of finding mercy and forgiveness with God; and the sooner thou beginnest a holy course, and the longer thou continuest therein, thou hast reason to expect a greater and more ample reward. Thou canst not by holding off hope to bring down pardon and mercy to lower rates, and to obtain these hereafter upon easier terms: No; the terms and conditions of God's mercy are already fixed and established, so as never to be altered.

So that whatever reason thou canst possibly alledge for taking up this resolution, it is every whit as forcible and powerful to persuade thee to put it speedily in execution.

And then there is this reason besides, and that a very considerable one, why thou shouldest immediately put this resolution in practice, and not delay it for a moment. Thou mayest at present do it much more certainly, and much more easily. Much more certainly; because thou art surer of the present time, than thou canst be of the future. The present is in thy power, but not one moment more. And thou mayest at present do it more easily; for the longer thou continuest in sin, thy resolution against it will still grow weaker, and the habit of sin continually stronger. Thou wilt every day be more enslaved by the power of thy lusts, and thy heart will every day be more " hardened through the deceitfulness " of sin." All the change that time makes will still be for the worse, and more to thy disadvantage. Sin will be as pleasant to thee hereafter, and thou more loth to leave it, than at present. Sin was never mortified by age. It will every day have more strength to bind thee and hold thee fast, and thou wilt have every day less to break loose from it. For

I

by

by every fin thou doft commit, thou addeft a new degree to the ftrength and force of it ; and fo much ftrength as thou addeft to it, fo much thou takeft from thy felf, and fo much thou lofeft of thine own power and liberty. For a man and his lufts are like nature and difeafe : fo much ftrength as the difeafe gains, nature lofeth, and the man is hereby doubly weakened : for he does not only lofe fo much of his own ftrength, but the enemy gets it.

Nay thou doft hereby likewife forfeit that auxiliary ftrength and affiftance which the grace of GOD is ready to afford to men, his reftraining and his preventing grace. For as a man goes on in fin, and advanceth in an evil courfe, the grace of GOD draws off by degrees, and his Holy Spirit doth infenfibly leave him : and when a finner is come to this, his beft refolutions will " vanifh like the morning cloud " and the early dew which paffeth away."

So that it cannot be a true and fincere refolution of leaving our fins, if it do not take place and have not it's effect prefently. For there is no man that takes up a refolution, upon weighty and confiderable reafons, of doing any thing ; but if the reafons upon which he takes it up urge him to do the thing at prefent, he will prefently fet about it : and that man is not refolved to do a thing, whatever he may pretend, who hath moft reafon to do it at prefent, and may beft do it now, and yet delays it.

And thus I have opened to you the nature of this holy refolution of leaving our fins, and returning to GOD and our duty ; and have fhewn what is neceffarily implied in fuch a refolution, if it be fincere and in good earneft ; that it be univerfal ; and that it be a refolution of the means, as well as of the end ; and that it prefently take place and be put in execution.

tion.   And theſe are three the beſt ſigns and marks that I know of, whereby a man may try and examine the truth and ſincerity of that reſolution of amendment, which we call repentance.   If it be againſt all ſin, and have an equal regard to every part of our duty ; if when we reſolve upon the end, that is, to avoid ſin, and to perform our duty, we are equally reſolved upon the means that are neceſſary to thoſe ends ; if the reſolution we have taken up commence preſently, and from that day forward be duly executed and put in practice, then is our repentance and reſolution of amendment ſincere : but if there be a defect in any of theſe, our reſolution is not as it ought to be.

SERMON CLXVIII.

The nature and neceſſity of holy reſolution.

JOB xxxiv. 31, 32.

Surely it is meet to be ſaid unto GOD, *I have born chaſtiſement, I will not offend any more : That which I ſee not, teach thou me ; if I have done iniquity, I will do no more.*

SERM. THESE words are the deſcription of the
CLXVIII.   temper and behaviour of a true penitent, and
Theſecond do contain in them the two eſſential parts of a true
ſermon on repentance.
this text.
        Firſt, An humble acknowlegment and confeſſion of ſin.

Secondly,

Secondly, A firm purpose and resolution of amendment and forsaking our sins for the future.

And this latter is so necessary a part of repentance, that herein the very essence and formal nature of repentance does consist. In handling of this argument, I proposed to consider,

I. What resolution in general is.

II. What is the special object or matter of this kind of resolution.

III. What is implied in a sincere resolution of leaving our sins, and returning to God and our duty.

· IV. To shew that in this resolution of amendment, the very essence and formal nature of repentance doth consist.

V. To offer some considerations to convince men of the necessity and fitness of this resolution, and of keeping stedfast to it.

VI. To add some directions concerning the managing and maintaining this holy resolution. The three first I have spoken to, I now proceed to the

IV. To shew that in this resolution the very essence and formal nature of repentance doth consist. A man may do many reasonable actions, without an explicit resolution. In things that are more easy and natural to us, judgment and resolution are all one; it is all one to judge a thing fit to be done, and to resolve to do it. But in matters of difficulty, when a man is to strive against the stream, and to oppose strong habits that have taken deep root, there is nothing to be done without an explicit resolution. No man makes any remarkable change in his life, so as to cross his inclinations and custom, without an express resolution. For though a man's judgment be never so much convinced of the reasonableness and necessity of such a change; yet unless a man's spirit

be

SERM. be fortified and fix'd by refolution, the power of
CLXVIII. cuftom, and the violence of his own inclinations will
carry him againft his judgment. Now there is no
change of a man's life can be imagined, wherein a
man offers greater violence to inveterate habits, and
to the ftrong propenfions of his prefent temper, than
in this of repentance. So that among all the actions
of a man's life, there is none that doth more neceffarily require an exprefs purpofe, than repentance does.

. And that herein repentance doth chiefly confift, I
fhall endeavour to make evident from fcripture, and
from the common apprehenfions of mankind concerning repentance.

The fcripture, befides the feveral defcriptions of
repentance, ufeth two words to exprefs it to us, μɛ-
ταμέλεια and μετάνοια. The former properly fignifies the inward trouble and difpleafure which men
conceive againft themfelves, for having done amifs ;
which if it be κατὰ Θεὸν λύπη, " a godly forrow,"
it worketh in us μετάνοιαν ἀμείαμέλητον, as St. Paul
calls it, " a repentance not to be repented of," that
is, fuch a change of our minds, which as we fhall
have no caufe to be troubled at, fo no reafon to alter
afterwards. And what is this, but a firm, ftedfaft,
and unalterable refolution ?

The fcripture likewife ufeth feveral phrafes of the
like importance to defcribe repentance by ; as forfaking and turning from fin, and converfion and turning to God. Forfaking and turning from fin. Hence
it is called " repentance from dead works," Heb.
vi. 1. and turning to God, Acts xxvi. 20. " I have
" fhewed to the Gentiles, that they fhould repent and
" turn to God," that is, from the worfhip of idols
to the true God. And we have both thefe together
in the defcription which the prophet gives of repentance,

ance, Isa. lv. 7. " Let the wicked forsake his ways, " and the unrighteous man his thoughts, and let " him return unto the LORD." Now this change begins in the sinner's resolution of doing this; and the " unrighteous man's forsaking his thoughts," is nothing else but changing the purpose of his mind, and resolving upon a better course. And thus Lactantius describes it: *Agere autem pœnitentiam nihil aliud est, quam affirmare & profiteri se non amplius peccaturum.* " To repent is nothing else, but for a " man to declare and profess that he will sin no " more." This is repentance before men. And repentance before GOD is a resolution answerable to this profession. And elsewhere saith the same author, " The Greeks do most fully express repentance by " the word μεϯάνοια, because he that repents reco- " vers his mind from his former folly, and is trou- " bled at it;" *& confirmat animam suam ad rectius vivendum,* " and confirms his mind for a better " course," And how is this done but by resolution?

And that this is the natural and true notion of repentance appears, in that the heathens did consent and agree in it. Gellius gives this description of it. *Pœnitere tum dicere solemus, cum quæ ipsi fecimus, ea nobis post incipiunt displicere, sententiamque in iis nostram demutamus.* " We are said then to repent, " when those things which we have done begin af- " terwards to displease us, and we change our reso- " lution about them." And so likewise one of the philosophers describes it; " repentance is the begin- " ning of philosophy, a flying from foolish words " and actions, ϗ τῆς ἀμεϯαμελήτε ζωῆς ἡ πρώτη " παρασκευὴ, and the first preparation of a life not " to be repented of."

It is true indeed, repentance supposeth the entire

VOL. IX.   19 Q   change
4

change of our lives and actions, and a continued state, as the proper consequence of it : but repentance is but the beginning of this change, which takes its rise from the purpose and resolution of our minds ; and if it be sincere and firm, it will certainly have this effect, to change our lives ; and if it be not so, it is not repentance. For though in the nature of the thing it be possible, that a man may sincerely resolve upon a thing, and yet let fall his resolution afterwards, before it come into act : yet in the phrase of scripture, nothing is called repentance, but such a resolution as takes effect, so soon as there is opportunity for it. If we change our resolution, and repent of our repentance, this is not that which St. Paul calls " repentance unto salvation." So that no man that reads and considers the bible, can impose upon himself so grosly, as to conceit himself a true penitent, and consequently to be in a state of salvation, who hath been troubled for his sins, and hath taken up a resolution to leave them, if he do not pursue this resolution, and act according to it.

V. I shall in the next place propound some arguments and considerations to persuade men to this holy resolution, and then to keep them firm and stedfast to it, so as never to change it after they have once taken it up.

First, I shall propound some arguments to persuade men to take up this resolution ; and they are these.

1. Consider that this resolution of repentance, is nothing but what, under the influence of God's grace and holy Spirit, which are never wanting to the sincere endeavours of men, is in your power. And it is necessary to premise this ; for unless this be cleared, all the other arguments that I can use will signify no-

3
thing.

thing. For nothing in the world could be more
vain, than to take a great deal of pains to perfuade men to do a thing which they cannot do, to entreat them to attempt an impoſſibility, and to urge and folicit them with all earneſtneſs and importunity to do that which is abſolutely and altogether out of their power. All the commands of God, and the exhortations of his word, and all the promiſes and threatnings, whereby theſe commands and exhortations are enforced, do plainly ſuppoſe, either that it is in our power to do the thing which God commands or exhorts us to : or elſe, if it be not (which I grant it is not) that God is ready by his grace and ſtrength, if we be not wanting to ourſelves, to aſſiſt and enable us to thoſe ends and purpoſes. For the goſpel ſuppoſeth a power going along 'with it, and that the holy Spirit of God works upon the minds of men, to quicken and excite and aſſiſt them to their duty. And if it were not ſo, the exhortations of preachers would be nothing elſe, but a cruel and bitter mocking of ſinners, and an ironical inſulting over the miſery and weakneſs of poor creatures ; and for miniſters to preach, or people to hear ſermons, upon other terms, would be the vaineſt expence of time, and the idleſt thing we do all the week ; and all our diſſuaſives from ſin, and exhortations to holineſs and a good life, and vehement perſuaſions of men to ſtrive to get to heaven and to eſcape hell, would be juſt as if one ſhould urge a blind man, by many reaſons and arguments taken from the advantages of ſight, and the comfort of that ſenſe, and the beauty of external objects, · by all means to open his eyes, and to behold the delights of nature, to ſee his way, and to look to his ſteps ; and ſhould upbraid him, and be very angry with him for not doing ſo. Why, it reſolu-

tion

tion be abfolutely impoffible to us, and a thing wholly out of our power, it is juft the fame cafe. But
then we ought to deal plainly and openly with men,
and to tell them, that what we fo earneftly perfuade
them to, is that which we certainly know they cannot
do. So that it is neceffary, if I intend that the following confiderations fhould do any good, to affure
men, that it is not impoffible for them to make a refolution of leaving their fins, and returning to GOD.

It is a power which every man is naturally inveft-
ed withal, to confider, and judge, and chufe. To
confider, that is, to weigh and compare things together. To judge, that is, to determine which is
beft. And to chufe, that is, to refolve to do it or
not. And there is nothing more evident and more
univerfally acknowledged in temporal cafes, and in
the affairs and concernments of this life. In thefe
matters refolution is a thing ordinary and of frequent
practice; it is the principle of all great and confiderable actions. Men refolve to be great in this world,
and by virtue of this refolution, when they have
once taken it up, what induftry will they not ufe!
what hazards will they not run in the purfuit of their
ambitious defigns! difficulties and dangers do rather
whet their courage, and fet an edge upon their fpirits. Men refolve to be rich; the apoftle fpeaks of
fome that will be rich, 1 Tim. vi. " they that will
" be rich: and though this be but a low and mean
defign, yet thefe perfons, by virtue of this refolution, will toil and take prodigious pains in it.

And as to fpiritual things, every man hath the
fame power radically, that is, he hath the faculties of underftanding and will; but thefe are ob-
ftructed and hindered in their exercife, and ftrongly
biaffed a contrary way by the power of evil inclinations

tions and habits ; so that as to the exercise of this power and the effect of it in spiritual things, men are in a sort as much disabled, as if they were destitute of it. For it is in effect all one, to have no understanding at all to consider things that are spiritual, as to have the understanding blinded by an invincible prejudice; to have no liberty as to spiritual things, as to have the will strongly biassed against them. For a man that hath this prejudice upon his understanding, and this bias upon his will, is to all intents and purposes as if he were destitute of these faculties. But then we are not to understand this impotency to be absolutely natural, but accidental ; not to be in the first frame and constitution of our souls, but to have happened upon the depravation of nature. It is not a want of natural faculties, but the binding of them up and hindering their operations to certain purposes. This impotency proceeds from the power of evil habits. And thus the scripture expresseth it, and compares an impotency arising from bad habits and customs to a natural impossibility ; nothing coming nearer to nature, than a powerful custom. " Can the Ethiopian change his skin, or the leo-
" pard his spots ? Then may ye also, that are ac-
" customed to do evil, learn to do well."

But now God by the gospel hath designed the recovery of mankind from the slavery of sin, and the power of their lusts ; and therefore, as by the death of Christ he hath provided a way to remove the guilt of sin, so by the spirit of Christ he furnisheth us with sufficient power to destroy the dominion of sin. I say sufficient, if we be not wanting to ourselves, but be " workers together with God," and be as diligent " to work out our own salvation," as he is ready " to work in us both to will and to do."

So

So that when we perſuade men to repent and change their lives, and to reſolve upon a better courſe, we do not exhort them to any thing that is abſolutely out of their power; but to what they may do, though not of themſelves, yet by the grace of GOD, which is always ready to aſſiſt them, unleſs by their former groſs neglects and long obſtinacy in an evil courſe, they have provoked GOD to withdraw his grace from them. So that though, conſidering our own ſtrength abſtractedly, and ſeparately from the grace of GOD, theſe things be not in our power; yet the grace of GOD puts them into our power.

And this is ſo far from derogating from the grace of GOD, that it is highly to the praiſe of it. For if the grace of GOD makes us able to repent and reſolve upon a new life, he that aſſerts this does not attribute his repentance to himſelf, but to the grace of GOD: nay he that ſays that GOD's grace excites, and is ready to aſſiſt men to do what GOD commands, repreſents GOD immenſely more good and gracious, than he that ſays that GOD commands men to do that which by their natural power they cannot do, and will condemn them for not doing it, and yet denies them that grace which is neceſſary to the doing of it.

Let this then be eſtabliſhed as a neceſſary conſideration to prevent diſcouragement, that to reſolve upon the change of our lives, is that which by the grace of GOD we are enabled to do, if we will. Reſolution is no ſtrange and extraordinary thing; it is one of the moſt common acts that belongs to us as we are men; but we do not ordinarily apply it to the beſt purpoſes. It is not ſo ordinary for men to reſolve to be good, as to be rich and great; not ſo common for men to reſolve againſt ſin, as to reſolve againſt poverty and ſuffering. It is not so usual for men to resolve to keep a good conscience, as to keep a good place. Indeed our corrupt nature is much more opposite to this holy kind of resolution. But then to balance and answer this, God hath promised greater and more immediate assistance to us in this case, than in any other. There is a general blessing and common assistance promised to resolution and diligence about temporal things ; and God's providence doth often advance such persons to riches and honour. The diligent hand, with God's blessing, makes rich, as Solomon tells us, Prov. x. 4. and xxii. 29. Seest thou" (says he) " a " man diligent in his business? He shall stand before " kings, he shall not stand before mean men." Now diligence is the effect of a great and vigorous resolution. But there is a special and extraordinary blessing and assistance, that attends the resolution and endeavour of a holy life. God hath not promised to strengthen men with all might in the way to riches and honours, and to assist the ambitious and covetous designers of this world, with " a mighty " and glorious power, such as raised up JESUS from " the dead :" but this he hath promised to those, who with a firm purpose and resolution do engage in the ways of religion. Let us then shake off our sloth and listlesness, and in that strength and assistance which God offers, let us resolve to leave our sins, and to amend our lives.

2. Consider what it is that you are to resolve upon; to leave your sins, and to return to God and goodness. So that the things I am persuading you to resolve upon are the strongest reasons that can be for such a resolution. Sin is such a thing, that there can be no better argument to make men resolve against it, than to consider what it is, and to think
seriously

ERM.
LXVIII.
ſeriouſly of the nature and conſequence of it. And God and goodneſs are ſo amiable and deſirable, that the very propoſal of theſe objects hath invitations and allurements enough to inflame our deſires after them, and to make us ruſh into the embraces of them. If we would but enter into the ſerious conſideration of them, we ſhould ſoon be reſolved in our minds about them.

Do but conſider a little what ſin is. It is the ſhame and blemiſh of thy nature, the reproach and diſgrace of thy underſtanding and reaſon, the great deformity and diſeaſe of thy ſoul, and the eternal enemy of thy reſt and peace. It is thy ſhackles and thy fetters, the tyrant that oppreſſes thee and reſtrains thee of thy liberty, and condemns thee to the baſeſt ſlavery and the vileſt drudgery. It is the unnatural and violent ſtate of thy ſoul, the worm that perpetually gnaws thy conſcience, the cauſe of all fears and troubles, and of all the evils and miſeries, all the miſchiefs and diſorders that are in the world ; it is the foundation and fuel of hell; it is that which puts thee out of the poſſeſſion and enjoyment of thyſelf, which doth alienate and ſeparate thee from God the fountain of bliſs and happineſs, which provokes him to be thine enemy, and lays thee open every moment to the fierce revenge of his juſtice, and if thou doſt perſiſt and continue in it, will finally ſink and oppreſs thee under the inſupportable weight of his wrath, and make thee ſo weary of thyſelf, that thou ſhalt wiſh a thouſand times that thou hadſt never been ; and will render thee ſo perfectly miſerable, that thou wouldeſt eſteem it a great happineſs to exchange thy condition with the moſt wretched and forlorn perſon that ever lived upon earth, to be perpetually upon a rack, and to lie

down

down for ever under the rage of all the most violent
diseases and pains that ever afflicted mankind. Sin is all this which I have described, and will certainly bring upon thee all those evils and mischiefs which I have mentioned, and make thee far more miserable than I am able to express, or thou to conceive. And art thou not yet resolved to leave it ? Shall I need to use any other arguments to set thee against it, and to take thee off from the love and practice of it, than this representation which I have now made of the horrible nature and consequences of it ?

And then consider on the other hand, what it is that I am persuading thee to turn to ; to thy God and duty. And would not this be a blessed change indeed ! To leave the greatest evil, and to return to the chief good ! For this resolution of returning to God, is nothing else but a resolution to be wise and happy, and to put thyself into the possession of that which is a greater good, if it is possible, than sin is an evil, and will render thee more happy, than sin can make thee miserable. Didst thou but think what God is, and what he will be to thee if thou wilt return to him, how kindly he will receive thee after all thy wandrings from him days without number, thou wouldst soon take up the resolution of the prodigal, and say, " I will arise and go to my father."

And consider likewise what it is to return to thy duty. It is nothing else but to do what becomes thee, and what is suitable to the original frame of thy nature, and to the truest dictates of thy reason and conscience, and what is not more thy duty, than it is thy interest and thy happiness. For that which God requires of us, is to be righteous and holy and good, that is, to be like God himself, who is the pattern of all perfection and happiness. It is to have

our lives conformed to his will, which is always perfect holiness and goodness, a state of peace and tranquillity, and the very temper and disposition of happiness. It is that which is a principal and most essential ingredient into the felicity of the divine nature,
and without which God would not be what he is,
but a deformed and imperfect and miserable being.

And if this be a true representation which I have
made to you, of sin and vice on the one hand, and
of God and goodness on the other, what can be
more powerful than the serious consideration of it,
to engage us to a speedy resolution of leaving our
sins, and of " turning and cleaving to the Lord
" with full purpose of heart ?" After this we
cannot but conclude with the penitent in the text;
" Surely it is meet to be said unto God, I will not
" offend any more : that which I see not, teach
" thou me ; and if I have done iniquity, I will do
" no more."

3. Consider how unreasonable it is to be unresolved in a case of so great moment and concernment.
There is no greater argument of a man's weakness,
than irresolution in matters of mighty consequence,
when both the importance of the thing, and exi-
gency of present circumstances require a speedy resolution.   We should account it a strange folly, for
a man to be unresolved in the clearest and plainest
matters that concern his temporal welfare and safety.
If a man could not determine himself whether he
should eat or starve ; if he were dangerously sick,
and could not determine whether he should take phy-
sick or die ; or if one that were in prison, could not
resolve himself whether he should accept of liberty,
and be content to be released ; or if a fair estate
were offered to him, he should desire seven years time

to

to consider whether he should take it or not : this would be so absurd in the common affairs of life, that a man would be thought infatuated, that should be doubtful and unresolved in cases so plain, and of such pressing concernment. If a man were under the sentence and condemnation of the law, and liable to be executed upon the least intimation of the prince's pleasure, and a pardon were graciously offered to him, with this intimation, that this would probably be the last offer of mercy that ever would be made to him ; one would think that in this case a man should soon be determined what to do, or rather that he should not need to deliberate at all about it ; because there is no danger of rashness in making haste to save his life.

And yet the case of a sinner is of far greater importance, and much more depends upon it, infinitely more than any temporal concernment whatsoever can amount to, even our happiness or misery to all eternity. And can there be any difficulty, for a man to be resolved what is to be done in such a case ? No case surely in the world can be plainer than this ; whether a man should leave his sins, and return to God and his duty, or not ; that is, whether a man should chuse to be happy or miserable, unspeakably and everlastingly happy, or extremely and eternally miserable.

And the circumstances and exigencies of our case do call for a speedy and peremptory resolution in this matter. The sentence of the law is already past, and God may execute it upon thee every moment, and it is great mercy and forbearance not to do it. Thy life is uncertain, and thou art liable every minute to be snatched away and hurried out of this world. However at the best, thou hast but a little time to

resolve

resolve in ; death and judgment and eternity cannot
be far off, and for ought thou knowest they may be
even at the door. Thou art upon the matter just
ready to be seized upon by death, to be summoned
to judgment, and to be swallowed up of eternity :
and is it not yet time, thinkest thou, to resolve ?
Wouldst thou have yet a little longer time to deliberate, whether thou shouldst repent and forsake thy
sins, or not ? If there were difficulty in the case, or
if there were no danger in the delay ; if thou couldst
gain time, or any thing else, by suspending thy resolution ; there were then some reason why thou
shouldst not make a sudden determination. But
thou canst pretend none of these. It is evident at
first sight, what is best to be done, and nothing can
make it plainer. It is not a matter so clear and out
of the controversy, that riches are better than poverty,
and ease better than pain, and life more desirable
than death ; as it is, that it is better to break off our
sins, than to continue in the practice of them ; to
be reconciled to God, than to go on to provoke
him ; to be holy and virtuous, than to be wicked
and vicious ; to be " heirs of eternal glory," than
to be " vessels of wrath fitted for destruction."

And there is infinite danger in these delays. For
if thy soul be any thing to thee, thou venturest
that ; if thou hast any tenderness and regard for thy
eternal interest, thou runnest the hazard of that ; if
heaven and hell be any thing to thee, thou incurrest
the danger of losing the one, and falling into the other.

And thou gainest nothing by continuing unresolved. If death and judgment would tarry thy leisure,
and wait till thou hadst brought thy thoughts to
some issue, and were resolved what to do, it were
something : but thy irresolution in this matter will
be

be fo far from keeping back death and judgment, that it will both haften and aggravate them, both make them to come the fooner, and to be the heavier when they come: becaufe thou abufeft the goodnefs of GOD, and "defpifeft his patience and "long-fuffering, which fhould lead thee" and draw thee on "to repentance," and not keep thee back. Hereby thou encourageft thyfelf in thy lewd and riotous courfes, and, becaufe thy "LORD delayeth his "coming," art the more negligent and extravagant. Hear what doom our LORD pronounceth upon fuch flothful and wicked fervants, Luke xii. 46. "the LORD "of that fervant will come in a day when he looketh "not for him, and at an hour when he is not aware, "and will cut him in funder, and will appoint him "his portion with the unbelievers." None fo like to be furprized, and to be feverely handled by the juftice of GOD, as thofe that trifle with his patience.

4. Confider how much refolution would tend to the fettling of our minds, and making our lives comfortable. There is nothing that perplexeth and difquieteth a man more, than to be unrefolved in the great and important concernments of his life. What anxiety and confufion is there in our fpirits, whilft we are doubtful and undetermined about fuch matters? How are we divided and diftracted, when our reafon and judgment direct us one way; and our lufts and affections biafs us to the contrary? When we are convinced and fatisfied what is beft for us; and yet are difaffected to our own intereft. Such a man is all the while felf-condemned, and acts with the perpetual regret of his reafon and confcience; and whenever he reflects upon himfelf, he is offended and angry with himfelf, his life and all his actions are uneafy and difpleafing to him; and there is no

way

way for this man to be at peace, but to put an end
to this conflict one way or other, either by conquering his reason or his will. The former is very difficult, nothing being harder than for a sinner to lay
his conscience asleep, after it is once thoroughly a-
wakened ; he may charm it for a while, but every
little occasion will rouze it again, and renew his trouble ; so that though a man may have some truce
with his conscience, yet he can never come to a firm
and settled peace this way : but if by a vigorous resolution a man would but conquer his will, his mind
would be at rest, and there would be a present calm
in his spirit. And why should we be such enemies
to our own peace, and to the comfort and contentment of our lives, as not to take this course, and
thereby rid ourselves at once of that, which really
and at the bottom is the ground of all the trouble and
disquiet of our lives ?

SERMON CLXIX.

The nature and necessity of holy
resolution.

JOB xxxiv. 31, 32.

Surely it is meet to be said unto GOD, *I have born
chastisement, I will not offend any more : That which
I see not, teach thou me ; if I have done iniquity,
I will do no more.*

SERM.
CLXIX.
The third
sermon on
his text.

THESE words are a description of the temper and behaviour of a true penitent, his confession of sins, and resolution of amendment. Concerning

cerning resolution I have shewn what it is in general: What is the special object or matter of this kind of resolution: What is implied in a sincere resolution of leaving our sins, and returning to GOD and our duty: That in this resolution the very essence and formal nature of repentance doth consist: and have offered some considerations, to convince men of the necessity and fitness of this resolution, and to keep them stedfast to it.   As,

1. That this resolution is nothing but what under the influence of GOD's grace is in our power.

2. The things themselves, which we are to resolve upon, are the strongest arguments that can be for such a resolution.

3. How unreasonable it is for men to be unresolved in a case of so great moment.

4. How much this resolution will tend to the settling of our minds, and making our lives comfortable.   I proceed to the considerations which remain.

5. Then be pleased to consider, that a strong and vigorous resolution would make the whole work of religion easy to us, it would conquer all difficulties which attend a holy and religious course of life, especially at our first entrance into it: Because resolution brings our minds to a point, and unites all the strength and force of our souls in one great design, and makes us vigorous and firm, couragious and constant in the prosecution of it; and without this it is impossible to hold out long, and to resist the strong propensions and inclinations of our corrupt nature, which, if we be not firmly resolved, will return and by degrees gain upon us; it will be impossible to break through temptations, and to gainsay the importunity of them; when the devil and the world solicit us, we shall not be able to say them nay, but shall be apt to yild to them.   _And the_

There are many, who have had faint wifhes and cold defires, and half purpofes of leading a new and better life: but having not taken up a firm refolution in the cafe, having not determined themfelves by a fevere purpofe, a little thing fways them, and brings them back to their former courfe; it is no hard matter to divert them and engage them another way; they are " fhaken with every wind" of temptation, every little blaft of oppofition and perfecution turns them back, and carries them to the ways of fin: whereas refolution fixeth a man's fpirit, and makes it moft ftedfaft and unmoveable, and fets him upon a rock, which, " when the winds blow, and the rain " falls, and the floods come," abides firm againft all impreffions.

If I would give the moft probable and ufeful advice to engage and continue a man in a good courfe, I would commend to him a deliberate and firm refolution.   David proved this way with very happy fuccefs, Pfal. cxix. 106. " I have fworn (fays he) " and will perform it, that I will keep thy righteous " judgments." This was a fecurity to him againft all affaults, and nothing could turn him from his courfe afterwards; not the dangers he was expofed to, ver. 109. " My foul is continually in my hand, " yet do I not forget thy law;" not the fnares of wicked men that were laid for him, ver. 110. " The " wicked have laid a fnare for me, yet I erred not " from thy precepts." By virtue of this refolution he could rife up in defiance of all thofe that would have tempted him to any finful action, ver. 115. " Depart from me ye evil doers : for I will keep the " commandments of my God."

When a man is thus refolved upon a holy courfe, he is not eafily diverted from it, and is able to refift
the

the importunity and flattery of temptations, and to say to them, as men are wont to do, when they are fully and firmly resolved upon any thing ; " Let " me alone, I am not to be moved, it is in vain to " urge me, I am resolved to the contrary." Thus stiff and resolute men can be in other cases, where there is not near that cause and reason for it : and if we would but take up a generous resolution to break off our sins, and to live better lives, this would be the way to conquer that listlesness and unwillingness, which hinders us from engaging in a good course, and is the cause of so many lame excuses and unreasonable delays. It is the want of resolution, and the weakness of our resolutions, which is the true reason why we are not more equal and constant and uniform in the ways of religion ; but are religious only by fits and starts, in a heat, and during some present trouble and conviction of mind. " The double " minded is unstable, says St. James, in all his ways." When a man is of several minds, he is easily moved one way or other.

6. And lastly, Consider the infinite danger of remaining unresolved. " The evil day may overtake " you," while you are deliberating whether you should avoid it or not. A state of sin is liable to so many hazards, hath so many dangers continually threatening it, and hanging over it, that it is the most imprudent thing in the world to linger in it. It is like Lot's staying in Sodom, when the LORD was going to destroy it, when fire and brimstone were just ready to be rained down from heaven upon it. Whilst men are lingering in a sinful state, if " the " LORD be not merciful to them," they will be consumed. Therefore it concerns thee sinner, to determine thy self speedily, and to make haste out of

this dangerous condition, " to escape for thy life," " left some evil overtake thee," and left death, finding thee unresolved, determine thy case for thee, and put it out of all doubt, and past all remedy.

How many have been cut off in their irresolution? And because they would not determine what to do, God hath concluded their case for them, and " sworn " in his wrath, that they should not enter into his " rest." It may be thou promisest thyself the space of many years to resolve in: " Thou fool, this " night thy soul may be required of thee," and whilst thou art unresolved what to do, God is resolving what to do with thee, and putting a period to his patience and long expectation of thy repentance: and thou knowest not how soon God may do this, and make an immutable determination concerning thee. And wo unto thee when God hath resolved thus.

Suppose thou shouldst be snatched out of the world, and hurried before the dreadful tribunal of God, in this doubtful and unresolved state. And this is possible enough ; because thou hast no certain tenure of thy life, thou art at no time secured from the stroke of death : nay it is probable enough ; because thou art every moment liable to ten thousand accidents, any one of which may snap in sunder the thread of thy life. And suppose this should happen to thee, what dost thou imagine would become of thee ? Wouldst not thou then wish a thousand times, that thou hadst resolved in time? How glad wouldst thou then be, that it were possible for thee to retrieve and call back but one of those days without number, which thou hast so vainly trifled away, that thou mightest resolve upon " the things of thy peace !" but " thou wouldest not" do it " in that thy day,"

which

which God afforded thee to this purpofe ; thou haft
let the opportunity flip out of thy hands, and it will
nvever be in thy power again, but " the things of
" thy peace will be" for ever " hid from thine eyes."

Why wilt thou then be fo foolifh, as to run thy
felf upon the evident hazard of lofing heaven, and
being miferable for ever ? Why wilt thou make work
for a fadder and longer repentance, than that which
thou doft now fo carefully decline? This was the
cafe of the foolifh virgins in the parable, Matt.
xxv. who made account to be ready " to meet the
" bridegroom" at his coming, but took no care in
time to get oil into their lamps. They thought the
bridegroom would tarry yet a while longer, and
therefore " they flumbered and flept" in great fecurity : but at midnight, when the cry was made,
" behold the bridegroom cometh ;" then they arofe,
and in a great hurry and confufion went about " trim-
" ming their lamps ;" they were refolved then, they
would have begged or bought oil, and would have
been at any pains or coft for it : but then it was too
late ; for the door was fuddenly fhut againft them,
and no importunity could prevail to have it opened
to them.

Canft thou be contented to have the door fhut
againft thee, and when thou fhalt cry, " Lord open
" unto me," to have him return this anfwer, " de-
" part from me, I know thee not ?" If thou canft
not, refolve to prevent this in time.

Didft thou but fee, and know, and feel, what the
miferable do in hell, thou couldft not linger thus,
thou couldft not continue fo long unrefolved. Why
the time will come, when thou wilt reflect feverely
upon thyfelf, and fay, that I fhould ever be fo ftupid
and fottifh, to be unrefolved in a matter of fuch in-

finite

finite concernment to me! How often was I ad-
moniſhed and convinced of the neceſſity of changing my courſe? How many inward motions had I
to that purpoſe? How often did my own reaſon and
conſcience, and the holy Spirit of God, by his frequent and friendly ſuggeſtions, put me upon this?
How often was I juſt upon the brink of reſolving?
I reſolved to reſolve; but ſtill I delayed it till death
ſeized upon me unreſolved: and now the opportunity
is loſt, and never to be recovered again. I would not
in time reſolve to be wiſe and happy: and now by
the ſentence of the juſt and unchangeable God, it is
reſolved that I muſt be miſerable to all eternity.

How ſhould theſe conſiderations quicken us, who
have yet theſe opportunities in our hands: which thoſe
who neglected and trifled them away, would now
purchaſe at any rate! I ſay, how ſhould theſe conſiderations which I have propoſed, move us to take
up a preſent reſolution in the matter! Conſider theſe
things, ſinner, and lay them ſeriouſly to heart, and
ſay to thy ſelf, fool that I have been, to be unreſolved ſo long; not to determine myſelf in a matter of
ſuch mighty conſequence; to continue ſo long in ſuf-
pence, whether I had beſt go to heaven or hell, and
which was moſt adviſable, to be happy or miſerable
for ever! Bleſſed be God that hath been pleaſed to
exerciſe ſo much patience and long-ſuffering towards
me, that hath ſpared me ſo long, when he might
have taken me away, and cut me off unreſolved.
My ſoul lies at ſtake, and for ought I know all eternity depends upon my preſent and ſpeedy reſolution.
And now by God's grace I will not delay one moment more, I will hang no longer between heaven and
hell. I ſhall now in the

Second place, offer ſome conſiderations to perſuade

suade those that have taken up this good resolution, to pursue it, and to promote it to practice and exe-cution, and to keep firm and stedfast to it. And to this end, be pleased to consider these three things.

1. What an argument it is of vanity and incon-stancy, to change this resolution, whilst the reason of it stands good and is not changed. I suppose that thou wert once resolved to leave thy sins, and to re-turn to God and thy duty. Why dost thou not pur-sue this resolution? Why dost thou not persist in it? Surely there appeared to thee some reason why thou didst take it up; and if the reason remain, and ap-pear still the same to thee that it did, how comes it to pass that thou hast altered thy mind, and chang-ed thy purpose? Either the case is the same it was, when thou tookest up this resolution; or it is not. If it be altered, then thou hast reason to change thy resolution: if it be not, thou hast the same reason to continue in it, that thou hadst to take it up. Shew then, if thou canst, wherein it is changed. Wert thou mistaken before about the nature of sin, and the per-nicious consequences of it; or about the nature of God and goodness? Hast thou any thing now to plead for sin, which thou didst not know or consider before? Art thou now satisfied that sin is not so evil and unreasonable a thing, as thou didst once appre-hend, or that it does not threaten thee with so much danger as thou didst fear? Hath God altered his opinion of it, or is he become more favourable to it than he was? Hast thou received any news lately from heaven by any good hands, that God hath re-versed his threatnings against sin, or that he hath ad-journed the judgment of the world, *sine die*, without any set time? That he hath set the devils at liberty, and releas'd them from their chains of darkness, and

hath

S E R M.
CLXIX

hath quenched and put out the fire of hell? Or art thou ſatisfied that there is no ſuch being as God in the world, or that he is not ſo good as thou didſt apprehend him to be, or that he will not reward thoſe that diligently ſerve him? Haſt thou found upon trial, that holineſs and virtue are but empty names, and that there is nothing in them? That there is not that pleaſure and peace in keeping the commandments of God, which thou wert told of? I am ſure thou canſt not with reaſon pretend any thing of all this. Thy reaſon and conſcience and experience cannot ſpeak one word on the behalf of ſin, or give any teſtimony againſt God and his holy ways. And if the caſe be the ſame it was, nothing but thine own vanity and fickleneſs, or ſome worſe reaſon, could move thee to alter thy purpoſe.

2. Let it be farther conſidered, that if we be not conſtant to our reſolution, all we have done is loſt. If thou repenteſt of thy repentance, it will not prove " a repentance to ſalvation." As good to have ſtayed in Sodom, as to look back after thou art come out of it. Thus God tells us by the prophet. Ezek. xxxiii. 12, 13. " Therefore thou Son of man, ſay " unto the children of thy people, the righteouſ- " neſs of the righteous ſhall not deliver him in the " day of his tranſgreſſion ; neither ſhall the righteous " be able to live in the day that he ſinneth. When " I ſay to the righteous, he ſhall ſurely live: if he " truſt to his own righteouſneſs, and commit ini- " quity, all his righteouſneſs ſhall not be remembred : " but for his iniquity that he hath committed, he " ſhall die for it." So that whatever we have done in the work of repentance, what reſolutions ſoever we have taken up: if afterwards we give over and let them fall, all that we have done is loſt, and will come to nothing.　　　　3. Let

3. Let us consider in the last place, that if we be SERM.
not constant to our resolution, we shall not only lose CLXIX.
all that we have done, but we shall thereby render
our condition much worse. " Remember Lot's
" wife," who, after she was escaped out of Sodom,
looked back, and was made a particular and lasting
monument of God's wrath and displeasure; which
seems to be meant by that expression of her being
" turned into a pillar of salt," that is, a lasting monument. Prov. xiv. 14. " The backslider in heart
" shall be filled with his own ways." "Shall be filled
" with his own ways;" this expression doth signify
a most heavy and dreadful curse upon those, who
fall off from their good purpose and resolution, that
they shall have sorrow and trouble enough upon it.
For so likewise Prov. i. 26, 27. where God threatens wilful and obstinate sinners with the heaviest judgments, that he would " laugh at their calamity, and
" mock when their fear comes, when their fear comes
" as desolation, and their destruction as a whirlwind,
" and fear and anguish cometh upon them;" he
adds, as the sum of all other judgments, that " they
" shall eat the fruit of their own ways, and be filled
" with their own devices." Heb. x. 38. " But if
" any man draw back, my soul shall have no plea-
" sure in him;" which words are a μείωσις, and
signify a great deal more than seems to be express'd.
" My soul shall have no pleasure in him;" that is,
let such an one expect the effects of God's fiercest
wrath and displeasure. For so the Hebrews are wont
to express things that are great and unspeakable;
when they cannot sufficiently set them forth; by saying less, they say more. So Psal. v. 4. where it is
said, " thou art not a God that hast pleasure in wick-
" edness," the Psalmist means, and would have us

I

to understand it so, that God is so far from taking any pleasure in the sins of men, that he bears the most violent hatred and displeasure against them. So when the apostle here says, " If any man draw back, my " soul shall have no pleasure in him," he means, that it is not to be express'd how God will deal with such persons, and how severely his justice will handle them. To the same purpose is that declaration, 2 Pet. ii. 20, 21. " For if after they have escaped " the pollutions of the world, through the know- " ledge of the Lord and Saviour Jesus Christ, " they are again entangled therein and overcome, " the latter end is worse with them than the begin- " ning. For it had been better for them, not to " have known the way of righteousness, than after " they have known it, to turn from the holy com- " mandment delivered unto them." The condition of all impenitent sinners is very sad ; but of apostates much worse : not only because the sins which they commit afterwards are much greater, receiving a new aggravation, which the sins of those who are simply impenitent are not capable of ; but likewise be- cause such persons are usually more wicked after- wards. For they that break loose from severe pur- poses and resolutions of a better course, do by this very thing in a great measure fear and conquer their consciences ; and then no wonder if afterwards " they " give up themselves to commit all iniquity with " greediness." When after long abstinence men return to sin again, their lusts are more fierce and violent; like a man who, after long fasting, returns to his meat with a more raging appetite. This our Saviour sets forth to us in the parable of the unclean spirit's returning again and taking possession of the man, after he had left him. Matt. xii, 43, 44, 45.
" When

" When the unclean spirit is gone out of a man, he
" walketh through dry places, seeking rest, and find-
" eth none. Then he saith, I will return into my
" house from whence I came out : And when he is
" come, he findeth it empty, swept, and garnish'd.
" Then goeth he, and taketh with himself seven
" other spirits more wicked than himself; and the
" end of that man is worse than his beginning."
The moral of which is, that when a man hath once
left his sins, if afterward he entertain thoughts of returning to them again, sin will return upon him with
redoubled force and strength, and his heart will be
so much the more prepared and disposed for the
entertaining of more and greater vices; and his leaving his sins for a time will be but like a running back,
that he may leap with greater violence into hell and
destruction.

Besides that such persons do the greatest injury to
God and the holy ways of religion, that can be, by
forsaking them after they have owned and approved
them. For it will not be so much regarded, what
wicked men, who have always been so, talk against
God and religion , because they do not talk from
experience, but " speak evil of the things which they
" know not :" whereas those who forsake the ways
of religion after they have once engaged in them, do
disparage religion more effectually, and reproach it
with greater advantage ; because they pretend to
speak from the experience they have had of it ; they
have tried both the ways of sin, and the ways of
religion, and after experience of both, they return
to sin again : which, what is it but to proclaim to the
world, that the ways of sin and vice are rather to
be chosen than the ways of holiness and virtue ; that
the devil is a better master than God, and that a

S. R. M. sinful and wicked life yields more pleasure and great-
CLXIX. er advantages, than are to be had in keeping the
commandments of God? And this must needs be a
high provocation, and a heavy aggravation of our
ruin. Let these considerations prevail with us, to
pursue this holy resolution, after we have taken it up,
and to persist in it. There remains only the

VI. And last particular which I proposed to be
spoken to, viz. to add some directions for the maintaining and making good of this resolution of repentance and amendment; and they shall be these
three.

1. Let us do all in the strength of God, considering our necessary and essential dependance upon
him, and that " without him," and the assistance of
his grace, " we can do nothing." " We are not (as
" the apostle tells us) sufficient of ourselves, as of
" ourselves," that is, without the assistance of God's
holy Spirit, " to think any thing" that is good ;
much less to resolve upon it. " It is God that
" worketh in us both to will and to do of his good
" pleasure," that is, of his own goodness, as the
same apostle speaks, Phil. ii. 13. It is God that up-
holds us in being, and from whom we have all our
power as to natural actions ; but as to spiritual things,
considering the great corruption and depravation of
human nature, we stand in need of a more especial
and immediate assistance.

If we know any thing of ourselves, we cannot but
know what foolish and ignorant creatures we are,
how weak and impotent, how averse and opposite to
any thing that is good. And therefore it is wise
counsel in all cases, but chiefly in spiritual matters,
which Solomon gives, Prov. iii. 5, 6. " Trust in
" the Lord with all thine heart, and lean not to
                                        " thine

" thine own underftanding. Acknowledge him in S E R M.
" all thy ways: and he fhall direct thy fteps." Let CLXIX.
us then addrefs ourfelves to God, in the words of
the holy prophet, Jer. x. 23. " O Lord, I know
" that the way of man is not in himfelf, and that it
" is not in man that walketh, to direct his fteps."
And let us beg of him, that he would confider our
cafe, commiferate our weaknefs, and pity our impotency, and that he would join his ftrength to us,
and grant us the affiftance of his grace and holy fpirit, to put us upon fincere refolutions of a new life,
and to keep us conftant and ftedfaft to them; " to
" open the eyes of our minds, and to turn us from
" darknefs to light, and from the power of Satan
" and our lufts, unto God; that we may repent and
" turn to God, and do works meet for repentance,
" that fo we may receive forgivenefs of fins, and an
" inheritance among them that are fanctified through
" faith that is in Christ."

And for our encouragement in this matter, God
hath bid us to apply ourfelves to him; and he hath
promifed not to be wanting to us, in words as exprefs
and univerfal as can well be devifed. Jam. i. 6.
" If any man lack wifdom, let him afk it of God,
" who giveth to all liberally, and upbraideth no
" man: but let him afk in faith, nothing waver-
" ing," that is, not doubting but that God is both
able and willing to give what he afks. And Luke
xi. 9, 10, 11, 12, 13. " I fay unto you, afk,
" and it fhall be given you; feek, and ye fhall
" find; knock, and it fhall be opened unto you.
" For every one that afketh, receiveth; and he that
" feeketh, findeth; and to him that knocketh, it
" fhall be opened. If a fon fhall afk bread of any
" of you that is a father, will he give him a ftone?

" Or if he aſk a fiſh, will he for a fiſh give him a
" ſerpent ? Or if he ſhall aſk an egg, will he offer
" him a ſcorpion? If ye then being evil, know how
" to give good gifts unto your children ; how much
" more ſhall your heavenly Father give the holy Spi-
" rit to them that aſk him ?" To encourage our
faith, our SAVIOUR uſeth ſuch an argument as may
give us the greateſt aſſurance. We are commonly
confident, that our earthly parents will not deny us
thoſe things that are good and neceſſary for us,
though they may be otherwiſe evil : " how much
" more then ſhall our heavenly Father," who is eſ-
ſentially and infinitely good, " give his holy Spirit
" to us ?" And if this be not enough, St. Matthew
uſeth a larger expreſſion, " How much more ſhall
" your heavenly Father give good things to them
" that aſk him ?" If there be any thing that is
good, and we ſtand in need of it, and earneſtly
pray to GOD for it, we may be confident that he
will give it us.

2. We ought to be very watchful over ourſelves,
conſidering our weakneſs and wavering, and inſta-
bility and fickleneſs, the treachery and deceitfulneſs
of our own hearts, and the malice of Satan. It will
be a great while before the habits of ſin be ſo weakened and ſubdued, as that we ſhall have no propenſi-
on to return to them again ; ſo that our hearts will
be often endeavouring to return to their former poſ-
ture, and like a deceitful bow, which is not firmly
ſtrong, to ſtart back. And beſides the deceitfulneſs of
ſin and our own hearts, the devil is very malicious,and
his malice will make him vigilant to watch all advantages againſt us ; and his great deſign will be to
ſhake our reſolution ; for if that ſtand, he knows
his kingdom will fall, and therefore he raiſeth all his
batteries

batteries againſt this fort, and labours by all means to undermine it; and nothing will be matter of greater triumph to him, than to gain a perſon that was revolted from him, and reſolved to leave his ſervice. If therefore thou expecteſt God's grace and aſſiſtance to keep thee ſtedfaſt to thy reſolution, do not neglect thyſelf, but " keep thy heart with all diligence," and watch carefully over thyſelf: for becauſe "God " worketh in us both to will and to do," therefore he expects that " we ſhould work out our ſalvation " with fear and trembling," leſt by our own careleſneſs and neglect we ſhould miſcarry.

3. Let us frequently renew and reinforce our reſolutions, more eſpecially when we think of coming to the ſacrament, and approaching the holy table of the Lord. Nothing is more apt to beget in us good reſolutions, and to ſtrengthen them, than to conſider the dreadful ſufferings of the Son of God for our ſins, which are ſo lively ſet forth and repreſented to us in his holy ſacrament, which as it is on God's part a ſeal and confirmation of his grace and love to us, ſo on our part it ought to be a ſolemn ratification of our covenant with God, " to depart " from iniquity, and to walk before him in holineſs " and righteouſneſs all the days of our lives."

SERMON CLXX.

The nature and neceſſity of reſtitution.

LUKE xix. 8, 9.

And if I have taken any thing from any man by falſe accuſation, I reſtore him fourfold. And JESUS *ſaid unto him, This day is ſalvation come to this houſe.*

SERM.
CLXX.
The firſt
ſermon on
this text.

ONE particular and eminent fruit of true repentance, is the making of reſtitution and ſatisfaction to thoſe whom we have injured. As for GOD, we can make no ſatisfaction and compenſation to him, for the injuries we have done him by our ſins ; all that we can do in reſpect of GOD, is to confeſs our ſins to him, to make acknowledgment of our miſcarriages, to be heartily troubled for what we have done, and not to do the like for the future. But for injuries done to men, we may in many caſes make reparation and ſatisfaction. And this, as it is one of the beſt ſigns and evidences of a true repentance ; ſo it is one of the moſt proper and genuine effects of it : for this is as much as in us lies, to undo what we have done, and to unſin our ſins.

But, becauſe the practice of this duty doth ſo interfere with the intereſt of men, and conſequently it will be very difficult to convince men of their duty in this particular, and to perſuade them to it ; therefore I deſign to handle this particular fruit and effect of a true repentance by itſelf, from theſe words, which contain in them,

I. The fruit and effect of Zaccheus his converſion

and

and repentance; " If I have taken any thing from " any man, I restore him fourfold."

II. The declaration, which our Saviour makes hereupon, of the truth of his repentance and conversion, and the happy state he was thereby put into. " And Jesus said unto him, This day is sal- " vation come to this house, for as much as he also " is the son of Abraham ;" as if he had said, by these fruits and effects it appears, that this is a repentance to salvation ; and this man whom you look upon as a sinner and a heathen, may by better right call Abraham father, than any of you formal pharisees and Jews, who glory so much in being the children of Abraham.

I. The fruit and effect of Zaccheus's conversion and repentance ; " If, &c.

This Zaccheus, as you find at the second verse, was chief of the publicans, which was an office of great odium and infamy among the Jews, they being the collectors of the tribute which the Roman emperor, under whose power the Jews then were, did exact from them. And because these publicans farmed this tribute of the emperor at a certain rent, they made a gain out of it to themselves, by exacting and requiring more of the people than was due upon that account; so that their calling was very infamous, upon three accounts.

1. Because they were the instruments of oppressing their countrymen; for so they looked upon the tax they paid to the Romans, as a great oppression.

2. Because they were forced by the necessity of their calling to have familiar conversation with heathens, whom they looked upon as sinners. Hence the phrase used by the apostle, of " sinners of the " Gentiles." And hence likewise probably it is, that

3 " publicans

SERM.   " publicans and sinners, publicans and heathens,"
CLXX.   are joined several times together, because of the occasions of frequent converse which the publicans had
with heathens.

3. But principally they were odious, because of
the common injustice and oppression, which they
used in the management of their calling, by fraud
and violence extorting more than was due, to in-
hance the profit of their places.   Hence it is, that
this sort of officers have been generally branded, and
reckoned among the worst sort of men.   So he in
the comedy, πάν]ες τηλῶναι, πάν]ες εἰσὶν ἅρπαγες,
" all publicans are rapacious or robbers." And this is
most probably the sin which Zaccheus here repents of,
and in regard to which he promises restitution, κỳ εἴ
τινὸς ἐσυκοφάν]ησα,   " and if I have taken any
" thing from any man by false accusation ;" so we
render the words in our translation : but the word
ἐσυκοφάν]ησα signifies more generally, " if I have
" been injurious to any one, if I have wronged any
" man," as appears by the constant use of this word
by the LXX, who by this word do translate the most
general Hebrew words, which signify any kind of
injury or oppression, either by fraud or violence or
calumny.   So that there is no reason here to restrain
it," wronging men by false accusation :" for Zaccheus
his sin being in all probability extorting more than
was due, this might as easily be done many other
ways, as by false accusation.   And that this was the
common sin of the publicans, appears by the counsel which John the Baptist gives them, Luke iii. 12,
15. " Then came also the publicans to be baptized,
" and said unto him, master, what shall we do ?
" And he said unto them, exact no more than that
" which is appointed you ;" that is, do not by fraud
                                                            or

or violence extort from any man, any more than the tribute which is laid upon him.

So that Zaccheus here promiſeth, that if he had been injurious to any man in his office, by extorting more than was due, he would reſtore to him four-fold. And if Zaccheus calculated his eſtate right, and intended to reſerve any part of it to himſelf, which is but reaſonable to ſuppoſe ; it could be no very great part of his eſtate which was injuriouſly got ; and I am afraid a far ſmaller proportion than many are guilty of, who yet paſs for very honeſt men in compariſon of the publicans. The text ſaith, he was a rich man. Suppoſe he was worth ten or twelve thouſand pounds ; half he gives to the poor ; that was well got, or elſe his whole eſtate could not have made fourfold reſtitution for it. Suppoſe he reſerved a thouſand or two to himſelf, then at the rate of re-ſtoring fourfold, not above a thouſand can be inju-riouſly got, that is about a penny in the ſhilling. I am afraid that now a-days there are few ſuch moderate oppreſſors : nay, it is poſſible that the proportion of his eſtate injuriouſly got might be much leſs ; more it could not eaſily be. But whatever it was, he does not plead that by way of excuſe for himſelf, he freely confeſſeth he had ſinned in this kind, and of-fers reſtitution to the utmoſt, much more than the law did require in ſuch caſes.

II. You have the declaration our SAVIOUR makes hereupon, of the truth of his repentance and con-verſion, and the happy ſtate he was thereby put in-to, " this day is ſalvation come to this houſe."

The obſervation I ſhall make from hence is this, that reſtitution and ſatisfaction for the injuries we have done to others, is a proper and genuine effect of true repentance. I know the text only ſpeaks of restitution in case of oppression and exaction : but because there is the same reason why restitution should be made for all other injuries, I think I may, without any force or violence to my text, very well make it the foundation of a more general discourse concerning restitution.

In the handling of this, I shall,

First, open to you the nature of this duty.

Secondly, confirm the truth of the proposition, by shewing the necessity of it.

Thirdly, endeavour to persuade men to the discharge of this necessary duty.

First, for the opening the nature of this duty, I will consider,

I. The act.

II. The latitude or extent of the object, as I may call it, or the matter about which it is conversant.

III. The manner how it is to be done.

IV. The measure of it.

V. The persons who are bound to make restitution ; and to whom it is to be made.

VI. The time in which it is to be done.

VII. The order of doing it, where more are injured, and restitution cannot be made at once to all.

I. For the act. Restitution is nothing else but the making reparation or satisfaction to another for the injuries we have done him. It is to restore a man to the good condition, from which, contrary to right and to our duty, we have removed him. Restitution is only done in case of injury. Another man may be damaged and prejudiced by us many ways, and we not be bound to make restitution ; because there are many cases, wherein a man deserves the prejudice we do to him. As when we are instruments of inflicting upon a man the punishment which the law doth

sen-

sentence him to. And there are many cases wherein we may be prejudicial to others, and cannot help it. As a man that is sick of a contagious disease, may infect others that are about him : but he is not injurious to them ; because it is not his fault, but his infelicity.

II. For the latitude and extent of the object, as I may call it, or the matter about which it is conversant. It extends to all kind of injuries, which may be reduced to these two heads ; either we injure a person with or without his consent.

1. Some injuries are done to persons with their consent. Such are most of those injuries which are done to the souls of men, when we command, or counsel, or incourage them to sin, or draw them in by our example. For the maxim *volenti non fit injuria*, " there's no injury done to a man that is " willing," is not so to be understood, as that a man may not in some sort consent to his own wrong : for absolute freedom and willingness supposeth that a man is wholly left to himself, and that he understands fully what he does. And in this sense no man sins willingly, that is, perfectly knowing and actually considering what he does ; and commands, and persuasion, and example are a kind of violence : yet none of these hinder, but that a man in these cases may sufficiently consent to what he does. But yet he is not so perfectly free, as to excuse him that draws him into sin by these ways. So likewise when a man refuseth to do that which is his duty without a reward ; for instance, to do justice to another ; he is injurious in so doing : but yet not altogether without the consent of him whom he injures.

2. Injuries are done to persons without their consent. And these, though they are not always the greatest mischiefs, yet they are the greatest injuries. And

these

these injuries are done either by fraud and cunning, or by violence and oppression; either by over-reaching another man in wit, or over-bearing him by power. And these usually either respect the bodies of men, or their estates, or their good name. The bodies of men. He that maims another, or does him any other injury in his limbs or health, either by fraud or force, is bound, so far as he is able, to make reparation for the injury. Or they respect the estates of men. If by cunning, or by violence, or by false testimony or accusation, thou hast hindered a man of any benefit, which otherwise would have come to him, thou art bound to restitution. If by thy power or interest, by thy knowledge in the law, or skill in business, thou hast directly and avowedly helped and assisted another to do injustice to his neighbour, thou art bound to restitution; though not as the principal, yet as the accessary. If thou hast over-reached thy brother in any contract, making advantage of his ignorance or unskilfulness; if thou hast made a gain of his necessity; if thou hast by thy power and interest, or by any more violent and forcible way detained his right, or taken away that which was his; thou art bound to make reparation for these injuries, to restore that which thou hast borrowed, to return the pledge which thou hast wrongfully kept, to release unconscionable forfeitures, to pay debts, to make satisfaction for frauds and cheats, to take off all unjust invasions and surprizals of estates: yea though the fraud be such that thou art not liable to make satisfaction by any human law, yet thou art as much bound to it in conscience to GOD and thy duty, as if thou hadst stoln, or taken it by violence from thy neighbour. For in truth and reality, fraud is as great an injury as violence, although human

3

laws

laws cannot take cognizance of it, fo as to relieve SERM.
every man that is over-reached in a bargain : nay of CLXX.
the two it is worfe; for whenever thou deceiveft a
man in this kind, thou doft not only wrong him in
point of eftate, but thou abufeft his underftanding.

And fo likewife in refpect of a man's fame and
reputation. If thou haft hurt any man's good name
by flander or calumny, by falfe witnefs, by rendring
him ridiculous, or any other way, thou art bound
to give fuch fatisfaction as the thing is capable of;
or if there be any other injury which I have not mentioned, thou art obliged to make reparation for it.

III. As to the manner how reftitution is to be
made.

1. Thou art bound to do it voluntarily, and of
thy own accord, though the perfon injured do not
know who it was that did him the injury, though
he do not feek reparation by law. When a man is
forced by law to make reftitution, it is not a virtue,
but neceffity; this is not a fruit of repentance and a
good mind, but of good law. And that thou doft
not do it, unlefs the law compel thee to it, is an argument thou wouldft not have done it, if thou couldft
have avoided it. And though the thing be done,
yet thou haft not done it, but the law; and unlefs
thou heartily repent of thy crime, the injury ftill lies
at thy door, and in GOD's account thou art as guilty
as if no reftitution had been made. Not that thou
art bound in this cafe to make new reftitution over
again; but thou art bound to bewail thy neglect, that
thou didft not do it voluntarily and without the com-
pulfion of the law.

2. Thou muft do it in kind, if the thing be capable of it, and the injured party demand it. Thou
muft reftore the very thing which thou hadft depriv-

cd

ed thy neighbour of, if it be fuch a thing as can be reftored, and be ftill in thy power ; unlefs he voluntarily accept of fome other thing in exchange.

3. If thou canft not reftore it in kind, thou art bound to reftore it in value, in fomething that is as good. As for fpiritual injuries done to the fouls of men, we are bound to make fuch reparation and compenfation as we can. Thofe whom we have drawn into fin, and engaged in wicked courfes, by our influence and example, or by neglect of our duty towards them, we are fo far as becomes the relation we ftand into them, to make acknowledgment of our fault, to endeavour by our inftruction and counfel to reclaim them from thofe fins we led them into, and " to recover them out of the fnare of the " devil;" and fhould never be at reft till we have done as much or more for the furtherance of their falvation, and helping them forwards towards heaven, as we did contribute before to their ruin and deftruction. If we have violated any one's chaftity, we are bound to marry them, if it was done upon that condition, and if they require it : thou art bound to keep and maintain thofe children which are the fruit of thy luft, and to make reparation to the perfon whom thou haft injured, by dowry or otherwife.

If thou haft defrauded and injured any man in his good name, thou art obliged to make him a compenfation by acknowledgment of thy fault, by a ftudious vindication of him, and by doing him honour and repairing his credit in all fitting ways. And if the injury be irreparable (as it frequently happens, that we can hardly fo effectually vindicate a man, as we can defame him ; and it is feldom feen that thofe wounds which are given to mens reputation are perfectly healed) I fay, if the injury be irreparable, efpecially

cially if it prove really prejudicial to a man in his calling and civil interest; if no other satisfaction will be accepted, it is to be made in money, " which, " Solomon says, answers all things;" and the rather, because the reason and equity of human laws hath thought fit to assign this way of satisfaction in many cases upon actions of scandal and defamation. And whatever the law would give in any case, if it could be proved, that is the least we are bound in conscience to do, when we are guilty to ourselves, though the law cannot take hold of us.

So likewise, if thou hast wounded a man, thou art bound to pay the cure, to repair to him and his relations the disability for his calling, and his way of livelihood and subsistence, which he hath contracted by thy injury. And so for false imprisonment, the real detriment which comes to him by it is to be made amends for: and so in all other cases, the injured person is so far as is possible to be restored to the good condition in which he was before the injury.

IV. As to the measure and proportion of the restitution we are to make. Zaccheus here offers fourfold, which was much beyond what any law required in like cases. The measure of restitution by the judicial law of the Jews, did very much vary according to the kind and degree of the injury. In some cases a man was only bound to simple restitution; but then he was to do it to the full, Exod. xxii. 5, 6. And so if that which is another man's be " delivered " unto his neighbour to keep, and be stoln from " him, he is to make restitution thereof," ver. 12. " And so if a man borrow ought of his neighbour, " and if it be hurt or die, the owner thereof not being " with it, he shall surely make it good," ver. 14. " But for all manner of trespasses by way of theft,
" whether

" whether it be for ox, for afs, for sheep, for rai-
" ment, or for any manner of loft thing, which ano-
" ther challengeth to be his, he whom the judge
" shall condemn, shall pay double to his neighbour,"
ver. 9. that is, if it be of " a living creature," if the
theft be " found in his hands alive, whether it be ox,
" or afs, or sheep, he shall restore double," ver. 4. But
if a man did " steal an ox or a sheep, and did kill it
" or fell it," he was to restore " five oxen for an ox,
" and four sheep for a sheep." And thus we find
David judged upon Nathan's parable of the rich man,
who had taken the poor man's only lamb, and kill'd
and dreft it for a traveller that came to him, 2 Sam.
xii. 6. " He shall restore the lamb fourfold." Now
the reason of this seems to be partly because of the
advantage and usefulness of those creatures above any
other; and partly because when they were once killed or alienated, a man could not without great trouble and difficulty make discovery, which hazard of
not-discovering seems to be accounted for in the restitution: but if a man did voluntarily offer restitution, before he was prosecuted, for any thing that
was taken by violence, or unjustly detained from his
neighbour, then he was only " to restore the prin-
" cipal, and to add a fifth part thereto, and to offer
" up an offering to the LORD, and so his atonement
" was made," Lev. vi. 1, &c.

So that the highest proportion was a fourth or
fifth part, and that only in the particular case of
sheep or oxen stoln away, and killed or alienated
afterwards. Indeed Solomon speaks of a sevenfold
restitution, Prov. vi. 31. where he saith, " If a thief
" be found, he shall restore sevenfold, even all the
" substance of his house;" where seven is only a
number of perfection, and the meaning is, he shall
                                        make

make perfect and full reſtitution according to the S E R M. law, ſo far as his ſubſtance or eſtate will reach.   CLXX.

So that it ſeems Zaccheus in reſtoring fourfold did out-do the utmoſt ſeverity of the law ; which in caſe of fraud and oppreſſion was but double, if demanded ; if voluntarily offered, was the principal and a fifth part added : but to teſtify the truth of his repentance, and his hearty ſorrow for the injuries he had done, he puniſheth himſelf beyond what the law would have done.

I do not ſay that this example binds as to this meaſure and proportion: nay, I do not ſay we are bound to the proportions of the law ; for that only concerned the nation of the Jews : but although we be free from the letter of the law, yet we are tied to the equity of it. As to the ſubſtance of the duty of reſtitution, we are bound to that by the law of nature. As to the meaſure and proportion, the equity of the judicial law in it's proportions, and of Zaccheus his example, ought to be conſiderable to us.

But to ſpeak more particularly concerning the meaſures and proportions of reſtitution, I ſhall lay down theſe propoſitions.

1. Where reſtitution can be made in kind, or the injury can be certainly valued, we are to reſtore the thing, or the value.

2. We are bound to reſtore the thing, with the natural increaſe of it, that is, to ſatisfy for the loſs ſuſtained in the mean time, and the gain hindered.

3. Where the thing cannot be reſtored, and the value of it is not certain, we are to give reaſonable ſatisfaction, that is, according to a middle eſtimation ; not the higheſt, nor the loweſt of things of the kind. The injured perſon can demand no more, and ſtrict juſtice requires no more. But it is ſafe for

him that hath done the injury, rather to exceed than
to fall short.

4. We are at least to give by way of restitution
what the law would give; for that is generally equal,
and in most cases rather favourable than rigorous.

5. A man is not only bound to restitution for the
injury which he did, but for all that directly follows
upon his injurious act, though it were beyond his
intention. For the first injury being wilful, thou art
presumed to will all that which directly followed upon it ; according to that rule, *Involuntarium ortum
ex voluntario censetur pro voluntario.* " We are pre-
" sumed to will that which follows upon a voluntary
" action, though we did not intend it." For instance, if a man maliciously and knowingly set fire
upon another man's house, though he intended only
an injury to that particular person, yet if a wind
come and drive the fire to his neighbours at some di-
stance, though he did not intend this, yet because
the first act was unlawful, he is liable to satisfy for
all the direct consequences of it. If a man wound
another without any intention of killing him, and
the wound prove mortal, though there was no probability that death would ensue upon it, the man is
bound, because the first act was injurious, to make
reparation to his relations for the damage they sustain
by his death ; and if they did depend solely upon
him, who died by such injury, thou art bound to
maintain them.

6. Because those who have lived in a trade and
course of injustice, can hardly remember all the particular injuries they have done, so as to make exact
satisfaction for them, it will not be amiss over and
besides to give something to the poor. So Zaccheus
does here, " half of my estate I give to the poor,
" and if I have taken any thing," &c.   V. The

V. The persons who are concerned in restitution. And here I shall consider,

First, The persons who are bound to make restitution.

Secondly, The persons to whom it is to be made.

First, The persons who are bound to make restitution. In general, they who have done the injury, or they who come into their stead, so as in law or equity the injury devolves and descends upon them. But for the clearer stating of this, I shall lay down several propositions, which may serve to resolve a great many cases, that may be put concerning persons obliged to make restitution.

1. If the injury be done solely by one, without accomplices and partakers in the crime, he alone is responsible, and wholly bound to make satisfaction; I mean, he only is bound so long as he lives; but if the injury descends as a burden upon the estate, then he who enjoys the estate becomes bound to make satisfaction; as I shall shew afterwards.

2. If the injury was done by more, who did all equally concur to the doing of it, they are all equally bound to make satisfaction; and they are bound to concur together to that purpose; and in case of such concurrence, every one is not bound to satisfy for the whole, but *pro ratâ parte*, for his share; provided they do among them make full satisfaction.

3. If all will not concur, those that are willing are bound among them to make reparation for the injury: nay, if all the rest refuse to join with thee in it, thou art bound *in solidum* to make full reparation so far as thou art able; because every one was guilty of the whole injury. For instance, if four men conspire together to cheat a man, or to rob him, any one of these, if the rest refuse, is bound to make en-

tire

tire satisfaction; yea, though he was only partaker in the benefit; because, as I said before, he is guilty of the whole injury.

4. If the injury be done by more, who do unequally concur to the doing of it, he that is principal is chiefly and principally bound to make satisfaction: and here I do not take principal, strictly in the sense of the law, but in the sense of equity; not for him always who is the more immediate cause of the injury, but for him who was the greatest cause, and by whose influence chiefly it was procured and done: but if the principal will not, the accessories and instruments are bound, at least for their share, and according to the proportion of the hand they had in it. But if the principal do satisfy in the name, and upon the account of the rest, then the accessories are free from an obligation to restitution, and are only bound to repentance.

5. If the injury devolve upon another, by descending as a burden upon the estate, he who enjoys the estate is bound to make satisfaction. And when injuries do thus descend as burdens and incumbrances upon estates, and when not, the civil laws of the place where we live must determine: but then where my case falls within the compass of the law, I am bound voluntarily to satisfy without the compulsion of the law. For instance, if an estate fall to me charged with a debt, which hath been unjustly detained, I am bound voluntarily to discharge the debt, so soon as it appears to me, before I am compell'd thereto by the law.

6. As for personal injuries which do not lye as burdens upon the estate, nor do by the law descend upon the son or heir, though in strict justice a man be not bound to make compensation for them, for

that

that would be endless, *& infinitum in lege repudia-tur*, " no law can take notice of that which is infi-
" nite and endless;" for *quæ exitum non habent ha-bentur pro impossibilibus*, " those things which have
" no end, to which no bounds can be set, are esteem-
" ed among things impossible," to which no man
can be obliged: but though in strict justice the heir
be not bound to make reparation, for the personal
injuries of him whom he succeeds in the estate, yet
in many cases it is equitable, and generous, and christian, for such persons to make some kind of reparation for palpable and notorious injuries. For instance, if I be heir to an estate, part of which I know
certainly was injuriously gotten, it is not only christian, but prudent, to make satisfaction in the case to
the party injured, if certainly known; if not, to give
it to the poor; for by this means I may take out the
moth, which was bred by injustice in the estate, and
rub off the rust, that sticks to the gold and silver,
which was got by oppression or fraud, and so free
the remaining part of the estate from that secret and
divine *Nemesis* which attends it and follows it. And
for the same reason, it is very noble and christian, for
the son and heir of an unjust father, to make some
reparation for his father's injuries by restitution, if
the thing be capable of it: if not, by doing all good
offices to the injured persons, which is some kind of
compensation. And in this case the obligation is
greater, because by this means a man does not only
do what in him lies, to cut off the curse, which by
his father's oppression and injustice is intail'd upon
the family and estate: but likewise, because a son
ought much more to be concern'd for his father, than
any other person, and to consult the honour and reputation both of him and his own family; and the

reparation

reparation which the son makes, is in some sort the father's act, because he succeeds him and comes into his stead.

Secondly, As to the persons to whom satisfaction is to be made. For the resolution of those cases which may fall under this head, I shall lay down these propositions.

1. If the injured person can be certainly known, and be alive and extant, the satisfaction is to be made to him.

2. If he be not alive, or which is all one, not to be found or come at, satisfaction is to be made to his nearest relations, his wife, or children, or brothers, or other nearest kindred. The reason is, because satisfaction being due, and I having no right to keep that which I injuriously gotten, if I cannot restore it to the party himself, I ought in all reason to place it there where I may most reasonably presume the party injured would have bestowed his estate, and this part of it amongst the rest, had he been possessed of it. And by the same reason that I am bound thus to restore the part of his estate which I have injuriously taken or detained from him, I am likewise obliged to give satisfaction to the same person for any other injury: for to whomsoever I would pay a debt due to one that is deceased, to the same person I ought to give satisfaction for the injuries, by which a debt is, though not formally, yet virtually contracted.

3. If the party injured be not certainly known, or have no near relations known to me, in that case I think it very advisable to give so much to the poor, or to some charitable use ; or if the party injured be not capable of proper satisfaction, as sometimes it is a community and body of men that you have injured, in this case it is proper to repair the injuries to com-

I   munities

munities or bodies of men, by equivalent good offices, or by some publick good work, which may be of common benefit and advantage. This is the fifth thing I proposed to speak to, the persons concern'd in restitution; both the persons who are bound to make restitution, and the persons to whom it is to be made. Of the rest hereafter.

SERMON CLXXI.

The nature and necessity of restitution.

LUKE xix. 8, 9.

And if I have taken any thing from any man by false accusation, I restore him fourfold. And Jesus *said unto him, This day is salvation come to this house.*

IN speaking to these words, I proposed to consider, S E R M.
Firft, The nature of this duty of restitution. CLXXI.
Secondly, To shew the necessity of it. The
Thirdly, To persuade men to the discharge of it. second
In treating of the nature of restitution, I have sermon on this text.
consider'd,

I. The act.

II. The extent of it.

III. The manner how it is to be perform'd.

IV. The measure of it.

V. The persons who are to make restitution; and the persons to whom restitution is to be made. I now proceed to consider.

VI. The time when restitution is to be made. In these cases a man is not tied up to an instant, not

just

just to the present time, unless the case be such, that he can never do it, if he do not do it then. As if a man lie upon his death-bed; that is a case that admits of no delay, a man should hasten restitution, as he would do the making of his will, and the disposal of his estate; lest if he do not do it presently, he lose his opportunity of doing it for ever: but ordinarily, a man is not so strictly tied up to moments, and to the present time. It is sufficient that a man be for the present resolved to do it, so soon as morally he can, so soon as he would do other actions of great moment and concernment. And to this purpose the text gives us an excellent pattern; Zaccheus, the same day he repented, took up this resolution, and to oblige himself effectually to put it in execution, he publickly declares it, and before all the people offers to make restitution to all whom he had injured.

Therefore take heed of all unnecessary delays in these matters: for though God would accept of a firm and sincere resolution in this case, if a person thus resolved should, before he could bring his resolution to effect, happen to be cut off by death, or be otherwise rendered incapable of doing it; I say, though God would accept such a resolution as this, yet he will not interpret that to be a sincere resolution, which a man is negligent to put in practice: for every neglect of putting our resolution in practice, is a degree of quitting and altering it; and he who did not do what he was resolved to do, when he had an opportunity and ability of doing it, is justly presumed to have let fall his resolution.

Therefore let no man presume upon his good intention and resolution in this kind; for they are only acceptable to God, so far as they are sincere and real;

and

and they are only so far sincere and real, as the man that makes them, is ready to put them in execution, so soon as morally he can. And if thou carelesly and supinely trifle away thy opportunities in this kind, God may likewise deprive thee of an opportunity for ever. For all the while thou wilfully neglectest to make restitution, thou art guilty of the injury ; and there are hardly two sins that cry louder to God for a quick and speedy revenge, than injustice and oppression, deceit and fraud. God many times takes such causes into his more immediate cognizance, 1 Theff. iv. 6. "Let no man deceive or "go beyond his brother in any thing : for God is "the avenger of such." And David tells us, that God in a peculiar manner "abhors the blood-thirsty "and deceitful man ;" and threatens that "he "shall not live out half his days." And God by the prophet, Mal. iii. 5. tells us, that "He will "be a swift witness against the oppressors." And if God be so swift to take vengeance upon such persons, surely then they are concerned to be very quick and speedy in making satisfaction for their injuries and oppressions, lest divine vengeance prevent them, and instead of making reparation to men, they be called upon to make satisfaction to the justice of God ; and you know who hath said it, that "it is a fear-"ful thing to fall into the hands of the living God."

You therefore that have hitherto neglected this duty, delay it no longer ; by all means discharge your consciences of this burden, before you come to lye upon a death-bed. Then the consciences of the worst of men begin to work, like a stomach oppressed and surcharged with meat, and then they are willing for their ease to vomit up those estates, which they have devoured by fraud and injustice ; then they begin to conſider the difficulty of being ſaved, and to fear that it will be impoſſible for them ever " to enter in at the ſtrait gate," thus laden with the ſpoils of violence and deceit ; even thoſe that have the hardeſt and moſt ſeared conſciences, will be touched with the ſenſe of ſuch great ſins at ſuch a time : but do not thou defer this work to that time, for theſe two reaſons.

1. Becauſe it cannot be ſo acceptable to GOD, to make reſtitution at ſuch a time, as when thou art in health and in hopes of longer life. To give a man his own, when thou canſt enjoy it and uſe it no longer, this is next to detaining of it.

2. Becauſe in all probability the reſtitution which is then made will not prove ſo effectual. What thou doſt thyſelf, that thou art ſure is done : but what thou leaveſt to be done by thy executors, and chargeſt upon them, thou art not ſure will be done ; ten to one but if they can find out any trick and evaſion in law, either to delay or avoid the doing of it, it ſhall either never be done, or very ſlowly. This is the ſixth thing, the time when reſtitution is to be made.

But before I leave this head, there is one caſe very proper to be conſidered, which relates to this circumſtance of time, and that is concerning injuries of a very ancient date ; that is, how far this duty of reſtitution is to look backward, and whether it doth not expire by tract of time ? For anſwer to this, I ſhall lay down theſe propoſitions.

1. At what diſtance of time ſoever the law would in the caſe make reparation and give ſatisfaction, we are undoubtedly bound in conſcience voluntarily to give it. I deliver this generally ; becauſe, though it be poſſible ſome civil laws may be in ſome caſes unreaſonable in this matter, yet they are our beſt rule

and

and guide ; and speaking generally and for the most part, they are as equitable as the reason of man could devise. Not that we are to tie ourselves strictly to the law, so as not to go farther, if reason and equity require ; for, as Seneca says, *Parum est ad legem bonum esse,* " it is no great argument of goodness, " to be just as good as the law requires." Therefore I think it will very well become a good man, in many cases, rather to be better than the law, than to keep strictly to it.

2. In cases where the law hath not determined the time, we may do well to observe a proportion to what the law hath determined in other cases, which come nearest our own case.

3. When the injury is so old, that the right which the injured person had to reparation is reasonably presumed to be quitted and forsaken, then the obligation to satisfaction ceaseth and expires. The reason is plain, because every man may recede from his own right, and give it up to another ; and where a man may reasonably be presumed to have parted with his right to another, the obligation to restitution ceaseth, and the right of claiming it. Now when a thing begins, *haberi pro derelicto,* that is, when a right may reasonably be presumed to be quitted and forsaken, cannot in general be determined : but this must be estimated according to the importance of the right and thing in controversy, as whether it be more or less considerable ; and according to the reason and determination of laws about things of this nature. To illustrate this rule by instances. The Saxons, Danes, and Normans, did at several times invade and conquer this nation, and conquered it we will suppose unjustly, and consequently did hold and possess that which truly belonged to others, contrary

to

to right ; and several of the posterity of each of
these do probably to this day hold what was then
injuriously gotten ; I say, in this case, the obligation to satisfaction and restitution is long since ex-
pired, and the original title, which those who were dif-
possessed had, is reasonably presumed to be long since
quitted and forsaken ; and that for very wise reasons
in law and government ; because it would confound
and unsettle all estates, if every thing, the original
title whereof is naught, were to be restored ; and it
is but equal to presume, that all mankind are so reasonable, as to quit their right in such cases, rather
than to cause endless disturbances, and to have the
guilt of injustice everlastingly perpetuated. And
though it be a rule in civil law, that *vitiosum initio,*
tractu temporis non convalescit, " a title originally
" bad can never by time be made just ;" it is only
true thus far, that time in itself doth not alter the
nature of things : but considering the necessities of
the world, and the infinite difficulties of retrieving
an ancient right, and the inconveniencies and disturbances that would thereby redound to human society,
it is better that an injury should be perpetuated, than
that a great inconveniency should come by endeavouring to redress it ; so that although considering a
thing simply in itself, an injury is so far from being
lessened or nulled by tract of time, that it is increased, and the longer it continues, the greater it is ;
yet by accident, and in compliance with the necessity of things, length of time may give a right to that
which was at first injuriously possess'd. Judg. xi.
26. Thus Jephthah reasons with the king of Am-
mon, who had made war for recovery of an ancient
right, as he supposed. And though the instances I have
given of the unjust conquest of a nation be great and
publick ;

publick; yet the same is to be determined propor-
tionably in less and particular cases. And thus I have done with the sixth thing.

VII. And lastly, as to the order of restitution. When we have injured a great many, and are not able to make restitution to all at once, our best prudence and discretion must govern us herein. Because no certain rule can be given, which will reach all cases, I will only say this in general, that it is reasonable first to make reparation for the oldest and greatest injuries; and *cæteris paribus*, if all other considerations be equal, to consider those first who are most necessitous, and if there be any other special reason and obligation arising from the nature of the injury, or the circumstances of the person injured, to have regard to them. I come now in the

Second place, to confirm the truth of the proposition, that to make restitution and satisfaction to those whom we have injured, is a proper and necessary fruit of a true repentance. And this will appear, if we consider these two things.

I. Our obligation to this duty.

II. The nature of repentance.

I. Our obligation to this duty. Upon the same account that we are obliged to repentance, we are obliged to restitution; and both these obligations arise from natural equity and justice. All sin is an injury done; and though repentance be not strictly satisfaction, yet it is the best we can make; and he is unjust, who having done an injury, does not make the best reparation he can. But now there are some sins, in which, besides the injury that is done to God by them, upon the general account, as they are sins and violations of his laws, there is likewise a particular injury done to men; and such are all those,

the

the effect whereof redounds to the prejudice of other men : such are fraud and oppreffion, and all other fins whereby others are injured. So that in thefe kinds of fins, there are two things confiderable, the irregularity and vitioufnefs of the act, and the evil effects of it upon other men : the former refpects the law, and calls for forrow and repentance for our violation of it ; the latter refpects the perfon that is injured, and calls for fatisfaction and reftitution. So that our obligation to reftitution is founded in the immutable and indifpenfable law of nature, which is " to " do that to another, which we would have another " do to us." We would have no man be injurious to us, or if he hath been fo, we would have him make fatisfaction and reparation to us of the injury he hath done ; and we take it grievoufly from him, if he do not. Now nothing is more juft and equitable, than that we fhould do that to others, which we in like cafe would expect from them : for the very fame obligation that lyes upon others towards us, does lye upon us in regard to others.

II. This will yet further appear, if we confider the nature of repentance, which is to be forry for what we have done, and not to do the like for the future. Now if thou be forry for what thou haft done, thou wifheft with all thy heart thou hadft not done it ; and if thou doft fo, thou wilt undo, as much as in thee lyeth, what thou haft done. Now the beft way to undo an injury, is to make reparation for it ; and till we do this, we continue in the fin. For if it was a fin, to do the injury at firft, it is the fame continued, not to make fatisfaction ; and we do not ceafe to commit the fin, fo long as we detain that which is another's right. Nothing but reftitution can ftop the progrefs of fin : for if it be a fin to

take

take that which is another man's from him by fraud or violence, it is the fame continued and virtually repeated, to detain and keep it from him ; and nothing more contrary to repentance, than to continue in the fin thou pretendeft to repent of. For how art thou forry for doing of it, if thou continueft to do it, if thou wilt go on to do it and do it again ? How doft thou hate thy fin, if thou enjoy the benefit and reap the advantage of it? If thou doeft this, it is an argument thou loveft thy fin ftill : for thou didft never love it for itfelf, but for the profit of it ; and fo long as thou retaineft that, thou canft not be quit of the fin. Thou holdeft faft thy fin fo long as thou refufeft to make fatisfaction for it; and repentance without reftitution differs as much from true repentance, as continuance in fin does from the forfaking of it. *Si res aliena non redditur, non agitur pœnitentia, fed fingitur* ; fo St. Auguftine " If we " do not reftore that which we have injurioufly de- " tained from another, our repentance is not real, " but feigned and hypocritical," and will not be effectual to the obtaining of our pardon. It is a very common, but a true and terrible faying, *Non dimittitur peccatum, nifi reftituatur ablatum*, " no re- " miffion without reftitution." If we will inherit the profit and advantage of fin, we cannot think it unreasonable or unjuft that we should inherit the punishment of it.

When the fcripture fpeaks of repentance, it frequently mentions reftitution as a proper fruit and effect of it, and as a neceffary and indifpenfable condition of pardon and life. Ezek. xxxiii. 14, 15, 16. " Again, when I fay unto the wicked, thou fhalt " furely die : if he turn from his fin, and do that " which is lawful and right; if the wicked reftore
" the

SERM. " the pledge, give again that he hath robbed," &c.
CLXXI. As if he had said, when I denounce death and destruction to the wicked, there is but this one way to
escape it, and that is by repentance; but then take
notice, what a repentance it is, that will avail to this
end; it is not a bewailing ourselves, and lamenting
over our sins, but a forsaking of them and returning
to our duty; "If we turn from our sin, and do that
" which is lawful and right." For instance, if he
have been guilty of injustice and oppression; if he
leave his course, and deal justly and righteously
with his neighbour, and not only so, but he also
make restitution for the injury he hath done, and restore what he hath unjustly detain'd and taken away;
" if he restore the pledge, and give again that he hath
" robbed," and do no injustice for the future, but
" walk in the statutes of life without committing
" iniquity;" upon these terms and no other " he
" shall live, he shall not die." Yea the very light
of nature could suggest thus much to the people of
Nineveh, that there was no hope, without this fruit
of repentance, of appeasing God's wrath. Therefore the king and the princes, after all the external
solemnity of fasting, and sackcloth, and crying
mightily, they decree that " every one should turn
" from the evil of his ways, and from the violence
" that was in their hands," *ut rapina manus vacue-*
faciat, & rapta restituat, sine quo non est vera pæni-
tentia; so Grot. upon the place, " that he empty
" his hands of the spoils of rapine and oppression,"
that is, " that he make restitution, without which
"there can be no repentance:" and upon their doing
this, it is said, that " God spared them, v. 10.
" and God saw their works, that they turned from
" their evil ways." It is not said, that he saw their
                                                    .ting

fasting and sackcloth, but he saw their works, the real
fruits and effects of their repentance ; and upon this
it was that " God repented of the evil he said he
" would do to them, and he did it not." And elsewhere we find, that God speaks with great indignation of the most solemn repentance, which is not accompanied with this fruit, Isa. lviii. 3, 4, 5, 6. The
people tell God how "they had fasted and afflicted their
" soul, and made their voice to be heard on high:"
but God despiseth all this, because it was not accompanied with the fruit of repentance, " it is such
" a fast as I have chosen," &c. There is so much of natural justice and equity in restitution, and it is so proper a fruit of repentance, that as Grotius observes, it
is not only the doctrine of the Jews and Christians,
but of Heathens and Mahometans, that the repentance which doth not produce this fruit is feigned, and
will never avail with God for pardon and mercy.
Thus much for confirmation of this doctrine.

The third and last thing I proposed was to persuade to the practice of this duty ; and this may serve
by way of application of the doctrine of restitution.
The use we shall make of it is,

First, To persuade men to the practice of this
difficult duty. I doubt not but the arguments I have
used are sufficient to convince us of the equity and
necessity of restitution ; but what arguments shall I
use to persuade to the practice and exercise of it?
When we press men to their duty, though we have
some advantages on our side, yet we have also great
disadvantages. We have this advantage, that we
have the reason and consciences of men on our side :
but then we have this disadvantage, that we have to
contend either with the lusts or interests of men, or
both : now that these are usually more powerful, is

SERM evident, in that the lusts and interests of men do so
CLXXI frequently bias and draw them to do things contrary
to reason and conscience. When we persuade men
to be just, and to make restitution to those whom
they have injured, it is true we have not to contend
with the lusts of men, with any corrupt and vicious
inclination of nature. There are some sins that have
their rise from mens natural tempers, as passion and
lust, and those sensual vices that abound in the world :
but there's nothing in any man's natural temper and
disposition that inclines him to be unjust, no man's
complexion doth particularly dispose him to lie or
steal, to defraud his neighbour, or detain his right
from him ; it is only the interests of men that prompt
them to these things ; and they are upon this account
the more inexcusable, because no man is inclined to
these sins from particular temper and constitution ;
so that an unjust man is in ordinary cases and circumstances a greater sinner, than a drunkard or a lustful
man, because no man can pretend to be hurried a-
way by the strong propension and inclination of his
nature, to cheat his brother ; but although when we
persuade men to be just, we have not the lusts of men
to contend withal, yet we have another powerful ad-
versary, and that is the interests of men, which is one of
the chief rulers and governors of this world ; so that
when we press men to restitution, we touch them in
their interest, which is a very touchy and tender
thing ; when we tell them that without restitution no
man can repent and be saved, they think this to be a
very hard saying, and they know not how to bear it.

But certainly it hath all the reason and equity in the
world on it's side. If it be so hard for them to restore that which is another man's, is it not much
harder for him whom thou hast injured, to lose that
which

which is his own? Make it thine own case; wouldst
thou not think it much harder to have thy right detained from thee by another, than for another to part
with that which is not his own?

But I am sensible how little it is, that reason will
sway with men against their interest ; therefore the
best argument that I can use will be to satisfy men,
that upon a true and just account, it is not so much
their interest, to retain what they have unjustly got,
as to make restitution.   And this I shall do by shewing men, that to make restitution is their true interest,
both in respect of themselves, and of their posterity.

I. In respect to themselves.   It is better both in
respect of our present condition in this world, and of
our future state.

1. In respect of our present condition in this world,
and that both in respect of our outward estate, and
our inward peace and tranquillity.

(1.) In respect of our outward estate.   If we have
any belief of the providence of GOD, that his blessing can prosper an estate, and his curse consume it
and make it moulder away, we cannot but judge it
highly our interest to clear our estates of injustice by
restitution ; and by this means to free them from
GOD's curse.   For if any of our estate be unjustly
gotten, it is enough to draw down GOD's curse upon
all that we have; it is like a moth in our estate,
which will insensibly consume it ; it is like a secret
poison, which will diffuse itself through the whole ;
like a little land *in capite*, which brings the whole
estate into wardship.

Hear how GOD threatens to blast estates unjustly
gotten, Job xx. 12, &c. concluding with these words;
" this is the portion of a wicked man," that is, of an
unjust man.   Jer. xvii. 11.   " As a partridge sitteth

" on eggs, and hatcheth them not, ſo he that getteth
" riches, and not by right, ſhall leave them in the
" midſt of his days, and at his end ſhall be a fool."
Men many times live to ſee the folly of their injuſtice
and oppreſſion, and their eſtates wither away before
their eyes ; and by the juſt revenge of GOD they are
deprived of them in the midſt of their days. So
that the beſt way to fix an eſtate, and to ſecure it to
ourſelves, is by reſtitution to free it from GOD's
curſe ; and when we have done that, how much ſoever we may diminiſh our eſtate by it, we may look
upon ourſelves as having a better eſtate than we had ;
better, becauſe we have GOD's bleſſing with that
which remains. If we believe the bible, we cannot
doubt of this. The Spirit of GOD tells us this from
the obſervation of the wiſeſt men, Pſal. xxxvii. 16.
" A little that a righteous man hath, is better than the
" riches of many wicked." Prov. xvi. 8. " Better
" is a little with righteouſneſs, than great revenues
" without right."

(2.) In reſpect of inward peace and tranquillity, it
is highly our intereſt to make reſtitution. No man
can enjoy an eſtate, that does not enjoy himſelf ;
and nothing puts a man more out of the poſſeſſion of
himſelf, than an unquiet conſcience ; and there are
no kind of ſins lye heavier upon a man's conſcience,
than thoſe of injuſtice ; becauſe they are committed
againſt the cleareſt natural light, and there is the
leaſt natural temptation to them. They have theſe
two great aggravations, that they are ſins moſt
againſt knowledge, and have moſt of will in them.
There needs no revelation to convince men of ſins of
injuſtice and oppreſſion ; every man hath thoſe principles born with him, which will ſufficiently acquaint
him, that he ought not to be injurious to another.
                                                    There

There is nothing that relates to our duty, that a man SER M.
can know with greater certainty than this, that in- CLXXI.
juſtice is a ſin. And as it is a ſin moſt againſt knowledge, ſo it hath moſt of will in it. Men are hurried
away to other ſins by the ſtrong and violent propen-
ſions of their nature : but no man is inclined by his
temper and conſtitution, to fraud and oppreſſion ;
and the leſs there is of nature in any ſin, there is the
leſs of neceſſity, and conſequently it is the more voluntary. Now the greater the aggravations of any
ſin are, the greater is the guilt ; and the greater the
guilt is, the more unquiet our conſciences will be :
ſo that if thou have any regard to the intereſt of thine
own peace, if that be conſiderable to thee, which to
wiſe men is the moſt valuable thing in the world, do
not for a little wealth continue in thoſe ſins, which
will create perpetual diſturbance to thee, and imbit-
ter all the pleaſures of thy life. Hear how Job de-
ſcribes the condition of the wicked oppreſſors in the
place before cited, Job xx. 12, &c. " He ſhall not
" rejoice in them, becauſe he hath oppreſſed, becauſe
" he hath violently taken away a houſe which he
" builded not, ſurely he ſhall not feel quietneſs in his
" belly :" that is, he ſhall have no inward peace and
contentment in the midſt of all his outward enjoyments ; but his ill-gotten eſtate will work in his conſcience, and gripe him, as if a man had taken down
poiſon into his belly.

2. But chiefly, in reſpect of our future eſtate in
another world, it is every man's intereſt to make reſtitution. Without repentance we are ruined for
ever, and without reſtitution no repentance. " No
" unrighteous man hath any inheritance in the king-
" dom of CHRIST." If thou continue in thy fraud
and oppreſſion, and carry theſe ſins with thee into
another

SERM. another world, they will hang as a milſtone about
CLXXI. thy neck, and ſink thee into eternal ruin. He that
wrongs his brother hates him, and "he that hateth his
" brother is a murderer, and ye know that no-mur-
" derer hath eternal life abiding in him," 1 John iii.
15. Rom. i. 18. " The wrath of God is revealed
" from heaven, againſt all ungodlineſs and unrigh-
" teouſneſs of men." So that if it be mens intereſt
to eſcape the wrath of God, it concerns us to make
reparation for thoſe injuries which will expoſe us to
it. That is a dreadful text, Jam. v. 1, 2, 3, 4. " Go
" to now ye rich men, weep and howl for your mi-
" ſeries that ſhall come upon you. Your riches are
" corrupted, and your garments moth-eaten: your
" gold and ſilver is cankered, and the ruſt of them
" ſhall be a witneſs againſt you, and ſhall eat your
" fleſh as it were fire: ye have heaped treaſure to-
" gether for the laſt days. Behold! the hire of the
" labourers which have reaped down your fields,
" which is of you kept back by fraud, crieth; and
" the cries of them which have reaped, are entered
" into the ears of the Lord of Sabaoth." Do not
by " detaining the treaſures of wickedneſs, treaſure
" up to yourſelves wrath againſt the day of wrath :"
do not make yourſelves " miſerable for ever," that
you may be " rich for a little while :" do not for a
little " ſilver and gold," forfeit " the eternal inhe-
" ritance," which " was not purchaſed with corrup-
" tible things, but with the precious blood of the
" Son of God :" And if this conſideration, which
is the weightieſt in the world, will not prevail with
men, I can only ſay with the angel, Rev. xxii. 11.
" He that is unjuſt, let him be unjuſt ſtill," let him
continue in his injuſtice at his peril, and remember
what is added at the 12th verſe, " Behold! I come
" quickly

" quickly, and my reward is with me, to give to
" every man according as his work shall be."

II. In respect of our children and posterity, it is
greatly our interest to make restitution. GOD many
times suffers an estate got by oppression to prosper
for a little while : but there is a curse attends it, which
descends upon the estate like an incumbrance ; and
parents many times when they think they entail an
estate, they entail poverty upon their children, Job
xx. 10. speaking of the children of the oppressor, he
saith, " his children shall seek to please the poor,
" and his hands shall restore their goods." And
Job xxi. 19. " GOD layeth up his iniquity for his
" children." Thou layest up riches for thy children ; and " GOD lays up thine iniquity" and injustice " for them," the curse that belongs to them.
Hab. ii. 9, 10, 11. " Wo unto him that coveteth
" an evil covetousness, or gaineth an evil gain to 'his
" house," &c. Thou thoughtest to raise thy family by those ways ; but " thou hast consulted shame
" to thy house." No such effectual way to ruin thy
family, as injustice and oppression. As then you
would not transmit a curse to your children, and devolve misery upon your family, free your estates from
the burden and weight of what is other mens, lest by
GOD's just judgment and secret providence, that little which you injuriously detain from others, carry
away your whole estate to them and their family.
GOD's providence many times makes abundant restitution, when we will not.

Having now endeavoured to satisfy men, that it
is their truest interest, to make restitution for the
injuries they have done to others, it remains only
that I should answer an objection or two, which men
are apt to make against this duty.

First,

First, Men say they are ashamed to do it.   Ans.
It is not matter of shame, but of praise and commendation.   But it may be thou wilt say, it is matter of shame to have injured another, and this is the
way to lay open thy shame.   Indeed if the injury
were publick, the restitution ought to be so too, as
the only way to take off the shame of the injury.
For thy restitution doth not in this case publish thy
shame, but thy honesty : but if the injury was private, thou mayst preserve thy own credit by concealing thyself ; and provided thou do the thing effectually, thou mayst be as prudent, as to the manner
of doing it as thou pleasest.

Secondly, Another objection is the prejudice it
will be to mens estates.   But this I have answered
already, by shewing that it is more their interest to
make restitution, than to continue in the sin.   I shall
only add, that, as our SAVIOUR reasons in another
case, " it is profitable for thee, that one of thy mem-
" bers should perish, rather than that thy whole
" body should be cast into hell :" it is true likewise
here, it is profitable for thee, that thou shouldst go
a beggar to heaven, rather than that thou shouldst go
to hell, laden with the spoils and guilt of rapine and
injustice.

Thirdly, The last objection that I shall mention,
is disability to make restitution.   This indeed is
something ; where nothing is to be had, every man
must lose his right: but then remember, that there
must be a hearty repentance for the sin ; and thy sorrow must be so much greater, by how much thy
ability to make restitution is less ; and there must be
a willing mind, a firm purpose and resolution of doing it, when GOD shall enable thee, and diligent endeavours to that purpose.   Under the law those who
were

were not able to make reſtitution, were ſold for ſix years, if their ſervice did not make reparation in leſs time. It is true indeed, ' the moderation of the goſpel does not ſuffer Chriſtians to deal ſo hardly with another: but if the goſpel remit of this rigour, and do not allow Chriſtians to challenge it, we ſhould voluntarily do in effect that which they were forced to, that is, we ſhould uſe our beſt endeavours and diligence to put ourſelves into a condition of making ſatisfaction; and we ſhould not look upon any thing beyond the neceſſary conveniencies of life as our own, till we have done it; unleſs the party injured will recede from his right, in whole or in part. For though the impoſſibility of the thing do diſcharge us for the preſent, yet the obligation ſtill lyes upon us to do it, ſo ſoon as we are able.

And here it will be proper to conſider the caſe of thoſe, who have compounded with their creditors for a ſmall part, whether they be in conſcience and equity releaſed from the whole debt. I am loth to lay unneceſſary burdens upon mens conſciences, therefore I am very tender in reſolving ſuch caſes: but I ought to have a more tender care of the ſouls of men, than of their eſtates: therefore to deal plainly, and to diſcharge my conſcience in this matter, I think ſuch perſons do, notwithſtanding the compoſition, ſtand oblig'd in equity and conſcience for the whole debt, and are bound to diſcharge it, ſo ſoon as they can with tolerable convenience. My reaſon is, becauſe, though they be diſcharged in law, yet the law does not intend to take off the obligation of conſcience or equity, which they are under; but leaves that as it found it. Thus the caſe ſtands; men who are in a way of trade are engaged by the neceſſities of their calling, to venture a great part of their

estate in other mens hands, and by this means become liable many times to be undone without their
own fault; therefore it is usual, when any man in a
way of trade becomes disabled, for the creditors to
make such a composition with him, as his estate will
bear, and upon this composition to give him a full difcharge, so as that they cannot afterwards by law require of him the remainder of their debt. Now though
this be a favour to the debtor, yet it is principally
intended for the benefit of the creditor; because it
being his act, it is to be presumed, that he intended
it as much as may be, for his own advantage; and
so it is, for the creditor has as much satisfaction at
present as can be had, and the debtor is hereby left
in a capacity of recovering himself again by his industry and diligence, which could not be, if he were not
fully discharged; for if he were still liable for the
rest, he would continually be obnoxious to imprifon-
ment, which would render him incapable of following his calling; or if he were at liberty, he could
have no credit to enable him to do any thing in his
calling; for who would trust a man with any thing,
who is liable every moment to have it taken from
him? So that the reason of this plenary discharge is
this, that men, who are otherwise hopeful, and in a
fair probability of recovering themselves, may not be
rendered incapable of getting an estate afterwards,
whereby they may support themselves, and discharge
their debts. Now this discharge being given in order to these ends, it cannot be imagined that it should
be intended to defeat them; but it is in all reason to
be supposed, that the creditors did not intend to take
off the obligation of equity and conscience, only to
put the man into a condition of doing something towards the enabling him to discharge his debt. So
that

that unless it were exprefs'd at the compofition, that the creditor would never expect more from him, upon any account of equity and confcience, but did freely forgive him the reft, the contrary whereof is ufually done; I fay, unlefs it were thus exprefs'd, there is no reafon why the creditor's favour in making a compofition fhould be abufed to his prejudice; and why a legal difcharge, given him on purpofe for this reafon among others, to put him into a capacity of recovering himfelf and giving full fatisfaction, fhould be fo interpreted, as to extinguifh the equitable right of the creditor to the remainder of his debt.

The fecond ufe of this doctrine of reftitution fhould be by way of prevention, that men would take heed of being injurious, and fo take away the occafion of reftitution, and free themfelves from the temptation of not performing fo difficult and fo unwelcome a duty. It is much eafier of the two, not to cozen or opprefs thy neighbour, than after thou haft done it, it will be to bring thyfelf to make reftitution : therefore we fhould be very careful, not to be injurious to any one in any kind; neither immediately by ourfelves, nor by aiding and affifting others, by our power and intereft, or fkill in the law, or by any other way, to do injuftice.

SERMON CLXXII.

The ufefulnefs of confideration, in order to repentance.

DEUT. xxxii. 29.

O that they were wife, that they underftood this, that they would confider their latter end!

THIS chapter is called Mofes his fong, in which he briefly recounts the various providences of GOD toward the people of Ifrael, and the froward carriage of that people towards him.

Firft, He puts them in mind how GOD had chofen them for his peculiar people, and had by a fignal care and providence conducted them all that tedious journey, for the fpace of forty years in the wildernefs, till he had brought them to the promifed land, which they had now begun to take poffeffion of.

And then he foretels, how they would behave themfelves after all this mercy and kindnefs GOD had fhewn to them, ver. 15. " Jefurun waxed fat, and " kicked, and forfook GOD which made him, and " lightly efteemed the rock of his falvation." Upon this he tells them, GOD would be extremely difpleafed with them, and would multiply his judgments upon them, ver. 19, 20. " When the LORD " faw it, he abhorred them, becaufe of the provok- " ing of his fons and of his daughters ; and he faid, " I will hide my face from them, I will fee what " their end fhall be : for they are a very froward " generation, children in whom is no faith." And ver. 23. " I will heap mifchief upon them, I will " fpend

" fpend mine arrows upon them." And then he
enumerates the particular judgments which he would
fend upon them: nay, he declares he would have
utterly confumed them, but that he was loth to give
occafion of fo much triumph to his and their enemies, v. 26, 27. " I faid, I would fcatter them
" into corners, I would make the remembrance of
" them to ceafe from among men: were it not, that
" I feared the wrath of the enemy, left their adver-
" faries fhould behave themfelves ftrangely, and left
" they fhould fay, our hand is high, and the LORD
" hath not done all this." And he adds the reafon
of all this feverity ; becaufe they were fo very ftupid
and inconfiderate, v. 28. " For they are a nation
" void of counfel, neither is there any underftand-
" ing in them."

And in the conclufion of all, he reprefents GOD
as it were breaking out into this vehement and affec-
tionate wifh, " O that they were wife, that they
" underftood this, that they would confider their
" latter end !"

" O that they were wife, that they underftood
" this!" What is that? This may refer to all that
went before. O that they were wife to confider
what GOD had done for them, and what they had
done againft him, and what he will do againft them,
if they continue or renew their former provocations!
O that they were but duly apprehenfive of this, and
would lay it ferioufly to heart!

But from what follows, it feems more particularly to refer to thofe particular judgments, which GOD
had threatened them withal, and which would certainly befal them, if they ftill continued in their difobedience. " O that they were wife, that they un-
" derftood this, that they would confider their lat-
" ter

" ter end !'' that is, the fad confequences of thefe
their provocations, that by the confideration thereof,
they might prevent all thofe evils and calamities, by
turning from thofe fins which would unavoidably
bring them upon them.

From the words thus explained, I fhall obferve
thefe four things.

I. That God doth really and heartily defire the
happinefs of men, and to prevent their mifery and
ruin. For the very defign of thefe words is to exprefs this to us, and it is done in a very vehement,
and, as I may fay, paffionate manner.

II. That it is a great point of wifdom to confider
ferioufly the laft iffue and confequence of our actions,
whither they tend, and what will follow upon them.
And therefore wifdom is here defcribed by " the con-
" fideration of our latter end.''

III. That this is an excellent means to prevent that
mifery, which will otherwife befal us. And this
is neceffarily implied in this wifh, that if they would
but confider thefe things, they might be prevented.

IV. That the want of this confideration is the
great caufe of mens ruin. And this is likewife implied in the words, that one great reafon of mens
ruin is, becaufe they are not fo wife, as to confider
the fatal iffue and confequence of a finful courfe. I
fhall fpeak briefly to each of thefe.

I. That God doth really and heartily defire the
happinefs of men, and to prevent their mifery and
ruin. To exprefs this to us, God doth put on the
vehemency of a human paffion, " O that they were
" wife,'' &c. The laws of God are a clear evidence of this ; becaufe the obfervance of them tends
to our happinefs. There is no good prince makes
laws with any other defign, than to promote the
" publick

publick welfare and happinefs of his people : and
with much more reafon may we imagine, that the
infinite good God does by all his laws defign the
happinefs of his creatures. And the exhortations of
fcripture, by which he enforceth his laws, are yet
a greater evidence how earneftly he defires the happinefs of his creatures. For it fhews that he is concerned for us, when he ufeth fo many arguments to
perfuade us to our duty, and when he expoftulates
fo vehemently with us for our neglect of it, faying
to finners, " Turn ye, turn ye, why will ye die, O
" houfe of Ifrael?" " Ye will not come unto me, that
" ye might have life," fays our bleffed SAVIOUR,
with great trouble to fee men fo obftinately fet a-
gainft their own happinefs ; and again, " How of-
" ten would I have gathered you, as a hen gathereth
" her chickens under her wings, and ye would not !"
And to fatisfy us yet farther, that it is his real defire, by our obedience to his laws, to prevent our
ruin, God does frequently in fcripture put on the
paffions of men, and ufe all forts of vehement expreffions to this purpofe, Deut. v. 29. " O that
" there were fuch a heart in them, that they would
" fear me, and keep all my commandments always,
" that it might be well with them, and with their
" children for ever !" And Pfal. lxxxi. 13. " O
" that my people had hearkned unto me, and Ifrael
" had walked in my ways ! I fhould foon have fub-
" dued their enemies, and turned my hand againft
" their adverfaries." Jer. xiii. 27. " O Ifrael ! wilt
" thou not be made clean ? When fhall it once be ?"
And to name but one text more, when our bleffed
SAVIOUR wept over Jerufalem, how paffionately
does he wifh that " fhe had known in that her day,
" the things that belonged to her peace !"

And

And if after all this we can doubt whether the faithful God means as he says, he hath for our farther assurance, and to put the matter out of all doubt, confirmed his word by an oath, Ezek. xxxiii. 11. "As I live, saith the Lord God, I have no "pleasure in the death of the wicked, but that the "wicked turn from his ways and live. Turn ye, "turn ye from your evil ways; for why will ye die, "O house of Israel?" So that if words can be any declaration of a hearty and sincere desire, we have no reason to doubt, but that God does really desire the happiness of men, and would gladly prevent their ruin and destruction.

If any now ask, Why then are not all men happy? Why do they not escape ruin and destruction? And particularly why the people of Israel, for whom God here makes this wish, did not escape those judgments which were threatened; the prophet shall answer for me, Hos. xiii. 9. "O Israel! thou hast "destroyed thyself." And David, Psal. lxxxi. 11. "My people would not hearken to my voice, Israel "would none of me." And our blessed Saviour, Matt. xxiii. 37. "How often would I have ga- "thered thee, as a hen gathereth her chickens un- "der her wings, and ye would not!" And John v. 40. "Ye will not come unto me, that ye might "have life." You see what account the scripture plainly gives of this matter; it rests upon the wills of men, and God hath not thought fit to force happiness upon men, and to make them wise and good whether they will or no. He presents men with such motives, and offers such arguments to their considera-tion, as are fit to prevail with reasonable men, and is ready to afford them all necessary assistance, if they be not wanting to themselves; but if they will not

be

be wife and confider, if they will ftand out againft all the arguments that God can offer, if they will receive the grace of God in vain, and refift his bleffed Spirit, and reject the counfel of God againft themfelves, God hath not in this cafe engaged himfelf to provide any remedy againft the obftinacy and perverfenefs of men, but " their deftruc-" tion is of themfelves, and their blood fhall be " upon their own heads." And there is no nicety and intricacy in this matter ; but if men will confider fcripture and reafon impartially, they will find this to be the plain refolution of the cafe.

So that no man hath reafon either to charge his fault, or his punifhment upon God ; he is " free " from the blood of all men ;" he fincerely defires • our happinefs ; but we wilfully ruin ourfelves : and when he tells, that " he defires not the death of " a finner, but rather that he fhould turn from his " wickednefs and live ; that he would have all men " to be faved, and to come to the knowledge of the " truth ; that he is not willing that any fhould pe-" rifh, but that all fhould come to repentance ; he plainly means as he fays, and doth not fpeak to us with any referve, or dark diftinction between his fecret and revealed will, he does not decree one thing, and declare another.

And if this be fo, no man hath reafon to be difcouraged from attempting and endeavouring his own happinefs, upon a jealoufy and furmife that God hath by any fatal decree put a bar to it from all eternity : for if he had fo abfolutely refolved to make the greateft part of mankind miferable, without any refpect to their actions in this world, he would never have faid, that " he defires that all fhould be faved ;" he would not have exhorted all men " to work out "their own salvation:" had he taken up any such resolution, he would have declared it to all the world: for he hath power enough in his hand, "to do what he pleaseth, and none can resist his will;" so that he did not need to have dissembled the matter, and to have pretended a desire to save men, when he was resolved to ruin them.

This is the first, that God doth really and heartily desire the happiness of men, and to prevent their misery and ruin. I proceed to the

II. That it is a great part of wisdom to consider seriously the last issue and consequence of our actions, and whither the course of life which we lead does tend, and what will follow upon it. And therefore wisdom is here explained by consideration, "O that they were wise, that they would consider their latter end!" that is, what will befal them hereafter, what will be the issue and consequence of all the sins and provocations which they are guilty of.

And this is a principal point and property of wisdom, to look forward, and not only to consider the present pleasure and advantage of any action, but the future consequence of it: and there is no greater argument of an imprudent man, than to gratify himself for the present in the doing of a thing, which will turn to his greater prejudice afterwards; especially if the future inconvenience be great and intolerable, as it is in the case we are speaking of. For eternal happiness or misery depends upon the actions of this present life, and according as we behave ourselves in this world, it will go well or ill with us for ever; so that this is a matter of vast importance, and deserves our most serious thoughts; and in matters of mighty consequence, a wise man will take all things into consideration, and look before him as far

as

as he can. And indeed this is the reason why things of great moment are said to be things of consequence, because great things depend and are likely to follow upon them : and then surely that is the greatest concernment, upon which not only the happiness of this present life, but our happiness to all eternity does depend; and if the good and bad actions of this life be of that consequence to us, it is fit every man should consider what he does, and whither the course of life he is engaged or about to engage in, will lead him at last. For this is true wisdom, to look to the end of things, and to think seriously beforehand, what is likely to be the event of such an action, of such a course of life : if we serve God faithfully and do his will, what will be the consequence of that to us in this world, and the other : and on the other hand, if we live wickedly, and allow ourselves in any unlawful and vicious practice, what will be the end of that course.

And to any man that consults the law of his own nature, or the will of God revealed in scripture, nothing can be plainer than what will be the end of these several ways. God hath plainly told us, and our own consciences will tell us the same, that "if we " do well, we shall be accepted" of God, and rewarded by him: but if we do ill, " the end of these things " is death ;" that " indignation and wrath, tribulati- " on and anguish will be upon every soul of man " that doth evil ; but honour and glory and peace " to every man that doth good, in the day when " God shall judge the secrets of men by Jesus " Christ, according to the gospel "

So that God hath given us a plain prospect of the different issues of a virtuous and a wicked life, and there wants nothing but consideration to make us to

attend

attend to these things, and to lay them seriously to heart. For while men are inconsiderate, they go on stupidly in an evil way, and are not sensible of the danger of their present course, because they do not attend to the consequence of it: but when their eyes are once opened by consideration, they cannot but be sadly apprehensive of the mischief they are running themselves upon. If men would take but a serious and impartial view of their lives and actions, if they would consider the tendency of a sinful course, and whither it will bring them at last; if the vicious and dissolute man would but look about him, and consider how many have been ruined in that very way that he is in, how many lye " slain and wounded " in it; that it is the way to hell, and leads down " to the chambers of death ;" the serious thought of this could not but check him in his course, and make him resolve upon a better life. If men were wise, they would consider the consequence of their actions, and upon consideration would resolve upon that which they are convinced is best. I proceed to the

III. Thing I propounded, which was, that consideration of the consequence of our actions is an excellent means to prevent the mischiefs, which otherwise we should run into. And this is necessarily implied in the wish here in the text, that if we would but consider these things, they might be prevented. For how can any man, who hath any love or regard for himself, any tenderness for his own interest and happiness, see hell and destruction before him, which, if he hold on in his evil course, will certainly swallow him up, and yet venture to go on in his sins? Can any man that plainly beholds misery hastening towards him " like an armed man, and destruction " coming upon him as a whirlwind," think himself
unconcerned

unconcerned to prevent it and flie from it? The moft dull and ftupid creatures will ftart back upon the fight of prefent danger. Balaam's afs, when fhe faw the angel of the LORD ftanding in the way, with his fword drawn ready to fmite her, ftarts afide, and could not be urged on. Now GOD hath given us, not only fenfe to apprehend a prefent evil, but reafon and confideration to look before us, and to difcover dangers at a diftance, to apprehend them as certainly, and with as clear a conviction of the reality of them, as if they threatened us the next moment: and will any confiderate man, who hath calculated the dangerous events of fin, and the dreadful effects of GOD's wrath upon finners, go on to " provoke " the LORD to jealoufy, as if he were ftronger than " he ?" It is not to be imagined, but that if men would ferioufly confider what fin is, and what fhall be the fad portion of finners hereafter, they would refolve upon a better courfe. Would any man live in the lufts of the flefh, and of intemperance, or out of covetoufnefs defraud or opprefs his neighbour, did he ferioufly confider, that " GOD is the " avenger of fuch ;" and that " becaufe of thefe " things the wrath of GOD comes upon the chil- " dren of difobedience."

I fhould have great hopes of mens repentance and reformation, if they could but once be brought to confideration : for in moft men it is not fo much a pofitive difbelief of the truth, as inadvertency and want of confideration, that makes them to go on fo fecurely in a finful courfe. Would but men confider what fin is, and what will be the fearful confequence of it, probably in this world, but moft certainly in the other, they could not chufe but fly from it as the greateft evil in the world.

I

And

And to shew what power and influence consideration will probably have to bring men to repentance,
and a change of their lives, I remember to have
somewhere met with a very remarkable story, of one
that had a son that took bad courses, and would not
be reclaimed by all the good counsel his father could
give him; at last coming to his father, who lay upon his death-bed, to beg his blessing, his father instead of upbraiding him with his bad life, and undutiful carriage toward him, spake kindly to him, and
told him he had but one thing to desire of him, that
every day he would retire and spend one quarter of
an hour alone by himself; which he promised his
father faithfully to do, and made it good. After
a while it grew tedious to him, to spend even so little time in such bad and uneasy company, and he
began to bethink himself, for what reason his father should so earnestly desire of him to do so odd
a thing for his sake, and his mind presently suggest-
ed to him, that it was to enforce him to consideration; wisely judging that if by any means he could
but bring him to that, he would soon reform his life
and become a new man. And the thing had its de-
sired effect; for after a very little consideration, he
took up a firm resolution to change the course of his
life, and was true to it all his days. I cannot answer
for the truth of the story, but for the moral of it I
will; namely, that consideration is one of the best
and most likely means in the world, to bring a bad
man to a better mind. I now come to the

IV. and last particular, namely, that the want of
this consideration is one of the greatest causes of mens
ruin. And this likewise is implied in the text; and
the reason why God does so vehemently desire that
men would be wise and consider, is, because so many
are

are ruined and undone for want of it. This is the S E R M.
defperate folly of mankind, that they feldom think CLXXII.
ferioufly of the confequence of their actions, and leaft
of all of fuch as are of greateft concernment to them,
and have the chief influence upon their eternal condition. They do not confider what mifchief and inconvenience a wicked life may plunge them into in
this world, what trouble and difturbance it may give
them when they come to die ; what horror and confufion it may fill them withal when they are leaving
this world, and paffing into eternity ; and what intolerable mifery and torment it may bring upon them
to all eternity. Did men ponder and lay to heart
death and judgment, heaven and hell ; and would
they but let their thoughts dwell upon thefe things,
it is not credible that the generality of men could
lead fuch profane and impious, fuch lewd and diffolute, fuch fecure and carelefs lives as they do.

Would but a man frequently entertain his mind
with fuch thoughts as thefe ; I muft fhortly die and
leave this world, and then all the pleafures and enjoyments of it will be to me as if they had never
been, only that the remembrance of them, and the
ill ufe I have made of them, will be very bitter and
grievous to me ; after all, death will tranfmit me out
of this world, into a quite different ftate and fcene
of things, into the prefence of that great and terrible,
that inflexible and impartial judge, who will " ren-
" der to every man according to his works ;" and
then all the evils which I have done in this life, will
rife up in judgment againft me, and fill me with everlafting confufion, in that great affembly of men and
angels, will banifh me from the prefence of God,
and all the happinefs which flows from it, and procure a dreadful fentence of unfpeakable mifery and
torment

torment to be paft upon me, which I can never get
reverfed, nor yet ever be able to ftand under the weight
of it.   If men would but enter into the ferious confideration of thefe things, and purfue thefe thoughts
to fome iffue and conclufion, they would take up
other refolutions ; and I verily believe, that the want
of this hath ruined more than even infidelity itfelf.
And this I take to be the meaning of that queftion
in the Pfalmift, "Have all the workers of iniquity
" no knowledge ?" that is, no confideration ; intimating that if they had, they would do better.

All that now remains, is to perfuade men to apply their hearts to this piece of wifdom, to look before them, and to think ferioufly of the confequence
of their actions, what will be the final iffue of that
courfe of life they are engaged in ; and if they continue in it, what will become of them hereafter, what
will become of them for ever.

And here I might apply this text, as God here
does to the people of Ifrael, to the publick condition
of this nation, which is not fo very unlike to that of
the people of Ifrael : for God feems to have chofen
this nation for his more peculiar people, and hath
exercifed a very particular providence towards us, in
conducting us through that wildernefs of confufion,
in which we have been wandring for the fpace of
above forty years ; and when things were come to
the laft extremity, and we feemed to ftand upon the
very brink of ruin, " Then (as it is faid of the
people of Ifrael, ver. 36. of this chapter) " God
" repented himfelf for his fervants, when he faw
" their power was gone :" that is, that they were
utterly unable to help themfelves, and to work
their own deliverance.   And it may be faid of us,
as Mofes does of that people, chap. xxxiii. 29.
" Happy

" Happy art thou, O Ifrael, O people faved by the S E R M.
" LORD, the fhield of thy help, and who is the CLXXII.
" fword of thy excellency !" Never did any nation
ftruggle with, and get through fo many and fo great
difficulties, as we have feveral times done.

And I fear we have behaved ourfelves towards GOD,
not much better than the people of Ifrael did, but
like Jefurun, after many deliverances and great mercies, " have waxed fat and kicked, have forfaken
" the GOD that made us, and little efteemed the
" rock of our falvation ;" by which we have " pro-
" voked the LORD to jealoufy," and have as it
were forced him to multiply his judgments, and to
fpend his arrows upon us, and " to hide his face from
" us, to fee what our end will be ;" fo that we have
reafon to fear, that GOD would have brought utter
ruin and deftruction upon us, and " fcattered us in-
" to corners, and made the remembrance of us to
" have ceafed from among men, had he not feared
" the wrath of the enemy, and left the adverfaries
" fhould have behaved themfelves ftrangely, and left
" they fhould fay, our hand is high, and the LORD
" hath not done all this ;" that is, left they fhould
afcribe this juft vengeance of GOD upon a finful and
unthankful nation to the goodnefs and righteoufnefs
of their own caufe, and to the favour and affiftance
of the idols and falfe gods whom they worfhipped,
tc the patronage and aid of the virgin Mary and
the faints, to whom, contrary to the will and command of the true GOD, they had offer'd up fo many
prayers and vows, and paid the greateft part of their
religious worfhip. But " the LORD hath fhewn
" himfelf greater than all gods, and in the things
" wherein they dealt proudly, that he is above them :

" for our rock is not as their rock, even our enemies
" themfelves being judges."

And we have been too like the people of Ifrael in
other refpects alfo, fo fickle and inconftant, that after
great deliverances we are apt prefently to murmur
and be difcontented, to grow fick of our own happinefs, and " to turn back in our hearts into Egypt;"
fo that GOD may complain of us, as he does of his
people Ifrael, that nothing that he could do would
bring them to confideration, and make them better,
neither his mercies nor his judgments. Ifa. i. 2, 3.
" Hear, O heavens! and give ear, O earth! For the
" LORD hath fpoken; I have nourifhed and brought
" up children, but they have rebelled againft me.
" The ox knoweth his owner, and the afs his mafter's
" crib: but Ifrael doth not know, my people doth
" not confider." And fo likewife he complains,
that his judgments had no effect upon them, ver. 5.
" Why fhould ye be fmitten any more? Ye will
" revolt more and more." Well therefore may it
be faid of us, as it was of them in the verfe before
the text, " they are a nation void of knowledge,
" neither is there any underftanding in them." And
the wifh that follows in the text is as feafonable for
us as it was for them, " O that they were wife, that
" they underftood this, that they would confider
" their latter end!"

And by parity of reafon, this may likewife be applied to particular perfons, and to perfuade every one
of us to a ferious confideration of the final iffue and
confequence of our actions, I will only offer thefe two
arguments.

I. That confideration is the proper act of reafonable creatures, and that whereby we fhew ourfelves
men. So the prophet intimates, Ifa. xlvi. 8. "Re-
                                          " member

" member this, and shew yourselves men ; bring it
" again to mind, O ye transgressors !" that is, consider it well, think of it again and again, ye that run
on so furiously in a sinful course, what the end and
issue of these things will be. If ye do not do this,
you do not " shew yourselves men," you do not
act like reasonable creatures, to whom it is peculiar to propose to themselves some end and design
of their actions ; but rather like " brute creatures,
" which have no understanding," and act only by
a natural instinct, without any consideration of the
end of their actions, or of the means conducing to it.

II. Whether we consider it or not, our latter end
will come ; and all those dismal consequences of a
sinful course, which God hath so plainly threatened,
and our own consciences do so much dread, will certainly overtake us at last ; and we cannot, by not
thinking of these things, ever prevent or avoid them.
Death will come, and after that the judgment, and
an irreversible doom will pass upon us, according to
all the evil that we have done, and all the good that
we have neglected to do in this life, under the heavy
weight and pressure whereof we must lye groaning,
and bewailing ourselves to everlasting ages.

God now exerciseth his mercy and patience and
long-suffering towards us, in expectation of our
amendment ; he reprieves us on purpose that we may
repent, and in hopes that we will at last consider and
grow wiser ; for " he is not willing that any should
" perish, but that all should come to repentance :"
but if we will trifle away this day of God's grace
and patience, if we will not consider and bethink
ourselves, there is another day that will certainly
come, " that great and terrible day of the Lord,
" in which the heavens shall pass away with a great

20 C 2   " noise,

" noife, and the elements fhall melt with fervent
" heat ; the earth alfo, and the works that are there-
" in fhall be burnt up."

" Seeing then all thefe things fhall be," let us confider ferioufly " what manner of perfons we ought to
" be in all holy converfation and godlinefs, waiting
" for and haftening unto the coming of the day of
" GOD ; to whom be glory now and for ever."

SERMON CLXXIII.

The danger of impenitence, where the gofpel is preached.

MATT. xi. 21, 22.

*Woe unto thee Chorazin, woe unto thee Bethfaida!
for if the mighty works which were done in you,
had been done in Tyre and Sidon, they would have
repented long ago in fackcloth and afhes. But I
fay unto you, It fhall be more tolerable for Tyre and
Sidon at the day of judgment, than for you.*

SERM.
LXXIII.
AFTER our bleffed SAVIOUR had inftructed,
and fent forth his difciples, he himfelf went
abroad to preach unto the cities of Ifrael ; particularly he fpent much time in the cities of Galilee, Chorazin, and Bethfaida, and Capernaum, preaching the
gofpel to them, and working many and great miracles among them ; but with little or no fuccefs :
which was the caufe of his denouncing this terrible
woe againft them, ver. 20. " Then began he to
" upbraid the cities, wherein moft of his mighty
" works

" works were done, becaufe they repented not. Woe
" unto thee Chorazin," &c.

In which words our SAVIOUR declares the fad and miferable condition of thofe two cities, Chorazin and Bethfaida, which had negle&ed fuch an opportunity, and refifted and withftood fuch means of repentance, as would have effeftually reclaimed the moft wicked cities and people that can be inftanced in any age, Tyre and Sidon and Sodom ; and therefore he tells them, that their condition was much worfe, and that they fhould fall under a heavier fentence at the day of judgment, than the people of thofe cities, whom they had always looked upon as the greateft finners that ever were in the world. This is the plain meaning of the words in general ; but yet there are fome difficulties in them, which I fhall endeavour to clear, and then proceed to raife fuch obfervations from them, as may be inftruftive and ufeful to us.

The difficulties are thefe :

I. What repentance is here fpoken of; whether an external repentance, in fhew and appearance only, or an inward and real and fincere repentance.

II. In what fenfe it is faid, that " Tyre and Sidon " would have repented."

III. What is meant by their " would have repent- " ed long ago."

IV. How this affertion of our SAVIOUR, that miracles would have converted Tyre and Sidon, is reconcilable with that other faying of his, Luk. xvi. 31. in the parable of the rich man and Lazarus, that " thofe who believed not Mofes and the prophets, " neither would they be perfuaded, though one rofe " from the dead."

I. What repentance is here fpoken of ; whether a mere external and hypocritical repentance in fhew

SERM. and appearance only, or an inward and real and fin-
CLXXIII. cere repentance.

The reafon of this doubt depends upon the different theories of divines, about the fufficiency of
grace accompanying the outward means of repentance, and whether an irrefiftible degree of God's
grace be neceffary to repentance : for they who deny
fufficient grace to accompany the outward means of
repentance, and affert an irrefiftible degree of God's
grace neceffary to repentance, are forced to fay, that
our Saviour here fpeaks of a mere external repentance : becaufe if he fpake of an inward and fincere
repentance, then it muft be granted, that fufficient
inward grace did accompany the miracles that were
wrought in Chorazin and Bethfaida, to bring men to
repentance ; becaufe what was afforded to them,
would have brought Tyre and Sidon to repentance.
And that which would have effected a thing, cannot
be denied to be fufficient ; fo that unlefs our Saviour here fpeaks of a mere external repentance, either
the outward means of repentance, as preaching and
miracles, muft be granted to be fufficient to bring
men to repentance, . without the inward operation of
God's grace upon the minds of men; or elfe a fufficient degree of God's grace muft be acknowledged
to accompany the outward means of repentance.
Again, if an irrefiftible degree of grace be neceffary
to true repentance, it is plain, Chorazin and Bethfaida had it not, becaufe they did not repent ; and
yet without this Tyre and Sidon could not fincerely
have repented ; therefore our Saviour here muft
fpeak of a mere external repentance. Thus fome argue, as they do likewife concerning the repentance of
Nineveh, making that alfo to be merely external, becaufe they are loth to allow true repentance to heathens.   But

But it feems very plain, that our SAVIOUR does
fpeak of an inward and true and fincere repentance;
and therefore the doctrines that will not admit this, are
not true. For our SAVIOUR fpeaks of the fame kind
of repentance, that he upbraided them with the want
of, in the verfe before the text. "Then began he
" to upbraid the cities wherein moft of his mighty
" works were done, becaufe they repented not;"
that is, becaufe they were not brought to a fincere
repentance by his preaching, which was confirmed
by fuch great miracles. It is true indeed, he mentions the outward figns and expreffions of repentance,
when he fays, "they would have repented in fack-
" cloth and afhes;" but not as excluding inward
and real repentance, but fuppofing it, as is evident
from what is faid in the next verfe, "It fhall be more
" tolerable for Tyre and Sidon at the day of judg-
" ment, than for you:" for though an external and
hypocritical repentance may prevail with GOD to put
off temporal judgments, yet furely it will be but a very
fmall, if any mitigation of our condemnation at the
day of judgment: fo that the repentance here fpoken
of cannot, without great violence to the fcope and
defign of our SAVIOUR's argument, be underftood
only of an external fhew and appearance of repentance.

II. The next difficulty to be cleared, is, in what
fenfe it is here faid, that "if the mighty works
" which were done" by our SAVIOUR among the
Jews, "had been done in Tyre and Sidon, they
" would have repented."

Some to avoid the inconvenience which they apprehend to be in the more ftrict and literal fenfe of
the words, look upon them as hyperbolical, as we
fay fuch a thing would move a ftone, or the like,
when we would exprefs fomething to be very fad and
grievous;

SERM grievous ; fo here to aggravate the impenitence of
CXXLIII. the Jews, our Saviour fays, that they refifted
thofe means of repentance, which one would think
fhould almoft have prevailed upon the greateft and
moft obdurate finners that ever were ; but not intending to affirm any fuch thing.

But there is no colour for this, if we confider that
our Saviour reafons from the fuppofition of fuch a
thing, that therefore the cafe of Tyre and Sidon
would really be " more tolerable at the day of judg-
" ment than theirs ;" becaufe they would have repented, but the Jews did not.

Others perhaps underftand the words too ftrictly,
as if our Saviour had fpoken according to what he
certainly foreknew would have happened to the people of Tyre and Sidon, if fuch miracles had been
wrought among them. And no doubt but in that
cafe God did certainly know what they would have
done : but yet I fhould rather chufe to underftand the
words as fpoken popularly, according to what in all
human appearance and probability would have happened, if fuch external means of repentance, accompanied with an ordinary grace of God, had been
afforded to them of Tyre and Sidon. And thus the old
Latin interpreter feems to have underftood the next
words, " if the mighty works which have been
" done in thee, had been done in Sodom, $\xi\mu\epsilon\iota\nu\alpha\nu$ $\overset{\,\prime\prime}{\alpha}\nu$, "
forte manfiffent, " it would perhaps have remained
" to this day, in all likelihood it had continued till
" now." Much the fame with that paffage of the
prophet, Ezek. iii. 5, 6. " Thou art not fent to a
" people of a ftrange fpeech, and of a hard lan-
" guage, but to the houfe of Ifrael : Surely had I
" fent thee to them, they would have hearkened un-
" to thee ;" that is, in all probability they would,

    I   there

there is little doubt to be made of the contrary. And
this is sufficient foundation for our SAVIOUR's reason-
ing afterwards, that " it shall be more tolerable for
" Tyre and Sidon in the day of judgment than for
" them." And if we may judge what they would
have done before, by what they did afterward, there is
more than probability for it : for we read in the 21st
chapter of the Acts, ver. 3. and ver. 27. that the inhabitants of Tyre and Sidon received the gospel, and
kindly entertained St. Paul, when the Jews rejected
them both. The

III. Thing to be cleared, is, what is meant by
long ago ; " they would have repented long ago."

Some understand this, as if our SAVIOUR had
said, they would not have stood out so long against
so much preaching, and so many miracles ; but would
at first have repented, long before our SAVIOUR
gave over Chorazin and Bethsaida for obstinate and
incorrigible sinners ; they would not only have repented at last, but much sooner and without so
much ado.

But this does not seem to be the meaning of the
words ; but our SAVIOUR seems to refer to those
ancient times long ago, when the prophets denounced judgments against Tyre and Sidon, particularly
the prophet Ezekiel ; and to say, that if in those days
the preaching of that prophet had been accompanied
with such miracles as our SAVIOUR wrought in the
cities of Galilee, Tyre and Sidon would in those
days have repented.

The last and greatest difficulty of all is, how this
assertion of our SAVIOUR, that miracles would have
converted Tyre and Sidon, is reconcilable with that
discourse of our SAVIOUR's, Luke xvi. in the parable of the rich man and Lazarus, that " those

" who would not believe Mofes and the prophets,
" would not have been perfuaded, though one had
" rofe from the dead."

The true anfwer to which difficulty in fhort is
this ; that when our SAVIOUR fays, " if they be-
" lieve not Mofes and the prophets, neither will
" they be perfuaded though one rofe from the dead,"
he does not hereby weaken the force of miracles, or
their aptnefs to convince men and bring them to repentance, but rather confirm it ; becaufe Mofes and
the prophets had the atteftation of many and great
miracles, and therefore there was no reafon to think,
that they who would not believe the writings and
doctrine of Mofes and the prophets, which had the
confirmation of fo many miracles, and was owned by
themfelves to have fo, fhould be wrought upon by
one particular miracle, " the coming of one from
" the dead, and fpeaking unto them:" or however
this might move and aftonifh them for the prefent,
yet it was not likely that the grace of GOD fhould
concur with fuch an extraordinary means, to render it effectual to their converfion and repentance,
who had wilfully defpifed and obftinately rejected
that which had a much greater confirmation, than the
difcourfe of a man rifen from the dead, and was appointed by GOD for the ordinary and ftanding means
of bringing men to repentance. So that our SAVI-
OUR might with reafon enough pronounce that Tyre
and Sidon, who never had a ftanding revelation of
GOD to bring them to repentance, nor had rejected
it, would upon miracles extraordinarily wrought a-
mong them, have repented ; and yet deny it elfewhere to be likely, that they who rejected a ftanding revelation of GOD, confirmed by miracles, which
called them to repentance, would probably be brought

to

to repentance by a particular miracle ; or that God should afford his grace to make it effectual for their repentance and salvation.

The words being thus cleared, I come now to raise such observations from them, as may be instructive and useful to us.

I. I observe from this discourse of our SAVIOUR, that miracles are of great force and efficacy to bring men to repentance.

This our SAVIOUR's discourse here supposeth ; otherwise their impenitence had not been so criminal and inexcusable upon that account, " that such " mighty works had been done among them," as would probably have prevailed upon some of the worst people that had been in the world ; for such were the inhabitants of Tyre and Sidon, guilty of great covetousness and fraud, pride and luxury, the usual sins of places of great traffick and commerce : and such to be sure was Sodom ; and yet our SAVIOUR tells us, that the miracles which he had wrought in the cities of Israel, would in all probability have brought those great sinners to repentance ; namely, by bringing them to faith, and convincing them of the truth and divinity of that doctrine which he preached unto them, and which contains such powerful arguments to repentance. and amendment of life.

II. I observe likewise from our SAVIOUR's discourse, that God is not always obliged to work miracles for the conversion of sinners. It is great goodness in him to afford sufficient means of repentance to men, as he did to Tyre and Sidon, in calling them to repentance by his prophet ; though such miracles were not wrought among them, as God thought fit to accompany our SAVIOUR's preaching withal.

10 D 2   THS

This I obferve, to prevent a kind of bold and faucy objection, which fome would perhaps be apt to make; if Tyre and Sidon would have repented, had fuch miracles been wrought among them, as our SAVIOUR wrought in Chorazin and Bethfaida, why were they not wrought, that they might have repented? To which it is fufficient anfwer to fay, that GOD is not obliged to do all that is poffible to be done, to, reclaim men from their fins; he is not obliged to overpower their wills, and to work irrefiftibly upon their minds, which he can eafily do; he is not obliged to work miracles for every particular man's conviction; nor where he vouchfafeth to do this, is he obliged always to work the greateft and moft convincing miracles; his goodnefs will not fuffer him to omit what is neceffary and fufficient to bring men to repentance and happinefs, nay beyond this he many times does more; but it is fufficient to vindicate the juftice and goodnefs of GOD, that he is not wanting to us, in affording the means neceffary to reclaim us from our fins, and to bring us to goodnefs. That which is properly our part, is to make ufe of thofe means which GOD affords us to become better, and not to prefcribe to him how much he fhould do for us; to be thankful that he hath done fo much, and not to find fault with him for having done no more.

III. I obferve farther from our SAVIOUR's difcourfe, that the external means of repentance which GOD affords to men, do fuppofe an inward grace of GOD accompanying them, fufficiently enabling men to repent, if it be not their own fault; I fay a fufficient grace of GOD accompanying the outward means of repentance, till by our wilful and obftinate neglect and refiftance and oppofition of ths grace, we provoke God to withdraw it from the means, or

I   elfe else to withdraw both the grace and the means from us; otherwise impenitence after such external means afforded, would be no new and special fault. For if the concurrence of God's grace with the outward means be necessary to work repentance, then the impenitence of those to whom this grace is not afforded, which yet is necessary to repentance, is neither any new sin, nor any new aggravation of their former impenitence. For no man can imagine that the just God will charge men with new guilt, and increase their condemnation, for remaining impenitent in such circumstances in which it is impossible for them to repent.

IV. I observe from this discourse of our SAVIOUR's, that an irresistible degree of grace is not necessary to repentance, nor commonly afforded to those who do repent. God may where he pleaseth, without injury to any man, over-power his will, and stop him in his course, and hinder him from making himself miserable, and by an irresistible right convince him of his error and the evil of his ways, and bring him to a better mind: But this God seldom does; and when he does it, it is very probable it is not so much for their own sakes, as to make them instruments of good to others. Thus by a secret but over-powering influence he over-ruled the disciples to follow our SAVIOUR, and to leave their calling and relations, and all their temporal concernments to do it. But one of the most remarkable examples of this extraordinary grace of God, is St. Paul, who was violently stopt in his course of persecuting the Christians, and convinced of his sin, and brought over to christianity, in a very extraordinary and forcible manner. And of this miraculous and extraordinary conversion, God himself gives this account, " that he " was a chosen vessel unto him, to bear his name
" before

" before the Gentiles and kings, and the children of
" Ifrael," Acts. ix. 15.   And St. Paul tells us, Gal.
i. 15, 16. " That for this end God had feparated
" him from his mother's womb, and called him by
" his grace, and revealed his Son to him" in that
extraordinary manner, " that he might preach him
" among the heathen."

But generally God does not bring men thus to repentance ; nor is it neceffary he fhould.   For if an
irrefiftible degree of grace were always neceffary to
bring men to repentance, there could be no difference
between the impenitence of Chorazin and Bethfaida,
and of Tyre and Sidon.   For according to this doctrine of the neceffity of irrefiftible grace to the converfion of every man, it is evident, that Tyre and
Sidon neither could, nor would have repented, without an irrefiftible degree of God's grace, accompanying the outward means of repentance which he afforded to them ; becaufe fuch a degree of grace is
neceffary to repentance, and without it, it is impoffible for any man to repent.   But then it is as plain
on the contrary, that if Chorazin and Bethfaida had
had the fame irrefiftible degree of God's grace, together with the outward means of repentance afforded to them, that they would have repented as certainly as Tyre and Sidon.   Where then is the reafon
of upbraiding the impenitence of the one, more than
of the other?   Where the aggravation of the one's
guilt above the other ?   Where the juftice of punifh-
ing the impenitence of Chorazin and Bethfaida,
more than theirs of Tyre and Sidon ?   For upon this
fuppofition, they muft either have repented both alike,
or have been both equally impenitent.   The fum of
what I have faid, is this, that if no man does, nor
can repent, without fuch a degree of God's grace as
                                                            cannot

cannot be resisted, no man's repentance is commendable, nor is one man's impenitence more blameable than another's ; Chorazin and Bethsaida can be in no more fault for continuing impenitent, than Tyre and Sidon were. For either this irresistible grace is afforded to men or not : if it be, their repentance is necessary, and they cannot help it ; if it be not, their repentance is impossible, and consequently their impenitence is necessary, and they cannot help it neither.

V. I observe from the main scope of our SAVIOUR's discourse, that the sins and impenitence of men receive their aggravation, and consequently shall have their punishment proportionable to the opportunities and means of repentance, which those persons have enjoyed and neglected.

For what is here said of miracles, is by equality of reason likewise true of all other advantages and means of repentance and salvation. The reason why miracles will be such an aggravation of the condemnation of men is, because they are so proper and powerful a means to convince them of the truth and divinity of that doctrine which calls them to repentance. So that all those means which GOD affords to us of the knowledge of our duty, of conviction of the evil and danger of a sinful course, are so many helps and motives to repentance, and consequently will prove so many aggravations of our sin and punishment, if we continue impenitent. The

VI. and last observation, and which naturally follows from the former, is this, that the case of those who are impenitent under the gospel, is of all others the most dangerous, and their damnation shall be heaviest and most severe.

And this brings the case of these cities here in the text home to ourselves. For in truth there is no material

terial difference between the cafe of Chorazin and Bethfaida and Capernaum, and of ourfelves in this city and nation, who enjoy the clear light of the gofpel, with all the freedom, and all the advantages that any people ever did. The mercies of GOD to this nation have been very great, efpecially in bringing us out of that darknefs and fuperftition, which covered this weftern part of the world; in refcuing us from that great corruption and degeneracy of the chriftian religion which prevailed among us, by fo early and fo regular a reformation; and in continuing fo long this great blefling to us. The judgments of GOD have been likewife very great upon us for our fins: " GOD hath manifefted himfelf by " terrible things in righteoufnefs;" our eyes have feen many and difmal calamities in the fpace of a few years, which call loudly upon us to repent and turn to GOD. GOD hath afforded us the moft effectual means of repentance, and hath taken the moft effectual courfe of bringing us to it. And though our blefled SAVIOUR do not fpeak to us in perfon, nor do we at this day fee miracles wrought among us, as the Jews did; yet we have the doctrine which our blefled SAVIOUR preached, faithfully tranfmitted to us, and a credible relation of the miracles wrought for the confirmation of that doctrine, and many other arguments to perfuade us of the truth of it, which thofe to whom our SAVIOUR fpake had not, nor could not then have, taken from the accomplifhing of our SAVIOUR's predictions, after his death; the fpeedy propagation and wonderful fuccefs of this doctrine in the world, by weak and inconfiderable means, againft all the power and oppofition of the world; the deftruction of Jerufalem, and the difperfion of the Jewifh nation, according to our SAVIOUR's prophecy;

phecy; besides many more that might be mentioned. And which is a mighty advantage to us, we are
free from those prejudices against the person of our
Saviour and his doctrine, which the Jews, by the
reverence which they bare to their rulers and teach-
ers, were generally possess'd withal; we are brought
up in the belief of it, and have drunk it in by education; and if we believe it, as we all profess to do,
we have all the obligation and all the arguments to
repentance, which the Jews could possibly have from
the miracles which they saw; for they were means of
repentance to them no otherwise than as they brought
them to the belief of our Saviour's doctrine, which
called them to repentance.

So that if we continue impenitent, the same woe
is denounced against us that is against Chorazin and
Bethsaida; and we may be said with Capernaum,
" to be lifted up to heaven," by the enjoyment of
the most excellent means and advantages of salvation,
that any people ever did, which if we neglect, and
still continue wicked and impenitent under them, we
may justly fear, that with them " we shall be thrown
" down to hell," and have our place in the lowest
part of that dismal dungeon, and in the very center
of that fiery furnace.

Never was there greater cause to upbraid the impenitence of any people, than of us, considering the
means and opportunities which we enjoy; and never
had any greater reason to fear a severer doom, than
we have. Impenitence in a heathen is a great sin;
else how should God judge the world? But God
takes no notice of that, in comparison of the impenitence of Christians, who enjoy the gospel, and are
convinced of the truth, and upon the greatest reason
in the world profess to believe it. We Christians

have all the obligations to repentance, that reason and revelation, nature and grace can lay upon us. Art thou convinced that thou haft finned, and done that which is contrary to thy duty, and thereby provoked the wrath of God, and incenfed his juftice againft thee ? As thou art a man, and upon the ftock of natural principles, thou art obliged to repentance. The fame light of reafon which difcovers to thee the errors of thy life, and challengeth thee for thy impiety and intemperance, for thy injuftice and oppreffion, for thy pride and paffion ; the fame natural confcience which accufeth thee of any mif-carriages, does oblige thee to be forry for them, " to " turn from thy evil ways, and to break off thy " fins by repentance." For nothing can be more unreafonable, than for a man to know a fault, and yet not think himfelf bound to be forry for it ; to be convinced of the evil of his ways, and not to think himfelf obliged by that very conviction, to turn from it and forfake it. If there be any fuch thing as a natural " law written in mens hearts," which the apoftle tells us the heathens had, it is impoffible to imagine, but that the law, which obligeth men not to tranfgrefs, fhould oblige them to repentance in cafe of tranfgreffion. And this every man in the world is bound to, though he had never feen the bible, nor heard of the name of CHRIST. And the revelation of the gofpel doth not fuperfede this obligation, but adds new ftrength and force to it : and by how much this duty of repentance is more clearly revealed by our bleffed SAVIOUR in the gofpel ; by how much the arguments which the gofpel ufeth to perfuade men, and encourage them to repentance, are greater and more powerful.; by fo much is the impenitence of thofe who live under the gofpel the more inexcufable. Had

Had we only some faint hopes of God's mercy, a doubtful opinion and weak persuasion of the rewards and punishments of another world; yet we have a law within us, which upon the probability of these considerations would oblige us to repentance. Indeed if men were assured upon good grounds, that there would be no future rewards and punishments; then the sanction of the law were gone, and it would lose it's force and obligation : or if we did despair of the mercy of God, and had good reason to think repentance impossible, or that it would do us no good ; in that case there would be no sufficient motive and argument to repentance : for no man can return to his duty, without returning to the love of God and goodness ; and no man can return to the love of God, who believes that he bears an implacable hatred against him, and is resolved to make him miserable for ever. During this persuasion no man can repent. And this seems to be the reason, why the devils continue impenitent.

But the heathens were not without hopes of God's mercy, and upon those small hopes which they had, they encouraged themselves into repentance ; as you may see in the instance of the Ninevites, " Let " them turn every one from his evil ways, and from " the violence that is in his hands. Who can tell, " if God will turn and repent, and turn away from " his fierce anger, that we perish not ?" Jonah iii. 8, 9. But if we, who have the clearest discoveries, and the highest assurance of this, who profess to believe that God hath declared himself placable to all mankind, that " he is in Christ reconciling the " world to himself," and that upon our repentance " he " will not impute our sins to us ," if we, to whom " the wrath of God is revealed from heaven, against

" all ungodlinefs and unrighteoufnefs of men," and to whom " life and immortality are brought to light " by the gofpel ;" if after all this, we ftill go on in an impenitent courfe, what fhall we be able to plead in excufe of ourfelves at that great day ? " The men " of Nineveh fhall rife up in judgment" againft fuch an impenitent generation, and condemn it ; be.- caufe they repented upon the terror of lighter threaten- ings, and upon the encouragement of weaker hopes.

And therefore it concerns us, who call ourfelves Chriftians, and enjoy the clear revelation of the gof- pel, to look about us, and take heed how we con- tinue in an evil courfe. For if we remain impenitent, after all the arguments which the gofpel, fuper-added to the light of nature, affords to us to bring us to repentance, it fhall not only " be more tolerable for " the men of Nineveh, but for Tyre and Sidon, for " Sodom and Gomorrah," the moft wicked and impenitent heathens, " at the day of judgment, " than for us." For becaufe we have ftronger ar- guments, and more powerful encouragements to repentance, than they had, if we do not repent, we fhall meet with a heavier doom, and a fiercer dam- nation. The heathen world had many excufes to plead for themfelves, which we have not. " The " times of that ignorance GOD winked at : but now " commands all men every where to repent ; becaufe " he hath appointed a day, in the which he will " judge the world in righteoufnefs, by that man " whom he hath ordained, whereof he hath given " affurance unto all men, in that he hath raifed him " from the dead."

SERMON CLXXIV.

Of the immortality of the foul, as difcovered by nature, and by revelation.

---

2 TIM. i. 10.

But is now made manifeft by the appearing of our
SAVIOUR JESUS CHRIST, *who hath abolifhed*
death, and hath brought life and immortality to
light, through the gofpel.

THE defign of the apoftle in thefe two epi-
ftles to Timothy, is to direct him how he
ought to demean himfelf, in the office which he
bore in the church ; which he does in the firft epiftle : and to encourage him in his work ; which he
does here in the fecond : in which, after his ufual
falutation, he endeavours to arm him againft the fear
of thofe perfecutions, and the fhame of thofe reproaches, which would probably attend him in the
work of the Gofpel, ver. 8. " Be not thou there-
" fore afhamed of the teftimony of our LORD, nor
" of me his prifoner ; but be thou partaker of the
" afflictions of the gofpel, according to the power
" of GOD, who hath faved us, and called us with an
" holy calling ;" as if he had faid, the GOD whom
thou ferveft in this employment, and by whofe power thou art ftrengthened, is he that " hath faved
" and called us with an holy calling," that is, it is
he who by JESUS CHRIST hath brought falvation to
us, and called us to this holy profeffion ; " not ac-
" cording to our works," that is, not that we by
any thing that we have done, have deferved this at

SERM.
CLXXIV.

The firft
fermon on
this text.

his

his hand, but " according to his own purpofe and " grace," that is, according to his own gracious pur- pofe, " which was given us in CHRIST before the " world began," that is, which from all eternity he decreed and determined to accomplifh by JESUS CHRIST ; " but is now made manifeft by the appear- " ing of our SAVIOUR JESUS CHRIST ;" that is, which gracious purpofe of his is now clearly difcover- ed by our SAVIOUR JESUS CHRIST's coming into the world, "who hath abolifhed death, and hath brought " life and immortality to light, through the gofpel."

Which words exprefs to us two happy effects of CHRIST's appearance : firft, " the abolifhing of " death ;" and, fecondly, " the bringing of life and " immortality to light." In the handling of thefe words, I fhall,

Firft, Open to you the meaning of the feveral ex- preffions in the text.

Secondly, Shew what our SAVIOUR JESUS CHRIST did towards " the abolifhing of death, and " bringing to light life and immortality."

For the firft, I fhall fhew,

I. What is here meant by " the appearing of " JESUS CHRIST."

II. What by the " abolifhing of death."

III. What by " bringing to light life and im- " mortality."

I. What is here meant by " the appearing of our " SAVIOUR JESUS CHRIST." The fcripture ufeth feveral phrafes to exprefs this thing to us. As it was the gracious defign of GOD the Father, fo it is call- ed the giving of his Son, or fending him into the world. John iii. 16. " GOD fo loved the world, " that he gave his only begotten Son." Gal. iv. 4. " In the fulnefs of time GOD fent his Son." As it was

was the voluntary undertaking of GOD the Son, fo it is called his coming into the world. In relation to his incarnation, whereby he was made vifible to us in his body, and likewife in reference to the ob-fcure promifes, and prophecies, and types of the old teftament, it is called his manifeftation or ap-pearance. So the apoftle expreffeth it, 1 John iii. 5. " Ye know that he was manifefted to take away " our fins ;" by which we are to underftand prima-rily his incarnation, his appearing in our nature, whereby he became vifible to us. As he was GOD, he could not appear to us, dwelling in light and glory, not to be approached by us in this ftate of mortality, and therefore he clothed himfelf in flefh, that he might appear and become manifeft to us.

I fay, by his appearing we are primarily to under-ftand his incarnation : yet not only that, but like-wife all that was confequent upon this, the actions of his life, and his death and refurrection ; becaufe all thefe concur to the producing of thefe happy ef-fects mentioned in the text.

II. What is meant by the abolifhing of death. By this we are not to underftand, that CHRIST by his appearance hath rooted death out of the world, fo that men are no longer fubject to it. For we fee that even good men, and thofe who are partakers of the benefits of CHRIST's death, are ftill fubject to the common law of mortality : but this expreffion of CHRIST's having abolifhed death, fignifies the con-queft and victory which CHRIST hath gained over death in his own perfon, in that after he was dead, and laid in his grave, he rofe again from the dead, he freed himfelf from the bands of death, and broke loofe from the fetters of it, they not being able to hold him, as the expreffion is, Acts ii. 24. and confe-

quently

quently hath, by this victory over it, given us an affurance of a refurrection to a better life. For fince
CHRIST hath abolifhed death, and triumphed over
it, and thereby over the powers of darknefs: (for
fo the apoftle tells us, that by his death, and that
which followed it, his refurrection from the dead,
" he hath deftroyed him that had the power of
" death, that is, the devil." The devil, he contri-
buted all he could to the death of CHRIST, by tempting Judas to betray him, and engaging all his inftruments in the procuring of it ; .as he had before
brought in death into the world, by tempting the
firft man to fin, upon which death infued ; thus far
he prevailed, and thought his kingdom was fafe,
having procured the death of him who was fo great
an enemy to it : but CHRIST, by rifing from
the dead, defeats the devil of his defign, and plainly conquers him, who had arrogated to himfelf the
power of death ;). I fay, fince CHRIST hath thus
vanquifhed death, and triumphed over it, and him
that had the power of it, death hath loft it's dominion, and CHRIST hath taken the whole power and
difpofal of it ; as you find, Rev. i. 18. " I am
" he that liveth and was dead, and behold I am
" alive for evermore, and have the keys of hell and
" of death." Now CHRIST hath not only thus
conquered death for himfelf, but likewife for all thofe
who believe on him ; fo that death fhall not be able
to keep them for ever under it's power : but CHRIST,
by the fame power whereby he raifed up himfelf from
the dead, will alfo " quicken our mortal bodies,"
and raife them up to a new life ; for he keeps " the
" keys of hell and death ;" and as a reward of his
fufferings and fubmiffion to death, he hath power conferred upon him, " to give eternal life to as many as
                                                    " he

" he pleases." In this sense, death, though it be not quite chased out of the world, yet it is virtually and in effect " abolished by the appearance of JESUS " CHRIST," having in a great measure lost it's power and dominion ; and since CHRIST hath assured us of a final rescue from it, the power of it is rendered insignificant and inconsiderable, and the sting and terror of it is taken away. So the apostle tells us in the forementioned place, Heb. ii. 14, 15. that CHRIST having " by death destroyed him who had the " power of death, that is, the devil, he hath deli- " vered those who through fear of death, were all " their life-time subject to bondage." And not only the power and terror of death is for the present in a great measure taken away ; but it shall at last be ut- terly destroyed. So the apostle tells us, 1 Cor. xv. 26. " The last enemy that shall be destroyed is " death ;" which makes the apostle, in the latter end of this chapter, to break forth into that triumph, ver. 54, 55. " So when this corruptible shall have " put on incorruption, and this mortal shall have " put on immortality, then shall be brought to pass " the saying that is written, death is swallowed up in " victory. O death, where is thy sting ? O grave, " where is thy victory ?"

III. What is here meant by " bringing life and " immortality to light." Life and immortality, is here by a frequent Hebraism put for immortal life ; as also immediately before the text, you find purpose and grace, put for GOD's gracious purpose. The phrase of bringing to light, is spoken of things which were before either wholly or in a great measure hid, either were not at all discovered before, or not so clearly. Now because the heathens by the light of nature, had some probable conjectures and hopes con-

cerning another life after this, they were in fome meafure perfuaded, that when men died, they were not wholly extinguifhed, but did pafs into another world, and did there receive rewards fuited to their carriage and demeanour in this life ; and becaufe the Jews alfo, before CHRIST, had thefe natural fuggeftions and hopes ftrengthened and confirmed by revelations, which GOD made unto them under the old teftament, therefore we cannot underftand this phrafe of CHRIST's, "bringing immortal life to light" abfolutely, as if it were wholly a new difcovery, which the world had no apprehenfion of before ; but only comparatively, as a thing which was now rendered, by the coming of CHRIST into the world, incomparably more evident and manifeft. *Quicquid enim philofophi, quicquid rabbini eâ de re dicunt, tenebræ funt, fi ad evangelii lucem comparentur* ; " what-
" ever the philofophers, whatever the rabbins fay of
" this matter, is but darknefs, compared to the
" clear light and revelation of the gofpel." I proceed to the

Second thing I propofed, viz. to fhew what CHRIST's coming into the world hath done towards " the abolifhing of death," and " bringing of life
" and immortality to light." I fhall fpeak diftinctly to thefe two.

I. What CHRIST's appearance and coming into the world hath done towards " the abolifhing of
" death," or how " death is abolifhed by the ap-
" pearance of CHRIST." I have already fhewn in the explication, that this phrafe, " the abolifhing of
" death," fignifies the conqueft which he made over death in his own perfon for himfelf; the fruit of which victory redounds to us. For in that CHRIST by his divine power did conquer it, and fet himfelf

2   free

free from the bands of it, this shews that the power
of it is now brought into other hands, that " CHRIST
" hath the keys of hell and death ;'' so that though
the devil, by tempting to sin, brought death into
the world, yet it shall not be in his power to keep
men always under the power of it; and hereby the
terror of this great enemy is in a good measure taken
away, and he shall at last be totally destroyed, by the
same hand that hath already given him his mortal
wound.

Now this is said to be done by " the appearing of
" JESUS CHRIST,'' for as much as by his coming
into the world, and taking our nature upon him, he
became capable of encountering this enemy and over-
coming him, in such a manner as might give us affurance of a final victory over it, and for the present
comfort and encourage us against the fears of it. For,

1. By taking our nature upon him, he became subject to the frailties and miseries of mortality, and liable to the suffering of death, by which expiation of
sin was made. Sin was the cause of death. So the
apostle tells us, " by man sin entered into the world,
" and death by sin, so that death came upon all.''
Now the way to cure this malady which was come
upon our nature, and to remove this great mischief
which was come into the world, is by taking away
the meritorious cause of it, which is the guilt of sin.
Now this CHRIST hath taken away by his death.
CHRIST, that he might abolish death, hath appeared
for " the abolition of sin.'' So the apostle tells us,
Heb. ix. 26, 27, 28. " But now once in the end of
" the world hath he appeared, to put away sin by
" the sacrifice of himself, εἰς ἀθέτησιν ἁμαρτίας, for
" the abolishing of sin .'' and to shew that this was
intended as a remedy of the great mischief and in-

conv.

convenience of mortality, which fin had brought
upon mankind, the apoftle immediately adds in the
next verfe, that " as it is appointed unto all men
" once to die, fo CHRIST was once offered to bear
" the fins of many :" and by this means the fting
of death is taken away, and death in effect conquered ; the confideration of which makes the apoftle
break out into that thankful triumph, 1 Cor. xv.
55, 56, 57. " O death, where is thy fting ? O grave,
" where is 'thy victory ? The fting of death is fin :
" But thanks be to GOD, which giveth us the vic-
" tory through our LORD JESUS CHRIST.".

2. As CHRIST by taking our nature upon him became capable of fuffering death, and thereby making
expiation for fin ; fo by dying he became capable of
rifing again from the dead, whereby he hath gained
a perfect victory and conqueft over death and the
powers of darknefs. And this account the apoftle
gives us of CHRIST's taking our nature upon him,
as being one of the principal ends and defigns of it,
Heb. ii. 14, 15, 16. " For as much then as the children are partakers of flefh and blood, he alfo himfelf
" likewife took part of the fame, that through death
" he might deftroy him that had the power of death,
" that is, the devil ;" that is, that by taking our
nature upon him, he might be capable of encountering this enemy, that is, of encountering death in his
own territories, and beating him in his own quarters ;
and by rifing out of his grave, he might give us full
and comfortable affurance of the poffibility of being
refcued from the power of the grave, and recovered
out of the jaws of death. And therefore the wifdom
of GOD pitched upon this way, as that which was
moft fit and proper to encourage and bear us up
againft the terrors of the enemy ; and by giving us
a lively

a lively inftance and example of a victory over death, atchieved by one clothed with mortality like our-felves, " we might have ftrong confolation and good " hope through grace," and might be fully affured that he who had conquered this enemy for 'himfelf, was able alfo to conquer him for us, and to deliver us from the grave. Therefore the apoftle reafons from the fitnefs and fuitablenefs of this difpenfation, as if no other argument could have been fo proper to arm us againft the fears of death, and to fatisfy us that we fhould not always be held under the power of it ; " for as much as the children are partakers " of flefh and blood, he alfo himfelf likewife took " part of the fame, that through death he might " deftroy him that had the power of death, and de- " liver them who through fear of death," &c. The force of which argument is this, that feeing men are of a mortal nature (for that he means by " being " partakers of flefh and blood") nothing can be a greater comfort to us againft the fears of death, than to fee death conquered by flefh and blood, by one of the fame nature with ourfelves. Therefore the apoftle adds, ver. 16. " For verily he took not on " him the nature of angels ; but the feed of Abra- " ham." If he had affumed the angelical nature, which is immortal, this would not have been fo fen-fible a conviction to us of the poffibility of it, as to have a lively inftance and example prefented us, of one in our nature conquering death, and triumphing over the grave. I proceed to the

II. thing, What CHRIST hath done towards " the " bringing of life and immortality to light." And becaufe I told you that this is comparatively fpoken, and fignifies to us a greater degree of evidence, and a firmer affurance given us by the chriftian religion,

than

than the world had before, therefore it will be requisite to inquire into thefe two things.

Firft, What affurance men had or might have had
of the immortality of the foul, and a future ftate,
before the coming of CHRIST into the world, and
the revelation of the gofpel.

Secondly, What greater evidence, and what higher degree of affurance the gofpel now gives us of
immortal life ; what greater arguments this new revelation and difcovery of GOD to the world doth furnifh us withal, to perfuade us of this matter, than the
world was acquainted withal before.

Firft, What affurance men had or might have had
of the immortality of the foul, and confequently of
a future ftate, before the revelation of the gofpel by
CHRIST's coming into the world. And here are two
things diftinctly to be confidered.

Firft, What arguments natural reafon doth furnifh
us withal, to perfuade us of this principle, that our
fouls are immortal, and that there is another ftate
remains for men after this life.

Secondly, What affurance *de facto* the world had
of this principle, before CHRIST's coming into the
world: what the heathens, and what the Jews had.
The reafon why I fhall fpeak to thefe diftinctly, is,
becaufe they are two very different inquiries; what
affurance men might have had from the principles of
natural reafon concerning this matter, and what affurance they had *de facto*. I begin with the

Firft, What arguments natural reafon doth furnifh us withal to perfuade us to this principle, that
our fouls are immortal, and confequently that another ftate remains for men after this life. And here
I fhall fhew,

I. How much may be faid for it.

II. How

II. How little can be faid againft it. But before I come to fpeak particularly to the arguments, which natural reafon affords us for the proof of this principle, I fhall premife certain general confiderations, which may give light and force to the following arguments. As,

Firft, By the foul we mean a part of man diftinct from his body, or a principle in him which is not matter. I chufe rather to defcribe it this way, than by the effential properties of it, which are hard to fix upon, and are more remote from common apprehenfion. Our SAVIOUR, when he would convince his difciples after his refurrection, that the body wherein he appeared to them was a real body, and that he was not a fpirit or apparition, he bids them " touch and handle him ; for, fays he, a fpirit hath " not flefh and bones, as ye fee me to have." So that by the foul or fpirit of a man, we mean fome principle in man, which is really diftinct from his vifible and fenfible part, from all that in man which affects our outward fenfes, and which is not to be defcribed by any fenfible and external qualities, fuch as we ufe to defcribe a body by : becaufe it is fuppofed to be of fuch a nature, as does not fall under the cognizance and notice of any of our fenfes. And therefore I defcribe it, by removing from it all thofe qualities and properties which belong to that which falls under our fenfes, viz. that it is fomething in man diftinct from his body, a principle in him which is not matter ; that principle which is the caufe of thofe feveral operations, which by inward fenfe and experience we are confcious to ourfelves of ; fuch are perception, underftanding, memory, will. So that the moft plain and popular notion that we can have of the foul, is, that it is fomething in us which we

never

never faw, and which is the caufe of thofe effects which we find in ourfelves ; it is the principle whereby we are confcious to ourfelves, that we perceive fuch and fuch objects, that we fee, or hear, or perceive any thing by any other fenfe ; it is that whereby we think and remember, whereby we reafon about any thing, and do freely chufe and refufe fuch things as are prefented to us. Thefe operations every one is confcious to himfelf of, and that which is the principle of thefe, or the caufe from whence thefe proceed, is that which we mean by the foul.

Secondly, By the immortality of the foul, I mean nothing elfe, but that it furvives the body, that when the body dies and falls to the ground, yet this principle which we call the foul, ftill remains and lives feparate from it ; that is, there is ftill a part of us which is free from the fate of the body, and continues to perform all thofe operations, to the performance of which the organs of the body are not neceffary ; that is, when our bodies are deftitute of life, and become a dead carcafe, there is ftill fomething that did belong to us, which retains the power of underftanding, which thinks, and reafons, and remembers, and does all thefe freely.

Thirdly, That he that goes about to prove the foul's immortality, fuppofeth the exiftence of a Deity, that there is a GOD. For although there be a very intimate and ftrict connexion between thefe two principles as to us, as being the two great pillars of all religion ; yet that which is firft and moft fundamental to all religion, is the exiftence of a God ; which if it be not firft proved, the beft arguments for the foul's immortality lofe their force. Therefore as to the prefent argument, I fuppofe the being of GOD as a thing acknowledged, and not now to be proved ;

which

which I may the better do, having formerly endeavoured to make good this grand principle of religion, against the pretensions of the Atheists.

Fourthly, The existence of a GOD being supposed, this doth very much facilitate the other, of the soul's immortality. For this being an essential property of the divine nature, that he is a spirit, that is, something that is not matter ; it being once granted that GOD is, thus much is gained, that there is such a thing as a spirit, as an immaterial substance, that is not liable to die or perish : so that he that goes about to prove the immortality of the soul, shall not need to prove that there may be such a thing as a spirit, that the notion of an immaterial substance does not imply a contradiction, because, supposing that there is a GOD, who is essentially a spirit, there can be no doubt of the possibility of such a thing as a spirit; and though there be this difference between GOD and all other spirits, that he is an infinite spirit, whereas others are but finite ; yet no man, that grants the existence of an infinite spirit, can with any pretence or colour of reason deny the possibility of a finite spirit.

Fifthly, and lastly, it is highly reasonable that men should acquiesce and rest satisfied in such reasons and arguments for the proof of any thing, as the nature of the thing to be proved will bear ; because there are several kinds and degrees of evidence, which all things are not equally capable of. It is sufficient that the evidence be such as the nature of the thing to be proved will admit of, and such as prudent men make no scruple to admit for sufficient evidence for things of the like nature, and such as, supposing the thing to be, we cannot ordinarily expect better or greater evidence for it.

There are two kinds of evidences, which are the

higheſt and moſt ſatisfactory that this world affords to us, and thoſe are the evidence of ſenſe, and mathematical demonſtration. Now there are many things, concerning which the generality of men profeſs themſelves to be well ſatisfied, which do not afford either of theſe kinds of evidence. There's none of us but doth firmly believe that we were born, though we do not remember any ſuch thing ; no man's memory does furniſh him with the teſtimony of his ſenſes from this matter, nor can any man prove this by a mathematical demonſtration, nor by any neceſſary argument, ſo as to ſhew it impoſſible that the thing ſhould be otherwiſe. For it is poſſible that a man may come into the world otherwiſe, than by the ordinary courſe of generation, as the firſt man did, who was created immediately by GOD ; and yet I know no man in the world who doubts in the leaſt concerning this matter, though he hath no other argument for it, but the teſtimony of others, and his own obſervation, how other perſons like himſelf came into the world. And it is reaſonable to acquieſce in this evidence, becauſe the nature of the thing affords no greater. We who never were at Jeruſalem, do firmly believe that there is ſuch a place, upon the teſtimony and relation of others : and no man is blamed for this, as being over-credulous ; becauſe no man, that will not take the pains to go thither, can have any other greater evidence of it, than the general teſtimony of thoſe who ſay they have ſeen it. And indeed almoſt all human affairs, I am ſure the moſt important, are governed and conducted by ſuch evidence, as falls very much ſhort both of the evidence of ſenſe, and of mathematical demonſtration.

To apply this then to my preſent purpoſe. Tha

2   the

the foul of man is of an immortal nature, is not capable of all kinds and degrees of evidence. It cannot be proved by our fenfes, nor is it reafonable to expect it fhould be fo proved ; becaufe the foul is fuppofed, by every one that difcourfeth of it, to be a thing of fuch a nature, as cannot be feen or handled, or fall under any other of our fenfes : nor can it be proved to us by our own experience, while we are in this world ; becaufe whoever dies, which is the only trial that can be made whether our fouls remain after our bodies, goes out of this world. As for mathematical demonftration, the nature of the thing renders it incapable of it. It remains then that we reft contented with fuch arguments as the nature of the thing will bear, and with fuch evidence as men are contented to accept of, and do account fufficient, in other matters ; fuch evidence as a prudent confidering man, who is not credulous on the one hand, and on the other is not prejudiced by any intereft againft it, would reft fatisfied in.

Having premifed thefe general confiderations, to clear my way, I now come to fpeak to the particular arguments, whereby the immortality of the foul may be made out to our reafon. And the beft way to eftimate the force of the arguments which I fhall bring for it, will be to confider before-hand with ourfelves, what evidence we can in reafon expect for a thing of this nature. Suppofe our fouls be immortal ; by what kind of arguments could we defire to be affured of it ? Setting afide miracles and divine revelation, could we defire more than this ?

I. That the thing be a natural notion and dictate of our minds.

II. That it doth not contradict any other principle that nature hath planted in us, but does very

w 'l

well accord and agree with all other the moſt natural notions of our minds.

III. That it be ſuitable to our natural fears and hopes.

IV. That it tends to the happineſs of man, and the good order and government of the world.

V. That it gives the moſt rational account of all thoſe inward actions, which we are conſcious to our-ſelves of, as perception, underſtanding, memory, will, which we cannot without great unreaſonable-neſs aſcribe to matter, as the cauſe of them. If all theſe be thus, as I ſhall endeavour to make it appear they are, what greater ſatisfaction could we deſire to have of the immortality of our ſouls, than theſe ar-guments give us? I do not ſay that any one of theſe arguments doth ſufficiently conclude this thing; nor is it neceſſary, that taken ſingly and by themſelves they ſhould do it; it is ſufficient that they concur to make up one entire argument, which may be a ſuf-ficient evidence of the ſoul's immortality. To il-luſtrate this by an inſtance. Suppoſe a man ſhould uſe theſe two arguments, to prove that ſuch a man deſerves to be credited in ſuch a relation. Firſt, be-cauſe he had ſufficient knowledge of the thing he relates; and, ſecondly, becauſe he is a man of in-tegrity and fidelity. Neither of theſe alone would prove the man to be worthy of credit; though both together make up a good argument. So it is in theſe arguments which I have produced; it may be, no one of them is a ſufficient inducement, taken ſingly and by itſelf, to ſatisfy a man fully that the ſoul is immortal; and yet they may concur together to make a very powerful argument. I begin with the

I. That our ſouls are of an immortal nature, that they do not die and periſh with our bodies, but paſs into another ſtate upon the diſſolution of our bodies,

is

is a natural notion and dictate of our minds. That I
call a natural notion, which the minds of all men do
naturally hit upon and agree in, notwithftanding the
diftance and remotenefs of the feveral parts of the
world from one another, notwithftanding the different tempers, and manner and ways of education.
The only way to meafure whether any thing be natural or not, is by inquiring whether it agree to the
whole kind or not : if it do, then we call it natural.
Omnium confenfus naturæ vox eft, " The confent of
" all is the voice of nature," fays Tully, fpeaking
of the univerfal agreement of all nations in this apprehenfion, that " the fouls of men remain after
" their bodies." And this he tells us he looks upon
as a very great argument, *Maximum verè argumen-*
tum eft, naturam ipfam de immortalitate animarum
tacitam judicare, quod omnibus curæ fint & maximè
quidem quæ poft mortem futura funt : " this is a very
" great argument that nature doth fecretly, and in
" mens filent thoughts determine the immortality of
" the foul, that all men are folicitous of what fhall
" become of them after death." *Nefcio quomodo*
inhæret in mentibus quafi feculorum quoddam augurium
futurorum, idque in maximis ingeniis altiffimifque ani-
mis & exiftit maxime & apparet facillime : " I know
" not how (faith he) there fticks in the mind a cer-
" tain kind of prefage of a future ftate, and this is
" moft deeply fixed and difcovers itfelf fooneft in
" the choiceft fpirits." Again the fame author, *Ut*
Deos effe naturâ opinamur fic permanere animos arbi-
tramur confenfu nationum omnium : " As this opinion
" is planted in us by nature, that there is a God, fo
" by the confent of all nations we believe that fouls
" remain after the body." I might multiply teftimonies to this purpofe out of the ancient heathen
writers;

SERM. writers; but thefe which I have produced out of
CLXXIV. this great author, are fo plain and exprefs, that I
need bring no other.

As for thofe barbarous nations which have been
difcovered in thefe latter ages of the world, and
which before the firft planting of America, were
never known to have held correfpondence with thefe
parts of the world, yet all thofe nations agree in this
principle, of the immortality of the foul ; nay even
the moft barbarous of thofe nations, thofe who are
moft inhuman and eat one another, thofe of Joupi-
namboult in Brafile, who are faid by fome authors,
but I think not upon fufficient grounds, not to acknowledge the being of a GOD ; yet even thefe (as
Lerius tells us, who lived among them) had a
very fixed and firm perfuafion of this principle of
religion, the immortality of the foul. " There is
" not, fays he, any nation in the world more remote
" from all religion than thefe were ; yet to fhew that
" there is fome light in the midft of this darknefs,
" I can, fays he, truly affirm, that they have not
" only fome apprehenfions of the immortality of
" the foul, but a moft confident perfuafion of it.
" Their opinion, fays he, is that the fouls of ftout
" and valiant men after death fly beyond the higheft
" mountains, and there are gathered to their fathers
" and grand-fathers, and live in pleafant gardens,
" with all manner of delights ; but the fouls of
" flothful and unactive men, and thofe who do no-
" thing for their country, are carried to Aygman
" (fo they call the devil) and live with him in perpe-
" tual torments." The like Xaverius and others,
who laboured in the converfion of the remote parts
of the Eaft-Indies, tell us concerning thofe nations,
that they found them generally poffeffed with this
principle, of the foul's immortality.   Now

Now what will we call a natural notion, if not that which mankind in all places of the world, in all ages, fo far as hiftory informs, did univerfally agree in ? What evidence greater than this can any man give, to fhew that any thing is natural ? And if we believe a God, (which I told you I do all a-long in this argument fuppofe to be already proved) can we imagine that this wife and good God would plant fuch a notion and apprehenfion in the under-ftandings of men, as would put an univerfal cheat and delufion upon human nature?

And that the univerfal confent of all nations in this principle, cannot be refolved either into the fears and groundlefs jealoufy and fuperftition of human nature, nor into univerfal tradition, which had it's original from fome impoftor, nor into reafon and policy of ftate, I might fhew particularly : but having former-ly done that, concerning the univerfal confent of all nations in the belief of a God, and the reafon being the very fame, as to this principle of the immorta-lity of the foul, I fhall not need to do this over again upon this argument.

And that fome perfons, and particular fects in the world, have difowned this principle, is no fufficient objection againft it. It cannot be denied, but the Epicureans among the philofophers, did renounce this principle ; and fome alfo among the Stoicks do fpeak doubtfully of it. The Sadducees likewife a-mong the Jews fell into this error, upon a miftake and mifapprehenfion of the doctrine of their mafter Sadoc, who, as Jofephus tells us, did ufe to incul-cate this principle to his fcholars, that though there were no rewards nor punifhments after this life, yet men ought to be good and live virtuoufly ; from whence in procefs of time, by heat of oppofition

againft

againſt the Phariſees, who brought in oral tradition, and made it equal with the written word of GOD, they fell into that error, and denied the ſoul's immortality, not finding ſuch clear texts for it in the Old Teſtament, as to them did ſeem fully convincing of this truth. Xaverius likewiſe tells us, that among the ſeveral ſects of religion which he found in Japan, there was one which denied the immortality of the ſoul, and that there were any ſpirits : but he ſays they were a ſort of notoriouſly wicked and vicious perſons.

To theſe inſtances, which are ſo few, and bear no proportion to the generality of mankind, I have theſe two things to ſay.

1. That no argument can be drawn, *à monſtro ad naturam.* A thing may be natural, and yet ſome inſtances may be brought to the contrary : but theſe are but few in compariſon, and like monſters, which are no argument againſt nature. No man will deny that it is natural for men to have two eyes, and five fingers upon a hand ; though there are ſeveral inſtances of men born but with one eye, and with four or ſix fingers.

2. But eſpecially in matters of religion and diſcourſe, which are ſubject to liberty, men may offer violence to nature, and to gratify their luſts and intereſts, may by falſe reaſonings debauch their underſtanding, and by long ſtriving againſt the natural bent and biaſs of it, may alter their apprehenſions of things, and perſuade others to the ſame : but nothing that is againſt nature can prevail very far, but nature will ſtill be endeavouring to recover itſelf, and to free itſelf from the violence which is offered to it. So that mens underſtandings left to themſelves, and not having ſome falſe biaſs put upon them, out of a
                                                        deſign

defign of pride and fingularity in opinion, which
was the cafe of Epicurus; or out of the intereft of
fome luft, and a defign to fet men at liberty to fin,
which is the cafe of moft who have renounced this
principle; I fay, nothing but one of thefe two can
ordinarily make men deny the immortality of the foul.
Thus I have done with the firft argument, namely,
that the immortality of the foul is a natural notion and
dictate of our minds.

SERMON CLXXV.

Of the immortality of the foul, as difcovered by nature, and by revelation.

2 TIM. i. 10.

*But is now made manifeft by the appearing of our
Saviour Jesus Christ, who hath abolifhed
death, and hath brought life and immortality to
light, through the gofpel.*

I Proceed to the fecond argument, that this notion
or principle of the immortality of the foul doth
not contradict any other principle that nature hath
planted in us, but doth very well accord and agree
with all thofe other notions which are moft natural.
I fhall mention two, which feem to be the moft natural notions that we have, and the moft deeply rooted in our natures; the one is the exiftence and the
perfections of God; and the other, the difference of
good and evil. Mankind do univerfally agree in
thefe two principles, that there is a God who is ef-

S E R M.
CLXXV.

The
fecond
fermon on
this text.

fentially good and juft; and that there is a real dif-ference between good and evil, which is not founded in the opinion and imagination of perfons, or in the cuftom and ufage of the world, but in the nature of things. Now this principle of the immortality of the foul, and future rewards after this life, is fo far from clafhing with either of thefe principles, that the contrary affertion, viz. that our fouls are mortal, and that there is nothing to be hoped for, or feared beyond this life, would very much contradict thofe other principles. To fhew this then particularly,

1. The immortality of the foul is very agreeable to the natural notion which we have of GOD, one part whereof is, that he is effentially good and juft.

(1.) For his goodnefs. It is very agreeable to that, to think that GOD would make fome creatures for as long a duration as they are capable of. The wifdom of GOD hath chofen to difplay itfelf, in creating variety of things of different degrees and perfections; things devoid of life and fenfe; and feveral degrees and orders of fenfitive creatures, of different fhapes and figures, of different magnitude, fome vaftly great, others extremely little, others of a middle fort between thefe. And himfelf being a pure fpirit, we have no reafon to doubt, but he could make creatures of a fpiritual nature, and fuch as fhould have no principle of felf-corruption in them. And feeing he could make creatures of fuch perfection, if we believe him to be effentially good, we have no reafon to doubt, but that he hath done fo. For it is the very nature of goodnefs, to communicate and diffufe itfelf, and to delight in doing fo; and we cannot imagine, but that the fame goodnefs which prompted and inclined him to give being to thofe creatures which are of an inferior degree of perfection, would

3　　　　　move

move him likewife to make creatures more perfect, and capable of greater degrees of happinefs, and of a longer enjoyment of it, if it were in his power to make fuch; and no man that believes the omnipotency of GOD can doubt of this. For he who by a pure act of his will can command things to be, and in an inftant to ftart out of nothing, can as eafily make one fort of creatures as another. Now the power of GOD being fuppofed, his goodnefs fecures us of his will: for we cannot imagine any fuch thing as envy, in a being which we fuppofe to be perfectly good; nothing being more inconfiftent with perfect goodnefs, than to be unwilling to communicate happinefs to others, and to grudge that others fhould partake of it.

Now this being fuppofed, that GOD could and would make creatures of a fpiritual and immortal nature, and the utmoft imaginable perfections of fuch creatures being knowledge and liberty, wherever thefe perfections are found, we have reafon to conclude that creature to be endowed with a principle that is of a fpiritual and immortal nature. Now thefe perfections of underftanding and will being found in man, this argues him to be endowed with fuch a principle, as is in it's own nature capable of an immortal duration.

It is true indeed, this fpiritual part of man, which we call his foul, is united to a vifible and material part, viz. his body; the union of which parts conftitutes a peculiar fort of creature, which is *utriufque mundi nexus,* " unites the material and immaterial " world, the world of matter and of fpirits." And as it is very fuitable to the wifdom of GOD, which delights in variety, that there fhould be a fort of creatures, compounded of both thefe principles, matter and spirit; so it is very agreeable to his goodness to think that he would design such creatures for as long a duration and continuance as they were capable of. For as it is the effect of goodness to bring creatures forth into the possession of that life and happiness which they are capable of; so to continue them in the enjoyment of it for so long as they are capable.

The sum of all this is, that as it is agreeable to the wisdom of GOD, which made the world, to display itself in all variety of creatures; so it is agreeable to his goodness, to make some of as perfect a kind as creatures are capable of being. Now it being no repugnancy nor contradiction, that a creature should be of a spiritual and immortal nature, we have no reason to think, but that the fruitfulness of the divine goodness hath brought forth such creatures; and if there be reason to conclude any thing to be of a spiritual and immortal nature, certainly the principle of understanding and liberty, which we are conscious of in ourselves, deserves to be reputed such.

(2.) It is very agreeable to the justice of GOD, to think the souls of men remain after this life, that there may be a state of reward and recompence in another world. If we believe GOD to be holy and just, we cannot but believe that he loves righteousness and goodness, and hates iniquity ; and that as he is governor and publick magistrate of the world, he is concerned to countenance and encourage the one, and to discountenance and discourage the other. Now the providences of GOD being in a great measure promiscuously administered in this world, so that no man can make any certain judgment of GOD's love and hatred towards persons, by what befals them in this world, it being the lot of good men many times to suffer and be afflicted, and of wicked men to live in a

flourishing

flourishing and prosperous condition ; I say, things being thus, it is very agreeable to these notions which we have of the divine holiness and justice, to believe that there will a time come, when this wise and just governor of the world will make a wide and visible difference between the righteous and the wicked ; so that though for a while the justice of God may be clouded, yet there will a time come when it shall be clearly manifested, and every eye see it and bear witness to it, when " judgment shall break forth as " the light, and righteousness as the noon-day." It is possible that sin for a while may go unpunished, nay, triumph and prosper ; and that virtue and innocence may not only be unrewarded, but oppressed and despised, and persecuted. And this may be reconcilable enough to the wisdom of God's providence, and the justice of it, supposing the immortality of the soul, and another state after this life, wherein all things shall be set strait, and every man shall receive according to his works : but unless this be supposed, it is impossible to solve the justice of God's providence. Who will believe that the affairs of the world are administered by him who loves righteousness, and hates all the workers of iniquity, who will not let the least service that is done to him pass unrewarded, nor on the other hand acquit the guilty, and let sin go unpunished, which are the properties of justice ; I say, who will believe this, that looks into the course of the world, and sees with how little difference and distinction of good and bad, the affairs of it are managed ? That sees virtue discountenanced and despised, poor and destitute, afflicted and tormented ; when wickedness is many times exalted to high places, and makes a great noise and ruffle in the world ? He that considers what a hazard many

t i..S

times good men run, how for goodnefs fake they venture, and many times quit all the contentments and
enjoyments of this life, and fubmit to the greateft
fufferings and calamities that human nature is capable
of; while in the mean time profperity is poured into
the lap of the wicked, and heaven feems to look plea-
fantly upon thofe that deal treacheroufly, and to be
filent whilft the wicked devours the man that is more
righteous than himfelf; he that confiders this, and
can without fuppofing another life after this, pretend
to vindicate the juftice of thefe things, muft be as
blind as the fortune that governs them.   Would not
this be a perpetual ftain and blemifh upon the divine
providence, that Abel, who offered up " a better
" facrifice than Cain, and had this teftimony, that
" he pleafed God," yet after all this, fhould have no
other reward for it, but to be flain by his brother,
who had offended God by a flight and contemptuous
offering? If there were no reward to be expected after this life, would not this have been a fad example
to the world, to fee one of the firft men that ferved
God acceptably, thus rewarded ? What a pitiful encouragement would it be to men to be good, to fee
profane Efau bleft " with the dew of heaven, and
" the fatnefs of the earth;" and to hear good old
Jacob in the end and conclufion of his days, to complain, " few and evil have the days of my pilgrimage
" been ?" If this had been the end of Efau and Jacob, it would puzzle all the wit and reafon of mankind, to wipe off this reproach from the providence
of God, and vindicate the juftice of it.   And therefore I do not wonder, that the greateft wits among
the heathen philofophers, were fo much puzzled with
this objection againft the providence of God ; if the
wife, and juft, and good God do adminifter the affairs

fairs of the world, and be concerned in the good or S F R M. bad actions of men, *cur bonis male & malis bene ?* CLXXV. " How comes it to pass, that good men many times " are miserable, and bad men so happy in the " world ?" And they had no other way to wipe off this objection, but by referring these things to another world, wherein the temporal sufferings of good men should be eternally rewarded ; and the short and transient happiness of wicked men should be rendered insignificant, and drowned in an eternity of misery.

So that if we believe the being of GOD, and the providence of GOD ; (which I do all along take for granted in this argument) there is no other way imaginable to solve the equity and justice of GOD's providence, but upon this supposition, that there is another life after this. For to say, that virtue is a sufficient and abundant reward for itself, though it have some truth in it, if we set aside those sufferings and miseries and calamities, which virtue is frequently attended with in this life ; yet if these be taken in, it is but a very jejune and dry speculation. For considering the strong propension and inclination of human nature to avoid these evils and inconveniencies, a state of virtue attended with great sufferings, would be so far from being a happiness, that it would be a real misery ; so that the determination of the apostle, 1 Cor. xv. 19. is according to nature, and the truth and reason of things, that, " if in this life only we " had hope, we were of all men most miserable." For although it be true, that as things now stand, and as the nature of man is framed, good men do find a strange kind of inward pleasure and secret satisfaction of mind in the discharge of their duty, and in doing what is virtuous ; yet every man that looks into himself, and consults his own breast, will find that

this

this delight and contentment springs chiefly from the hopes which men conceive, that a holy and virtuous life shall not be unrewarded: and without these hopes virtue is but a dead and empty name: and notwithstanding the reasonableness of virtuous actions compared with the contrary of them, yet when virtue came to be encumbered with difficulties, and to be attended with such sufferings and inconveniencies, as were grievous and intolerable to human nature, then it would appear unreasonable to chuse that for a happiness, which would rob a man of all the felicity of his life. For though a man were never so much in love with virtue, for the native beauty and comeliness of it; yet it would strangely cool his affection to it, to consider that he should be undone by the match, that when he had it he must go a begging with it, and be in danger of death, for the sake of that which he had chosen for the felicity of his life. So that how devout soever the woman might be, yet I dare say she was not over-wise and considerate, who going about with a pitcher of water in one hand, and a pan of coals in the other, and being asked what she intended to do with them, answered: " that she " intended with the one to burn up heaven, and " with the other to quench hell, that men might love " God and virtue for their own sakes, without hope " of reward, or fear of punishment."

And the consequence of this dry doctrine does sufficiently appear in the sect of the Sadducees, which had its rise from this principle of Sadoc, the master of the sect, who out of an indiscreet zeal to teach something above others, and indeed above the pitch of human nature, inculcated this doctrine upon his scholars, that religion and virtue ought to be loved for themselves, though there were no reward of virtue

to be hoped, nor punifhment of vice to be feared in another world; from which his difciples inferred, that it was not neceffary to religion to believe a future ftate, and in procefs of time, peremptorily maintained that there was no life after this. For they did not only deny the refurrection of the body, but as St. Paul tells us, they faid, that " there was nei-
" ther angel nor fpirit;" that is, they demed that there was any thing of an immortal nature, that did remain after this life. And what the confequence of this was, we may fee in the character which Jofephus gives of that fect; for he tells us, that the commonalty of the Jews were of the fect of the Phari-
fees, but moft of the great and rich men were Sadducees; which plainly fhews, that this dry fpeculation of loving religion and virtue for themfelves, without any expectation of future rewards, did end in their giving over all ferious purfuit of religion : and becaufe they hoped for nothing after this life, therefore laying afide all other confiderations, they applied themfelves to the prefent bufinefs of this life, and grafped as much of the prefent enjoyment of its power and riches, as they could by any means attain to.

And for a farther evidence of this, that it is only or principally the hopes of a future happinefs that bear men up in the purfuit of virtue, that give them fo much comfort and fatisfaction in the profecution of it, and make men encounter the difficulties, and oppofitions, and perfecutions they meet withal in the ways of religion, with fo much undauntednefs and courage, I fay, for the farther evidence of this, I fhall only offer this confideration, that according to the degree of this hope and affurance of another life, mens conftancy and courage in the ways of virtue and religion have been. Before Chrit's coming

VOL. II.

into the world, and " the bringing of life and im-
" mortality to light by the gofpel," we do not find
in all ages of the world, fo many inftances of patience and conftant fuffering for religion, as happened
in the firft age after CHRIST. GOD did not think
fit to try the world fo much in this kind, till they
were furnifhed with a principle which would bear
them up under the greateft fufferings, which was nothing elfe but the full affurance which the gofpel gave
the world of a bleffed immortality after this life ; the
firm belief and perfuafion of which, made Chriftians
dead to the world, and all the contentments and enjoyments of it, and by raifing them above all the
pleafures and terrors of fenfe, made them to defpife
prefent things, " in hopes of eternal life, which
" GOD that could not lye had promifed." This
was that which fet them above the fears of death, fo
that they were not to be frighted out of their religion by the moft exquifite torments, and all the moft
horrid and fearful fhapes that the malice of men and
devils could drefs up mifery and affliction in. Whereas under the old difpenfation of the law, before the
revelation of the gofpel, when the promifes of eternal life were not fo clear, and mens hopes of it more
weak and faint, the exprefs encouragement to obedience was founded in the promifes of temporal bleffings ; GOD herein complying with the neceffity of
human nature, which is not to be wrought upon to
any great purpofe, but by arguments of advantage.

The fum of this argument, which I have thus
largely dilated upon, becaufe I look upon it as one of
the moft ftrong and convincing of the foul's immortality, is this ; that the juftice of GOD's providence
cannot fufficiently be vindicated, but upon the fup-
pofal of this principle of the foul's immortality :
whereas

whereas if this principle be admitted, that men paſs out of this life into an eternal ſtate of happineſs or miſery, according as they have behaved themſelves in this world ; then the account of the unequal providences of God in this world is eaſy. For if we look upon this life as a ſtate of probation, of trial to wicked men, and of exerciſe to good men in order to a future and eternal ſtate ; and if we conſider withal, how vaſt the difference is between time and eternity, it will be eaſy then to apprehend how all .things may be ſet ſtrait in another world, and how the righteouſneſs of God may appear, in giving an abundant recompence to good men for all their temporal ſervice and ſufferings, which do but prepare them the moɾe for a quicker reliſh of the glory and happineſs which is reſerved for them ; and on the other hand, in puniſhing wicked men, whoſe ſhort eaſe and proſperity in this world will, by the juſt judgment of God for their abuſe of the bleſſings of this life, ſet out their miſery and torment to the greateſt diſadvantage. For as nothing commends happineſs more than precedent ſorrow ; ſo nothing makes pain and ſuffering more bitter and intolerable, than to ſtep into them out of a ſtate of eaſe and pleaſure ; ſo that the pleaſures and proſperity of wicked men in this life, conſidered with the puniſhment of the next, which will follow upon them, is an addition to their miſery. This is the very ſting of the ſecond death ; and in this ſenſe alſo that of the wiſe man is true, " the eaſe of the ſimple will ſlay them, " and the proſperity of" theſe " fools" ſhall be the great aggravation of their deſtruction.

2. Another notion which is deeply rooted in the nature of man, is, that there is a difference between good and evil, which is not founded in the imagi-

nation of perfons, or in the cuftom and ufage of the world, but in the nature of things; that there are fome things which have a natural evil, and turpitude, and deformity in them; for example, impiety and profaneneſs towards God, injuſtice and unrighteouſneſs towards men, perfidiouſneſs, injury, ingratitude, theſe are things that are not only condemned by the poſitive laws and conſtitutions of particular nations and governments, but by the general verdict and ſentiments of humanity. Piety and religion towards God, juſtice, and righteouſneſs, and fidelity, and reverence of oaths, regard to a man's word and promiſe, and gratitude towards thoſe who have obliged us, theſe and the like qualities, which we call virtues, are not only well ſpoken of, where they are countenanced by the authority of law, but have the tacit approbation and veneration of mankind: And any man that thinks theſe things are not naturally and in themſelves good, but are meerly arbitrary, and depend upon the pleaſure of authority, and the will of thoſe who have the power of impoſing laws upon others; I ſay, any ſuch perſon may eaſily be convinced of his error, by putting this ſuppoſition; ſuppoſe wickedneſs were eſtabliſhed by a law, and the practice of fraud, and rapine, and perjury, falſeneſs in a man's word and promiſes, were commended and rewarded, and it were made a crime for any man to be honeſt, to have any regard to his oath or promiſe, and the man that ſhould dare to be honeſt or make good his word ſhould be ſeverely puniſhed and made a publick example; I ſay, ſuppoſe the reverſe of all that which we now call virtue, were ſolemnly enacted by a law, and publick authority ſhould enjoin the practice of that which we call vice; what would the conſequence of this be, when

the

the tables were thus turned? Would that which we now call vice, gain the efteem and reputation of virtue; and thofe things which we now call virtue, grow contemptible and become odious to human nature? If not, then there is a natural and intrinfical difference between good and evil, between virtue and vice; there is fomething in the nature of thefe things which does not depend upon arbitrary confti-tution. And I think nothing can be more evident, than that the authority which fhould attempt fuch an eftablifhment, would thereby be render'd ridiculous, and all laws of fuch a tendency as this, would be hift out of the world. And the reafon of this is plain, becaufe no government could fubfift upon thefe terms : for the very forbidding men to be juft and honeft, the enjoining of fraud, and violence, and perjury, and breach of truft, would apparently deftroy the end of government, which is to preferve men and their rights againft the encroachments and inconveniencies of thefe; and this end being de-ftroyed, human fociety would prefently difband, and men would naturally fall into a ftate of war; which plainly fhews that there is a natural, and immutable, and eternal reafon for that which we call goodnefs and virtue, and againft that which we call vice and wickednefs.

To come then to my purpofe, it is very agreeable to this natural notion of the difference between good and evil, to believe the foul's immortality. For no-thing is more reafonable to imagine, than that good and evil, as they are differenced in their nature, fo they fhall be in their rewards; that it fhall one time or other be well to them that do well, and evil to the wicked man. Now feeing this difference is not made in this world, but all things happen alike to

all,

all, the belief of this difference between good and evil, and the different rewards belonging to them, infers another ftate after this life, which is the very thing we mean by the foul's immortality, namely, that it does not die with the body, but remains after it, and paffeth into a ftate wherein it fhall receive a reward fuitable to the actions of this life.

And thus I have done with the fecond argument for the foul's immortality, namely, that this principle doth not contradict thofe other principles which nature hath planted in us, but doth very well accord and agree with thofe natural notions which we have of the goodnefs of God, and of the juftice of his providence, and of the real and intrinfical difference between good and evil.

III. This principle of the foul's immortality, is fuitable to the natural hopes and fears of men.

To the natural hopes of men. Whence is it that men are fo defirous to purchafe a lafting fame, and to perpetuate their memory to pofterity, but that they hope that there's fomething belonging to them, which fhall furvive the fate of the body, and when that lies in the filent grave, fhall be fenfible of the honour which is done to their memory, and fhall enjoy the pleafure of the juft and impartial fame, which fhall fpeak of them to pofterity without envy or flattery? And this is a thing incident to the greateft and moft generous fpirits ; none fo apt as they to feed themfelves with thefe hopes of immortality. What was it made thofe great fpirits among the Romans, fo freely to facrifice their lives for the fafety of their country, but an ambition that their names might live after them, and be mentioned with honour when they were dead and gone ? Which ambition of theirs, had it not been grounded in the hopes of

immor-

immortality, and a natural opinion of another life after this, in which they might enjoy the delight and ſatisfaction of the fame which they had purchaſed, nothing could have been more vain and unreaſonable. If there were no hopes of a life beyond this, what is there in fame that ſhould tempt any man to forego this preſent life, with all the contentments and enjoyments of it ? What is the pleaſure of being well ſpoken of, when a man is not ? What is the happineſs which men can promiſe to themſelves, when they are out of being, when they can enjoy nothing, nor be ſenſible of any thing, becauſe they are not ? So that the ſpring of all thoſe brave and gallant actions, which the heathens did with the hazard of their lives, out of a deſire of after-fame and glory ; I ſay, the ſpring of all thoſe actions, could be no other than the hopes of another life after this, in which they made account to enjoy the pleaſure of the fame, which they purchaſed with the expence and loſs of this preſent life.

But this ardent deſire and impatient thirſt after fame, concerns but a few of mankind in compariſon. I ſhall therefore inſtance in ſomething which is more common and general to mankind, which plainly argues this hope of immortality. What is the ground of that peace, and quiet, and ſatisfaction, which good men find in good and virtuous actions, but that they have a ſecret perſuaſion and comfortable hopes that they ſhall ſome time or other be rewarded ? And we find that they maintain theſe even when they deſpair of any reward in this world. Now what do theſe hopes argue, but a ſecret belief of a future ſtate, and another life after this, wherein men ſhall receive the reward of their actions, and inherit the fruit of their doings ? Whence is it elſe, that good

men,

men, though they find that goodness suffers, and is perfecuted in this world, and that the best designs are many times unsuccessful; what is it that bears them up under these disappointments, and makes them constant in a virtuous course, but this hope of another life, in a better state of things hereafter? They have some secret presage in their own minds of a life after death, which will be a time of recompence, as this is of trial.

2. The same may be argued from the natural fears of men. Whence is the secret shame, and fear, and horror, which seizeth upon the minds of men, when they are about a wicked action; yea, though no eye see them, and though what they are doing do not fall under the cognizance of any human court or tribunal? Whence is it that they meet with such checks and rebukes in their own spirits, and feel such a disturbance and confusion in their minds, when they do a vile and unworthy thing; yea, although it be so secretly contrived and so privately managed, that no man can charge them with it, or call them to account for it? What art thou afraid of, man, if there be no life after this? Why do thy joints tremble, and thy knees knock together, if thou be'st in no danger from any thing in this world, and hast no fears of the other? If men had not a natural dread of another world, and sad and dreadful presages of future vengeance, why do not men sin with assurance, when no eye sees them? Why are not men secure, when they have only imagined a mischief privately in their own hearts, and no creature is privy and conscious to it? Why do mens own consciences lash and sting them for these things, which they might do with as great impunity from men in this world, as the most virtuous actions? Whence is it
that

that *cogitare, peccare eft*, as *Min. Felix* expreffeth it, *& non folum confcios timet, fed & confcientiam?* " Whence is it that a wicked man is guilty upon " account merely of his thoughts, and is not only " fearful becaufe of thofe things which others are " confcious of, but becaufe of thofe things which " no body knows but his own confcience ?" Whence is it, that,

> *Scelus intra fe tacitum qui cogitat ullum,*
> *Facti crimen habet,*

That " he that does but imagine and devife fecret " mifchief in his heart is guilty to himfelf, as if the " fact had been committed;" and when no man can charge and accufe him for it, yet,

> *Noête dieque fuum geftat in pectore teftem,*

"he carries his accufer in his breaft, who does night " and day inceffantly witnefs againft him?"

And that thefe fears are natural, the fudden rife of them is a good evidence. They do not proceed from deliberation, men do not reafon themfelves into thefe fears, but they fpring up in mens minds they know not how ; which fhews that they are natural Now a man's natural actions, I mean fuch as furprize us, and do not proceed from deliberation, are better arguments of the intimate fenfe of our minds, and do more truly difcover the bottom of our hearts, and thofe notions that are implanted in our natures, than thofe actions which are governed by reafon and difcourfe, and proceed from deliberation. To de-monftrate this by an inftance; If a man upon a fud-den fight of a fnake, do recoil and ftart back, trem-ble and grow pale; this is a better argument of a natural antipathy and fear, than it is of a natural courage, if afterward, when he hath commanded down his fear, he fhould by his reafon perfuade himfelf to take up the fnake into his hand. If you would know what a man's natural apprehenfions are, take him on the fudden, and give him no time to deliberate. Therefore fome cunning politicians have ufed this way of furprize and fudden queftions, to dive into the hearts of men, and difcover their fecrets.

In like manner, if we would know what mens natural apprehenfions are concerning the immortality of the foul, and a future ftate, obferve what mens firft thoughts are, whether a man's confcience does not fuggeft to him fuch fears upon the commiffion of fin. There's no doubt but men may offer violence to their natures, and reafon themfelves into great doubts about the foul's immortality ; nay, men may be bribed into the contrary opinion : but this man who in his deliberate difcourfes denies any rewards after this life, fhall by his natural actions acknowledge them, by thofe fears and terrors, which his guilty confcience is ever and anon furprized withal.

The fum of this argument is, that it is natural for men that live pioufly and virtuoufly, that do juft and honeft and worthy actions, to conceive good hopes that it fhall fome time or other be well with them ; that however they may meet with no reward and recompence in this world, yet verily there will be a reward for the righteous : and on the other hand, wicked men, though they flourifh and profper in their wickednefs, yet they are not free from guilt, they are fearful and timorous, even when their condition fets them above the fear of any man upon earth. Now what doth this fignify, but that they have fome fecret prefages of an after-punifhment? Nature fuggefts this thought to them, that there will

be

be a time when all the fins which they have committed, and the wickednefs which they have done, fhall be accounted for.

And it is no prejudice to this truth, that fome men fin againft their confciences, and by frequent acts of fin, and offering notorious violence to their own light, bring themfelves into a brawny and infenfible condition, fo that they have not thofe ftings and lafhes, are not haunted with thofe fears and terrors which purfue common finners. This is but reafonable to be expected, that men by frequent acts of fin, fhould lofe the tender fenfe which mens confciences naturally have of good and evil ; that men that lay wafte their confciences by grofs and notorious fins, fhould lofe the fenfe of good and evil, and that their confciences fhould grow hard like the beaten road ; nay, it is fuitable to the juftice of God, to give up fuch perfons to a reprobate fenfe, to an injudicious mind, that they who would not be awakened and reclaimed by the natural fear of divine juftice, which God hath hid in every man's confcience, fhould at laft lofe all fenfe and apprehenfion of thefe things, and be permitted fecurely and without remorfe to perfect their own ruin.

IV. This doctrine of the immortality of the foul, does evidently tend to the happinefs and perfection of man, and to the good order and government of the world ; to the happinefs and perfection of man, both confidered fingly, and in fociety.

1. To the happinefs and perfection of man, confidered in his fingle capacity. If it be a thing defirable to be at all, then it is a thing defirable to be continued in being as long as may be, and for ever if it be poffible. If life be a perfection, then eternal life is much more fo; efpecially if the eternal

SERM. ſtances of this preſent life be conſidered, together
LXXV. with the ſtate which we hope for hereafter. The
condition of men in this preſent life, is attended with
ſo many frailties, liable to ſo great miſeries and ſufferings, to ſo many pains and diſeaſes, to ſuch various cauſes of ſorrow and trouble, of fear and vexation, by reaſon of the many hazards and uncertain-
ties, which not only the comforts and contentments
of our lives, but even life itſelf is liable to, that the
pleaſure and happineſs of it is by theſe very much re-
bated ; ſo that were not men trained on with the
hopes of ſomething better hereafter, life itſelf would to
many men be an inſupportable burden ; if men were
not ſupported and born up under the anxieties of this
preſent life, with the hopes and expectations of a
happier ſtate in another world, mankind would be
the moſt imperfect and unhappy part of GOD's creation. For although other creatures be ſubjected to
a great deal of vanity and miſery, yet they have this
happineſs, that as they are made for a ſhort duration and continuance, ſo they are only affected with
the preſent, they do not fret and diſcontent themſelves about the future, they are not liable to be
cheated with hopes, nor tormented with fears, nor
vexed at diſappointments, as the ſons of men are.

But if our ſouls be immortal, this makes abundant amends and compenſation for the frailties of
this life, and all the tranſitory ſufferings and inconveniencies of this preſent ſtate ; human nature, conſidered with this advantage, is infinitely above the
brute beaſts that periſh.

As for thoſe torments and miſeries which we are
liable to in another world, far greater than any thing
that men ſuffer in this life, this ought not in reaſon
to be objected againſt the immortality of the ſoul, as
if

if this doctrine did not tend to the happiness and
perfection of man : for if this be truly the case of
mankind, that God hath made mens souls of an immortal nature, and designed them for a perpetual duration and continuance in another state after this life,
in order to which state, he hath placed every man in this
world, to be as it were a candidate for eternity, he
hath furnished every man with such helps and advantages, such opportunities and means for the attaining of everlasting happiness, that if he be not
grosly wanting to himself, he shall not miscarry ; if
this be the case, then an immortal nature is a real
and mighty privilege. If God puts every man into
a capacity of happiness, and if no man becomes miserable but by his own choice, if no man falls short
of eternal happiness but by his own fault, then immortality is a privilege in itself, and a curse to none
but those who make it so to themselves.

2. This doctrine tends to the happiness of man
considered in society, to the good order and government of the world. I do not deny, but if this principle of the immortality of the soul were not believed in the world, if the generality of mankind
had no regard to any thing beyond this present life ;
I say, I do not deny notwithstanding this, but there
would be some kind of government kept up in the
world ; the necessities of human nature, and the
mischiefs of contention would compel men to some
kind of order : but I say withal, that if this principle were banished out of the world, government
would want it's most firm basis and foundation ;
there would be infinitely more disorders in the world,
were men not restrained from injustice and violence
by principles of conscience, and the awe of another
world. And that this is so, is evident from hence,

that all magiftrates think themfelves concerned to cherifh religion, and to maintain in the minds of men the belief of a God, and of a future ftate.

This is the fourth argument, that this doctrine does evidently tend to the happinefs of man, and the good order and government of the world. I grant, that this argument alone, and taken fingly by itfelf, is far from enforcing and neceffarily concluding the foul's immortality : but if the other arguments be of force to conclude, this added to them is a very proper inducement to perfuade and incline men to the belief of this principle ; it does very well ferve the purpofe for which I bring it, namely, to fhew that if there be good arguments for it, no man hath reafon to be averfe or backward to the belief of it ; if by other arguments we be convinced of the fuitablenefs of this principle to reafon, this confideration will fatisfy us, that it is not againft our intereft to entertain it. And no man that is not refolved to live wickedly, hath reafon to defire that the contrary fhould be true. For what would a man gain by it, if the foul were not immortal, but to level himfelf with the beafts that perifh, and to put himfelf into a worfe and more miferable condition than any of the creatures below him ?

SERMON CLXXVI.

Of the immortality of the foul, as difcovered by nature, and by revelation.

2 TIM. i. 10.

But is now made manifeft by the appearing of our SA-
VIOUR JESUS CHRIST, *who hath abolifhed death,
and hath brought life and immortality to light,
through the gofpel.*

THE fifth and laft argument is, that this fuppofition of the foul's immortality gives the
faireft account and eafieft folution of the phænomena
of human nature, of thofe feveral actions and operations which we are confcious to ourfelves of, and
which, without great violence to our reafon, cannot
be refolved into a bodily principle, and afcribed to
meer matter; fuch are perception, memory, liberty,
and the feveral acts of underftanding and reafon.
Thefe operations we find in ourfelves, and we cannot imagine how they fhould be performed by mere
matter; therefore we ought in all reafon to refolve
them into fome principle of another nature from matter, that is, into fomething that is immaterial, and
confequently immortal, that is, incapable in it's
own nature of corruption and diffolution.

And that the force of this argument may the better appear, I fhall fpeak fomething of thefe diftinctly, and fhew that none of thefe operations can be
performed from mere matter. I begin with the

1. And loweft, which is fenfitive perception,
which is nothing elfe but a confcioufnefs to ourfelves
of

SERM.
CLXXVI.

The third
fermon on
this text.

of our own senfations, an apprehenfion of the impreffions which are made upon us; and this faculty is that which conftitutes the difference between senfitive and infenfitive creatures. A ftone may have several impreffions made upon it, as well as the living creature endowed with senfe: but with this difference, that whatever impreffions are made upon a ftone, by knocking, cutting, or any other kind of motion or action, the ftone is ftupid, and is not in the leaft confcious of any of thofe impreffions, does not perceive what is done to it; whereas thofe creatures which are endowed with senfe, do plainly perceive their own and other motions, they are affected with the impreffions which are made upon them.

Now we can give no account of this operation from mere matter. It is plain, that matter is not in its own nature senfible: for we find the greateft part of the world to confift of infenfible parts, and fuch as have no perception. Now if matter be granted in itfelf to be infenfible, it is utterly unimaginable, how any motion or configuration of the parts of it, fhould raife that which hath no senfe to a faculty of perception. Epicurus fancied thofe particles of matter, of which fouls were framed, to be the fineft and fmalleft; and for their fmoother and eafier motion, that they were all of a round figure. But fuppofing matter not to be naturally and of itfelf senfible, who can conceive what that is which fhould awaken the drowfy parts of it, to a lively senfe of the impreffions made upon it? It is every whit as eafy to imagine how an inftrument might be framed and tuned fo artificially, as to hear its own founds, and to be marveloufly delighted with them; or that a glafs might be polifhed to that finenefs, as to fee all thofe objects which are reflected upon it.

But

But there is one difficulty in this: for it may be said, if sensitive perception be an argument of the soul's immateriality, and consequently immortality, then the souls of beasts will be immortal, as well as the souls of men. For answer to this, I shall say these things.

(1.) That the most general and common philosophy of the world hath always acknowledged something in beasts besides their bodies, and that the faculty of sense and perception, which is in them, is founded in a principle of a higher nature than matter. And as this was always the common philosophy of the world, so we find it to be a supposition of scripture, which frequently attributes souls to beasts as well as to men, though of a much inferior nature. And therefore those particular philosophers, who have denied any immaterial principle, or a soul to beasts, have also denied them to have sense, any more than a clock or watch, or any other engine; and have imagined them to be nothing else but a finer and more complicated kind of engines, which, by reason of the curiosity and tenderness of their frame, are more easily susceptible of all kind of motions and impressions from without, which impressions are the cause of all those actions, that resemble those sensations which we men find in ourselves; which is to say, that birds, and beasts, and fishes, are nothing else but a more curious sort of puppets, which by certain secret and hidden weights and springs do move up and down, and counterfeit the actions of life and sense. This I confess seems to me to be an odd kind of philosophy; and it hath this vehement prejudice against it, that if this were true, every man would have great cause to question the reality of his own perceptions: for to all appearance the sensations of beasts are as real as ours, and in many things their

fenfes much more exquifite than ours ; and if nothing
can be a fufficient argument to a man, that he is really
endowed with fenfe, befides his own confcioufnefs of
it, then every man hath reafon to doubt whether all
men in the world befides himfelf be not mere engines ; for no man hath any other evidence, that
another man is really endowed with fenfe, than he
hath that brute creatures are fo ; for they appear to us
to fee, and hear, and feel, and fmell, and tafte things
as truly and as exactly as any man in the world does.

(2.) Suppofing beafts to have an immaterial principle diftinct from their body, it will not from hence
follow, that they are immortal, in the fenfe that we
attribute immortality to men. For immortality,
when we afcribe it to men, fignifies two things.

1. That the foul remains after the body, and is
not corrupted and diffolved together with it.

2. That it lives in this feparate ftate, and is fenfible of happinefs or mifery.

1. Immortality imports that the foul remains after the body, and is not corrupted or diffolved together with it. And there is no inconvenience in at-
tributing this fort of immortality to the brute creatures. And here it is not neceffary for us, who know
fo little of the ways and works of GOD, and of the
fecrets of nature, to be able to give a particular account what becomes of the fouls of brute creatures
after death ; whether they return into the foul and
fpirit of the world, if there be any fuch thing, as fome
fancy ; or whether they pafs into the bodies of other
animals which fucceed in their rooms ; I fay, this is
not neceffary to be particularly determined ; it is fufficient to lay down this in general as highly probable, that they are fuch a fort of fpirits, which, as to
their operation and life, do neceffarily depend upon
matter,

matter, and require union with it, which union being diffolved, they lapfe into an infenfible condition, and a ftate of inactivity. For being endowed only with a fenfitive principle, the operations of which do plainly depend upon an organical difpofition of the body, when the body is diffolved, all their activity ceafeth ; and when this vifible frame of the world fhall be diffolved, and this fcene of fenfible things fhall pafs away, then it is not improbable that they fhall be difcharged out of being, and return to their firft nothing: for though in their own nature they would continue longer, yet having ferved the end of their being, and done their work, it is not unfuitable to the fame wifdom that made them, and commanded them into being, to let them fink into their firft ftate.

2dly, Immortality, as applied to the fpirits of men, imports that their fouls are not only capable of continuing, but living in this feparate ftate, fo as to be fenfible of happinefs and mifery. For the foul of man being of an higher nature, and not only endowed with a faculty of fenfe, but likewife other faculties which have no neceffary dependance upon, or connexion with matter ; having a fenfe of God, and of divine and fpiritual things, and being capable of happinefs in the enjoyment of God, or of mifery in a feparation from him ; it is but reafonable to imagine, that the fouls of men fhall be admitted to the exercife of thefe faculties, and the enjoyment of that life which they are capable of in a feparate ftate. And this is that which conftitutes that vaft and wide difference between the fouls of men and beafts : and this degree of immortality is as much above the other, as reafon and religion are above fenfe.

2. Another faculty in us, which argues an immaterial, and confequently an immortal principle in

man,

man, is memory; and this likewife is common in fome degree to feveral of the brute creatures, and it feems to be nothing elfe but a kind of continued fenfation of things. And of this we can give no account from mere matter. For if that which we call the foul, were nothing elfe but, as Epicurus imagined, a little wild-fire, a company of fmall round particles of matter in perpetual motion, it being a fluid thing, it would be liable to a continual diffipation of its parts, and the new parts that come would be altogether ftrangers to the impreffions made upon the old ; fo that fuppofing the foul liable but to thofe changes which the groffer parts of our bodies, our flefh and blood, continually are liable to; by the evaporation and fpending of the old, and an acceffion of new matter ; (and if we fuppofe the foul to be fluid matter, that is, confifting of particles, which are by no kind of connexion linked to one another, it will in all probability be more eafily diffipable, than the groffer parts of the body, and) if fo, how is it imaginable that thefe new and foreign particles fhould retain any fenfe of the impreffions made upon thofe which are gone many years ago?

3. Another faculty which I fhall inftance in, is the will of man, which is endowed with liberty and freedom, and gives a man dominion over his own actions. Matter moves by neceffary and certain laws, and cannot move if it be at reft, unlefs it be moved by another; and cannot reft, that is, cannot but move, if it be impelled by another. Whence then are voluntary motions ? Whence is the αὐ]εξύσιον, the arbitrary principle which we find in ourfelves, the freedom of action to do or not to do, to do this or that, which we are intimately confcious to ourfelves of? Of all the operations of our minds, it is the hardeft to give an
account

account of liberty from mere matter. This Epicu- rus was fenfible of, and infinitely puzzled with it, as we may fee by the queftion which Lucretius puts,

Unde eft hæc inquam fatis avulfa voluntas?

" How comes the foul of man to have this pecu-
" liar privilege of freedom and liberty, above all
" other forts of matter that are in the world? whence
" is it, that when all things elfe move by a fatal ne-
" ceffity, the foul of man fhould be exempted from
" that flavery?" He does indeed attempt to give
an account of it from a motion of declination which
is proper and peculiar to the particles of the foul :
but that is a more unintelligible riddle than liberty
itfelf. The

4. And laft operation I fhall inftance in, is that
of reafon and underftanding. Not to mention the
activity and nimblenefs of our thoughts, in the ab-
ftracted notions of our minds, the multitude of diftinct ideas and notions which dwell together in our
fouls, none of which are accountable from matter, I
fhall only inftance in two particulars.

(1.) Thofe acts of reafon and judgment whereby
we over-rule the reports of our fenfes, and correct
the errors and deceptions of them.

(2.) The contemplation of fpiritual and divine
things.

(1.) Thofe acts of reafon and judgment whereby
we over-rule the reports and determinations of fenfe.
Our fenfe tells us, that things at a diftance are lefs,
than our reafon tells us they are really in themfelves ;
as that the body of the fun is but about a foot dia-
meter : but our reafon informs us otherwife. Now
what is the principle that controls our fenfes, and cor-
rects the deception of them? If the foul of man is

r r:

mere matter, it can only judge of things according
to the impreffions which are made upon our fenfes :
but we do judge otherwife, and fee reafon to do fo
many times. Therefore it muft be fome higher
principle which judges of things, not by the material
impreffions which they make upon our fenfes, but by
other meafures. And therefore to avoid this inconvenience, Epicurus was glad, to fly the abfurdity,
to affirm that all things really are what they appear
to us, and that in truth the fun is no bigger than it
feems to be.

(2.) The contemplation of things fpiritual and divine, is an argument that the foul is of a higher original than any thing that is material. To contemplate the nature of GOD, and the divine excellencies
and perfections ; the meditation of a future ftate, and
of the happinefs of another world ; thofe breathings
which good men feel in their fouls after GOD, and
the enjoyment of him, argue the fpiritual nature of
the foul. *Hoc habet argumentum divinitatis fuæ* (faith
Seneca) *quòd eam divina delectant, nec ut alienis intereft fed ut fuis.* " The foul of man hath this argu-
" ment of it's divine original, that it is fo ftrangely de-
" lighted, fo infinitely pleafed and fatisfied with the
" contemplation of divine things, and is taken up
" with thefe thoughts, as if they were it's proper
" bufinefs and concernment." Thofe ftrong inclinations and defires after immortality, and the pleafure which good men find in the fore-thoughts of the
happinefs which they hope to enter into, when their
fouls fhall quit thefe manfions ; the reftlefs afpirings
of our fouls toward GOD, and thofe bleffed manfions
where he dwells, and where the fpirits of good men
converfe with him and one another, thefe fignify
our fouls to be of a nobler extraction than the earth,

that

that they are descended from above, and that heaven is their country, their thoughts are so much upon it, and they are so desirous to return to it.

I shall conclude this argument from the noble and excellent operations of our souls, of which we are conscious to ourselves, with a passage of Tully to this purpose. *Animarum nulla in terris origo inveniri potest : nihil enim est in animis mixtum atque concretum, aut quod ex terrâ natum atque fictum esse videatur.* " The souls of men have not their original " from the earth, it is in vain to seek for it there : " for there is nothing in the mind of man of a ma- " terial mixture and composition, which we can ima- " gine to be born or formed out of the earth. For, " says he, among material and earthly things there " is nothing," *quod vim memoriæ, mentis, cogitationis habeat, quod & præterita teneat, & futura provideat, & complecti possit præsentia.* " There is no " earthly thing which hath the power of memory, " of understanding, of thought, which retains things " past, foresees and provides for things future, com- " prehends and considers things present." *Singularis est igitur quædam natura atque vis animi, sejuncta ab his usitatis notisque naturis ;* " so that the nature " and power of the soul are of a peculiar and singu- " lar kind, different from all those natures which " we are acquainted with in this world." He concludes, *Itaque quicquid est quod sentit, quod sapit, quod vult, quod viget, cœleste & divinum est, ob eamque rem æternum sit necesse est.* " Therefore what- " ever that is which is endowed with a power of " perception, with wisdom, with liberty, with so " much vigour and activity as the soul of man, is of " heavenly and divine original, and for that reason " is necessarily immortal, and to continue for ever."

I

Thus

Thus I have reprefented to you, as briefly and
plainly as I could, thofe which I account the chief
and ftrongeft arguments of this great principle of religion, the foul's immortality. Some of them are
plain and obvious to every capacity ; the reft, though
they be above common capacities, yet were not to
be neglected, becaufe they may be ufeful to fome,
though not to all ; and as thofe who are more wife
and knowing fhould have patience, whilft the moft
common and plaineft things are fpoken for the inftruction of ordinary capacities, fo thofe of lower capacities fhould be content that many things fhould
be fpoken which may be ufeful to others, though
they be above their reach.

To fum up then what has been faid from reafon, for
the proof of the foul's immortality. It is a natural
dictate and notion of our minds, univerfally entertained in all ages and places of the world, excepting
fome very few perfons and fects ; it doth not contradict any other principle that nature hath planted in
us, but doth very well agree with thofe other notions which are moft natural ; it is moft fuitable to
the natural hopes and fears of men ; it evidently tends to the happinefs and perfection of man,
and to the good order and government of the world ;
laftly, it gives the faireft account of the phænomena
of human nature, of thofe feveral actions and operations which we are confcious to ourfelves of.

Now fuppofing the foul were immortal, what
greater rational evidence than this can we expect for
it ? How can we without a revelation have more affurance of the things of this nature, than thefe arguments give us, not taken fingly, but as they concur
together to make up an entire argument, and to give
us fufficient evidence of this ?

                                                I do

I do not fay that thefe arguments do fo neceffarily conclude it, that there is an abfolute impoffibility the thing fhould be otherwife: but fo as to render it fufficiently certain to a prudent and confiderate man, and one that is willing to accept of reafonable evidence. For the generality of the papifts do pertinacioufly maintain this unreafonable principle, that there can be no certainty of any thing without infallibility: yet fome of the wifer of them have thought better of it, and are pleafed to ftate the bufinefs of certainty otherwife; particularly Melchior Canus, one of the moft learned of their writers determines thofe things to be fufficiently certain, which no man can without imprudence and obftinacy difbelieve. *Certa apud homines ea funt quæ negari fine pervicaciâ & ftultitiâ non poffunt.* " Men efteem thofe things " certain, which no man that is not unreafonably " obftinate and imprudent can deny." And I think the arguments I have brought for the foul's immortality, are fuch as no man that is unprejudiced and hath a prudent regard to his own intereft can refift.

Thus I have done with the firft thing I propounded to do for the proof of the foul's immortality, which was to fhew what evidence of reafon there is for it. I fhall fpeak briefly to the

Second thing I propounded, which was to fhew how little can be faid againft it, becaufe this will indirectly give a ftrength and force to the arguments I have brought for it. For it is very confiderable in any queftion or controverfy, what ftrength there is in the arguments on both fides: for though very plaufible arguments may be brought for a thing, yet if others as plaufible and fpecious may be urged againft it, this leaves the thing in æquilibrio, it fets the balance even, and inclines the judgment neither way;

nay, if the objections againſt a thing be conſiderable, though not ſo ſtrong as the arguments for it,
the conſiderableneſs of the objections does ſo far
weaken the contrary arguments : but where the arguments on one hand are ſtrong, and the objections
on the contrary very ſlight, and ſuch as may eaſily be
anſwered, the weakneſs of the objections contributes
to the ſtrength of the argument for the other ſide of
the queſtion.

To come then to the buſineſs, I know but three
objections, which have any colour againſt this principle.

I. That the notion of a ſpirit, or an immaterial
ſubſtance, does imply a contradiction.

Anſw. 1. This is only boldly ſaid, and not the
leaſt colour of proof offered for it by the author that
aſſerts it.   This objection had indeed been conſiderable, if it had been made out as clearly, as it is con-
fidently affirmed.   In the mean time I think we may
take leave to deny, that the notion of a ſpirit hath
any repugnancy in it, till ſome body think fit to
prove it.

2. I told you that this queſtion about the ſoul's
immortality, ſuppoſeth the exiſtence of God to be
already proved ; and if there be a God, and it be an
eſſential property of the divine nature, that he is a
ſpirit, then there is ſuch a thing as a ſpirit and immaterial ſubſtance, and conſequently the notion of a
ſpirit hath no contradiction in it ; for if it had, there
could be no ſuch thing.

II. It is ſaid, there is no expreſs text for the ſoul's
immortality in the old teſtament.

Anſw. This doth not properly belong to the in-
trinſical arguments and reaſon of the thing, but is
matter of revelation.   And this I ſhall fully ſpeak to,
when I come to ſhew what evidence the Jews had
                                                    for

for the soul's immortality. In the mean time this may be a sufficient answer to this objection, that there is no absolute necessity why it should be exprefly revealed in the old testament, if it be, as I have shewn, a natural notion of our minds : for the scripture supposeth us to be men, and to have an antecedent notion of those truths which are implanted in our nature, and therefore chiefly designs to teach us the way to that eternal happiness which we have a natural notion and hope of. The

III. Objection is from the near and intimate sympathy which is between the soul and the body, which appears in the vigour and strength of our faculties; as understanding and memory do very much depend upon the temper and disposition of the body, and do usually decay and decline with it.

Answ. The utmost that this objection signifies, is, that there is an intimate union and conjunction between the soul and the body, which is the cause of the sympathy which we find to be between them: but it does by no means prove, that they are one and the same essence. Now that there is such an intimate union and connexion between the soul and matter in all creatures endowed with life and sense, is acknowledged by all who affirm the immateriality of souls; though the manner of this union be altogether unknown to us; and supposing such an union, it is but reasonable to imagine that there should be such a sympathy, that the body should be affected with the delights and disturbances of the mind, and that the soul should also take part in the pleasures and pains of the body, that by this means it may be effectually excited and stirred up to provide for the supply of our bodily wants and necessities : and from this sympathy, it is easy to give account .... it .. ' to

pafs, that our faculties of underftanding, and memory, and imagination, are more or lefs vigorous,
according to the good or bad temper and difpofition
of our bodies. For by the fame reafon that the
mind may be grieved and afflicted at the pains and
fufferings of the body, it may likewife be difordered
and weakened in it's operations by the diftempers of
the body. So that this objection only proves the
foul to be united to the body; but not to be the fame
thing with it.

SERMON CLXXVII.

Of the immortality of the foul, as difco-
vered by nature, and by revelation.

2 TIM. i. 10.

But is now made manifeft by the appearing of our
SAVIOUR JESUS CHRIST, *who hath abolifhed
death, and hath brought life and immortality to
light, through the gofpel.*

SERM.
CLXXVII.

Thefourth
fermon on
this text.

HAVING in my three former difcourfes fhewed, what arguments natural reafon doth furnifh us with, for the immortality of our fouls, I
come now to the fecond thing I propounded, which
is to fhew what affurance the world had *de facto*, of
this great principle of religion, the foul's immortality, before the revelation of the gofpel.

Before our SAVIOUR's coming into the world,
there were but two different religions; that of the
heathens, and that of the Jews. The religion of the
heathens

heathens was natural religion, corrupted and dege-
nerated into idolatry : the religion of the Jews was
revealed and inftituted by God; but did fuppofe
natural religion, and was fuperadded to it. Therefore I fhall confider the heathens and the Jews diftinctly. And,

Firft, Shew what affurance the heathens had of
this principle of the foul's immortality.

Secondly, What the Jews had of it.

Firft, What affurance the heathens had of the
foul's immortality.

1. It is evident, that there was a general inclination in mankind, even after it's greateft corruption
and degeneracy, to the belief of this principle ;
which appears in that all people and nations of the
world, after they were funk into the greateft degeneracy, and all (except only the Jews) became idola-
ters, did univerfally agree in this apprehenfion, that
their fouls did remain after their bodies, and pafs into a ftate of happinefs or mifery, according as they
had demeaned themfelves in this life. Not that they
did generally reafon themfelves into this apprehenfion, by any convincing arguments, but did herein
follow the bent and tendency of their natures, which
did incline them thus to think. For no other reafon
can be given of the univerfal confent, even of the
moft rude and barbarous nations in this principle,
befides the inclination of human nature to this opinion; that is, either men come into the world with
this notion imprinted upon their minds, or elfe (which
comes all to one) the underftanding of man is naturally of fuch a frame and make, that left to itfelf,
and the free exercife of it's own thoughts, it will
fall into this apprehenfion.

2. The unlearned and common people among
the

the heathen, feem to have had the trueft and leaft wavering apprehenfions in this matter; the reafon of which feems to be plain, becaufe their belief fol-lowed the biafs and inclination of their nature, and they had not their natural notions embroiled and difordered by obfcure and uncertain reafonings about it, as the philofophers had, whofe underftandings were perplexed with infinite niceties and objections, which never troubled the heads of the common peo-ple. By which means the vulgar had this advantage, that the natural dictates of their minds had their free courfe; and as they did not argue themfelves into this principle, fo neither were their natural hopes and fears check'd and controlled by any objections to the contrary.

But then, this principle being only a kind of na-tural inftinct in them, which did not awaken their minds by any deep confideration and reafoning about it, it had no great influence on their lives. For as they were not much troubled with doubts concerning it, fo neither did they deeply attend to the confe-quences of it: but as they followed the inclination of nature in the entertaining of this notion, fo be-caufe it was not entertained upon deep confideration, it had no great effect upon them.

3. The learned among the heathen did not fo ge-nerally agree in this principle, and thofe who did confent in it, were many of them more wavering and unfettled than the common people. Epicurus and his followers were peremptory in the denial of it: but by their own acknowledgment, they did herein offer great violence to their natures, and had much ado to diveft themfelves of the contrary apprehen-fions and fears. Therefore the poet, in the perfon of the epicurean, reprefents it as a rare piece of hap-pinefs,

piness, and that which few attained to, to quit themselves of the notions of another state after this life.

Felix qui potuit rerum cognoscere causas,
Atque metus omnes & inexorabile fatum
Subjecit pedibus, strepitumque acherontis avari.

The Stoicks were very inclinable to the belief of
a future state ; but yet they almost every where speak
very doubtfully of it. Seneca and Antoninus often
speak to this purpose, that if the soul remain after
this life, there's no doubt but that good men shall
be happy, and bad men miserable ; but whether the
soul out-live the body or not, that they could not po-
sitively determine. Aristotle hath some express pas-
sages for the soul's immortality ; but it seems he was
not constant to himself in this matter, or else they
have done him a great deal of wrong, who have
wrote so many books on both sides, concerning
his opinion in this point. Pythagoras, Socrates,
and Plato, and many others of the most eminent
philosophers, as Tully tells us, were full, not of assurance, but of very good hopes of the soul's immortality and a future state. Socrates, who was
one of the best and wisest of all the heathens, does
in his discourses before his death, (as Plato relates
them) support and bear up himself against the terrors of death, only with this consideration, that he
was full of hopes that when he left this world, he
should pass into a far happier and more perfect state ;
that he should go to G o d and live with him, and
keep company with the spirits of good men : and
that he is not positive and peremptory in it, is no
argument that he doubted of this more than any
thing else ; for that was his fashion in all his dif-
courses, to speak modestly, and with some shew of
doubt-

doubting, even concerning thofe things whereof he had the greateft affurance : but this is plain, that he was fo well affured of it as to die chearfully, and to leave the world without any kind of disturbance, upon the hopes that he had conceived of another life ; and furely they muft be pretty confident hopes, that will bear up a man's fpirit to fuch a height when he comes to die. In fhort, he told his friends the morning before he died, that he had as good affurance of the foul's immortality as human reafon could give, and that nothing but a divine revelation could give him greater fatisfaction. And to mention no more, Tully, the chief philofopher among the Romans, expreffeth himfelf with a good degree of confidence in this matter. He argues excellently for it in feveral parts of his works ; but particularly in his book *de Senectute*, he declares his own opinion of it, where, fpeaking to Scipio and Lælius, he fays, " I do not fee why I may not ad-
" venture to declare freely to you, what my thoughts
" are concerning death ; and perhaps I may difcern
" better than others what it is, becaufe I am now
" by reafon of my age not far from it. I believe,
" fays he, that the fathers, thofe eminent perfons
" and my particular friends, are ftill alive, and that
" they live the life which only deferves the name of
" life." And afterward, *Nec me folum ratio ac difputatio impulit ut ita crederem, fed nobilitas etiam fummorum philofophorum & authoritas ;* " nor has
" reafon only and difputation brought me to this
" belief, but the famous judgment and authority of
" the chief philofophers." And having mentioned Pythagoras, Socrates, and Plato, he breaks out into this rapture, *Oh præclarum diem quum in illud animorum concilium cœtumque proficifcar, & cum ex*
L 's

hâc turbâ & colluvione discedam! "Oh glorious day,
" when I shall go unto the great council and assem-
" bly of spirits, when I shall go out of this tumult
" and confusion, and quit the sink of this world,
" when I shall be gathered to all those brave spirits
" who have left this world, and meet with Cato, the
" greatest and best of mankind !" What could a
Christian almost say with more extasy? And he concludes, *Quòd si in hoc erro, quod animos hominum
immortales esse credam, libenter erro, nec mihi hunc
errorem quo delector, dum vivo, extorqueri volo : sin
mortuus, ut quidam minuti philosophi censent, nihil sen-
tiam, non vereor ne hunc errorem meum mortui philosophi irrideant.''* "But if after all I am mistaken
" herein, I am pleased with my error, which I
" would not willingly part with whilst I live : and
" if after my death (as some little philosophers sup-
" pose) I shall be deprived of all sense, I have no
" fear of being exposed and laughed at by them,
" for this my mistake in the other world.''

Thus you see what assurance the heathens had of
this principle, and that there was a general inclination and propension in them to the belief of it ; and
as it was not firmly and upon good grounds believed
among the common people ; so neither was it doubted of or called in question among them. Among
the philosophers it was a matter of great uncertainty,
being stiffly denied by some, doubted of by others ;
and those who were most inclinable to the entertain-
ment of it, do rather express their desires and hopes of
it, than their full assurance concerning it. I come
therefore,

Secondly, To the enquiry, what assurance the
Jews had of the soul's immortality and a future

ſtate ? And of this, I ſhall give you an account in
theſe following particulars.

1. They had all the aſſurance which natural light,
and the common reaſon of mankind does ordinarily
afford men concerning this matter ; they had common to them with the heathens, all the advantage
that nature gives men to come to the knowledge of
this truth. But that which I chiefly deſign to enquire into, is, what ſingular advantage they had
above the heathens, by means of thoſe ſpecial revelations which were made to them from GOD.
Therefore,

2. They had by divine revelation a fuller aſſurance
of thoſe truths which have a nearer connexion with
this principle, and which do very much tend to facilitate the belief of it ; as namely, concerning the
providence of GOD, and his intereſting himſelf particularly in the affairs of the world. In the hiſtory
of Moſes they had a ſatisfactory account of the original of the world, that GOD made it, and that he
had eminently interpoſed in the government of it ;
and had given ſeveral eminent teſtimonies of his
providence, in the general deluge which was brought
upon the world, and in the dreadful particular judgment from heaven upon Sodom and Gomorrah, and
the neighbouring cities ; in his ſpecial providence towards Abraham, and Iſaac, and Jacob ; in that ſeries
of miracles whereby their deliverance was wrought
out of Egypt, and they were carried through the
wilderneſs to the promiſed land ; and in thoſe two
ſtanding miracles of the fruitfulneſs of every ſixth
year, becauſe the land was to reſt the ſeventh ; and
preſerving the land from the invaſion of enemies,
when they came up to Jeruſalem three times a year ;
by which GOD did teſtify a very particular and immediate

mediate providence toward them. Now whatever
gives affurance of GOD's providence, does very much
facilitate the belief of a future ftate. Epicurus was
well aware of the connexion of thefe principles , and
therefore in order to the freeing of the minds of men
from the fears of a future ftate, he makes way for it,
by removing the providence of GOD, and denying
that he either made the world, or concerned himfelf
in the government of it.

And then befides this, the Jews had affurance of
the exiftence of fpirits, by the more immediate miniftry of angels among them. And this does directly make way for the belief of an immaterial principle, and confequently of the foul's immortality.
And this the Sadducees, who were a kind of Epicureans among the Jews, were fenfible of ; and therefore as they faid that there was no refurrection and no
future ftate after this life, fo they denied that there
was either angel or fpirit, as the apoftle tells us, Acts
xxiii. 7. From whence by the way we may take
notice of the great miftake of thofe, who, from the
opinion of the Sadducees, argue that eternal life was
not at all believed under the old teftament ; becaufe
if it had been fo, it is not credible that it would have
been difowned by thofe who acknowledged the authority of thofe books ; whereas we fee that they denied, to ferve their hypothefis, other things which
were moft exprefly revealed in the old teftament, as
the doctrine of angels and fpirits.

3. There were fome remarkable inftances in the
old teftament, which did tend very much to perfuade
men to this truth ; I mean the inftances of Enoch
and Elias, who did not die like other men, but were
tranflated, and taken up into heaven in an extraordinary manner. From which inftances it was obvi-

ous to confiderate men, to reafon, that GOD did intend by thefe examples to encourage good men with
the hopes of another ftate after this life. And accordingly the apoftle to the Hebrews makes the belief of future rewards a neceffary confequence from
this inftance of Enoch's tranflation, Heb. xi. 5, 6.
" By faith Enoch was tranflated, that he fhould not
" fee death, and was not found, becaufe GOD had
" tranflated him : for before his tranflation he had
" this teftimony, that he pleafed GOD. But with-
" out faith it is impoffible to pleafe him : for he that
" cometh to GOD, muft believe that he is, and that
" he is a rewarder of them that diligently feek him."

4. This was typified and fhadowed forth to them
by the legal adminiftrations. The whole œconomy
of their worfhip and temple, of their rites and ceremonies, and fabbaths, did fhadow out fome farther
thing to them, though in a very obfcure manner :
The land of Canaan, and their coming to the poffeffion of it, after fo many years travel in the wildernefs, did reprefent that heavenly inheritance which
good men fhould be poffeffed of after the troubles of
this life. And thefe were intended by GOD to fignify
thofe greater and better things to them, and fo underftood by thofe who were more devout and knowing among them ; elfe the apoftle, in his epiftle to
the Hebrews, had gone upon a very ill ground, when
he all along takes it for granted, that the difpenfation of the law, and all the ceremonies of it, were
of a farther fignification, Heb. x. 11. " The law
" having a fhadow of good things to come."

5. This was in general, and by good confequence,
though not obvious to all, yet fufficiently to prudent
and difcerning men, revealed in the book of the law
taken precifely ; I mean the five books of Mofes. It

I   is

is faid of Abel, that God was pleafed with his facrifice, though with Cain's he was not well pleafed,
Gen. iv. Upon this Cain was angry at his brother,
and flew him. Now if the immortality of the foul
and a future ftate, be not fuppofed and taken for
granted in this ftory, this very paffage is enough to
cut the finews, and pluck up the roots of all religion.
For if there were no rewards after this life, it were
obvious for every man to argue from this ftory, that
it was a dangerous thing to pleafe God; if this were
all that Abel got by it, to be knocked on the head
by his brother, who offended God.

But I fhall chiefly infift on the general promifes,
which we find in thefe books of Mofes, of God's bleffing good men, and declaring that he was their God,
even after their death. Now I fhall fhew that thefe
promifes did involve the happinefs of another life,
and were intended by God to fignify thus much,
and were fo underftood by good men under that difpenfation. That thefe general promifes did contain
this fenfe under them, and were intended by God to
fignify thus much, is evident from our Saviour's
citation of that text, to confute the Sadducees, " I
" am the God of Abraham, the God of Ifaac, and
" the God of Jacob;" from whence he reafons
thus, " now God is not the God of the dead, but
" of the living; for all live to him:" the force of
which argument was directly and immediately levelled againft the main error of the Sadducees, which
was the denial of a future ftate. This our Saviour
immediately proves from this text, and by confequence the refurrection, which the Sadducees did not
deny upon any other account, but becaufe they did
not * believe a future ftate. *See fermon xxxvi. Vol. III.

6. Toward the expiration of the legal difpenfation,

tion, there was yet a clearer revelation of a future state. The text in Daniel seems to be much plainer than any in the old testament, Dan. xii. 2. "And "many of them that sleep in the dust of the earth "shall awake; some to everlasting life, and some "to shame and everlasting contempt." And to this text the seven brethren, who were cruelly put to death under the persecution of Antiochus, seem to refer, when they comfort themselves with the hopes of another life, 2 Mac. vii. 9. where one of them, ready to die, says thus to Antiochus, "thou like a fury "takest us out of this present life; but the king of "the world shall raise us up, who have died for his "laws, unto everlasting life." To the same purpose another of them, ver. 14. when he was tormented, expresseth his confidence thus, "it is good, "being put to death by men, to look for hope from "GOD, to be raised up again by him: but as for "thee (speaking of Antiochus) thou shalt have no "resurrection to life." Where he seems to allude to the twofold resurrection mentioned by Daniel. And though this history of the Maccabees be not canonical, yet the apostle hath warranted the truth of it to us, at least in this particular, for he plainly refers to this story, Heb. xi. 35. "Others were tor- "tured, not accepting deliverance, that they might obtain a better resurrection.

7. Notwithstanding this, I say, that the immortality of the soul, and a future state, was not expresly and clearly revealed in the old testament, at least not in Moses his law. The special and particular promises of that dispensation, were of temporal good things; and the great blessing of eternal life, was but somewhat obscurely involved and signified in the types and general promises: for considering that
the

the particular promises were plainly of temporal things, it was very obvious to those who were not so prudent and discerning to interpret the general promises, so as to comprehend only that kind of blessings, which were express'd in the special and particular promises, and so likewise to understand the general threatnings. And upon this account, the apostle to the Hebrews principally advanceth the new covenant of the gospel, above the old dispensation; because the gospel had clear, and express, and special promises of eternal life, which the law had not, Heb. viii. 6. "But now hath he obtained a more excel-
" lent ministry, by how much also he is the Medi-
" ator of a better covenant, which was established
" upon better promises." For the same reason CHRIST is said here in the text, " by his appearance
" to have abolished death, and brought life and
" immortality to light through the gospel." And so I proceed to the

Second thing I propounded, which is to shew what farther evidence and assurance the gospel gives us of it, than the world had before; what clearer discoveries we have by CHRIST's coming, than the heathens or Jews had before.

That the gospel hath brought to us a clearer discovery of this than they had, is here expresly said; that GOD's gracious purpose concerning our salvation, which was, before the world began, decreed to be accomplished in CHRIST, is now made manifest by his coming into the world; ver. 9. " Who hath
" saved and called us with an holy calling, not ac-
" cording to our works, but according to his own
" purpose and grace, which was given us in CHRIST
" JESUS before the world began, but is now made
" manifest, &c." Which is emphatically spoken,
now,

now, and not till now, importing that before the appearing of our SAVIOUR, it was in great meafure hid from the world, and that men had very dark and obfcure apprehenfions of it, till it was " brought to " light by the gofpel." And this is not only affirmed in this place, but very frequently all over the new teftament. I will mention fome of the moft exprefs places to this purpofe, John vi. 8. When many of CHRIST's followers left him, he afks the twelve, " will ye alfo go away?" To whom Peter anfwers, " LORD, to whom fhall we go? thou haft " the words of eternal life." As if he had faid, what mafter fhould we chufe to follow rather than thee, who bringeft to the world the glad tidings of eternal life? What difcipline or inftitution is there in the world, that gives fuch encouragement to its followers? Others may promife great things in this world; but in the declarations and promifes of another life, we cannot rely upon any one but him that comes from GOD, as we are fully perfuaded thou doft; for it follows in the next verfe, " and we be- " lieve, and are fure that thou art the CHRIST, the " Son of the living GOD."

Tit. ii. 10, &c. " The grace of GOD which brings " falvation hath appeared to all men, &c." Where the revelation of the gofpel is called " the grace of " GOD which brings falvation," that is, which difcovers to the world that eternal happinefs, which was in a great meafure hid from it before, and encourageth men by the hopes of that bleffing to live a holy life. The apoftle to the Hebrews doth all along in his epiftle, ufe this as an argument to the Jews, to take them off from the Mofaical inftitution, and to perfuade them to entertain the doctrine of the gofpel, as making clearer difcoveries, and giving greater affurance

furance of eternal life and falvation, than the law did, Heb. ii. 2, 3, 4, 5. " For if the word fpoken by " angels was ftedfaft, and every tranfgreffion and " difobedience received a juft recompence of reward : " how fhall we efcape, if we neglect fo great falva- " tion, which at the firft began to be fpoken by the " Lord, and was confirmed unto us by them that " heard him ; God alfo bearing them witnefs, both " with figns and wonders, and with divers miracles " and gifts of the Holy Ghoft, according to his own " will ? For unto the angels hath he not put in fub- " jection the world to come, whereof we fpeak." That is, if the promifes and threatnings of the law, which was delivered but " by the miniftry of angels," were made good, and the offenders under that dif- penfation were feverely punifhed, what fhall become of us, if we neglect the difpenfation of the gofpel, which reveals to us greater things, even eternal life and falvation, and which receiveth fo great a confir- mation both from Christ himfelf, by whom it was firft delivered, and alfo from his apoftles, who pub- lifhed it to the world, and gave teftimony to it by fo many miracles ? And it follows, at ver. 5. " For " unto the angels hath he not put in fubjection the " world to come, whereof we now fpeak." The meaning of which is this, the promifes and threat- nings of the law which was delivered by angels were temporal, and fuch as refpected this world ; but now God hath fent his fon, he hath in him made pro- mifes of a greater falvation, he hath put into his hands the great things of another world, and hath given him power to promife eternal life, and to give it to as many as he pleafes. So the danger of con- temning the gofpel muft needs be much greater than that of the law, becaufe the happinefs which the

gofpel promifes, is fo much greater: For unto the
angels, who delivered the law, GOD gave no power
and commiffion to make clear and exprefs promifes
of the rewards of another world. " Unto the angels
" did he not put in fubjection the world to come ;"
but fo hath he done to his Son, " he hath commit-
" ted all judgment to him, and hath given him
" power to raife up thofe who have done good, un-
" to the refurrection of life, and thofe that have done
" evil, unto the refurrection of damnation :" As
our SAVIOUR himfelf fpeaks, John v. 22. and thus,
" he hath put the world to come in fubjection unto
" his Son," having impowered him to encourage
and argue men to the obedience of his laws, by the
rewards and punifhments of another world : whereas
the law delivered by angels had only the fanction of
temporal threatnings and promifes. Heb. vii. 16.
The gofpel is called " the power of an eternal life,"
in oppofition to the law, which is called " a carnal
" commandment ;" not only becaufe the precepts
of it refpected the body, but becaufe the promifes of
it were of temporal good things which belong to this
life ; and at the 19th verfe, the gofpel, in oppofition
to the Mofaical difpenfation, is called " the bringing
" in of a better hope. The law made nothing per-
" fect : but the bringing in of a better hope did ;
" ἐπεισαγωγὴ, the fuperinduction of a better hope ;"
by which the apoftle plainly fignifies, that this was
the imperfection of the Mofaical difpenfation, that it
did not give men firm hopes and affurance of eternal life ; but the gofpel hath fuperinduced this hope,
and thereby fupplied the great defect of the former
adminiftration. To the fame purpofe he tells us,
chap. viii. 6. that CHRIST " hath now obtained a
" more excellent miniftry, for as much as he is the
2   " mediator

" Mediator of a better covenant, established upon
" better promises." How better promises? why,
instead of the promises of a temporal Canaan, and
earthly blessings, CHRIST hath given us promises of
eternal life and happiness. Therefore in the next
chapter he is called " an high priest of the good things
" to come :" and ver. 15. " For this cause" he is
said to be " the mediator of the new testament, that
" they which are called might receive the promise
" of the eternal inheritance." Once more the apostle, chap. x. 1. makes this the great imperfection of
the law, in opposition to the gospel, that it " had
" only a shadow of good things to come, but not
" the very image of the things ;" that is, it did but
darkly typify and shadow forth the things of another
life, not give us so express an image, and lively representation of the rewards of another world, as the
gospel does. Therefore St. John makes eternal life
to be the great promise of the gospel, the great blessing which CHRIST hath revealed to the world,
1 John ii. 25. " this is the promise which he hath
" promised, even eternal life." So that you see, that
the full and clear discovery of eternal life is every
where in the new testament attributed to CHRIST,
and to the revelation which by him was made to the
world.

It remains now, that I shew more particularly,
wherein the gospel hath given the world greater evidence and assurance of a future state, than they had
before.

1. The rewards of another life are most clearly
revealed in the gospel. That GOD hath made a revelation of this by CHRIST is an advantage which
the heathen wanted, who were destitute of divine
revelation. There are many truths which men may

be

be well inclined to believe, and for the proof of which, the wiser and more knowing sort of men may be able to offer very fair and plausible arguments; and yet for all this, they may have no confident assurance of them, or at least may be very far from a well-grounded certainty, such as will give rest and satisfaction to the mind of a considerate and inquisitive man. All men are not capable of the force of a reason; nay, there are very few who can truly judge of the weakness or strength of an argument. There are many things which admit of very plausible arguments on both sides; and the generality of men are very apt to be imposed upon by very slight arguments, to be moved any way with some little shew and appearance of reason. So that when this principle of the soul's immortality came to be disputed in the world, and the sects of the philosophers, the learned men of those times, came to be divided in opinion about it, some disputing directly against it, others doubting very much of it, and scarce any pretending to any great assurance of it, it was no wonder, if by this means many came to be in suspence about it; but now divine revelation, when that comes, it takes away all doubting, and gives men assurance of that, concerning which they were uncertain before. For every man that believes a God, does firmly believe this principle, that whatever is revealed by him is true: But especially if the revelation be clear and express, then it gives full satisfaction to the mind of man, and removes all jealousy and suspicions of the contrary. And this is a great advantage which the gospel gives us in this matter, above what the Jews had. They had some kind of revelation and discovery of this under the dispensation of the law; but very darkly, in types and shadows; but the gospel gives us a most express revelation

velation of it, is full of special promises to this pur-pose, made in clear words, free from all ambiguity, or liableness to be interpreted to another sense. So that if we compare the law and the gospel together, we shall see a vast difference as to this matter. Under the law, the promise of eternal life was only comprehended in some general words, from which a man that had true notions of GOD and religion might be able to infer, that GOD intended some reward for good men, and punishment for wicked men, beyond this life : but the promises of temporal good things were special and express, and their law was full of them. Contrariwise in the new testament, the most special and express promise is that of eternal life, and this the books of the new testament are full of : as for temporal blessings, they are but sparingly and obscurely promised in comparison of the other.

2. The rewards of another life, as they are clearly and expresly revealed by the gospel, so that they may have the greater power and influence upon us, and we may have the greater assurance of them, they are revealed with very particular circumstances. And herein the gospel gives us a great advantage, both above the heathens and Jews. For though a man was satisfied in general of a state after this life, that mens souls should survive their bodies, and pass into another world, where it shall be well with them that have done well in this world, and ill to those that have done ill; yet no man, without a revelation, could conjecture the particular circumstances of that state. What wild descriptions do the heathen poets, who were their most ancient divines, make of heaven and hell, of the Elysian fields, and the infernal regions! But now the gospel, for our greater assurance and satisfaction, hath revealed many particular circumstances

SERM.
CLXXVII.
cumftances of the future ftate to us; as that all men
at the end of the world fhall be fummoned to make
a folemn appearance before the LORD JESUS CHRIST,
whom GOD hath made judge of the world, as a reward of his patience and fufferings; that the bodies
of men fhall, in order to that appearance, be raifed up
by the mighty power of GOD, and united to their
fouls, that as they have been inftruments of the foul
in acts of holinefs and fin, fo they may take part likewife in the happinefs and torments of it. There are
feveral other circumftances the gofpel hath revealed
to us concerning our future ftate, which had they not
been revealed, we could never have known, hardly
have conjectured; in all which, befides the affurance
that they are revealed, it is a great fatisfaction to us,
that there is nothing in them that is unworthy of
GOD, or that favours of the weaknefs and vanity of
human imagination.

3. The gofpel gives us yet farther affurance of
thefe things, by fuch an argument as is like to be the
moft convincing and fatisfactory to common capacities; and that is by a lively inftance of the thing to
be proved, in " raifing CHRIST from the dead,"
Acts xvii. 30, 31.

It is true indeed, under the old teftament there
were two inftances fomewhat of this nature; Enoch
and Elias were immediately tranflated, and taken up
alive into heaven; but thefe two inftances do in many
refpects fall fhort of the other. For after CHRIST
was raifed from the dead, he converfed forty days
with his difciples, and fatisfied them that he was
rifen; after which he was in their fight vifibly taken
up into heaven: and as an evidence that he was poffeffed of his glorious kingdom, he fent down, according to his promife, his holy Spirit in miraculous
gifts,

gifts, to affure them by thofe teftimonies of his roy-
alty, that he was in heaven, and to qualify them by
thofe miraculous powers to convince the world of the
truth of their doctrine.

Now what argument more proper to convince
them of another life after this, than to fee a man raifed
from the dead, and reftored to a new life ? What
fitter to fatisfy a man concerning heaven, and the
happy eftate of thofe there, than to fee one vifibly
taken up into heaven ? And what more fit to affure
us, that the promifes of the gofpel are real, and fhall
be made good to us, than to fee him who made thefe
promifes to us, raife himfelf from the dead, and go
up into heaven, and from thence to difpenfe miraculous gifts and powers abroad in the world, as evidences of the power and authority which he was in-
vefted withal ? All the philofophical arguments that
a man can bring for the foul's immortality, and another life, will have no force upon vulgar apprehenfions, in comparifon of thefe fenfible demonftrations,
which give an experiment of the thing, and furnifh
us with an inftance of fomething of the fame kind,
and of equal difficulty with that which is propounded
to our belief.

4. And laftly, the effects which the clear difcovery
of this truth had upon the world, are fuch, as the
world never faw before, and are a farther inducement
to perfuade us of the truth and the reality of it. After the gofpel was entertained in the world, to fhew,
that thofe who embrace i it did fully believe this principle, and were abundantly fatisfied concerning the
rewards and happinefs of another life, they did for
the fake of their religion defpife this life and all the
enjoyments of it, from a thorough perfuafion of a
far greater happinefs than any this world could afford,

ford, remaining in the next life. With what chear-
fulnefs did they fuffer perfecutions, with what joy
and triumph did they welcome torments, and embrace death, " knowing in themfelves that they had
" in heaven a better and more enduring fubftance !"
Thus when " life and immortality was brought to
" light by the gofpel," death was as it were quite
abolifhed ; thofe of the weakeft age and fex, wo-
men and children, did familiarly encounter it with
as great a bravery, and bore up againft the terrors
of it with as much courage, as any of the greateft
fpirits among the Romans ever did : and this not in
a few inftances, but in vaft numbers. No emperor
in the world ever had fo numerous an army of perfons refolved to fight for him, as this " captain of
" our falvation, this prince of life and glory" had
of perfons couragioufly refolved, and chearfully contented to die for him.

Now this wonderful effect, the like of which the
world never faw before, was very fuitable to the nature of this doctrine. Suppofe that GOD from heaven fhould have given men affurance of another life
after this, in which good men fhould be unfpeakably happy : what more reafonable to imagine, than
that perfons fo affured fhould defpife this life, and
all the enjoyments of it, in comparifon of the eternal
and unconceivable happinefs, which they were perfuaded they fhould be made partakers of in another
world ? So that whatever affurance an exprefs and
clear revelation from GOD of the foul's immortality
and another life, together with the particular circumftances of that ftate ; whatever affurance a lively inftance and example of the thing, in the perfon of
him who brings this doctrine to the world ; whatever confequent miracles, and fuitable effects upon
the

the minds of men to such a principle : I say, whatever assurance and satisfaction these can give of this principle, all this the gospel hath given us, beyond whatever the heathens or Jews had before.

The inference I shall make from this discourse shall be only this ; that if there be such a state after this life, then how does it concern every man to provide for it? Every action that we do in this life will have a good or bad influence upon our everlasting condition, and the consequences of it will extend themselves to eternity. Did men seriously consider this, that they carry about them immortal souls that shall live for ever, they would not trifle away the opportunities of this life, bend all their thoughts, and imploy their designs in the present gratification of their senses, and the satisfaction of their fleshly part, which shall shortly die and moulder into dust : but they would make provision for the state which is beyond the grave, and lay designs for eternity, which is infinitely the most considerable duration ; they would not, like children, take care for the present, without any prospect to the future, and lay out all they have to please themselves for a day, without any regard to the remaining part of their lives. Nothing can be more unbecoming Christians, whose whole religion pretends to be built upon the firm belief of another world, than to be intent upon the things of this present life, to the neglect of their souls and all eternity.

Seeing then we pretend to be assured of immortal life, and to have clear discoveries of everlasting happiness and glory, as we hope to be made partakers of this portion, let us live as it becomes the candidates of heaven, those that are heirs of another world, and " the children of the resurrection, that this

" grace

" grace of God, which hath brought falvation, may
" teach us to deny ungodlinefs and worldly lufts,
" and to live foberly, righteoufly, and godly in this
" prefent life, looking for that bleffed hope, and the
" glorious appearing of the great God, and our
" Saviour Jesus Christ."

SERMON CLXXVIII.

Of the certainty of a future judgment.

---

2 COR. v. 10.

For we muſt all appear before the judgment-ſeat of
Christ, *that every one may receive the things*
done in his body, according to that he hath done,
whether it be good or bad.

THE apoftle, in the beginning of this chapter, expreffeth his earneft defire, if God faw it fit, to quit " this earthly tabernacle, for a houfe not " made with hands, eternal in the heavens, to be " abfent from the body, and prefent with the Lord." But however God fhould difpofe of him, he tells us that he made it his conftant endeavour, fo to behave himfelf, that both in this prefent ftate, whilft he continued in the body, and when he fhould quit it, and appear before God, he might be approved and accepted of him. And that which made him fo careful was, becaufe there was a day certainly coming, wherein every man muft give an account of himfelf to the great judge of the world, and receive the juft recompence of his actions done in this life, v. 9, 10. " Wherefore we labour, that whether
" prefent

" prefent or abfent, we may be accepted of him.
" For we muft all appear before the judgment-feat
" of CHRIST, that every one may receive the things
" done in the body, according to that he hath done,
" whether it be good or bad."

Which words are fo plain and powerful, fo eafy
to be underftood, and of fuch a mighty force and
influence, if thoroughly believed, that the very re-
peating of them is fufficient to awaken men to a
ferious care of their lives and actions, and a powerful confideration to perfuade them to do every thing,
with refpect to that folemn account they muft one
day make to GOD of all the actions done in this life.

But that the truth contained in them, may make
the greater impreffion upon us, I fhall diftinctly confider the words, and handle, as briefly as I can, the
feveral propofitions contained in them.

The general and principal propofition contained
in thefe words is, the certainty of a future judgment.

But befides this principal propofition, which comprehends the general meaning and intention of thefe
words, there are four other more particular propofitions contained in them.

Firft, That the adminiftration of this judgment
will be committed to the LORD JESUS CHRIST; for
which reafon the tribunal before which we muft appear, is called, " the judgment-feat of CHRIST.
" We muft all appear before the judgment-feat of
" CHRIST."

Secondly, That all men are liable to this judgment; no perfon of what condition foever fhall be
exempted from it. " We muft all appear."

Thirdly, That all the actions which men have
done in this life fhall then come to account, and they

fhall be judged for them. " That every one may " receive the things done in the body."

Fourthly, That fentence will then be paft according to the quality of mens actions, whether good or bad : " every one fhall receive according to that he " hath done, whether it be good or evil."

But I fhall at prefent only fpeak to the principal propofition contained in the words, concerning the certainty of a future and general judgment, viz. That at the end of the world, there fhall be a general and publick affize, when all perfons that have lived in this world (except only the judge himfelf, our bleffed SAVIOUR, who is " the man ordained " by GOD to judge the world)" fhall come upon their trial, and all the actions which they have done fhall come under a ftrict examination ; and according as men have demeaned themfelves in this world towards GOD and man, they fhall receive fentence, and rewards fhall be diftributed to them, according to the nature and quality of their actions. And though all thefe particulars be not expreffed in the text, yet they are virtually contained in the general expreffions of it, and fully and clearly delivered in other texts of fcripture.

The truth and certainty of a future and general judgment, I fhall endeavour to confirm from thefe three heads of arguments.

I. From the acknowledgments of natural light.

II. From the notions which men generally have of GOD and his providence.

III. From exprefs and clear revelation of holy fcripture.

I. From the acknowledgments of natural light. And I might fhew the general confent of mankind in this matter, by all forts of human teftimonies, and

from

from all kinds of writers in all ages: but this would be almoft endlefs, and not fo proper for a plain and practical difcourfe upon this fubject. And therefore paffing by teftimonies, I fhall mainly infift upon this, that the confciences of men do fecretly acknowledge a difference between good and evil. Hence it is that men find great peace and quiet and fatisfaction of mind, in the doing of good and virtuous actions, and have fecret and comfortable hopes, that this kind of actions will fome time or other be confidered and rewarded; and they are apt to maintain thefe hopes, and to fupport themfelves with them, even when they defpair to meet with any reward of their good and honeft actions in this world.

And on the other hand, men find a fecret fear and horror, and are inwardly afhamed and confounded in their own minds, when they are about a wicked enterprize, and engaged in an ill defign; their confciences check them and terrify them, and their own minds bode ill to them, as if mifchief and vengeance would overtake them one time or other; and this, when no eye fees them, and what they are a doing does not fall under the cognizance of any human court or tribunal, nor is liable to any cenfure or punifhment from any human authority; yet for all that, they have many ftings and lafhes from their own minds, feel many checks and rebukes from their own confciences, when they do any thing which they ought not to do, though no man can charge them with it, or call them to an account for it.

Now thefe hopes and fears do argue, if not the firm belief and perfuafion of a future judgment, yet great fufpicions and mifgivings of it in bad men; and in good men, fecret and comfortable apprehenfions concerning it. From whence elfe can it be, that

SERM.
LXXVIII.
that good men, though they find that virtue is difcountenanced, and goodness many times suffers, and
is persecuted in this world, and that the best actions
and designs are often unsuccessful; whence I say, is
it that good men, notwithstanding this, bear up and
persist in their course, but because they have this inward apprehension and persuasion, that there will be
a time, when virtue and goodness will be considered
and rewarded, though not in this world? And
whence is it, that bad men, though they prosper in
their impiety, are yet guilty and fearful and timorous; but because they stand in awe of a being,
greater and more righteous and more powerful than
themselves; but because they have some secret apprehensions of an invisible judge, and inward presage
of a future vengeance, which sooner or later will
overtake them; and because they believe there will
be a time when all the wickedness they have done
shall be accounted for? Insomuch that when they
have done what they can, they cannot shake off these
fears, nor quit themselves of these apprehensions of
divine justice, threatening and pursuing them for
their evil deeds. All which are plain acknowledgments of a natural apprehension and persuasion born
with us, and riveted in our minds, concerning a future judgment.

II. This will farther appear from the natural notions which men have of a God, and his providence.
This is essential to the notion of a God, that he is
good, and holy, and just; and consequently, that
he loves goodness, and hates iniquity; and therefore it must be agreeable to his nature, to countenance the one, and to discountenance the other, in
such a manner as becomes the wise sovereign and
governor of the world. Now this cannot be solemnly

ly and openly done, but by a publick diftribution of rewards and punifhments ; and this we fee is not done in this world. The difpenfations of God's providence in this world, toward good and bad men, are many times very promifcuous, and very crofs, and contrary to what might be expected from the wife and juft fovereign of the world, from one whom we believe to love righteoufnefs, and to hate iniquity. For virtuous and holy men are often ill treated in this world, grievoufly haraffed and afflicted, and that " for righteoufnefs fake ;" and bad men many times flourifh, and are profperous, "they are not in trouble " like other men, neither are they plagued like other " men." And this is a very great objection againft the providence of God ; if there were no other confi- deration had of virtue and vice, no other kind of retribution made to good and bad men, but what we fee in this world. And therefore the juftice of the divine providence feems to require, that there fhould be a day of recompence, and a folemn and publick diftribution of rewards and punifhments to the righteous and to the wicked. For this is plainly a ftate of trial and probation, of patience, and for- bearance to finners, and of exercife to good men ; and being a ftate of trial, it is not fo proper a feafon for the diftribution of publick juftice. But fince the juftice of God doth not appear in this world, it feems very reafonable to believe, that there will be a time when it will be made manifeft, and every eye fhall fee it ; that God will one day fully vindicate his righteoufnefs, and acquit the honour of his juftice, and that there fhall be a general affize held, when all men fhall have a fair and open trial, and " God will " render to every man according to his works."

Now the juftice of God's providence is in a

great

great measure hid and covered, but there will come ἡμέρα ἀποκαλύψεως (as the apostle calls the day of judgment, Rom. ii. 5.) " a day of the revelation " of the righteous judgment of GOD, when he will " bring forth his righteousness as the light, and his " judgment as the noon-day, and every mouth " shall be stopped," and every conscience and heart of man acknowledge " the righteous judgment of " GOD."

And in the mean time GOD contents himself to give some particular and remarkable instances of his rewarding and punishing justice, in this world, which may be to us an earnest of a future and general judgment ; he is pleased sometimes in the dispensations of his providence, clearly to separate and distinguish " the precious from the vile," remarkably to deliver good men, and " to snare the wicked in the " works of their own hands." Sometimes he gives good men some foretastes of heaven, some earnest of their future happiness in this life : and on the other hand, he many times gives sinners some *præjudicia divini judicii*, some intimations of a future judgment, and shadows of that " utter darkness," where they are to dwell for ever ; he drops down now and then a little of hell into the conscience of a sinner. That fire which is kindled in some mens consciences in this life, that unspeakable anguish, and those inexplicable horrors, which some sinners have felt in this world, may serve to give us notice of the extreme severity of the divine justice towards impenitent sinners ; that miraculous deluge that swept away the old world ; those stupendous and terrible showers of fire and brimstone, which consumed Sodom and Gomorrah, and the cities about ; that dreadful earthquake, which swallowed

up

up Corah and his company, and let them down as it were quick into hell, may serve for pledges and earnests to us of the dismal punishments and torments of the next world.

But notwithstanding all these particular and remarkable instances of the divine justice, yet considering how unequal and promiscuous the greatest part of God's providences are in this world, it is highly requisite, that there should be a general judgment, for a more clear and full manifestation of the justice and equity of the divine providence.

II. But this will most evidently appear from the clear and express revelation of the holy scripture. I will not cite texts out of the old testament to this purpose, because these things were but obscurely revealed to the Jews in comparison, " life and immor-
" tality being brought to light by the gospel." Yet St. Jude tells us, that there was an early revelation of this to the old world, ver. 14, 15. " And Enoch
" also the seventh from Adam prophesied of these,
" saying, behold the LORD cometh with ten thou-
" sands of his saints, to execute judgment upon all,
" and to convince all that are ungodly." But whether this refer to the flood, or the final judgment of the world, is not so clear and certain ; however this is most plainly revealed by our blessed LORD and SAVIOUR, in the new testament. The process of this great day, with several of the particular circumstances of it, are fully described by our SAVIOUR, Matt. xxv. and in the vision of St. John, Rev. xx. 11, 12, 13. And the apostles of our LORD and SAVIOUR do most frequently declare and inculcate it. Acts xvii. 30, 31. " But now commandeth all men every where
" to repent : because he hath appointed a day, in the
" which he will judge the world in righteousness, by

" that man whom he hath ordained, whereof he hath
" given affurance unto all men, in that he hath raifed
" him from the dead." Rom. ii. 5, 6, 7, 8, 9.
where fpeaking of the day of judgment, he calls it,
" the day of wrath, and revelation of the righteous
" judgment of God ; who will render to every man
" according to his deeds : to them, who by patient
" continuance in well-doing feek for glory, and ho-
" nour, and immortality, eternal life : but unto them
" that are contentious, and do not obey the truth,
" but obey unrighteoufnefs ; indignation and wrath,
" tribulation and anguifh upon every foul of man
" that doth evil."   1 Pet. i. 17. " And if ye call on
" the father, who without refpect of perfons judgeth
" according to every man's work."   2 Pet. iii. 10.
" But the day of the LORD will come, in which the
" heavens fhall pafs away with a great noife, &c."

Thus you fee the truth and certainty of a future
judgment confirmed, from the acknowledgments of
mens natural hopes and fears, from the natural notions which men have concerning God and his providence, and from plain revelation of fcripture.

All that I fhall do farther at prefent fhall be to
make fome reflections upon what hath been delivered, concerning the certainty of a future general judgment.   And,

I. If there be fuch a day certainly a coming, it
may juftly be matter of wonder and aftonifhment to
us, to fee the general impiety and ftupidity of men,
how wicked they are, and how carelefs of their lives
and actions, and how infenfible of that " great and
" terrible day of the LORD," which is coming upon
all flefh, and for any thing we know to the contrary,
may be very near us, and " even at the door." How
fecurely do the great part of men pafs away their time,
                                                    fome

fome in worldly bufinefs, others in worldly pleafures and vanity, and a great many in wickednefs and vice? Surely fuch men have no apprehenfions of a future judgment; furely they do not believe that there will be any memorial of their actions in another world, and that they fhall be called to a ftrict and fevere account for all the actions of this life; they do not think that there is a juft and powerful being above them, who now obferves every thing that they do, and will one day judge them for; that there is a pen always writing, and making a faithful record of all the paffages of their lives; and that thefe volumes fhall one day be produced and " opened, and men fhall be " judged out of the things that are written in them;" and all our thoughts, words, and actions fhall pafs under a moft fevere trial and examination.

Or if men do believe thefe things, they ftifle and fupprefs this belief, and " detain this great truth of " GOD in unrighteoufnefs;" they do not attend to it, and confider it, that it may have it's due awe and influence upon their lives. For it is not imaginable, that if men were poffefs'd with a firm belief and perfuafion of this "great and terrible day of the LORD," they fhould be fo carelefs and fecure, as we fee they are, and have fo little regard to what they do; that they fhould pafs whole days, and weeks, and years, in the grofs neglect of GOD and religion, and of their immortal fouls; that they fhould " fpend their days " in vanity, and their years in pleafure;" that they fhould live in a continued courfe of impiety and profanenefs, of leudnefs and intemperance, in the curfed habits of fwearing and curfing; which are now grown fo common among us, that a man cannot walk in the ftreet, without having his ears grated with this hellifh noife; and that they fhould go on in

thefe

SERM.
LXXVIII.
these courses, without any great regret or disturbance, as if no danger attended them, as if justice were asleep, and all their actions would be buried with them, and never rise up against them.

What can we resolve this into, but either into habitual or actual atheism and infidelity? Either men do not at all believe a judgment to come; or else they do not actually consider it, and attend to the natural and proper consequences of such a belief. One of these two is necessary. It seems very hard to charge the generality of wicked men with habitual atheism and unbelief, but that the Spirit of God in scripture so often does it. Psal. xiv. 1. " The fool " hath said in his heart, there is no God." How doth that appear? It follows, " they are corrupt, " they have done abominable works, there is none " that doth good." And Psal. xxxvi. 1. " The " transgression of the wicked saith within my heart, " there is no fear of God before his eyes." David speaks as if the wicked practices of men did convince him, that they had no belief and apprehension of a God.

Nay, even after those clear discoveries which the gospel hath made of a future judgment, our SAVI-OUR seems to foretel a general infidelity among men, at least as to this particular article of a future judgment, Luke xviii. 8. " Nevertheless when the Son of " man shall come, shall he find faith upon the earth?" And St. Peter tells us, 2 Pet. iii. 3, 4. that " there " shall come in the last days scoffers, walking after " their own lusts, and saying, where is the promise " of his coming?" that is, deriding the belief and expectation which the Christians had of a future judgment.

But to be sure, if the generality of men be not already sunk thus low, as to disbelieve these things, yet

yet this at leaft is evident from the lives of men, that they are ftrangely inconfider'ate, and guilty of the moft grofs and ftupid inadvertency that can befal reafonable creatures. For I dare appeal to any man of underftanding and ferious confideration, whether a greater folly and madnefs can be imagined, than for men to profefs in good earneft to believe, that there is a day fhortly coming, wherein they fhall appear before the impartial tribunal of the great judge of the world, and all the actions of their lives fhall be ranfacked and laid open, and that there is not any thing that ever they did, that fhall efcape a fevere cenfure; yea, and farther to be perfuaded, that as it fhall upon that trial appear, that they have demeaned themfelves in this world, they fhall be fentenced to an eternal and unchangeable ftate, of happinefs or mifery, in the other world; and yet after all this conviction, to live at fuch a mad and carelefs rate, as no man in reafon can live, but he that is undoubtedly certain of the contrary. of all this, and verily perfuaded in his heart, that not one fyllable of what the gofpel fays concerning thefe matters, is true; this is fo incredible a ftupidity and folly, that did not frequent and undeniable experience make us fure of the truth of it, out of mere charity and refpect to human nature, it were not to be believed. " Confider this " all ye that forget Gop, and put far from you the " evil day; confider and fhew yourfelves men, O ye " tranfgreffors !" who profefs to believe a future judgment, and yet run the hazard of it, as if ye had no fear and fufpicion of any fuch thing.

II. Having confidered, not without wonder and aftonifhment, what manner of perfons the generality of men are, notwithftanding all the affurance we have of a future judgment, let us in the next place confi-

der,

SERM. der, " feeing thefe things fhall be, what manner of
CLXXVIII. " perfons we ought to be in all holy converfation
" and godlinefs, waiting for, and haftening unto the
" coming of the day of GOD," as the apoftle argues,
2 Pet. iii. 11, 12. How fhould the ferious belief of
this great principle of religion work upon us, that
" we muft all appear before the judgment feat of
" CHRIST, that every one may receive the things
" done in the body, according to that he hath done,
" whether it be good or evil?" St. Paul tells us,
that the confideration of it had a mighty awe and
influence upon him, to be careful of himfelf, and to
be concerned for others : to be careful of himfelf, in
the verfe before the text, " wherefore we labour that
" whether prefent or abfent, we may be accepted of
" him. For we muft all appear before the judg-
" ment feat of CHRIST." And to be concerned for
others, that they may prevent the terrors of that day,
in the verfe immediately after the text, " knowing
" therefore the terror of the LORD, we perfuade
" men. Knowing the terror of the LORD ;" it were
no difficult matter to make fuch a dreadful reprefentation of this "great and terrible day of the LORD,"
as would affright the ftouteft finner, and make every
joint of him to tremble : but it is much more defirable, that men fhould be wrought upon by reafon,
and convinced and perfuaded by a calm and fober
confideration of things ; becaufe that is likely to have
a better and more lafting effect, than prefent terror
and amazement ; and therefore I fhall content myfelf with the naked reprefentation of the thing, in the
plain and powerful expreffions of the holy fcriptures.
Imagine then thou faweft " the Son of man coming
" in great power and great glory, and all his holy
" angels with him ;" that thou heardeft the great
trumpet

trumpet found, and a mighty voice piercing the heavens and the earth, faying, " Arife, ye dead, and
" come to judgment." Suppofe thou faweft " the
" thrones fet, and the great judge fitting upon the
" throne of his glory, and all nations gathered be-
" fore him, and all the dead, both fmall and great,
" ftanding before God, the books opened, and the
" dead judged out of the things written in thofe
" books :" and the feveral fentences pronounced
from the mouth of Christ himfelf, " Come ye blef-
" fed of my Father, inherit the kingdom prepared
" for you, from the foundation of the world ;" and,
" Depart ye curfed into everlafting fire, prepared for
" the devil and his angels." Would not this be a
dreadful and amazing fight ! Why the gofpel plainly declares that all this fhall be, and thou pro-
feffeft to believe it. Why then doft thou not live as
if thou didft believe thefe things ; Why fhould not
that which will certainly be, have to all reafonable
purpofes the fame effect upon thee, as if it were already and actually prefent ? Why do men fuffer
themfelves to be diverted from the attentive confideration of fo important a matter, by the impertinent
trifles of this world ? Why do we not make wife and
fpeedy preparation for " that day," which " will cer-
" tainly come ?" but we are uncertain when it will
come, for " it will come as a thief in the night, and
" as a fnare upon all them that dwell on the face of
" the whole earth." Why doft thou ftifle thy confcience, and drown the loud cries of it, with the din
and noife of worldly bufinefs ? Why doft thou at any
time check and fupprefs the thoughts of a future
judgment, and " put far from thee the evil day ?"
and not rather fuffer the terrors of it to haunt and
purfue thee, till they have made thee weary of thy
wicked

S E R M. wicked life, till they have reclaimed thee to thy duty, CLXXVIII and effectually perfuaded thee, " to break off thy " fins by repentance;" and to refolve upon fuch a holy and virtuous courfe of life, that thou mayft be able, not only with peace and comfort, but with joy and triumph, to entertain the thoughts of that day?

Reafon thus with thyfelf, if this day be fo dreadful at a diftance, that I can hardly now bear the thoughts of it, how infupportable will the thing itfelf be, when it comes to be prefent; and if it will come neverthe-lefs, nor the later for my not thinking of it, is it not reafonable, inftead of putting away the thoughts of it, to endeavour by all poffible means to prevent the terrors of it?

We efpecially, who profefs ourfelves Chriftians, and live in the clear light of the gofpel, ought to confider, that we cannot plead ignorance for our ex-cufe, as the heathen world might. We read and hear the gofpel every day, " wherein the wrath of " God is clearly revealed againft all ungodlinefs and " unrighteoufnefs of men:" So that if we continue impenitent, we have no cloak, no excufe for our-felves; wo unto as above all others! " It fhall be " more tolerable for Tyre and Sidon, for Sodom and " Gomorrah, in the day of judgment, than for us. " The times of ignorance," faith St. Paul, fpeaking of the heathen world, " the times of this ignorance " God winked at; but now he commands all men " every where to repent, becaufe he hath appointed " a day, in which he will judge the world in righ- " teoufnefs, by that man whom he hath ordained, " whereof he hath given affurance unto all men, in " that he hath raifed him from the dead." Thus much concerning the general propofition, the certain-ty of a future judgment.

S E R-

SERMON CLXXIX.

Of the perfon by whom the world fhall
be judged.

---

2 COR. v. 20.

For we muft all appear before the judgment-feat of
CHRIST, that every one may receive the things done
in his body, according to that he hath done, whether
it be good or bad.

IN thefe words, befides the general point mainly
intended, concerning the certainty of a future and
general judgment, there are likewife feveral particular propofitions.

First, That the adminiftration of this judgment
is committed to the LORD JESUS CHRIST.

Secondly, That all men are liable to this judgment.

Thirdly, That all the actions which men have done
in this life fhall then come to account, and they fhall
be judged for them.

Fourthly, That this fentence fhall be paft upon
men according to the nature and quality of their
actions, whether good or evil. I have handled the
general point, the certainty of a future judgment : I
fhall now proceed to the particular propofitions contained in the text, and fhall handle them in the order
in which I have propofed them.

First, That the adminiftration of this judgment is
committed to the LORD JESUS CHRIST, and that he
is the perfon conftituted and ordained of GOD, to be
the judge of the world. The tribunal before which

SERM.
CLXXIX.

The
fecond
fermon on
this text.

SERM.
CLXXIX.
we muſt ſtand, is here in the text called " the judg-
" ment ſeat of Christ." " We muſt all appear
" before the judgment-ſeat of Christ." In the
proſecution of this I ſhall,

Firſt, Endeavour to confirm and illuſtrate the truth
of this propoſition.

Secondly, Draw ſome inferences from it, by way
of application.

Firſt, For the confirmation of it, I ſhall do theſe
two things.

I. Prove it from clear teſtimony of ſcripture.

II. Endeavour to give ſome account of this oeco-
nomy and diſpenſation ; why God hath committed
the adminiſtration of this great work to the Lord
Jesus Christ ; in all which I ſhall rely only upon
ſcripture, the thing being capable of no other proof
or evidence. And indeed the whole mediatory undertaking of our bleſſed Saviour, and all the circumſtances of it, are matter of pure revelation ; this
is " the hidden and manifold wiſdom of God, which
" none of the princes and philoſophers of this world
" knew," and which we could not poſſibly have
found out and diſcovered, had not God been pleaſed
to reveal it to us.

I. I ſhall prove this from expreſs teſtimony of
ſcripture, that the Lord Jesus Christ is the perſon conſtituted and ordained by God, to adminiſter
the judgment of the great day. Matt. xiii. 40, 41,
42, 43. " So ſhall it be in the end of this world.
" The Son of man ſhall ſend forth his angels, and
" they ſhall gather out of his kingdom all things
" that offend, and them which do iniquity ; and
" ſhall caſt them into a furnace of fire : there ſhall be
" wailing and gnaſhing of teeth. Then ſhall the
" righteous ſhine forth as the ſun in the kingdom of
" their

" their father." Here our SAVIOUR is reprefented
as the chief minifter of GOD's juftice, in the diftribution of rewards to the righteous and the wicked;
and though the effect and execution of the fentence
only be exprefs'd, yet it fuppofeth a judicial procefs
preceding. So likewife Matt. xvi. 27. " For the
" Son of man fhall come in the glory of his Father,
" with his holy angels, and then he fhall reward every
" man according to his work." " Shall come in the
" glory of his Father," that is, with his authority
committed to him. Matt. xxiv. 30. where our SA-
VIOUR fpeaking of his coming to judge the world,
it is faid, " then fhall appear the fign of the Son of
" man in heaven, and then fhall all the tribes of the
" earth mourn ; and they fhall fee the Son of man
" coming in the clouds of heaven with power and
" great glory ;" that is, in order to the judgment of
the world. But moft fully and exprefly, Matt. xxv.
31. where you have the manner of his coming particularly defcribed, together with the folemn reprefentation of the procefs of that day. " When the
" Son of man fhall come in his glory, and all the
" holy angels with him, then fhall he fit upon the
" throne of his glory : And before him fhall be ga-
" thered all nations, and he fhall feparate the one from
" another, as the fhepherd divideth his fheep from
" the goats : And he fhall fet the fheep on his right
" hand, but the goats on the left. Then fhall the
" king fay to them on his right hand, &c." You fee
the whole adminiftration of this judgment, and the
management of every part of it, is committed to
CHRIST. John v. 22. Our SAVIOUR there produceth his commiffion, and tells us from whence this
authority was derived to him. " The Father judg-
" eth no man, but hath committed all judgment to

" the Son." And ver. 27. " He hath given him
" authority alfo to execute judgment, becaufe he is
" the Son of man." Acts x. 42. " And he com-
" manded us to preach unto the people, and to tef-
" tify that it is he that is ordained of GOD, to be the
" judge of quick and dead." Acts xvii. 31. " He
" hath appointed a day in the which he will judge the
" world in righteoufnefs, by that man whom he hath
" ordained," that is, by JESUS CHRIST ; for it follows, " whereof he hath given affurance unto all men,
" in that he hath raifed him from the dead." Rom.
ii. 16. " In the day when GOD fhall judge the fecrets
" of men by JESUS CHRIST." Rom. xiv. 10.
" We fhall all ftand before the judgment feat of
" CHRIST." 2 Theff. i. 7, 8, 9. The apoftle there
fpeaking of the day of judgment, defcribes it thus ;
" When the LORD JESUS fhall be revealed from
" heaven with his mighty angels, in flaming fire,
" taking vengeance on all them that know not GOD,
" and obey not the gofpel of his Son ; who fhall be
" punifhed with everlafting deftruction from the pre-
" fence of the LORD, and from the glory of his
" power." 2 Tim. iv. 1. " I charge thee, faith St.
" Paul there to Timothy, before GOD, and the LORD
" JESUS CHRIST, who fhall judge the quick and the
" dead at his appearing, and his kingdom." Rev.
xxii. 12. " Behold I come quickly, faith our LORD,
" and my reward is with me, to give to every man
" according as his work fhall be." I proceed to the

II. Thing I propofed, namely, to give fome account, why GOD hath committed the adminiftration
of this work, into the hands of the LORD JESUS
CHRIST. And of this I fhall give an account in
thefe two particulars.

1. GOD thought fit to confer this honour upon
                                        CHRIST,

CHRIST, as a suitable reward of his patience and sufferings.

2. He thought fit likewise hereby to declare the righteousness and equity of his judgment, in that mankind is judged by one in their own nature, a man like themselves.

1. GOD hath thought fit to confer this honour upon CHRIST, as a suitable reward of his obedience and sufferings, of his coming into the world by his appointment, to undertake the work of our redemption, and to mediate a reconciliation between GOD and us, of his voluntary submission to a condition so mean and low, to that poverty and contempt, and to those extreme sufferings which he did so patiently undergo, in the prosecution of this great design.

That GOD hath committed all power to CHRIST, with design to put an honour upon him, our SAVIOUR himself tells us, John v. 22, 23. " The Fa-
" ther judgeth no man, but hath committed all
" judgment to the Son ; that all men should honour
" the Son, even as they honour the Father." The scripture speaks of this matter, as if when CHRIST undertook the great work of our redemption, it were expresly covenanted between GOD the Father and him, that he should undertake this work, and submit to all those grievous things, which were necessary to be done and suffered, in order to the effecting of it ; and that when he had accomplished it, GOD would confer this glory upon him, that in his human nature he should be " exalted to the right-hand
" of GOD, and have power given him over all flesh,
" to judge the world, and to give eternal life to as
" many as he pleased ;" and when he had received this reward, that then his mediatory office should cease, and he should " g. . up th . . . . . to

(o)

" God the Father, that God might be all in all."
This is the fcope and defign of the feveral texts of
fcripture concerning this matter.

With relation to this covenant and agreement between him and his Father, he prays, John xvii. 1,
2. that he would not be unmindful of the glory
which he had promifed to inveft him withal. " Fa-
" ther, the hour is come, glorify thy Son ; as thou
" haft given him power over all flefh, that he fhould
" give eternal life to as many as thou haft given
" him." And ver. 4, 5. " I have glorified thee
" on the earth : I have finifhed the work which
" thou gaveft me to do." And then he claims the
reward of it. " And now, O Father, glorify thou
" me with thine own felf." And the apoftle to the
Hebrews, chap. xii. 2. tells us, that the hopes of
this did encourage, and bear up our Lord under his
fufferings, " who for the joy that was fet before
" him, endured the crofs, defpifing the fhame, and
" is fet down at the right-hand of the throne of
" God." And St. Peter tells us, 1 Pet. i. 11.
that " the prophets of old teftified before-hand the
" fufferings of Christ, and the glory that fhould
" follow." And St. Paul tells us what this glory
is, " Eph. i. 20, 21. viz. that " God hath fet
" him at his own right-hand in heavenly places, far
" above all principality, and power, and might, and
" dominion, and every name that is named, not
" only in this world, but in that which is to come"
But moft exprefly, Phil. ii. 7, 8, 9, 10, 11. the fame
apoftle tells us, that in confideration of the great
humiliation and fufferings of Christ, " God
" hath highly exalted him. He made himfelf of
" no reputation, (he emptied himfelf) and took
" upon him the form of a fervant, and was made

3   " in

" in the likenefs of men. And being found in fa-
" fhion as a man, he humbled himfelf, and became
" obedient unto death, even the death of the crofs.
" Wherefore God alfo hath highly exalted him,
" and given him a name, which is above every
" name : that at the name of Jesus every knee
" fhould bow, of things in heaven, and things in
" earth, and things under the earth : and that every
" tongue fhould confefs that Jesus Christ is
" Lord, to the glory of God the Father" And
that the giving of this name and authority to Christ,
upon account whereof all creatures fhould be fubject
to him, doth principally import that power of judging the world which was committed to him, is evident from the explication of thefe phrafes, of "bow-
" ing the knee to Christ, and of confeffing to
" him with the tongue," which the fame apoftle
tells us elfewhere do fignify our being judged by
him. Rom. xiv. 10, 11. " We fhall all ftand be-
" fore the judgment-feat of Christ : for it is writ-
" ten, As I live, faith the Lord, every knee fhall
" bow to me, and every tongue fhall confefs to God.
" So then every one of us fhall give an account of
" himfelf to God."

So that you fee that the glorious reward of
Christ's felf-denial and fuffering, doth principally
confift in having the judgment of the world committed to him, which therefore is called " his king-
" dom. Matth. xvi. 28. where our Saviour expreffeth it by " the Son of man's coming in his
" kingdom. 2 Tim. iv. 1. " I charge thee there-
" fore," faith St. Paul to Timothy, " before God
" and the Lord Jesus Christ, who fhall judge
" the quick and the dead at his appearing, and his
" kingdom." And it is with relation to this pow-

SERM.
CLXXIX.

er and authority, that the title of king is given to him, Matth. xxv. 34. " Then fhall the king fay " unto them on his right-hand, &c." And the fcripture almoft every where, when it fpeaks of CHRIST's coming, calls it his "glorious appearance." Matth. xvi. 27. " They fhall fee the Son of man " coming in the glory of his Father. Mat. xxiv. 30. " They fhall fee the Son of man coming with power " and great glory." Mat. xxv. 31. " When the " Son of man fhall come in his glory." And Tit. " ii. 13. it is called, " the glorious appearance of the " great GOD, and our SAVIOUR JESUS CHRIST."

And this is a very fuitable reward of his great fubmiffion and fufferings, that he who lived in fo mean and obfcure a condition, fhould come in great glory ; that he who was rejected and defpifed of men, fhould be attended on by mighty angels ; that he who was arraigned and condemned by the powers of the world, fhould have authority given him to fummon all, both fmall and great, the kings and great men, and judges of the earth, to appear at his bar, and to receive fentence at his mouth.

And this fhall be the laft act of his mediatorfhip, to fit in judgment upon the world, to diftribute rewards to his faithful fervants, and to punifh his obftinate and implacable enemies. And when this work is finifhed, then this authority fhall expire, and the office and kingdom of the mediator fhall ceafe ; for " when he fhall have fubdued all things to himfelf," as the apoftle exprefly tells us, 1 Cor. xv. 24, 25, &c. " then cometh the end, when he fhall have de- " livered up the kingdom to GOD, even the Father, " when he fhall have put down all rule, and all au- " thority, and power. For he muft reign, till he hath " put all enemies under his feet. And when all things " fhall

" shall be subdued unto him, then shall the Son also
" himself be subject unto him that hath put all things
" under him, that GOD may be all in all."

2. GOD hath committed the administration of this judgment to CHRIST, that he might hereby declare the righteousness and equity of it, in that mankind is judged by one in their own nature, a man like themselves. And therefore we find that the scripture, when it speaks of CHRIST as judge of the world, doth almost constantly call him man, and " the Son of man." In the places I have mentioned before, Matth. xiii. 41. " The Son of man shall " send forth his angels." And Matth. xvi. 27. " The Son of man shall come in the glory of his " Father." Matth. xxiv. 30. " Then shall appear " the sign of the Son of man in heaven, and they " shall see the Son of man coming in the clouds of " heaven, with power and great glory." Matth. xxv. 31. " When the Son of man shall come in his glory." Acts xvii. 31. " He hath appointed a day, in which " he will judge the world in righteousness, by that " man whom he hath ordained." By the constant use of which expression, the scripture doth give us plainly to understand, that this great honour of being judge of the world was conferred upon the human nature of CHRIST. For as he is GOD, he is over all, and judge of the world, and could not derive this power from any, it being originally inherent in the Deity. Which likewise appears in those expressions of his being ordained a judge, and having " all " authority and judgment committed and given to " him." Acts xvii. 31. " He will judge the " world in righteousness by that man, whom he " hath ordained." And John v. 22. " The Fa- " ther hath committed all judgment to the Son."

And ver. 27. " He hath given him authority to
" execute judgment." Now this cannot be ſaid of
CHRIST as GOD, but in reſpect of his human nature. And this is clear beyond all exception, by
what our SAVIOUR adds, as a reaſon why this authority is committed to him ; " he hath given him
" authority to execute judgment, becauſe he is the
" Son of man ;" that is, becauſe in that reſpect, and
no other, he is capable of having this authority derived to him ; for as he is the Son of GOD, he hath
it in himſelf. And perhaps for this reaſon likewiſe,
becauſe in reſpect of his human nature, he is viſible ;
and man being part of the viſible creation of GOD,
and the judgment of the great day being to be adminiſtered in a viſible manner, and to that end the bodies
of men to be raiſed and united to their ſouls, in order
to their viſible appearance at this judgment ; it ſeems
very congruous, that the Son of man, clothed in our
nature and inveſted with a human body, ſhould ſit
in judgment upon mankind.

But principally becauſe nothing can more effectually declare the equity of this judgment, and that
it ſhall be adminiſtered in righteouſneſs, than that
GOD hath ordained a man like ourſelves to ſit in
judgment upon us. In human judgments, it is
reckoned a great piece of equity, for men to be tried
by their peers, to be acquitted or condemned by
thoſe, who are as near as may be to them, and in
the ſame circumſtances of rank and condition with
themſelves ; becauſe ſuch are like to underſtand their
caſe beſt, and to have a fair and equitable conſideration of all the circumſtances belonging to it. Now
CHRIST, as he is " the Son of man," is near to us,
" bone of our bone, and fleſh of our fleſh, made
" in all things like unto us, only without ſin ;"
which

which was neceffary to qualify him to be our judge; he dwelt among us, and underftands all our circum- ftances, and whatever may have influence upon our cafe, to extenuate or aggravate our guilt. What the apoftle to the Hebrews fays of CHRIST as an high- prieft, may be applied to him as a judge, Heb. iv. 15. " We have not a judge, which cannot be " touched with the feeling of our infirmities ; but " was in all points tempted like as we are, yet with- " out fin."

That which now remains, is to draw fome infe- rences from what I have difcourfed to you upon this argument.

1. If the LORD JESUS CHRIST fhall judge the world, and we muft " all appear before his judg- " ment-feat," then it greatly concerns every one of us fo to demean ourfelves in this world, that we may be accepted of him in the next. If a man be to be tried for his life, how will he court the favour of the judge, that when he comes to ftand at his bar, he may receive a gracious fentence from his mouth ? Why there is a day certainly coming, when every one of us muft appear before the tribunal of the great judge of the world ; and therefore we fhould with all poffible care and diligence endeavour to approve our confciences, and all the actions of our lives to him. " Wherefore we labour," faith the apoftle immediately before my text, " that whether prefent " or abfent, we may be accepted of him. For we " muft all appear before the judgment-feat of " CHRIST." This is that which makes his accept- ance and approbation fo valuable and confiderable, that he is to be our judge, to him we muft ftand or fall, by his fentence we fhall be caft or cleared for ever

oo S o   We

We are very apt to court the favour of great men, of the princes and judges of this world, that when we come to stand in need of it, we may have the benefit and comfort of it. But this is not our great interest ; for the sentence that men can pass upon us, doth but operate for a little while, the effect and consequences of it do not reach beyond this world, it is not final and conclusive as to our eternal state. To allude to that saying of Solomon's, " many seek the " prince's favour : but every man's judgment is of " the LORD." We seek the favour of the great men of this world : but there is a greater man than any of these, whom we are apt to despise and neglect, " the prince of the kings of the earth, the " man who is ordained of GOD, to be judge both " of quick and dead." Every man's judgment shall be from him, it is his sentence which above all other we have most reason to desire or dread. Therefore we should have regard to him, and by submitting to his scepter, and yielding a willing obedience to the laws of his holy gospel, seek his favour, lest " he " break us with a rod of iron, and dash us in pieces " like a potter's vessel." This advice we find given " to the kings and rulers of the earth," Psal. ii. 10, 11, 12. " Be wise now therefore, O ye kings ; " and be instructed, ye judges of the earth. Serve " the LORD with fear, and rejoice with trembling. " Kiss the Son lest he be angry, and ye perish from " the way, when his wrath is kindled but a little : " blessed are all they that put their trust in him."

2. This is matter of great comfort to all sincere Christians, that CHRIST shall judge the world ; as it likewise is of great terror to all that disobey the gospel, and by their wicked lives confute their profession, and pretended belief of it. CHRIST is " the

" the author of eternal falvation to them that obey
" him," and to none elfe. He hath not only purchafed this falvation for us, but by a publick, and
folemn, and authoritative fentence, will confer it upon us.

Indeed it is juftly matter of great terror to the
wicked of the world, who live in ungodlinefs and
worldly lufts, and under the name and title of Chriftians, have "trampled under foot the Son of God"
and by their lives have openly declared, that " they
" would not have this man rule over them." Sure
it cannot but be matter of great horror and amazement to fuch perfons, to think of this judge, and to
confider, that he, whom by their lewd lives and practices they have fo contemned in this world, will fit
as judge upon them, and condemn them in the next.
And therefore our SAVIOUR tells us, Luke xxi. 25,
&c. that when the day of judgment fhall furprize
the world, and "they fhall fee the Son of man
" coming in the clouds of heaven, with power and
" great glory ;" then the wicked of the earth fhall
be in great diftrefs and perplexity, and " their hearts
" fhall fail them for fear, and for looking after thofe
" things which are coming upon the earth:" but
that to good men it fhall be a day of great joy, and
that the approach of it fhall revive their fpirits, and
raife their heads, ver. 28. " But when thefe things
" fhall begin to come to pafs, then lift up your heads
" with joy, becaufe your redemption draws nigh."

And this confideration is matter of great comfort
to all good men, both upon account of their fufferings and fervices for CHRIST. In refpect of their
fufferings for him. In this world they are expofed
to great trials and perfecutions for him : but he, for
whofe name we fu..r, is to give us our reward ; he,

who is of the fame nature with us, and " took part " of flefh and blood," and fuffered himfelf " in the " flefh," more grievoufly than any of us can fuf- fer ; he it is, to whom GOD hath referred it, to con- fider our fufferings, and give what rewards to them he thinks fit. And then in refpect of our fervices. Though the beft of them be imperfect, and nothing that we do is able to abide the feverity of his juftice, yet by virtue of his meritorious facrifice and fatis- faction, the imperfection of them is pardoned, and the fincerity of them is accepted. For he being our judge, who was our facrifice, and is our " advocate. " with the Father," we may reft affured, that he will plead our caufe for us, and the merit of his own fuffer- ings, in bar of that fentence which ftrict juftice would pafs upon us.

3. And laftly, this fhews what reafon the mini- fters of CHRIST have, to be earneft and importunate with finners, to repent and turn to GOD, to believe and obey the gofpel of CHRIST, that they may have him their friend, who will certainly be their judge. This inference the apoftle makes from this doctrine, in the words immediately after the text. " Know- " ing therefore the terror of the LORD, we per- " fuade men ;" we who are employed by CHRIST, to warn finners of the danger and terror of a future judgment, who are ambaffadors fent from this great king and judge of the world, to treat with finners, and to offer peace to them, and " in CHRIST's " ftead to befeech them to be reconciled to GOD," as the apoftle fpeaks in the latter part of this chap- ter. So that if we ourfelves believe what we preach to others, to be the word and law of him who fhall fhortly judge us, and them that hear us, can we for- bear with all poffible importunity to folicit their re-

pentance,

pentance, and to warn them " to flee from the wrath " which is to come ?" Can we let them fleep in their fins, when we fee them neglect fo great a happinefs, and run themfelves upon fo intolerable a mifery ? If we believe that holy book out of which we preach, and the difcoveries and revelation there made, we may take an eafy profpect of another world, and fee " the " wrath of God revealed from heaven, againft all " ungodlinefs and unrighteoufnefs of men." For the gofpel hath made a more particular and clear dif-covery to us of the ftate of the next world, and the proceedings of the great day, than ever the world was acquainted with before. It tells us who is the perfon that fhall fit in judgment upon us, even " Je- " sus Christ, whereof God hath given affurance " unto all men, in that he hath raifed him from the " dead." Now if we know this, and be affured of it, we cannot but deal plainly with finners, and out of tender pity and compaffion to them, endeavour to make them fenfible of the fad iffue and event of a wicked life, and that without repentance and amend-ment they will not be able to ftand in the judgment of the great day. When we fee men in the high-way to ruin and deftruction, and the evil day mak-ing hafte towards them, we cannot but warn them of that fad fate which hangs over them, and endea-vour by all means to refcue them from that extreme and endlefs mifery, which is ready to overtake them.

Confider then, finner, whom it is thou now reject-eft and defpifeft, and whofe laws thou cafteft behind thy back. It is he, who for all his mean appearance in the world, is " the Lord of glory," into whofe hand " the Father hath committed all judgment." And can there be a greater madnefs, than to provoke and make him thine enemy, who fhall be thy judge?

than

S E R M. than to defpife him, who can deftroy thee? He ap-
CLXXIX. peared once as "a lamb to take away the fins of the
"world:" but if through our obftinacy and im-
penitency we render this appearance of his ineffectual for our recovery, he will appear a fecond time in
a more terrible manner, as "a lion to tear us in
"pieces." He came once as "a light into the world,"
in a ftill and gentle way, to convince and convert
finners: but if we refift this light, he will come
"in flaming fire to take vengeance on all them that
"know not GOD, and obey not the gofpel of his
"Son."

And this is that which will make us fpeechlefs, and
fill our faces with everlafting confufion, at the fecond
coming of CHRIST, that we have fruftrated and made
void the end of his firft coming. What fhall we be able
to fay to him, when he comes to judge us, who rejected him, when he came to fave us? With what
reafon can we hope that he will deliver us from hell,
when we would not be faved by him "from our fins,
"and redeemed from our vain converfation?"

I will conclude all with that merciful warning
which the judge himfelf hath given us, and left upon record, Luke xxi. 34, 35, 36. ". Take heed
"to yourfelves, left at any time your hearts be over-
"charged with furfeiting, and drunkennefs, and
"cares of this life, and fo that day come upon you
"unawares. For as a fnare fhall it come on all them
"that dwell on the face of the whole earth. Watch
"ye therefore and pray always, that ye may be ac-
"counted worthy to efcape all thefe things that fhall
"come to pafs, and to ftand before the Son of man."

30, 31. is that which doth, as it were, make repentance to be a new doctrine that did come with the gospel into the world, because it was never before enforced with this powerful argument ; " the times " of that ignorance God winked at ; but now he " calls upon all men every where to repent ; be- " caufe, &c." When the world was in ignorance, and had not such affurance of a future ftate, of eternal rewards and punifhments after this life, the arguments to repentance were weak and feeble in comparifon of what they now are, the neceffity of this duty was not fo evident. But now God hath affured us of a future judgment, now exhortations to repentance have a commanding power and influence upon men ; fo that repentance, both as it is that which is very much preffed and inculcated in the gofpel, and as it hath it's chief motives and enforcements from the gofpel, may be faid to be one of the great doctrines of the gofpel.

Query 2. Whether the preaching of faith in CHRIST, among thofe who are already Chriftians, be at all neceffary ? Becaufe it feems very improper, to prefs thofe to believe in CHRIST, who are already perfuaded that he is the Meffias, and do entertain the hiftory and doctrine of the gofpel.

Anf. The faith which the apoftle here means, and which he would perfuade men to, is an effectual belief of the gofpel ; fuch a faith as hath real effects upon men, and makes them to live as they believe ; fuch a faith as perfuades them of the need of thefe bleffings that the gofpel offers, and makes them to defire to be partakers of them, and in order thereto to be willing to fubmit to thofe terms and conditions of holinefs and obedience, which the gofpel requires. This is the faith we would perfuade men to, and there is nothing more neceſſary to be preſſed upon the greateſt part of Chriſtians than this ; for how few are there, among thoſe who profeſs to believe the goſpel, who believe it in this effectual manner, ſo as to conform themſelves to it? The faith which moſt Chriſtians pretend to is merely negative ; they do not diſbelieve the goſpel, they do not conſider it, nor trouble themſelves about it, they do not care, nor are concerned whether it be true or not ; but they have not a poſitive belief of it, they are not poſſeſſed with a firm perſuaſion of the truth of thoſe matters which are contained in it ; if they were, ſuch a perſuaſion would produce real and poſitive effects. Every man naturally deſires happineſs, and it is impoſſible that any man that is poſſeſſed with this belief, that in order to happineſs it is neceſſary for him to do ſuch and ſuch things ; and that if he omit or neglect them he is unavoidably miſerable, that he ſhould not do them. Men ſay they believe this or that, but you may ſee in their lives, what it is they believe. So that the preaching of this faith in CHRIST, which is the only true faith, is ſtill neceſſary.

I. Infer. " If repentance towards GOD, and faith in " the LORD JESUS CHRIST," be the ſum and ſubſtance of the goſpel, then from hence we may infer the excellency of the chriſtian religion, which inſiſts only upon thoſe things that do tend to our perfection and our happineſs. Repentance tends to our recovery, and the bringing of us back as near as may be to innocence. *Primus innocentiæ gradus eſt non peccaſſe; ſecundus, pœnitentia :* and then " faith in the LORD " JESUS CHRIST," though it be very comprehenſive, and contains many things in it, yet nothing but what is eminently for our advantage, and doth very much conduce to our happineſs. The hiſtorical part

of

of the goſpel acquaints us with the perſon and actions of our SAVIOUR, which conduceth very much to our underſtanding of the author and means of our ſalvation. The doctrinal part of the goſpel contains what GOD requires on our part, and the encouragements and arguments to our duty, from the conſideration of the recompence and rewards of the next life. The precepts of CHRIST's doctrine are ſuch as tend exceedingly to the perfection of our nature, being all founded in reaſon, in the nature of GOD, and of a reaſonable creature ; I except only thoſe poſitive inſtitutions of the chriſtian religion, the two ſacraments, which are not burthenſom, and are of excellent uſe. This is the firſt.

II. We may learn from hence what is to be the ſum and end of our preaching, to bring men to repentance and a firm belief of the goſpel ; but then it is to be conſidered, that we preach repentance, ſo often as we preach either againſt ſin in general, or any particular ſin or vice ; and ſo often as we perſuade to holineſs in general, or to the performance of any particular duty of religion, or to the exerciſe of any particular grace ; for repentance includes the forſaking of ſin, and a ſincere reſolution and endeavour of reformation and obedience. And we preach repentance ſo often as we inſiſt upon ſuch conſiderations and arguments, as may be powerful to deter men from ſin, and to engage them to holineſs. And we preach "faith towards our LORD JESUS CHRIST," ſo often as we declare the grounds of the chriſtian religion, and inſiſt upon ſuch arguments as tend to make it credible, and are proper to convince men of the truth and reaſonableneſs of it ; ſo often as we explain the myſtery of CHRIST's incarnation, the hiſtory of his life, death, reſurrection, aſcenſion, and

interceſſion

interceffion, and the proper ends and ufe of thefe; fo often as we open the method of GOD's grace for the falvation of finners, the nature of the covenant between GOD and us, and the conditions of it, and the way how a finner is juftified and hath his fins pardoned, the nature and neceffity of regeneration and fanctification; fo often as we explain the precepts of the gofpel, and the promifes and threatenings of it, and endeavour to convince men of the equity of CHRIT's commands, and to affure them of the certainty of the eternal happinefs which the gofpel promifes to them that obey it, and of the eternal mifery which the gofpel threatens to thofe that are difobedient; all this is preaching "faith in our LORD " JESUS CHRIST."

III. This may correct the irregular humours and itch in many people, who are not contented with this plain and wholefom food, but muft be gratified with fublime notions and unintelligible myfteries, with pleafant paffages of wit, and artificial ftrains of rhetorick, with nice and unprofitable difputes, with bold interpretations of dark prophecies, and peremptory determinations of what will happen next year, and a punctual ftating of the time when Anti-chrift fhall be thrown down, and Babylon fhall fall, and who fhall be employed in this work. Or if their humour lies another way, you muft apply yourfelf to it, by making fharp reflections upon matters in prefent controverfy and debate, you muft dip your ftile in gall and vinegar, and be all fatyr and invective againft thofe that differ from you, and teach people to hate one another, and to fall together by the ears; and this men call gofpel preaching, and fpeaking of feafonable truths.

Surely St. Paul was a gofpel preacher, and fuch
an

an one as may be a pattern to all others; and yet he S E R M.
did none of these; he preached what men might CLIX.
understand, and what they ought to believe and
practise, in a plain and unaffected and convincing
manner; he taught " such things as made for peace,"
" and whereby he might edify and build up men in
" their holy faith." The doctrines that he preached will never be unseasonable, that men should leave
their sins, and believe the gospel, and live accordingly.

And if men must needs be gratified with disputes
and controversies, there are these great controversies
between God and the sinner to be stated and determined; whether this be religion, to follow our own
lusts and inclinations, or to endeavour to be like God,
and to be conformed to him, in goodness, and mercy, and righteousness, and truth, and faithfulness?
Whether Jesus Christ be not the Messias and Saviour of the world? Whether faith and repentance and
sincere obedience be not the terms of salvation, and the
necessary conditions of happiness? Whether there
shall be a future judgment, when all men shall be
sentenced according to their works? Whether there
be heaven and hell? Whether good men shall be
eternally and unspeakably happy, and wicked men
extremely and everlastingly miserable? These are the
great controversies of religion, upon which we are
to dispute on God's behalf against sinners. God
asserts, and sinners deny these things, not in words,
but which is more emphatical and significant, in their
lives and actions. These are practical controversies
of faith, and it concerns every man to be resolved
and determined about them, that he may frame his
life accordingly.

And so for repentance; God says, repentance is a
forsaking of sin, and a thorough change and amendment

ment of life; the sinner says, that it is only a formal confession, and a slight asking of God forgiveness: God calls upon us speedily and forthwith to
repent; the sinner saith it is time enough, and it
may safely be deferred to sickness or death; these are
important controversies, and matters of moment.
But men do not affect common truths; whereas these
are most necessary: And indeed whatever is generally useful and beneficial, ought to be common, and
not to be the less valued, but the more esteemed for
being so.

And as these doctrines of faith and repentance are
never unseasonable, so are they more peculiarly proper when we celebrate the holy sacrament, which
was instituted for a solemn and standing memorial
of the christian religion, and is one of the most
powerful arguments and persuasives to repentance
and a good life.

The faith of the gospel doth more particularly
respect the death of Christ; and therefore it is called " faith in his blood," because that is more especially the object of our faith; the blood of Christ,
as it was a seal of the truth of his doctrine, so it is
also a confirmation of all the blessings and benefits
of the new covenant.

And it is one of the greatest arguments in the world
to repentance. In the blood of Christ we may
see our own guilt, and in the dreadful sufferings of
the Son of God, the just desert of our sins; " he
" hath born our griefs, and carried our sorrows, he
" was wounded for our transgressions, and bruised
" for our iniquities; therefore the commemoration
of his sufferings should call our sins to remembrance,
the representation of his body broken, should melt
our hearts; and so often as we remember that " his
" blood

" blood was fhed for us, our eyes" fhould " run
" down with rivers of tears;" fo often as we "look
" upon him whom we have pierced," we fhould
" mourn over him." When the fon of GOD fuffered, " the rocks were rent in funder;" and fhall
not the confideration of thofe fufferings be effectual
to break the moft ftony and obdurate heart?

What can be more proper when we come to this
facrament, than the renewing of our repentance?
When we partake of this paffover, we fhould " eat
" it with bitter herbs." The moft folemn expreffions of our repentance fall fhort of thofe fufferings,
which our bleffed SAVIOUR underwent for our fins.
If " our head were waters, and our eyes fountains
" of tears," we could never fufficiently lament the
curfed effects and confequences of thofe provocations
which were fo fatal to the Son of GOD.

And that our repentance may be real, it muft be
accompanied with the refolution of a better life; for
if we return to our fins again, " we trample under
" foot the Son of GOD, and profane the blood of
" the covenant," and out of " the cup of falvation
" we drink our own damnation," and turn that
which fhould fave us into an inftrument and feal of
our own ruin.

SERMON CLX.

Of confeſſing and forſaking ſin, in or-
der to pardon.

PROV. xxviii. 13.

He that covereth his ſins ſhall not proſper: but who-
ſo confeſſeth and forſaketh them, ſhall have mercy.

SINCE we are all ſinners, and liable to the juſtice of GOD, it *is* a matter of great moment
to our comfort and happineſs, to be rightly inform-
ed by what means, and upon what terms, we may
be reconciled to GOD, and find mercy with him.
And to this purpoſe the text gives us this advice and
direction, " whoſo confeſſeth and forſaketh his ſins
" ſhall have mercy."

In which words there is a great bleſſing and benefit declared and promiſed to ſinners, upon certain
conditions. The bleſſing and benefit promiſed, is
" the mercy and favour of GOD," which comprehends all the happy effects of GOD's mercy and goodneſs to ſinners. And the conditions upon which this
bleſſing is promiſed are two, " confeſſion of our ſins,
" and forſaking of them;" and theſe two contain in
them the whole nature of that great and neceſſary
duty of repentance, without which a ſinner can have
no reaſonable hopes of the mercy of GOD.

I. Here is a bleſſing or benefit promiſed, which is
" the mercy and favour of GOD." And this in the
full extent of it, comprehends all the effects of the
mercy and goodneſs of GOD to ſinners, and doth primarily import the pardon and forgiveneſs of our ſins.
And

men, thou shall not escape the judgment of God. It may be thou art a prince, and bearest rule over others : but thou also art liable to the judgment of God, and therefore oughtest to remember, that " they that rule over men, must be just, ruling in the " fear of God," and of that great account which they must one day give of that high charge committed to them. It may be now thou judgest others, and canst call them before thy bar, and make them tremble, having power and authority to absolve or condemn them : but remember, that for all this thou must come into judgment thyself, and give an account how thou hast judged others, and whether thou hast sat and proceeded in these inferior courts, as one mindful of the high tribunal of God, and with a just sense of the judgment of the great day, when all the causes which thou hast tried here upon earth, will be reviewed and severely scanned in that higher court, from which there can be no appeal.

It may be thou art rich and powerful, and one of those great flies that can break through the cobwebs of human laws, and escape the judgment of them : but the judgment of God will take fast hold of thee, and in despite of all thy interest, and might, will take a severe revenge upon thee. As powerful as thou art, thou art but a man, and God is infinitely too strong for thee, thou canst not escape out of his hands. " Thinkest thou, O man ! that thou shalt " escape the judgment of God ?" says the apostle ; looking upon it as a foolish and absurd imagination, for any man to think, that he can by any means avoid the judgment of God.

So that so long as we are men, whatever else we are, we ought to stand in awe of the judgment of the great day ; because, let our rank and condition be what it will, we are all equally obnoxious to that, and can upon no account whatfoever plead any privilege and exemption from it.

II. The confideration of this confounds all thofe differences and diftinctions of men, which make fuch a noife in this world, and whatever they may fignify in this world, makes them very inconfiderable as to the other. Why then fhould men be puft up, and look fo big upon account of any of thefe things, when there is a day not far off, and which will certainly, and for ought we know, fhortly overtake us, which will level men in all thefe refpects, and fet them upon even ground, before an impartial bar ; where none of thefe things will be had in any confideration, and where the foolifh pride and arrogance of men fhall be confounded, and thofe who were wont to look down with fo much fcorn upon others, as fo infinitely below them, fhall find themfelves upon an equal level with the pooreft and moft abject part of mankind, and fhall be ready to fay with the wife man, in the wifdom of Solomon, chap. v. 8. " What hath pride profited us, or what hath " riches with our vaunting brought us ? All thefe " things are paffed away as a fhadow, and as a poft " that hafteth by." So that we ought to ufe well all thofe advantages which we have above others in this world : if we do not, they will be of no ufe and benefit to us in the other. " Riches profit not " in the day of wrath."

All thefe petty civil differences and difcriminations of high and low, rich and poor, honourable and bafe, they only hold in this world, and are in vogue on this fide the grave : but when we come into the other world, they will all ceafe and fignify nothing. There the powerful oppreffor can do nothing to the

injury

injury of the pooreft man that ever lived in this
world, and as little to his own fafety and fecurity.
All that power and intereft which is now fo confiderable, and makes it's way every where, and does
what it pleafeth, will be of no ufe and fignificancy in
the other world. The great and the mighty, when
death hath once arrefted them, and bound them over
to the judgment of the great day, their glory and
ftrength departs from them, and they are then but
like other men. Job elegantly defcribes the ftate of
men after death, Job iii. 17, 18, 19. " There the
" wicked ceafe from troubling; and there the weary
" be at reft. There the prifoners reft together, they
" hear not the voice of the oppreffor. The fmall
" and the great are there, and the fervant is free
" from his mafter." While we are upon the ftage
of this world, we fuftain feveral perfons ; one is a
prince and a great man, another is a captain and a
mighty man ; and whilft this life lafts, thefe differences are confiderable : but when we retire and go
off the ftage, we fhall then be undreft, we fhall be
ftrip'd of all our titles, and of all our glory, and
go out of the world as naked as we came into it.
Death and judgment level all mankind, and when
we come to appear before the judgment-feat of
CHRIST, we fhall all ftand upon equal terms. For
GOD refpects not the perfons of the mighty in judgment, he will fhew no reverence to the great ones of
this world, but will deal impartially and alike with
all. Matth. xxv. 32. You may there fee how the
judge himfelf reprefents the univerfality and impar-
tiality of his dealings with men in that day. " Be-
" fore him fhall be gathered all nations, and he fhall
" feparate them one from another, as a fhepherd
" divideth his fheep from the goats." All man-

kind fhall then be gathered into one common flock, among which there fhall no other diftinction be made, but of fheep and goats ; the feparation which fhall then be made, fhall not be of the high from the low, of the rich from the poor, of the honourable from the bafe, of the learned from the ignorant ; there fhall be but one diftinction then made, of the good from the bad, and the righteous from the wicked ; there fhall no confideration be then had, but only of the moral differences of men ; all civil difference will then vanifh and be of no account in that day, either to exempt any man from that judgment, or to gain any favour and refpect to him in the hearing or decifion of his caufe.   This fhould make all men very modeft and humble in this world, to confider how they fhall be levelled in the next.

III. How fhould the confideration of this dafh all our fenfual mirth and jollity, and put a damp upon our fpirits, when they are too light and vainly tranfported with the pleafures and delights of this world ! If a man be to prepare himfelf to be tried for his life after a few days, how will he look about him, with what care and ferioufnefs will he provide for fo folemn an occafion, and neglect nothing that may ftand him in ftead, and help to bring him off when he fhall receive his trial ! The thoughts of this will fpoil all his mirth, and turn the lightnefs of his fpirit into fober fadnefs. Much more ought the confideration of a judgment infinitely more terrible, and in the confequence of it of far greater concernment to us, to compofe our minds into a ferious frame. For if we believe a future and general judgment, and that none of us can by any means poffibly efcape it, then certainly it highly concerns every one of us to be ferious, and to pafs the time of his life in a

perpetual

perpetual awe of it. So that St. Peter argues from this confideration, 1 Pet. i. 17. " And if ye call " on the Father, who without respect of persons " judgeth every man, pass the time of your sojourn- " ing here in fear." This thought should interpose itself in all our mirth," that " we must appear be- " fore the judgment-seat of CHRIST." And there- fore Solomon admonisheth young men, in the midst of their sports and pleasures, to think of a future account, Ecclef. xi. 9. " Rejoice, O young man, " in thy youth, and let thy heart chear thee in the " days of thy youth, and walk in the ways of thy " heart, and in the sight of thine eyes : but know " that for all these things GOD will bring thee into " judgment."

IV. And lastly, from hence we learn, that the bufinefs of religion does equally concern every man. For if we muft all be judged, we are all concerned to prepare and provide for it ; and a religious and virtuous life is the only preparation for it. How should we order our lives with a respect to this great and general affize, when every one of us shall be brought upon his trial, and stand at the bar of GOD to be judged by him ? Many live as if they thought the bufinefs of religion below them, and not at all appertaining to them : but if the judgment of GOD will equally reach all perfons, then I am sure it e- qually concerns all to mind religion, and a holy and virtuous life ; for that alone will make us worthy, as our SAVIOUR himself expresseth it, " to escape " all these things that shall come to pass, and to stand " before the Son of man."

And this is the refult of Solomon's enquiry, and of his long difcourfe upon that argument, what is the great work and bufinefs, the great interest and

SERM. concernment of men in this life; which we find in
CLXXX. the conclusion of his sermon, called the book of the
preacher, Eccles. xii. 13, 14. " Let us, says he, hear
" the conclusion of the whole matter. Fear GOD,
" and keep his commandments ; for this is the
" whole of man." Religion is the great business
and concernment of men in this world, because
" GOD will bring every man, and every work into
" judgment, whether it be good or evil."

SERMON CLXXXI.

Of the actions for which men will be accountable.

2 COR. v. 10.

For we must all appear before the judgment-seat of
CHRIST, *that every one may receive the things done*
in his body, according to that he hath done, whether
it be good or bad.

SERM. I Proceed to the third proposition contained in these
CLXXXI. words, viz. That all the actions which men have
The fourth done in this life shall then come to account, and
sermon on men shall be judged for them. " That every man
this text. " may receive the things done in the body, τὰ ἴδια
" τȣ̃ σώμαΙ©-, the things proper and due to the
" body;" so some very good copies have it : and
then the meaning will be, that every one may receive the reward due to him; the word body, by a
frequent Hebraism ; being put for the person ; as if
he

he had said, " the reward due to himself," according to the actions he hath done in this life, good or
bad : but in most copies it is, τὰ διὰ τῦ σώμα]Ꙩ,
" the things done in, or by the body," as our translation renders it, that every one may receive the reward of the actions which he hath done in this life ;
and then this phrase doth import what it is that shall
be the matter of our account at the day of judgment,
viz. " The things done in the body," that is, all
the actions of this life, while we are in this world,
in this state of union of the soul and body.

Whether there be any peculiar emphasis in this
phrase, τὰ διὰ τῦ σώμα]Ꙩ, " the things done by,
" or in the body," as if it did exclude those things
which shall be done after death, in the state of sepa-
ration of our souls from our bodies, from being accounted for at the resurrection in the day of judgment ; I say, whether there be any such emphasis in
those words, " the things done in the body," I cannot certainly affirm, though according to the nature
and reason of the thing it seems very probable, as the
schoolmen have generally determined in this case,
that *meritum est viatoris,* " merit and demerit are pro-
" per to this state of trial ;" and that wicked men
when they are in *termino,* and their state is finally
concluded, and the trial of their obedience is at an
end, do not demerit by their sins, nor increase their
Punishment. For although that hatred and enmity of
God which is in the damned spirits, be a monstrous
irregularity in a creature, yet it cannot well in reason
be otherwise, but that a creature which is extreamly
miserable, and withal desperate, and past all hopes
of remedy and recovery out of that dismal state ; I
say, it cannot well in reason be otherwise expected,
but that a creature in such a condition should rage
against

SERM.
CLXXXI.

against the author of its torment and punishment, and do all the despite to him that he can, and wish that he were not, though it be in vain to wish so; and it seems probable that God will not bring this to a new account, because it seems so natural and necessary a consequent of a miserable and desperate state: but though all this be probable, I am far from being peremptory in it, much less am I confident that it is the meaning of this phrase here in the text, and I do not love to build an opinion upon a single and doubtful phrase of scripture. I only mention it by the by, not intending to insist upon it, being much of his mind, who said, *Non amo nimis argutam theologiam,* " I am no lover of great subtilty and nicety " in divinity."

It is sufficient to my purpose, that this phrase of " every man's receiving the things done in the body," does at least import thus much, that we shall be accountable at the day of judgment, for all the actions that we have done in this life, and receive the due recompence and reward of them; which is the proposition I intend as briefly as I can to illustrate and confirm.

And, first, for the illustration of this point, I shall instance in the several heads of action, as they take their difference and variety from the principle, or matter, or object, or other circumstances of them. We must render an account to this great judge for our inward as well as outward actions; for the acts of our minds, and every thought springing up there, especially if it be cherished and entertained by us; for all our secret designs, purposes and intentions, as well as for the words which we speak, and the outward actions which we do: whatever we have thought and designed, spoken and declared, accom-

plished

plifhed and done, will then be confidered and examined, and we fhall be judged for it. We muft
likewife give an account of all our civil as well as
religious actions, of our behaviour toward men in
all our dealing and intercourfe with them, as well as
of our demeanour toward G o d in the duties of
his more immediate worfhip and fervice. The neglects and omiffions of our duty in any kind will alfo
come under confideration, as well as our commif-
fions of evil. A ftrict account likewife will be exacted of all the talents which God hath entrufted
us with, of all the abilities, opportunities and advantages we ever had of doing fervice to God, and
good to men, and whether we have made anfwerable improvements of them, for the glory of God
and the benefit and advantage of men.

We muft be accountable likewife for words and
actions of lefs moment and confequence, as well as
for thofe of greater weight and concernment ; for
thofe which were done in fecret, and in the greateft
darknefs and privacy, as well as for thofe which
were done in publick, and in the open view and light
of the world ; for the good and evil which hath been
done by ourfelves, and in our own perfons, and for
what hath been done by others by our command and
countenance, and from the influence of our counfel
and perfuafion, or example, or which we have been
any ways acceffary to hinder or promote ; and laftly,
for the manner and circumftances of our actions, as
well as for the matter and fubftance of them ; all thefe
will be furveyed and ftrictly fearched into, and weighed in an exact balance, that we may receive a reward
or punifhment proportionable to them.

Secondly, for the confirmation of this, I fhall
make it evident both from fcripture and reafon.

I. From fcripture : which in general tells us, that " God will bring every work into judgment ;" and that in order thereto, God ftrictly obferves and takes notice of what we do ; that " his eyes are upon the " ways of man, and that he feeth all his goings ; " that there is no darknefs or fhadow of death, " where the workers of iniquity may hide ,them- " felves," Job xxxiv. 21, 22. That " the ways " of man are before the eyes of the Lord, and he " pondereth all his goings, Prov. v. 21. That " he knoweth our paths, and our lying down, and " is acquainted with all our ways." That " there " is not a word in our tongue, but he knoweth it " altogether, and that he underftands even our " thoughts afar off," Pfal. cxxxix. 2, 3, 4. That all the actions of men are recorded in books, which fhall be " produced and opened at the great day, " and the dead, both fmall and great, fhall be judged " from thofe things, which fhall be written in thofe " books, Rev. xx. 12."

And more particularly the fcripture tells us, that thofe words and actions of men which feem moft inconfiderable, and are moft likely to be exempted, fhall be accounted for, and feverely fcanned and weighed. Matt. xii. 36, 37. fays our Lord there, " I fay " unto you, that every idle word," by which if our Saviour do not mean every unprofitable, to be fure every " wicked word that men fhall fpeak, they fhall " give an account thereof in the day of judgment. " For by thy words thou fhalt be juftified, and by " thy words thou fhalt be condemned." By which faying, our Saviour defignedly confutes an opinion too current among many, that mens words fignify little, and that no account will be taken of them at the day of judgment ; that God will not be fo fevere

2   **as**

as to make them matter of charge and accufation, and to punifh us for them in the other world; and therefore to obviate this miftake, he purpofely adds, " for by thy words thou fhalt be juftified, and by " thy words thou fhalt be condemned." And therefore men muft not think, that all their lewd and filthy talk, all their rafh oaths and imprecations, all their atheiftical difcourfe, and profane jefts upon religion and the holy fcriptures, all their calumnies and flanders of good men, all their officious lies to ferve a prefent turn and occafion, will pafs for nothing at the judgment of the great day. No, the judge himfelf hath exprefly told us, that of all fuch " words men " fhall give an account in the day of judgment." And St. Jude tells us, out of an ancient prophecy of Enoch, that " the LORD fhall come with ten thou- " fands of his faints, to execute judgment upon all, " and to convince all that are ungodly, not only of " all their ungodly deeds which they have ungodly " committed, but likewife of all their hard fpeeches " which ungodly finners have fpoken againft him."

Our moft fecret thoughts and actions alfo, as well as our open and publick deeds, fhall then be brought upon the ftage, Ecclef. xii. 14. " For GOD will " bring every work into judgment, with every fecret " thing, whether it be good, or whether it be evil." Rom. ii. 16. " In the day, when GOD fhall judge " the fecrets of men by JESUS CHRIST, according to " my gofpel." And this likewife is the meaning of that proverbial fpeech fo often ufed by our SAVIOUR, " there is nothing covered, that fhall not be re- " vealed ; neither hid, that fhall not be known." There is nothing fo fecret which fhall not be difclofed and made manifeft in that great day of revelation, and be laid open in the face of the whole world; efpecially the cunning, diffimulation and hypocrify of men with GOD and men. Men are apt to think themfelves fafe enough, if they can but efcape the eye of men, and commit their fins fecretly, and in the dark. But this is either direct atheifm, or down-right folly; becaufe the eye of GOD is continually upon us, and " the darknefs hideth not from him, " but the night fhineth as the day, the darknefs and " the light are both alike to him." And if we be always under the infpection of our judge, if all that we think, and fay, and do, be " open and naked to " the eye of him, πρὸς ὃν ἡμῖν ὁ λόγος, to whom we " muft give an account," what will it profit us to diffemble before men, and to conceal any of our ac-tions from them? Nay, if we could hide them from ourfelves (as we cannot our wilful and deliberate fins) yet that would be of no advantage to us, becaufe GOD " is greater than our hearts, and knows all things."

And then likewife, we muft be accountable to GOD for all the neglects and omiffions of our duty, as well as for the pofitive commiffion of fin, and that in pro-portion to the advantages and opportunities we have had of doing more and greater good. So our SA-VIOUR tells us, that " unto whomfoever much is " given, of him much fhall be required," Luke xii. 48. Many are apt to think, that if they do but abftain from notorious and fcandalous vices, if they do no body harm, though they do not ferve GOD fo fervently and conftantly as others do, though they feldom think of him and pray to him, though they have no manner of activity or concernment to do good, either to the bodies or fouls of men, yet that this negative virtue will ferve their turn at the day of judgment. But the matter is quite otherwife, as our SAVIOUR hath moft exprefly declared. " A good
" tree,

" tree, faith he, will bring forth good fruit." And by the parable of the foolish virgins, who for want of " oil in their lamps" were shut out of the kingdom of God, he declares to us the dangerous state of those who slumber away their lives in a drowsy inactivity, and are not careful either to keep alive grace in their hearts, or to shew forth the light of good works in their conversation. And in the parable of the talents, Matt. xxv. he passeth a most severe sentence upon that " slothful servant, who hid his lord's " talent in a napkin, and buried it in the earth," without making any manner of improvement of it ; ver. 30. " Cast ye the unprofitable servant into outer " darkness, there shall be weeping and gnashing of " teeth." And in the same chapter, where our SAVIOUR represents to us the proceedings of the great day, the charge there drawn up against them, consists of sins of omission, and gross neglects to do the good which they had the ability and opportunity to do, ver. 41, 42, 43, &c. " Depart from me, ye cursed, " into everlasting fire, prepared for the devil and his " angels. For I was hungry, and ye gave me no " meat ; thirsty, and ye gave me no drink ; a stran- " ger, and ye took me not in ; naked, and ye cloth- " ed me not ; sick and in prison, and ye visited me " not." Not that sins of commission shall then be past by and left out of the account ; it is taken for granted, that they shall be reckoned for in the first place : but the wisdom of our SAVIOUR chuseth to instance in those sins, which many hope they shall not be called to account for, the omissions and neglects of their duty, that he might hereby root out of the minds of men effectually that false opinion, which they are so apt to entertain concerning such sins, as if they were of a very light and venial nature.

II. This

II. This is evident likewise from reason; because all the actions of reasonable creatures, as such, are under the regulation and government of law, by which, as by a rule, every thing that we do is to be measured. And we have all the reason that can be to expect, that he who gave us this law, will look to the observance of it, and take an account of all breaches and transgressions of it, so as to reward those that keep it, and to punish the bold transgressors of it; and if this were not so, the law would want it's proper sanction and enforcement, and had been given to no purpose.

And this law of God reacheth all our actions, inward and outward, religious and civil, secret and open, positive and negative, with all the circumstances of commendation or aggravation that belong to them. And as this law is the rule of all human actions now, and by which we ought to live in this world; so it will be the rule by which we and all our actions shall be examined and judged in the next. The judgment of God will be of the same extent with his law.

And thus I have, as briefly as I could, illustrated and confirmed the truth of this proposition, that all the actions which men have done in this life, shall come to account in the next, and they shall be judged for them.

And if so, then certainly no consideration that can be presented to the mind of man, ought in reason to be more powerful to beget in us a strict care and conscience of all our thoughts, words, and actions, than this, that after a little while, when a few days or years are over, all that we ever did in this world, shall be strictly examined and looked into, and be approved or condemned by the impartial judgment of God. And therefore, if we have any grain of true wisdom in us, any

love

love to ourselves, any sense of our great and everlasting interest, that great day of account should always
be before us, and present to our minds, and we should
govern every action of our lives with a serious and
awful regard to it. And if we be conscious to ourselves that " there is any way of wickedness in us,"
that we have been grosly culpable in the violation of
any known law of God, or in the neglect of any
part of our duty, how can we without dread think of
coming to so severe an account, and falling under so
heavy a sentence, as will then be pronounced upon
the workers of iniquity ?

Indeed, if we could do any thing now, of which
we were to give no account hereafter, and which
would not be taken into consideration at the great
day, we then might be secure and careless as to such
actions : But when nothing we do is exempted from
the judgment of God, when we are assured beyond
all doubt, that he will one day take cognizance of
every thought, word, and action ; how circumspect
should we be, " what manner of persons we are in
" all holy conversation and godliness !" how nearly
does it concern us, " to take heed to our ways, lest
" at any time we offend : to keep our hearts with all
" diligence, and to set a watch to the door of our
" lips !" that we may not think or speak any thing
in the sight or hearing of our judge, by which we
may incur his censure and condemnation. This is
the consideration which the wise man proposeth to
us, as of all other the most likely to awe men to the
careful obedience and observance of God's laws.
" Fear God, and keep his commandments : for God
" will bring every work into judgment, and every
" secret thing, whether it be good, or whether it be
" evil."

SERM.
CLXXXI.

Can we be negligent of our lives and actions, when we confider that all the paffages of our lives are upon record, and that there is a moft exact regifter kept of them, written in indelible characters with "a pen " of iron, and the point of a diamond?" as the ex- preffion is, Jer xvii. 1. " I remember all their wick- " ednefs, and their doings are before me," fays God, Hof. vii. 2. And chap. viii. 7. " The Lord " hath fworn by the excellency of Jacob, furely I " will not forget any of their works." We fin, and forget that we have finned : but God chargeth himfelf with the remembrance of all our evil doings, and they can never flip out of his mind.

Did men ferioufly believe thefe things, and were they affected with them as they ought, they could not but have a wonderful effect upon their lives, to make us more watchful over our ways, and to tread every ftep of our lives more warily. We could not " commit iniquity with fo much greedinefs and " pleafure, and rufh into fin, as the horfe rufheth " into battel," without any fear or confideration, were we verily perfuaded, that every evil action that we do in this life, will be matter of charge and accu- fation in the day of judgment.

Therefore when we are doing any thing, we fhould afk ourfelves, will not this alfo come into judgment? When we are engaged in any wicked defign, or vi- cious courfe, we fhould confider, with what face will this act of violence and oppreffion, of fraud and cozenage, of filthy leudnefs and brutifh intemperance, appear at the great day ? how will it look, when " God fhall arife to judgment?" When we are care- lefs and remifs, flight and fuperficial in the fervice of God, and the duties of his worfhip, we fhould re- member that God takes notice of all this, and we

must

muft give an account to him for the manner, as well as the matter of our actions.

If the actions of our lives were tranfient, and the confequence of them were over fo foon as they are done, and no memorial of them would remain hereafter; if they would die with us, and never rife up in judgment againft us; we needed not to take fuch heed to them: But we do all things for eternity, and every action of this life will have a good or bad influence upon our everlafting ftate.

More particularly, the confideration of this fhould have an influence upon us, more efpecially to thefe purpofes.

1. To make us afraid of leffer fins, as well as greater, becaufe thofe alfo, as well as thefe, will come into judgment; and we fhould not efteem any thing little, which God fhall think fit to take into confideration, and to bring upon the ftage at the great day.

2. The confideration of this fhould likewife deter us from fecret fins. We are apt to think, that if we can but fin in fecret, and hide what we do from the eyes of men, we are fecure and fafe enough: but alas! our great danger is not from men, but God; not now, but hereafter. We are now very folicitous to conceal our wickednefs, that we may avoid fhame, and efcape punifhment from men: but God will one day produce all our fecret fins, and bring them forth into the light, for all our ftudious concealment of them now. Now we are afraid of the eye of men, and therefore chufe fecrecy, that we may commit our fins privately and unfeen. Vain man! The day is at hand, when all thy fecret leudnefs and fraud will be brought upon the publick ftage of the world, and be matter of publick infamy to thee, and an everlafting reproach that can never be wiped off; and though

thou now " coverest thy transgression as Adam, " and hidest thine iniquity in thy bosom," yet the time is coming, when all thy secret wickedness shall be exposed to the view of angels and men; and then, sinner, what wilt thou do, when thou shalt appear before this all-seeing Judge? None of thine arts of concealment will then stand thee in stead. Canst thou hide thy sins from his eye, so that he cannot search them out? or thy self from his wrath? If thou canst not, what matters it to have any secret from others when all is known to thy Judge?

3. This should likewise dispose us to great sincerity in all our words and actions, and make us always to speak as we think, to perform what we promise and profess, and in all things to be what we would seem to be, since there is a day coming when " the " secrets of all hearts shall be disclosed," and every mask of hypocrisy and dissimulation shall be pluck'd off, and our most close and cunning designs shall be brought into the open light. In that great day of revelation, nothing will be matter of comfort and rejoicing to us, but " the testimony of our consciences, " that in all simplicity and godly sincerity, we have " had our conversation in the world."

4. This should make us faithfully to improve all the talents and opportunities which God affords to us, because we are but stewards, and must give an account of them. We are apt to covet great wealth, and to aspire after great places and power: but do we consider what it is that we so eagerly desire and pursue? All this will but bring upon us the burden of a greater and heavier account, if we do not improve these talents and advantages to the end for which they were given, to relieve the wants of the poor and miserable, and to serve the great ends of religion and

virtue;

virtue; and if we fail herein, a dreadful account will be exacted of us, and we shall wish that we had been the poorest and meanest, the most ignorant and unlearned persons in the world.

5. This should restrain us from uncharitable censures of others. " Thou art therefore inexcusable, O " man, whosoever thou art, that judgest another: " for thinkest thou, that thou shalt escape the judg- " ment of God?" as the apostle reasons, Rom. ii. 1.

6. This may help to support us under the unjust censures and reproaches of men. If we be innocent, God will one day " bring forth our righteousness as " the light, and our judgment as the noon-day." " With me, saith St. Paul, 1 Cor. iv. 3. it is a very " small thing that I should be judged of you, or of " man's judgment. He that judgeth me is the " Lord." It is desirable to approve ourselves and our actions to men: but if we cannot, it is a great satisfaction to approve them to our own consciences, and to God who is " greater than our hearts, and " knows all things."

Lastly, This will teach us not to measure our condition by the good opinion which others have of us; but by the law of God, which will be the standard and measure of our judgment. He will consider every thing exactly, and weigh all the circumstances of our case, and make all the allowances that equity requires. Men can but judge according to appearance; but the judgment of God will be according to truth: therefore we should above all " labour to be " accepted of him in that day."

S E R-

SERMON CLXXXII.

Of the sentence to be passed at the day of judgment.

2 COR. v. 10.

For we must all appear before the judgment-seat of CHRIST, *that every one may receive the things done in his body, according to that he hath done, whether it be good or bad.*

SERM.
CLXXXII.

The fifth sermon on this text. I Proceed to the fourth and laft propofition contained in the text, viz. that at the day of judg-
ment, fentence fhall be paffed upon men according to
the nature and quality of their actions done in this
world, whether good or evil. The reward of happinefs or mifery which men fhall be fentenced to at
that day, fhall bear a proportion to the good or evil
which they have done in this life.

In the profecution of this argument, I fhall enquire
into thefe two things.

Firft, What proportion the rewards of the next
world fhall bear to the actions of men in this life.

Secondly, The grounds and reafons of it. And
then make fome application of this truth to the confciences of men.

Firft, What proportion the rewards of the next
world fhall bear to the actions of men in this life. I
mean, whether the rewards of the next life fhall only
be proportioned to the kind and quality of our actions confidered in general, as good or evil, that is,
that good men fhall be rewarded with everlafting
glory

glory and happinefs, and wicked men with eternal punifhment and torment: or whether the degrees of thefe rewards fhall likewife bear a proportion to the degrees of the good or evil of our actions, fo that a more eminent degree of piety and holinefs, fhall have a proportionable fhare of glory and happinefs ; and greater and more hainous fins, fhall be loaded with greater and heavier punifhments.

I. It is clear, and out of all controverfy, that men fhall be rewarded according to the quality and kind of their actions ; good fhall be rewarded to the good, and evil to the evil. And this is the conftant tenor of the bible. Pfal. i. 6. " The LORD knoweth the " way of the righteous," that is, doth approve it, and will reward it : " but the way of the ungod- " ly fhall perifh ;" which is of the fame importance with the expreffion in the verfe before, " the wicked " fhall not ftand in the judgment." Ifa. iii. 10, 11. " Say ye to the righteous, it fhall be well with them, " for they fhall eat of the fruit of their doings. Wo " unto the wicked, for it fhall be ill with him, for " the reward of his hands fhall be given him;" which if it be meant of the rewards and punifhments of this life, is much more conftantly and univerfally true of the other. Matt. xvi. 27. " The Son of man " fhall come in the glory of his Father, with his an- " gels with him, and fhall reward every man ac- " cording to his works." Rev. xxii. 12. " Behold " I come quickly, and my reward is with me, to " render to every man according as his work fhall " be," that is, whether good or evil. Rom. vi. 23. " The wages of fin is death : but the gift of GOD is " eternal life, that is, to thofe who have their fruit " unto holinefs," as he had faid immediately before. Hither likewife belong thofe innumerable texts, in

which glory and happiness and eternal life are promised to those who live " soberly, righteously, and
" godly in this present world ;" and wickedness and
disobedience are threatened with dreadful and eternal
punishment. But I shall only take notice of two or
three of the most remarkable of them. Matt. xiii. 40,
41, 42. " The Son of man shall send forth his angels
" and they shall gather out of his kingdom all things
" that offend, and them which do iniquity, and shall
" cast them into a furnace of fire, there shall be
" wailing and gnashing of teeth. Then shall the
" righteous shine forth as the sun in the kingdom of
" their Father." But this is most fully represented
in that particular description, which our LORD himself makes of the process of that day, Matt. xxv. 34.
where the sentence that shall be past on the righteous
is this, " Come ye blessed of my Father, inherit the
" kingdom prepared for you before the foundation
" of the world." And on the wicked, ver. 41.
" Depart from me, ye cursed, into everlasting fire,
" prepared for the devil and his angels." And
ver. 46. " And these, speaking of the wicked, shall
" go away into everlasting punishment : but the
" righteous into life eternal." John v. 28, 29.
" The hour is coming in which all that are in their
" graves shall hear his voice, and shall come forth,
" they that have done good unto the resurrection of
" life, and they that have done evil unto the resur-
" rection of damnation." Rom. ii. 6, 7, 8, 9.
speaking of " the revelation of the righteous judg-
" ment of GOD, who, says the apostle, shall render
" to every man according to his works ; to them
" who by patient continuance in well-doing seek for
" glory and honour and immortality, eternal life :
" but to them that are contentious and obey not the
                              " truth,

" truth, but obey unrighteousness, indignation and
" wrath, tribulation and anguish, upon every soul
" of man that doth evil."

II. That the rewards and recompences of the next
world shall likewise bear a proportion to the degrees
of good or evil which we have done in this life,
though it have been controverted, seems also to be
sufficiently clear from scripture. And to this purpose I shall,

1. Produce such texts as will fully prove it. And,
2. Answer the grounds of the contrary opinion.

1. The scripture doth plainly assert, that the rewards of the next life will bear a proportion, not only to the kind and quality of our actions, but to the
degree of them; that good men shall receive a reward proportionable to the degree of their holiness
and obedience, of their service and sufferings for
God : and that the torments of the wicked shall be
greater or less, according to the degree and aggravation of their sins.

(1.) As for good men; that the reward, that
shall be bestowed upon them, shall bear a proportion
to the degree of their service and sufferings for God.
This seems to be intimated in those metaphorical
expressions used by the prophet Daniel, chap. xii. 3.
" They that be wise shall shine as the brightness of the
" firmament ; and they that turn many to righteous-
" ness, as the stars for ever and ever." Which is much
the same with what St. Paul expresly affirms, concerning the different glory of the saints at the resurrection,
1 Cor. xv. 41. " There is one glory of the sun, ano-
" ther glory of the moon, and another glory of the
" stars : for one star differeth from another star in
" glory. So also is the resurrection of the dead."
Matt. v. 10, 11. " Blessed are ye, when men shall
" revile

" revile you, and persecute you, and speak all man-
" ner of evil against you for my name's sake. Re-
" joice, and be exceeding glad: for great is your
" reward in heaven." Which words, if they do not
signify a more glorious reward to those who suffer
persecution for CHRIST, have no emphasis or encouragement in them. For what cause of " exceeding
" joy and gladness" is it, to be persecuted and suffer for CHRIST, if a peculiar reward did not belong
to those who suffer for him? If there do not, then
those who suffer for CHRIST, are plainly in a worse
condition in this world, than other good men who
escape these sufferings; and yet are in no better condition, than others in the next world: and then why
should any man be glad to suffer? Matt. x. 41, 42.
" He that receiveth a prophet, in the name of a pro-
" phet, shall receive a prophet's reward: and he
" that receiveth a righteous man, in the name of a
" righteous man, shall receive a righteous man's re-
" ward." Where you see a difference intimated between " the reward of a prophet, and a righteous
" man," namely, that a prophet shall have a greater
reward than an ordinary good man. Matt. xix. 28,
29. where our blessed SAVIOUR tells us, that all that
denied themselves for CHRIST," shall inherit everlast-
" ing life;" but for his disciples, who were continually attendants upon him, and sufferers for him, that
a more eminent degree of glory should be conferred
on them; which is express'd by their " sitting upon
" twelve thrones, to judge the twelve tribes of Is-
" rael." But most plainly in the parable of the talents, where every man's reward is according to the
improvement of his talents. " He that had gained
" five talents, is made ruler over five cities; and he
" that had gained ten talents, ruler over ten cities,"

I
Luke

Luke xix. 15. 1 Cor. xv. 58. " Be ye stedfast, un-
" moveable, always abounding in the work of the
" LORD; forasmuch as you know that your labour
" is not in vain in the LORD." But if our reward
should not hold a proportion to the degree of our
service, it would be in vain to be " abundant in the
" work of the LORD." 2 Cor. iv. 17. " Our light
" affliction which is but for a moment, worketh for
" us a far more exceeding and eternal weight of glo-
" ry;" that is, our affliction contributes to our glory, and adds to the degree of it. 2 Cor. ix. 6. The
apostle useth this as an argument to persuade the Corinthians to be very liberal and bountiful to their dif-
tressed brethren, because according to the degree of
their charity, would be the degree of their reward.
" This I say, he that soweth sparingly, shall reap
" sparingly, and he that soweth plentifully, shall reap
" plentifully:" than which I cannot imagine any
thing can be spoken more plainly to this purpose.
And the same argument he useth to the Philippians,
to stir them up to charity, Phil. iv. 17. " Not be-
" cause I desire a gift: but I desire fruit that may
" abound to your account;" clearly implying, that
the more good we do in this world, the more abundant shall be our reward in the next.

(2.) It is likewise as plain from scripture, that the
punishment and torment of wicked men will be abated or increased proportionably to the degree and aggravation of their sins. Upon this account our SA-
VIOUR threatens those who continue impenitent under the gospel, with more heavy and dreadful punishments, and tells us, that " in the day of judgment"
their condition shall be far worse than theirs of " Tyre
" and Sidon, of Sodom and Gomorrah," Matt. xi.
20, 21. And Matt. xxiv. 51. he threatens that ser-

vant, who, because " his LORD delayed his coming,"
presumed so much upon the patience of GOD, with a
more severe punishment: " The LORD of that ser-
" vant shall cut him in sunder, and appoint him his
" portion with the hypocrites;" intimating that the
punishment of hypocrites will be very severe, and as
it were the standard of the highest punishment. And
so likewise, Luke xii. 47, 48. our SAVIOUR tells us,
that according to the degree of light and knowledge
which men sin against, shall be the degree of their
torment. " The servant that knew his LORD's will,
" and prepared not himself to do according to it,
" shall be beaten with many stripes: but he that
" knew it not, and did commit things worthy of
" stripes, shall be beaten with few stripes." And in
general he tells us, that the punishment of sinners
takes it's aggravation from the advantages and opportunities which men have neglected. " For unto
" whomsoever much is given, of him much shall be
" required, and to whom men have committed much,
" of him they will ask the more." So likewise the
apostle to the Hebrews tells us, that GOD will vindicate the contempt of the gospel more severely than
of the law of Moses, Heb. ii. 2, 3, 4. " If the word
" spoken by angels was stedfast, and every trans-
" gression and disobedience received a just recom-
" pence of reward; how shall we escape, if we ne-
" glect so great salvation?" And chap. x. 28, 29.
" He that despised Moses's law died without mercy,
" under two or three witnesses; of how much sorer
" punishment, think ye, shall he be thought worthy,
" who hath trodden under foot the Son of GOD?"

So that it seems very evident from scripture, that
the degree of happiness or misery which men shall
be sentenced to in the next world, shall be correspondent

dent to the degree of good or evil, which they have done in this world; and I can hardly imagine any thing more clear. But it feems the fchoolmen, and other divines who have been at leifure to tie knots, and to make objections againft the plaineft truths, have called this alfo into queftion. And therefore I fhall, in the

ᐟ IId. Place, briefly examine the grounds of the contrary opinion; which though they do but imme-diately ftrike at the degrees of glory and happinefs, yet by a parity of reafon and confequence, they like-wife overthrow the degrees of punifhment; and they are thefe two.

I. They fay, that the merits of CHRIST, by which eternal life and happinefs is purchafed for us, are e-qual to all thofe who have any intereft in them, and are of value fufficient to purchafe the higheft degree of glory for them; and the meritorious caufe being the fame, there is no reafon to imagine any diffe-rence of degrees in the effect.

Anfw. The weaknefs of this objection, how fpe-cious foever it may appear, will be evident to any one that confiders, that eternal life and happinefs doth not accrue to us by way of neceffary and natural refult from the merit of CHRIST's obedience and fuf-ferings, but of voluntary compact and agreement, and therefore is only available fo far as it pleafed GOD the Father and him that it fhould be. Now the fcripture hath declared that "CHRIST is the author "of eternal falvation to them that believe and obey "him:" but it hath declared likewife, that accord-ing to the degrees of our holinefs and obedience fhall be the degrees of our happinefs; becaufe the happinefs which CHRIST hath purchafed for us, is not beftowed upon us but upon certain terms and

con-

conditions to be performed on our part, upon the performance whereof, and the degrees of that performance, the degrees of our happiness do depend.

II. The other objection is from the parable of the labourers in the vineyard, Matth. xx. where it is said, that " they that came in at the last hour re-
" ceived as much, as they that came in at the first,
" and had borne the heat and burden of the day,
" every one his peny." For answer to this, It is a known rule among divines, that *theologia parabolica non est argumentativa* ; by which they mean, that we cannot argue in divinity from every circumstance of a parable, but only from the main scope of it. Now this parable seems plainly directed against the envious Jews, who murmured because the Gentiles were to partake of the blessing of the Messias, and that they who were called in the last age of the world should share in this benefit, as well as the ancient people of God ; so that by the murmurers, the Jews are designed, who were offended that salvation should come to the Gentiles. And then the scope of the parable is not, that all good men shall have equal degrees of glory ; but that the Gentiles, which were called long after the Jews, should be saved as well as they. I proceed to the

Second thing I proposed to enquire into, viz. the grounds and reasons of this, why the rewards which shall be distributed at the day of judgment, shall bear a proportion to the good or evil which men have done in this life ? And,

1. That they shall be correspondent to the nature and quality of our actions, the justice and equity of the divine providence doth plainly require. For justice is to give to every one that which of due belongs to him : now of equity it belongs to them that
do

do well, that it fhould go well with them ; and to the evil, that it fhould be ill with them, that every one fhould " receive the fruit of his doings." Not that we can ftrictly merit any thing at the hand of God. It is goodnefs to reward an innocent creature, and it is goodnefs to reward the good actions of thofe who have been finners ; but juftice requires that good and bad men fhould not fare alike. Thus Abraham reafons from the juftice of God, " that " the righteous fhould be as the wicked, that be far " from thee : fhall not the judge of all the world " do right ?" And confidering the promifes which the goodnefs of God hath made freely to good men, for their encouragement in goodnefs, and the performance of thefe promifes is founded in the righ-teoufnefs and faithfulnefs of God.

2. That the rewards of the next life fhould bear a proportion to the degree of the good or evil done by us in this life, is clearly founded in the equity and reafonablenefs of the thing ; it being very much for the encouragement of holinefs and goodnefs, to be affured that whatever we do for God now, will be fully confidered and rewarded hereafter ; that he will take notice of the leaft fervice that we do for him, and that every degree of grace and holinefs fhall be crowned with an anfwerable degree of glory and happinefs. And fo on the other hand, it tends very much to difcountenance fin, and to keep men from running to the height of impiety ; to confider that every fin will aggravate their mifery, and that every degree of wickednefs will add to the weight of their torment, and that though they be " children of " wrath" already, yet by " adding iniquity to tranf-" greffion," they may caufe the " wrath of God " and his jealoufy to fmoke againft them," and bring

more

Of the sentence to be passed

more curses upon themselves, and make themselves " ten times more the children of wrath."

And indeed in the nature of the thing it cannot be otherwise, but that the better and more holy any man is, the more capable he should be of happiness, and the more disposed for the enjoyment of GOD ; and the more wicked any man is, the more he should exasperate his own conscience, and awaken those furies which rage in his breast. " He treasures up " more wrath against the day of wrath," and piles up more fuel for everlasting burnings. The torments of hell are in scripture compared to fire ; now the more fuel and greater store of combustible matter is cast into it, the more fierce and raging it must be.

I have done with the explication, and shall now apply what hath been delivered.

I. If sentence shall be past at the great day according to the good or bad actions of men, this shews us what should be the great care of every man in this life ; to attend to the nature and quality of our actions, and to observe that difference between them in our practice now, which our judge will certainly make in the sentence which he will pass upon them at the great day. And yet so blind and mistaken is the greatest part of the world, that they make this the least part of their care and business. Men are generally very solicitous to be rich and great, and to be in a healthful and prosperous condition, and do with all possible care seek to avoid sickness and poverty and meanness : but how few are concerned to be virtuous and good, and to avoid wickedness and vice ! And yet these moral differences of men at the day of judgment will only be taken into consideration : other things will not " profit us in the day of " wrath."

" wrath." God in that day will not proceed with men according to their outward quality and condition in this life, their eternal ſtate ſhall not then be decided according to their wealth or poverty, their height and meanneſs in this world : it will not then be enquired what office a man bore, what titles of honour, what manors or lordſhips he was owner of, but how he hath behaved himſelf in thoſe circumſtances, what uſe he hath made of his wealth and power, what good or evil he hath done ; whether he hath glorified God, and ſerved the great ends of his creation ; whether he hath obeyed or diſobeyed the truth ; whether he hath lived in " ungodlineſs " and worldly luſts, or ſoberly and righteouſly and " godly in this preſent world ;" in a word, whether we have been righteous or wicked. This will be the great enquiry at that day, and theſe qualities, according as they are found with us, will determine our condition for ever.

II. The conſideration of this may comfort good men under the promiſcuous diſpenſations of God's providence in this world. Now " all things gene- " rally happen alike, and there is the ſame event to " the righteous and to the wicked :" but things will not be always thus. Have but a little patience, and the juſtice of God's providence, which is now under a cloud, will clear up ; the day is coming which will make a wide and vaſt difference between good and bad men, " between thoſe that ſerve God, and " thoſe that ſerve him not ; thoſe that ſwear, and " thoſe that fear an oath ;" between the lewd and the chaſte, the ſober and debauched, the meek of the earth and the murderers ; between the proud and the humble, the juſt and the oppreſſors ; between thoſe that perſecute, and thoſe who are perſecuted for righteouſneſs. Now

SERM.
CLXXXII.

Now the difference is frequently on the wrong side ; good men suffer and are afflicted, the wicked flourish and are prosperous : but " go into the fan- " ctuary of GOD, and there thou shalt see their " end." Let us but look a little before us, beyond " the things which are seen and are but temporal, " unto the things which are not seen and are eter- " nal," and we shall see all things straight ; that the end of the wicked," who flourished in this world, " is to be destroyed for ever ; and that the " righteous," who were so distressed and afflicted in this world, " shall enter into rest and joy : when " the days of refreshing shall come from the presence " of the LORD, these shall be comforted and the " other tormented."

III. If the reward of the next life shall bear a pro- portion to the degrees of good or evil which we have done in this world, then on the one hand here is matter of great comfort and encouragement to us in the ways of holiness and obedience. This is a mighty argument to good men to grow in grace, and to press forward toward perfection, " to be sted- " fast and unmoveable and abundant in the work of " the LORD, because they know that their labour " shall not be in vain in the LORD ;" but that ac- cording to the degrees of our service and obedience, of our virtue and goodness, shall be the degree of our glory and happiness. We serve a good master, who will confider every thing that we do for him ; " who is not unrighteous, to forget our work and " labour of love," and will not let the least service pass unrewarded. Let us not then content ourselves with any low degree of goodness ; but be continual- ly aspiring after the highest perfection we are capa- ble of. Since we have such a prize in our view,

3

" let

" let us run with patience," and with all our might,
" the race which is fet before us." For by the fame
reafon that any man defires happinefs, he cannot but
defire the higheft degrees of it that are attainable ;
and will confequently endeavour to make himfelf capable of the greateft degree of glory: and though
no degree of holinefs can merit everlafting life and
happinefs, yet greater degrees of holinefs will certainly
be rewarded with a larger portion of happinefs. God
is not bound antecedently to his promife, to give fo
great a reward to any man for his works ; yet he
hath promifed to reward every man according to
them.

So that there is no reafon why a good man, when
he is once come to this, that by the grace and affiftance of God, he can refrain from grofs fins, and
refift the temptations to them, and perform the great
duties of religion, why he fhould with Efau, fit
down and fay, " I have enough," I have fo much as
will carry me to heaven, and I defire no more. It is
a fad prefage of apoftafy, to ftand ftill in religion.
He that once ftops, the next thing is to look back.
This is the remedy which St. Peter prefcribes againft
apoftafy, 2 Pet. iii. 18. " Take heed left ye fall
" from your own ftedfaftnefs ;" and then it follows, " but grow in grace, and in the knowledge of
" our LORD and SAVIOUR JESUS CHRIST." The
beft remedy againft apoftafy, is growth in goodnefs.
It is a rule in policy, that an ambitious man fhould
never ftay at any ftep of preferment, till he come at
the top, becaufe it is fome fecurity to be in motion.
Our afcent to heaven is fteep and narrow, and we are
fafeft when we do not ftand ftill: temptation cannot
fo well take it's aim at us.

Let us therefore prefs after the higheft degree of

virtue and holinefs, and labour to be as good as we
can in this world, that in the next our happinefs
may be the greater ; that when the day of recompence fhall come, we may receive an ample reward,
and GOD the righteous judge may fet a bright and
glorious crown upon our heads.

We ought likewife to confider, that if any man
can be content only to be faved, and defire no more
but juft to get heaven, that fuch a degree of holinefs
and virtue as will fave a man that can attain no more,
will perhaps not fave that man who lazily refts in the
loweft degree, and defires no more. To be " leaft
" in the kingdom of GOD," is next to being fhut
out of it. It is not to be expected that GOD fhould
beftow heaven and happinefs upon thofe who are fo
indifferent about it, as to defire heaven for no other
reafon, but becaufe they would not go to hell. Men
muft not think to drive fo near and hard a bargain,
in fo defirable and advantageous a purchafe.

And then on the other hand, it is matter of great
terror to great finners. " The wages of every fin
" is death," eternal death ; and every degree of
hell and damnation is dreadful : but there are fins
more heinous in themfelves, and fome that are attended with heavier aggravations in fome perfons ;
thefe do inflame hell, and heat that furnace feven
times hotter. There are fome moderate finners in
comparifon ; thefe fhall have a moderate doom, and a
cooler hell : but there are others, who are extravagant
and enormous finners, that " drink up iniquity, as
" the ox drinks up water ; that let themfelves loofe
" to commit all wickednefs with greedinefs ;" fuch
as fin above the common rate of men, with full confent, and upon deliberation, with great defign and
contrivance, in defpite of the cleareft convictions,

of

of the beft counfels and reproofs; thefe make hafte to ruin, and take hell by violence. Now fuch " migh-
" ty tranfgreffors fhall be mightily tormented ;"
they fhall not be punifhed at the common rate of
finners, their confciences will breed more and fharp-
er ftings, and wilder furies to torment them, and
they fhall fink into a deeper mifery.

More particularly this concerns us Chriftians, who
continue impenitent, and live in our fins, notwithftanding the clear revelation of the gofpel, and
" the wrath of God revealed from heaven, againft
" all ungodlinefs and unrighteoufnefs of men; not-
" withftanding life and immortality fo clearly brought
" to light by the gofpel. How fhall we efcape, if
" we neglect fo great falvation?" What condemnation will be heavy enough for thofe, who wilfully refufe
to be faved ? This is the condemnation, fays our
SAVIOUR, " that light is come into the world, and
" men love darknefs rather than light." All the
fins which we now commit, are infinitely aggravated
above the fins of thoufands in the world, who never
enjoyed that light, and thofe advantages and opportunities which we have done. " The ignorance of
" thefe God winked at, but now he expects, he
" commands all men every where to repent ; be-
" caufe he hath appointed a day, in which he will
" judge the world in righteoufnefs." What ftripes
do we deferve, who have " known our mafter's
" will, but have not prepared ourfelves to do accord-
" ing to it ?" All that light and knowledge which
we have, all thofe counfels and inftructions which
we have read and heard out of God's word, will
inflame our account, and heighten our condemnation, and the very means of our falvation will be the
faddeft aggravation of our ruin. What our SAVI-

our said of the impenitent and unbelieving Jews, holds as well concerning impenitent Christians ; that " it shall be more tolerable for Tyre and Sidon, for " Sodom and Gomorrah in the day of judgment, " than for them. But, beloved, I hope better things " of you, and things that accompany salvation." Let us but remember and seriously consider, that " we must all appear before the judgment-seat of " Christ, to receive the things done in the body, " according to what we have done, whether good " or evil;" and this will certainly have a mighty awe and influence upon our lives, and all the actions of them.

" Now the God of peace, &c."

The END of the NINTH VOLUME.

THE
CONTENTS.

SERM. CLVII.

God the firſt cauſe, and laſt end.

ROM. xi. 36.

FOR of him, and through him, and to him are all things, to whom be glory for ever, Amen.
Page 3761.

SERM. CLVIII.

Of doing good.

Being a ſpital ſermon preach'd at *Chriſt-Church* on *Eaſter-Tueſday, April* 14. 1691.

Let us not be weary in well-doing, for in due ſeaſon we ſhall reap, if we faint not: as we have therefore opportunity, let us do good unto all men, eſpecially unto them who are of the houſhold of faith,
P. 3776.

SERM. CLIX.

The neceſſity of repentance and faith.

ACTS xx. 21.

Teſtifying both to the Jews, and alſo to the Greeks, repentance toward God, and faith toward our Lord Jesus Christ.
P. 3797.

SERM. CLX.

Of confeſſing and forſaking ſin, in order to pardon.

Preached on Aſh-Wedneſday.

PROV

The CONTENTS.

SER-

The CONTENTS.